Multilingual Development

English as a global lingua franca interacts with other languages across a wide range of multilingual contexts. Combining insights from linguistics, education studies, and psychology, this book addresses the role of English within the current linguistic dynamics of globalization. It takes Singapore, Hong Kong, and Dubai as case studies to illustrate the use of English in different multilingual urban areas, arguing that these are places where competing historical assessments, and ideological conceptions of monolingualism and multilingualism, are being acted out most forcefully. It critically appraises the controversial concept of multilingual advantages, and studies multilingual cross-linguistic influence in relation to learning English in bilingual heritage contexts. It also scrutinizes multilingual language policies in terms of their impact on attitudes, identities, and investment into languages. Engaging and accessible, this book is essential reading for academic researchers and advanced students of bi- and multilingualism, globalization, linguistic diversity, World Englishes, sociolinguistics, and second/third language acquisition.

PETER SIEMUND is Professor and Chair of English Linguistics at the University of Hamburg. His publications include *Varieties of English* (2013) and *Speech Acts and Clause Types* (2018).

Multilingual Development

English in a Global Context

Peter Siemund

University of Hamburg

CAMBRIDGE
UNIVERSITY PRESS

CAMBRIDGE
UNIVERSITY PRESS

Shaftesbury Road, Cambridge CB2 8EA, United Kingdom

One Liberty Plaza, 20th Floor, New York, NY 10006, USA

477 Williamstown Road, Port Melbourne, VIC 3207, Australia

314–321, 3rd Floor, Plot 3, Splendor Forum, Jasola District Centre, New Delhi – 110025, India

103 Penang Road, #05-06/07, Visioncrest Commercial, Singapore 238467

Cambridge University Press is part of Cambridge University Press & Assessment, a department of the University of Cambridge.

We share the University's mission to contribute to society through the pursuit of education, learning and research at the highest international levels of excellence.

www.cambridge.org
Information on this title: www.cambridge.org/9781108844024

DOI: 10.1017/9781108915540

First published 2023

A catalogue record for this publication is available from the British Library.

Library of Congress Cataloging-in-Publication Data
Names: Siemund, Peter, 1965- author.
Title: Multilingual development : English in a global context / Peter Siemund.
Description: Cambridge, United Kingdom ; New York, NY : Cambridge University Press, 2022. | Includes bibliographical references and index.
Identifiers: LCCN 2022025739 (print) | LCCN 2022025740 (ebook) | ISBN 9781108844024 (hardback) | ISBN 9781108926089 (paperback) | ISBN 9781108915540 (epub)
Subjects: LCSH: Multilingualism. | English language–Globalization.
Classification: LCC P115 .S486 2022 (print) | LCC P115 (ebook) | DDC 306.44/6–dc23/eng/20220608
LC record available at https://lccn.loc.gov/2022025739
LC ebook record available at https://lccn.loc.gov/2022025740

ISBN 978-1-108-84402-4 Hardback
ISBN 978-1-108-92608-9 Paperback

One only sees what one looks for. One only looks for what one knows.

—Goethe

Contents

Figures

Tables

Preface

This book is about the multilingual upbringing and development of individuals in their respective societies, adopting a perspective of English as the current hub language of the world. It is placed at the intersection of language acquisition research, sociolinguistics, language contact studies, education, psychology, and the study of World Englishes. The book analyses the linguistic outcomes of current and historical globalization processes, with a focus on the special role of English in relation to its status as a native language, learner language, foreign language, second language, additional language, New English variety, and lingua franca. It tries to harness the multiple aspects of a person's multilingual reality and experience, such as their language biographies, repertoires and attitudes, language acquisition and learning, language dominance, language contact and cross-linguistic influence, language ideologies and policies, issues of identity and prestige, metalinguistic awareness, and multilingual advantages. In a nutshell, the book discusses how individuals grow up in this global, multilingual world, and which aspects determine their linguistic development and outcomes. Each chapter takes up a selection of these problems for discussion.

The book is written from the perspective of English, as this language increasingly pervades all aspects of our lives and can be expected to influence nearly everyone on this planet in one way or another. English is the language that is responsible for the greatest number of language contact situations in history and occurs in highly diverse multilingual ecologies. It heavily influences other languages, but also changes and diversifies rapidly. Currently, English is the most widely used and studied lingua franca. The book is especially interested in the role that English plays in today's multilingual urban ecologies and the ways in which it interacts with other languages.

Multilingualism represents a complex problem that eschews simple interpretations. Accordingly, this book does not communicate a single message. However, it argues that it is beneficial and profitable to develop one's innate language ability in all possible directions. Multilingualism is a vital glue that keeps diverse societies together and ensures that they remain functional.

Acknowledgements

Although strictly speaking I only started writing this book in 2019, it had a much longer gestation period that can in fact be traced back to the initial stages in my career. My interest in linguistic diversity and language typology was aroused when I embarked on my PhD project and never ceased. Language contact and multilingualism were intensely researched in the Hamburg-based Collaborative Research Centre on Multilingualism (1999–2011). I profit from that experience even today. The social and educational perspectives of multilingualism were then strengthened during the Cluster of Excellence on Linguistic Diversity Management in Urban Areas (2009–2013) and the follow-up project on Multilingual Development: A Longitudinal Perspective (2014–2019). Several research projects on multilingualism in Singapore and the United Arab Emirates, funded by the German Research Foundation, added expertise from crucial international multilingual melting pots. All of these research strands are weaved together in this book, and I wish to extend my gratitude to everyone from whom I had the privilege to gain inspiration on my way.

My former doctoral student, Eliane Lorenz, deserves a very special word of gratitude for patiently reading and meticulously commenting on the text while I was writing it. I further wish to thank Aikaterina Koufopoulou, Lijun Li, Alexander Onysko, and Tugba Elif Toprak for reading and commenting on various draft versions of the manuscript. Ashleigh Brito substantially increased the stylistic level and the readability of the text. Sarah El Kafi carefully examined the references and the index. Hans-Olav Enger, Nicholas Evans, Robert Fuchs, and Jakob Leimgruber helped at various points with insightful discussions and other crucial inputs. Finally, I wish to express my sincere gratitude to Helen Barton and the three anonymous Cambridge University Press reviewers who placed my initial book proposal on the right track. They believed in me and I hope that the final work does not disappoint them.

The book is a homage to all the people in the world who are torn between the opportunities that English offers and their attachment to their often multiple native and local tongues. The demands imposed by our modern super-efficient, technology-based written cultures are extremely high and it is easy to conceive linguistic diversity as an obstacle to efficiency and progress. I wish to assure these very people that this conflict can be managed and even be considered an enrichment. The book describes the avenues along which this can be achieved as well as the various pitfalls that need to be circumnavigated. I believe that this endeavour needs guidance, as linguistic and cultural diversity can easily be sacrificed on the altar of lopsided ideologies that can produce severe problems in the long run.

About the Author

Peter Siemund has been Professor of English Linguistics at the University of Hamburg since 2001. He pursues a cross-linguistic typological approach in his work on reflexivity and *self*-intensifiers, pronominal gender, interrogative constructions, speech acts and clause types, argument structure, tense and aspect, varieties of English, language contact, and multilingual development. His publications include, as author, *Intensifiers in English and German: A Comparison* (Routledge, 2000), *Pronominal Gender in English: A Study of English Varieties from a Cross-Linguistic Perspective* (Routledge, 2008/2013), *The Amazing World of Englishes: A Practical Introduction* (with Julia Davydova and Georg Maier; Mouton de Gruyter, 2012), *Varieties of English: A Typological Approach* (Cambridge University Press, 2013), and *Speech Acts and Clause Types: English in a Cross-Linguistic Context* (Oxford University Press, 2018), and, as editor, *Language Contact and Contact Languages* (with Noemi Kintana; John Benjamins, 2008), *Linguistic Universals and Language Variation* (Mouton de Gruyter, 2011), *Multilingualism and Language Diversity in Urban Areas: Acquisition – Identities – Space – Education* (with Ingrid Gogolin, Monika Schulz, and Julia Davydova; John Benjamins, 2013), *Foreign Language Education in Multilingual Classrooms* (with Andreas Bonnet; John Benjamins, 2018), and *Multilingual Global Cities: Singapore, Hong Kong, Dubai* (with Jakob Leimgruber; Routledge, 2021).

1 Multilingualism

Past and Present

The first chapter provides an introduction to the field of multilingual development explaining its scientific and societal relevance. The discussion begins with an overview of current globalization and migration processes (Section 1.1) where, based on Organization for Economic Co-operation and Development (OECD) data of the past ten years, international migration streams receive illustration and substantiation. The exposition distinguishes between foreign-born and foreign populations, but also details population inflows and the relevant source countries.

Section 1.2 then focuses on a selection of urban areas as the specific locus where the concomitant increase in linguistic diversity plays out most forcefully. This survey takes the reader from London and Hamburg, as European metropolises, to the Canadian migration centres of Toronto and Vancouver. It continues with New York City and San Francisco as two prominent urban centres located on the East and West Coast of the United States. We proceed along the Pacific Rim to Sydney and Melbourne in Australia and Auckland in New Zealand. The survey closes with an assessment of the multilingual textures of Singapore, Hong Kong, and Dubai. Data have been drawn from the relevant national and municipal censuses.

After that, in Section 1.3, the reader is invited to partake in a historical survey of multilingualism. It is argued that while multilingualism represents a very old, and perhaps even the most natural form of social organization, linguistic diversity has been curtailed through the development of asymmetrical power relations and identity issues across different social groups. History has seen such asymmetries culminate in nations, nation states, and national languages with widespread monolingualism as an important outcome. While certain parts of the world (e.g. the countries that make up the Western World) have witnessed a recent increase in (primarily urban) multilingualism, other parts are rapidly losing linguistic diversity, sometimes in conjunction with the promotion of monolingual ideologies. English as the current global lingua franca is completely undisputed in the special status it enjoys.

Section 1.4 problematizes the diverging academic and political assessments of monolingualism and multilingualism. It examines different views and ideologies, especially the idea that bilingualism and multilingualism are associated with certain cognitive deficits. Recent history has witnessed a radical reassessment of this deficit perspective, with current scientific work highlighting the positive aspects of a multilingual experience for cognitive development and reserve, educational attainment, as well as subsequent language learning processes. However, Section 1.4 also voices scepticism regarding the question of whether multilingualism can develop into the preferred ideology and social form of organization, as the linguistic texture of modern societies is under strong pressure from forces pushing for homogenization, especially through the education systems.

Another important determinant of multilingual development is the status or prestige associated with different languages, as these form highly complex social value networks. This social hierarchy of languages and the special role of English is addressed in Section 1.5. The hierarchy is proof of extensive social power asymmetries that, as argued here, are the seeds producing monolingualism.

The chapter ends with a brief explication of key concepts such as additive and subtractive bilingualism, heritage speakers, dominance, cross-linguistic influence, as well as different language acquisition processes (Section 1.6). This is followed by a description of the intended readership as well as the structure of the book (Section 1.7), and a summary of the main issues (Section 1.8).

1.1 Globalization and Migration

Even though migration has been a hallmark of the human species from its very beginnings (Evans 2018a), there has been an unprecedented increase in global traffic and migration during recent decades. The reasons are obvious and include, inter alia, a sharp increase in human population, momentous political developments such as the fall of the Iron Curtain, fast and cheap air traffic, economic and demographic imbalances, labour shortages in boom regions, as well as warfare, famines, and related crises. Generally speaking, the source areas of population movements are characterized by economic and human hardship, while migration moves to areas of economic prosperity and stability. Target areas include Europe, North America, Australia, New Zealand, the Middle East, and Singapore, while there is a wide variety of source areas, inter alia several African countries, China, India, Kazakhstan, Pakistan, the Philippines, Russia, Poland, Ukraine, Viet Nam, as well as several others. Notwithstanding this generalization, there is also substantial migration within Africa, China, India, the Philippines, as well as other territories and countries, especially from rural to urban areas.

The OECD has been monitoring international migration for a considerable period of time and makes a host of information publicly available. Crucial to interpreting the OECD migration figures is the distinction between foreign and foreign-born populations. The OECD (2019: 340) defines these concepts as follows:

The foreign-born population can be viewed as representing first-generation migrants, and may consist of both foreign and national citizens. The size and composition of the foreign-born population is influenced by the history of migration flows and mortality amongst the foreign-born.

The concept of foreign population may include persons born abroad who retained the nationality of their country of origin but also second and third generations born in the host country.

These definitions are the result of diverging immigration statistics used by different countries. European countries, Japan, and Korea have a tradition of counting 'foreign' people, whereas settlement countries like Australia, Canada, New Zealand, and the United States count 'foreign-born' people (OECD 2019: 340). The latter group comprises both nationals and non-nationals of the target (host) country (first generation migrants). Great care needs to be exercised in the interpretation of these figures, since the OECD countries use different sources to count and estimate these population groups (population registers, residence permits, labour force surveys, and censuses; OECD 2019: 340).

1.1.1 Foreign-Born Populations

The data on foreign-born percentage of the population are shown in Figure 1.1 and provide a rough indication of the people with a migration background from 2008 to 2018.[1] Data are only presented for a selection of the foundational OECD countries. For ease of presentation, the individual country data has been bundled into bigger units that belong together regionally, culturally, and economically. Here, besides North America (Canada, United States) and Australasia (Australia, New Zealand), I group together the British Isles (United Kingdom, Ireland), Central European countries (Austria, Belgium, France, Germany, the Netherlands), Southern European countries (Greece, Italy, Portugal, Spain), and Northern European (Scandinavian) countries (Denmark, Finland, Iceland, Norway, Sweden). Moreover, Luxembourg and

[1] The percentages were calculated using the data on "Stocks of foreign-born population in OECD countries and in Russia" (OECD 2019: 341–342) and the respective population counts for each country as indicated in the OECD database on historical population (stats.oecd.org/Index.aspx?DataSetCode=HISTPOP, accessed on 17 March 2020). A few figures in the stocks of foreign-born population had to be interpolated due to missing data. This concerns Canada (1 cell), Ireland (4 cells), Italy (1 cell), and New Zealand (1 cell). Interpolation averages the annual changes in stocks of foreign-born population across the data points available. In such cases, the percentages were produced with the interpolated figures calculated against the populations counts.

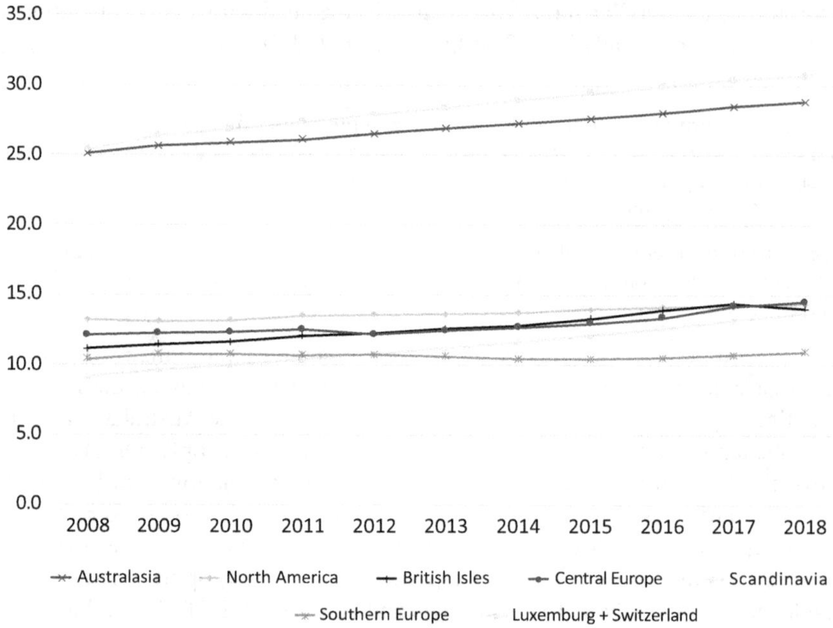

Figure 1.1 Foreign-born population as per cent of the population according to OECD figures (OECD 2019).

Switzerland are treated as one unit, as they are the only officially multilingual countries in the sample. All in all, the data offer an instructive overview of foreign-born population developments.[2]

One can gather from Figure 1.1 that Luxembourg and Switzerland show the highest number of foreign-born people, totalling 30.7 per cent in 2018. They are closely followed by Australia and New Zealand with an aggregate percentage of 28.8, again measured in 2018 (29.4% and 25.9%, respectively). Luxembourg taken on its own boasts a share of 46.2 per cent of foreign-born people (2018); the value for Switzerland is 29.6 per cent (2018). The remaining four groups of European countries (British Isles, Central European, Southern European, Northern European) as well as the United States, in combination with Canada, range between 10 and 15 per cent, again in 2018. The figure for Canada alone is 21.2 per cent in 2018. Austria reported a population of 19.2 per cent foreign-born residents in 2018, and Sweden 18.4 per cent.

[2] Technically this meant adding up the foreign-born populations as well as the overall population counts of the respective countries. Percentages were calculated on the basis of these aggregate values. The percentages calculated here diverge slightly from those given in OECD (2019: 341–342).

All groups of countries shown in Figure 1.1 manifest an upward trend in their foreign-born populations, though for some it is more pronounced than for others. The increase is relatively noticeable for Luxembourg and Switzerland, Australia and New Zealand, as well as the Scandinavian countries. One can also detect a slight upward trend for the other four groups.

1.1.2 Foreign Populations

While Australia and New Zealand do not offer separate statistics for their foreign populations, one does find figures for the other OECD countries included here. However, it is unclear to what extent these foreign populations overlap with the foreign-born populations. Consider Figure 1.2, for example, in the case of Luxembourg for 2018. The OECD data allow one to calculate a share of 46.2 per cent of the population in the category 'foreign-born' and 47.4 per cent in that of 'foreign', that is, an aggregate of 93.6 per cent of the population is non-indigenous in a technical sense (OECD 2019: 341, 363). The relevant graph in Figure 1.2 under-reports as it was averaged with the data from Switzerland. There, the foreign population was at 24.1 per cent in 2018.[3] In neighbouring Germany, the corresponding figures are 15.9 per cent for foreign-born and 12.8 per cent for foreign populations, that is, a combined total of 28.7 per cent (OECD 2019: 341, 363).[4] Here, the distinction between foreign and indigenous is still meaningful, while for Luxembourg it appears difficult to maintain. The OECD report warns that their statistics may "underestimate the number of immigrants" (OECD 2019: 340).

Apart from the combined values for Switzerland and Luxembourg, the other group values hover between 5 and 10 per cent, with there being a slight increase over time. Some of these countries reported shares of foreign populations above 10 per cent in 2018 (Austria 15.8%, Belgium 12.2%, Germany 12.8%, Iceland 10.7%, Ireland 12.2%, Norway 10.7%). These differences disappear in the averages.

[3] The population of Switzerland is much bigger than that of Luxembourg. In 2018, the OECD data listed a population of 8,513,227 for Switzerland and 607,950 for Luxembourg.

[4] These percentages again represent my own calculations based on the stocks of foreign population provided by the OECD data (OECD 2019: 363–364) and the historical population data (stats.oecd.org/Index.aspx?DataSetCode=HISTPOP, accessed on 17 March 2020). As with foreign-born populations, the percentages diverge slightly from those listed in OECD (2019: 363–364). Figures for Canada are only available for 2011 and 2016. I interpolated the remaining values, but there may be a more fundamental problem here. Figures for Greece had to be interpolated for 2018. Figures for Australasia are zero due to missing data.

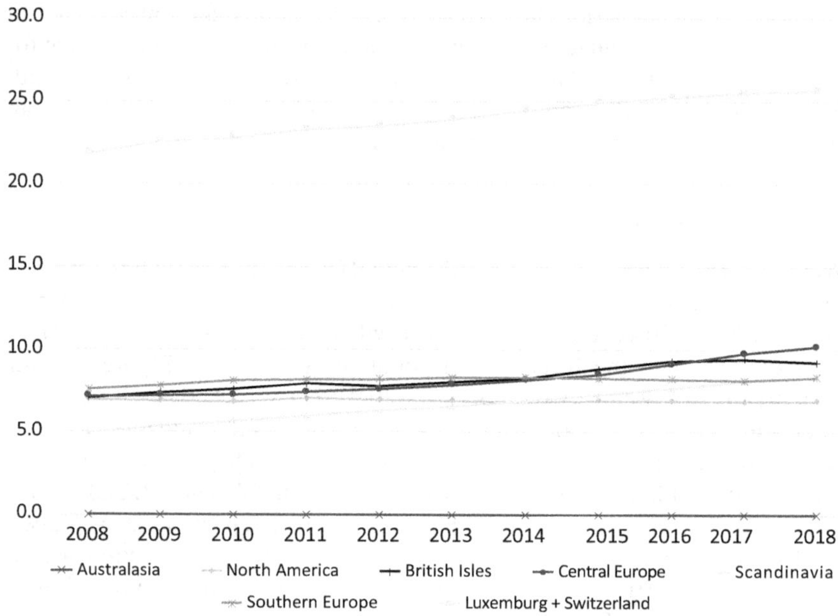

Figure 1.2 Foreign population as per cent of the population according to OECD figures (OECD 2019).

1.1.3 Foreign Population Inflow

It is also revealing to consider the development of the inflow of foreign population over time (2007–2017), measured in per cent of the entire population.[5] The relevant graphs for the groups of countries distinguished here can be found in Figure 1.3.

At around 0.4 per cent, the figures for the United States and Canada are quite stable and the lowest of all. The United States generally reported higher figures than Canada (0.8% vs. 0.3% in 2017, with similar values in the earlier years). At the opposite end of the spectrum, we find Luxembourg and Switzerland with relatively high inflow rates of around 2 per cent. The values for Luxembourg range between 3 and 4 per cent. The Central European countries

[5] Percentages were calculated using the foreign population inflow data offered in OECD (2019: 295) and the historical population data available at stats.oecd.org/Index.aspx?DataSetCode=HISTPOP, accessed on 17 March 2020. According to OECD (2019: 294), population flows were estimated on the basis of population registers, residence and/or work permits, and specific surveys such as household or passenger surveys. Given the scope of international population flows, figures need to be interpreted with care.

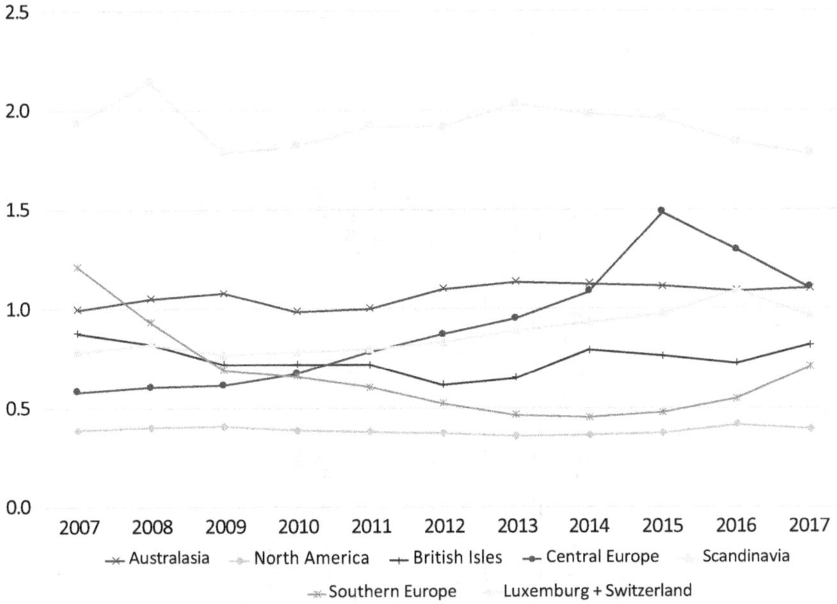

Figure 1.3 Population inflow as per cent of the population according to OECD figures (OECD 2019).

experienced an increase in the period considered here. The 2015 peak in this group of countries is primarily attributed to Austria and Germany (2.3% and 2.5%, respectively), apparently as a result of the Syrian refugee crisis. Australia and New Zealand portray stable inflow rates hovering at around 1 per cent. To be sure, this population inflow is subject to complex political decisions and economic demands.[6]

1.1.4 *Source Countries*

Table 1.1 lists the seven top-most important source countries for a selection of OECD member states in the category of foreign-born residents.[7] This small selection of source countries already reveals substantial diversity. In addition,

[6] Furthermore, OECD (2019: 314) provides data on the outflow of foreign populations. Although a comparison with the inflow data is interesting, this is beyond the current concern.

[7] The ranking is based on the "Stocks of foreign-born population by country of birth," as listed in OECD (2019: 343–360). The ranking generally uses the 2018 figures except for Canada, where due to missing data the 2016 figures are given. Equally, the ranking for Ireland represents stocks of foreign-borns in 2016 due to missing data for 2018. The New Zealand ranking uses 2013 figures, which are the only ones provided in OECD (2019: 354).

Table 1.1. *The top seven source countries of foreign-born populations in a selection of OECD countries (OECD 2019).*

Australia	Canada	Germany	Ireland	New Zealand	UK	US
United Kingdom	India	Poland	United Kingdom	United Kingdom	India	Mexico
China	China	Turkey	Poland	China	Poland	India
India	Philippines	Russia	Lithuania	India	Pakistan	China
New Zealand	United Kingdom	Kazakhstan	Romania	Australia	Romania	Philippines
Philippines	United States	Romania	United States	South Africa	Ireland	El Salvador
Viet Nam	Italy	Syria	India	Fiji	Germany	Viet Nam
South Africa	Hong Kong	Italy	Latvia	Samoa	Italy	Cuba

some pairings of target and source country enjoy a considerable time depth, as, for example, India for the United Kingdom, China for Canada, or Mexico for the United States. Poland is a very important source country in Europe, while Chinese immigration is strong in North America and Australasia. Hong Kong was the seventh most important source region for Canada in 2016. The United Kingdom appears to be an attractive destination for Germans.

Table 1.2 offers lists of the seven top source countries in the category of foreign populations for the same target countries, except Australia and New Zealand, as the OECD data are silent on these.[8] Instead, the relevant source countries for Japan and (South) Korea are listed here, as they are quite informative regarding the East Asian population movements. Evidently, China is a very strong export country here, but also Viet Nam and the Philippines. Korea attracts many immigrants from Viet Nam, Uzbekistan, and Cambodia. Brazil is an important source country for Ireland and Japan (and less surprisingly also for Portugal). Interestingly, amongst the top seven source countries for foreign populations we also find China for Finland, Hungary, Italy, Mexico, Portugal, and Spain (based on 2018 figures provided in OECD 2019).[9]

The above surveyed global migration has also important consequences for the attested number of languages in specific locales. Especially attractive target locations are major conurbations, and it is here where we currently find the greatest language diversity. Again, there are specific preference pairings of migrant groups and target cities, but on the whole, major urban areas like Vancouver, London, Sydney, or Hamburg have become home to people from nearly all 193 member states of the United Nations.[10] Since many – if not most – of these states are multi-ethnic and multilingual, the number of languages travelling globally and now residing in certain urban areas is much higher than the number of recognized nationalities. Some cities have turned into modern Babels.

1.1.5 Summary

The preceding survey has shown that many Western European countries have in fact become immigrant countries. The relevant OECD figures reveal trends that are similar to those for the traditional settler and immigrant countries of Canada, the United States, Australia, and New Zealand. The population inflows remain relatively stable with the exception of certain crisis-induced

[8] The ranking uses the data provided in OECD (2019: 365–381). The figures for 2018 were used, except for Canada (2016) and Ireland (2016), due to missing data.

[9] Some of the information is not included in Table 1.2.

[10] Retrieved from www.un.org/en/about-us/growth-in-un-membership, accessed on 23 March 2021.

Table 1.2. *The top seven source countries of foreign populations in a selection of OECD countries (OECD 2019).*

Canada	Germany	Ireland	Japan	Korea	UK	US
China	Turkey	Poland	China	China	Poland	Mexico
India	Poland	United Kingdom	Korea	Viet Nam	Romania	India
Philippines	Syria	Lithuania	Viet Nam	Uzbekistan	India	China
United States	Italy	Romania	Philippines	Cambodia	Ireland	El Salvador
United Kingdom	Romania	Latvia	Brazil	Philippines	Italy	Guatemala
France	Croatia	Brazil	Nepal	Indonesia	Portugal	Philippines
Korea	Greece	Spain	Chinese Taipei	Nepal	Pakistan	Cuba

peaks. The shares of foreign and foreign-born populations have been increasing slowly over time. Each receiving country appears to possess its unique array of source countries, apparently contingent on historical connections, geographical proximity, and government relations.

1.2 Multilingualism in Urban Areas

An important concomitant of these migration processes is an increase in individual and societal multilingualism, as languages travel with people and migrants face the need to learn new languages in the respective target areas of migration (Aronin & Singleton 2012; Blommaert 2010; Edwards 2012; Gogolin et al. 2013; Montrul 2016; Piller 2016; Polinsky 2018; Siemund et al. 2013; Singleton & Aronin 2019; Stavans & Hoffmann 2015). Home language and majority language come to differ, a complex fabric of heritage languages develops (Montrul 2016; Polinsky 2018), diglossic or triglossic situations arise, language vitality and attrition become an issue (Montrul 2008), educational challenges develop as students with diverse language repertoires enter the school system (Bonnet & Siemund 2018a; Cummins 2000), with similar challenges also developing for administration, businesses, the legal system, and the health system (Bührig & Meyer 2013).

Urban areas lead the trend, with several scores of languages being present in certain cities (London, Toronto, Melbourne, Dubai, Hamburg, etc.). Such conurbations accumulate linguistic density better known from high-contact areas such as Papua New Guinea or the Amazon Basin. Neighbourhoods and blocks correspond to villages and entire villages are squeezed vertically into multistorey apartment buildings. However, urban multilingualism in the Western World obeys rules different from the aforementioned, mostly rural, contexts.

Prosperous Western cities like London, Paris, Amsterdam, Hamburg, Toronto, and Vancouver now harbour immigrant communities from nearly all nations and many different ethnicities. Current research emphasizes the super-diverse networks of languages, cultures, ethnicities, rights, and levels of integration and participation (Blommaert 2010; Vertovec 2007). Buzzwords like diversity, fluidity, heterogeneity, mobility, and multilingualism dominate the discourse.

The following sections substantiate how the preceding generalizations manifest in a selection of important urban areas from different parts of the world. The information was culled from official, publicly available, census reports. Although they are unique in many respects, the city of London (Greater London) as well as the Free and Hanseatic City of Hamburg are taken here to reflect the situation in Europe. Toronto and Vancouver represent Canada, while for the United States, New York City and San Francisco were selected. Continuing with traditional immigrant countries, the overview then turns to

Australia and New Zealand, focusing on Sydney, Melbourne, and Auckland. As for Asia, the current situation in the former colonial cities of Singapore and Hong Kong will be explored. Finally, we will venture a glimpse onto the Middle East describing the multilingual landscape of Dubai.

1.2.1 London and Hamburg

The London 2011 Census lists a total population of 8.17 million (London Census 2011a; around nine million in 2020).[11] The 2011 Census asked respondents to indicate their "main language" (London Census 2011b). According to reported figures, "22.1 per cent of Londoners list a language other than English as their main language, a total of 1.73 million people," "41.6 per cent of non-English speakers in England & Wales live in London," and "9 of the top 10 most linguistically diverse local authorities in England & Wales are in London." Polish is widely spoken being the main language of 147,816 people (8.6%), the most important South Asian language is Bengali (6.6%), and Somali is the most spoken African language (3.2%). Other widely attested main languages are Gujarati (5.9%), French (4.9%), Urdu (4.6%), as well as Arabic, Portuguese, Spanish, Tamil, and Turkish (all equally at 4.1%), and Punjabi (4.0%). London harbours European languages (French, Polish, Portuguese, Spanish, etc.), languages of the Middle East (Arabic, Turkish, etc.), South Asian languages (Bengali, Gujarati, Urdu, etc.), East and Southeast Asian languages (Cantonese, Malay, Mandarin, Tagalog/Filipino, Thai, Vietnamese, etc.), and African languages (Igbo, Kiswahili, Somali, Yoruba, etc.). Without any doubt, it is a modern Babel. With regard to household languages, "74 per cent of households in London contain occupants who all have English as their main language, compared to 91 per cent nationally" (London Census 2011c). In addition, we are informed that "London is the region with the highest proportion of households where no one has English as a main language. There are 422,000 households in London where this is the case." Not surprisingly, there are severe differences in language distribution and home language use across the city.

With approximately 1.8 million inhabitants, the Free and Hanseatic City of Hamburg is the second largest city in Germany (after Berlin) and in many respects quite representative in regard to the ethnic and linguistic diversity currently found in Germany (and also other European countries). In the official statistics available for 2019 (Statistisches Amt für Hamburg und Schleswig-Holstein 2020),[12] 330,165 inhabitants were registered as foreign citizens, with

[11] The London 2011 Census contains the most recent data at the time of writing. The London 2021 Census will offer updated figures.

[12] I would like to express my gratitude to the Statistisches Amt für Hamburg und Schleswig-Holstein for granting me access to their data.

Europeans contributing 61.3 per cent, Asians 26.1 per cent, Africans 7.2 per cent, and people from the Americas 4.1 per cent. Australia and Oceania are only weakly represented at 0.3 per cent. Numerically important European source countries are Bulgaria, Poland, Portugal, Romania, and Turkey. Ghana stands out as the single most important African source country. Afghanistan, China, India, Iran, Iraq, the Philippines, and Syria represent principal Asian source countries. There are more males than females and the majority of people are of working age. A total of 670,016 inhabitants of Hamburg possessed a migration background according to the 2018 figures, amounting to approximately 35 per cent of the total population.[13] The most important source countries of this more encompassing group are Turkey (14.1%), Poland (11.4%), Afghanistan (6.6%), the Russian Federation (5.2%), Iran (3.6%), Kazakhstan (3.1%), Syria (2.6%), Romania (2.3%), Ghana (2.1%), Italy (2.0%), and Portugal (2.0%).

To be sure, the above figures reveal little about the relevant mother tongues and home languages. This information, however, can be approximated from school surveys. The cohort of 199,731 grade one students in the school year of 2019/2020 attests a share of 72.4 per cent of primarily German home language use (assessed before school entry). Other important primary home languages are Turkish (4.8%), Arabic (3.2%), Russian (2.4%), Dari (2.1%), Polish (1.6%), Farsi (1.4%), Albanian (1.1%), and Kurdish (1.0%). A total of 55,029 students indicated their heritage language as their primary home language. A total of 22,774 out of these 55,029 students use German as another home language besides the respective heritage language (Behörde für Schule und Berufsbildung, Hamburg 2020).[14]

1.2.2 Toronto and Vancouver

The 2016 census of Toronto reports that 92.8 per cent of the population speak English as their first official language (Statistics Canada 2017a). The other official language, French, is spoken unilingually by 1.5 per cent, while 0.9 per cent say that they speak English and French.[15] A total of 4.8 per cent of the population speak neither of the official languages, while 9.1 per cent of the population claim knowledge of English and French. Knowledge of English is

[13] This figure includes the foreigners mentioned before. The definition of "migration background" is complicated, but largely refers to foreign-borns with German citizenship as well as children under eighteen years with German citizenship of whom at least one parent is foreign-born (Statistisches Amt für Hamburg und Schleswig-Holstein 2020).

[14] I wish to thank the Behörde für Schule und Berufsbildung, Hamburg, for sharing their data with me.

[15] Knowledge of the official languages is very different in Montréal, where in the 2016 census 10.1 per cent claimed knowledge of English only, 29.9 per cent of French only, 57.4 per cent of both English and French, and 2.5 per cent knowledge of neither of the official languages (Statistics Canada 2017c).

reported by 95.0 per cent of the population; that of French by 9.2 per cent. Regarding mother tongues in the section "single responses" of the census, 50.9 per cent state English, 1.3 per cent French, and 43.9 per cent one of a host of non-official languages. The latter group attests a great variety of language families and languages, although it does not contain any native American ("aboriginal") languages (Afro-Asiatic 2.4%; Austro-Asiatic 1.0%; Austronesian 3.7% of which 3.1% is contributed by Tagalog; Dravidian 2.5%; Indo-European 21.8%; Korean 1.2%; Sino-Tibetan 9.3%).[16] In the group of Indo-European languages, Indo-Iranian languages represent the biggest subgroup contributing 7.2 per cent. African languages are practically absent. The distribution of languages spoken most often at home is strongly tilted towards English, with 64.3 per cent using English, 0.6 per cent French, and 25.9 per cent one of the non-official languages. In the section "knowledge of languages," the census lists 54.4 per cent for the non-official and 95.1 per cent for the official languages (mostly English). Like London, Toronto is a linguistically highly diverse territory.

Vancouver, although only less than half the size of Toronto in terms of population, is the biggest Canadian conurbation on the Pacific coast and shows important similarities in its linguistic landscape. The following figures are also based on the 2016 census (Statistics Canada 2017b). English is the (single) mother tongue of 51.3 per cent of its population, while it is the first official language spoken for 91.1 per cent. French as the other official language is reported by 1.6 per cent; both English and French by 0.6 per cent; neither English nor French by 6.7 per cent. Knowledge of English lies at 93.1 per cent; that of French at 10.0 per cent. These figures correspond to those for Toronto. Non-official languages as mother tongues are reported by 44.0 per cent of the population. For 25.7 per cent they represent the languages spoken most often at home, while 54.0 per cent claim knowledge of them. Due to its geographical location, the share of Sino-Tibetan languages is much higher than in Toronto (21.6% vs. 9.3% as single mother tongue). Cantonese is especially prominent with 13.7 per cent. Conversely, the share of Indo-European language is lower (12.5% vs. 21.8%). The other language families are distributed as follows: Austro-Asiatic 1.8 per cent; Austronesian 3.9 per cent (mostly Tagalog at 3.1%); Japanese 1.1 per cent; Korean 1.3 per cent.[17] In Vancouver we find, furthermore, that 0.1 per cent of its population speaks an aboriginal (native American) language as their mother tongue, though these are apparently not spoken at home. Like Toronto, African languages are rarely reported.

It is difficult to assess the exact levels of bilingualism or multilingualism for Toronto and Vancouver, as the census does not reveal this. However, with knowledge of English at more than 90 per cent and knowledge of the

16 Only language families equal and above 1 per cent are listed here.
17 Only language families equal and above 1 per cent are listed here.

non-official languages reported by more than 50 per cent of the population, one can assume levels of bilingualism or multilingualism to be above 50 per cent.[18]

1.2.3 New York City and San Francisco

To offer a glimpse of the situation in the United States, the major conurbations of New York City and San Francisco will be considered (US Census Bureau 2018).[19] They are located on the East Coast and West Coast, respectively, and provide suitable points of comparison to Toronto and Vancouver. The subsequent statistical information is based on the New York-Newark-Jersey City NY-NJ-PA Metro Area as well as the San Francisco-Oakland-Hayward, CA Metro Area (2018). With approximately 19 million people, the former metropolitan statistical area is considerably bigger than the latter (around 4.5 million). Home language use of only English is reported by 61.0 per cent of the population for the New York metro area and by 58.6 per cent of the San Francisco region.

An important difference to the language distribution in Canada is that Spanish occurs as a major category in the census. In New York, 19.8 per cent of the population use Spanish as their home language. The corresponding figure for San Francisco is 15.7 per cent. Other Indo-European languages excluding Spanish and Indian languages account for 7.3 and 3.6 per cent, respectively. As in the Canadian context, Chinese languages are more strongly represented on the West Coast than on the East Coast (9.0% vs. 3.5%).[20] Indian languages (Gujarati, Hindi, Urdu, Punjabi, Bengali, etc.) contribute 2.8 per cent of home language use in New York and 3.0 per cent in San Francisco. Tagalog and other Austronesian languages are quite strongly represented in the San Francisco area with 4.1 per cent of home language use. A total of 1.2 per cent of the population in the home language report of this area speak a Dravidian language (Telugu, Tamil, Malayalam, Kannada) and 1.1 per cent say that their home language is Vietnamese. A total of 3,878 people in the New York region speak a native American language at home, contrasting with 786 people in the San Francisco area.

[18] Knowledge of language is defined as the ability to conduct a conversation in a language (see Statistics Canada 2017a, 2017b, 2017c).

[19] I would like to express my gratitude to the US Census Bureau's American Community Survey for their assistance in finding suitable data. The data is based on the 2018 American Community Survey Table B16001 "Language Spoken at Home by Ability to Speak English for the Population 5 Years and over." The data on English ability is not used here. Percentages represent my own calculations.

[20] In the eleven districts of the City of San Francisco itself, Chinese outranks Spanish according to the San Francisco Office of Civic Engagement & Immigrant Affairs (sfgov.org/oceia/language-diversity-data, accessed on 22 April 2020).

1.2.4 Sydney, Melbourne, and Auckland

In what follows, Australia and New Zealand are treated as one unit. The cities of Sydney, Melbourne, and Auckland belong to the so-called 'Pacific Rim' and thus show some overlap regarding their economic orientation and immigration policies. Sydney and Melbourne are the largest Australian cities in terms of their population (both around 5 million; Australian Bureau of Statistics 2016a, 2016b), while Auckland is the main conurbation in New Zealand with a populace of about 1.5 million people (Statistics New Zealand 2018).

The 2016 Census of Population and Housing by the Australian Bureau of Statistics states that the majority of homes in both Sydney and Melbourne use only English (Australian Bureau of Statistics 2016a, 2016b).[21] The figure for Sydney (55.8%) is lower than that of Melbourne (61.2%). The main other languages spoken in Sydney homes are Mandarin (5.1%), Arabic (4.3%), Cantonese (3.1%), Vietnamese (2.2%), Greek (1.7%), Hindi (1.4%), Italian (1.4%), Korean (1.3%), and Spanish (1.2%). As for Melbourne, the major non-English languages are Mandarin (4.3%), Greek (2.5%), Italian (2.3%), Vietnamese (2.3%), Arabic (1.8%), Cantonese (1.8%), Hindi (1.1%), and Punjabi (1.2%).[22] A total of 4.7 per cent of the other languages spoken in Sydney homes are not specified in the census; 4.9 per cent for Melbourne. 5.8 per cent of the Sydney homes did not disclose their home languages; similarly 5.6 per cent for Melbourne. Interestingly, the Arabic-speaking community is much bigger in Sydney than in Melbourne, while the Greek-speaking community is bigger in Melbourne than in Sydney. The share of Chinese languages is more substantial in Sydney (8.6%) than in Melbourne (6.5%). The census data reveal that about half of the populations of Sydney and Melbourne are bilingual or multilingual.[23]

As far as Auckland is concerned, the 2018 census informs us that 92.8 per cent of the population speak English (Statistics New Zealand 2018). We need to bear in mind, though, that this figure indicates language knowledge and not home language use. Moreover, it includes people who speak other languages besides English and does not represent those who only speak English. The percentages for the other languages found in Auckland need to be interpreted

[21] The Australian Bureau of Statistics (ABS) needs to be credited for providing assistance in accessing their data. For Sydney, I used "GCP_1030 Sydney Significant Urban Area;" for Melbourne "GCP_2010 Melbourne Significant Urban Area." The data was extracted from Table G13 "Language Spoken at Home by Proficiency in Spoken English/Language by Sex." The data on English proficiency is not used. Percentages represent my own calculations.

[22] Only languages equal and above 1 per cent are listed here. There are several other languages spoken in the two cities that range below 1 per cent of the population.

[23] Piller (2016: 1) draws attention to a certain multilingual rivalry between Sydney and Melbourne – and also certain cities in Canada and the United States – over the highest levels of linguistic diversity.

with the same caveats: Samoan (4.4%), Northern Chinese (4.4%), Hindi (3.0%), Māori (2.4%), Yue (2.3%),[24] other Sinitic languages (2.3%), Tagalog (1.3%), French (1.2%), Tongan (1.9%), Punjabi (1.3%), Afrikaans (1.1%), Spanish (1.0%), German (0.8%), and other languages 12.2%).[25]

Statistics New Zealand furthermore provides information in regard to how many languages people speak. Here, 69.1 per cent claim to speak only one language, which can be assumed to be English in most cases. A total of 25.7 per cent report being bilingual, while trilingualism is attested by 4.2 per cent. Four and five languages are reported by 0.8 and 0.2 per cent of the Auckland population, respectively.[26] Hence, levels of multilingualism are relatively high.

1.2.5 Singapore, Hong Kong, and Dubai

The present survey of multilingual urban areas will now revert to three cities that do not belong to the typical targets of immigration in the Western World. Nevertheless, as former colonies or protectorates of the British Empire, Singapore, Hong Kong, and Dubai developed into important trading hubs whose strong demands for labour could only be satisfied by immigration. As a consequence, all three cities experienced a substantial increase in ethnic and linguistic diversity, to be briefly described in what follows (Siemund & Leimgruber 2021).

In 2019, Singapore's population consisted of 15.0 per cent Malays, who represent the indigenous population of the island cum city state, 76.0 per cent Chinese, 7.5 per cent Indians, and 1.5 per cent of other ethnic groups (Singapore Department of Statistics 2021). The Chinese and Indian populations primarily hailed from Southern China and the southern parts of India, bringing with them the local languages from these regions (Hokkien, Teochew, Cantonese, Tamil, etc.). They enjoy a long history in Singapore starting immediately with the arrival of the British in 1819, partly even earlier (Siemund and Li 2020; see Chapter 6.3). When Singapore was founded as an independent country in 1965, these languages used to be very prominent and were widely spoken. Over the past decades and as a consequence of tightly planned government language policy, the relative share of English and Mandarin Chinese has increased significantly, whereas the use of the other Chinese languages or vernaculars (referred to as "Chinese dialects" in the Census of Population) has been marginalized. These developments can be

24 It is not entirely clear what Yue here refers to. The label as such tends to be used as an umbrella term for the dialects spoken in the Guangdong and Guangxi provinces of Southern China, while Cantonese is used for the urban vernaculars of Hong Kong, Macau, and Guangzhou (the capital city of Guangdong). However, the two terms may also be used synonymously (Lijun Li, personal communication).

25 Percentages represent my own calculations.

26 Percentages represent my own calculations.

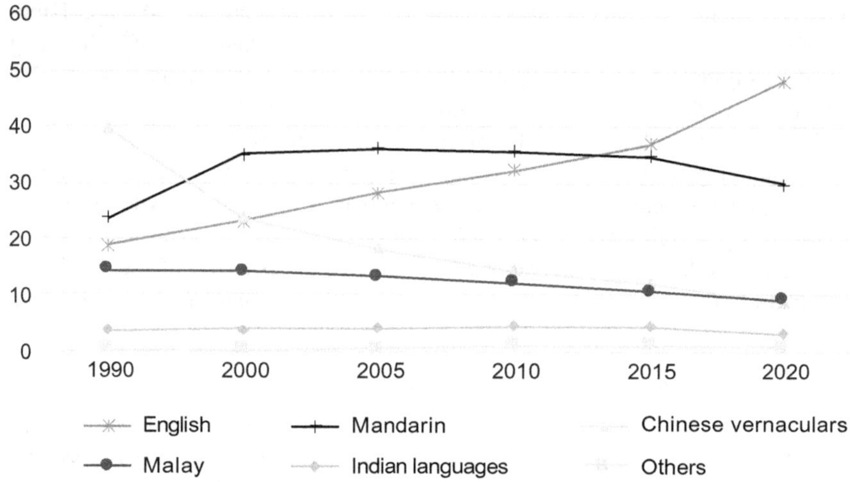

Figure 1.4 Home language use in Singapore from 1990 to 2020, in per cent (Singapore Department of Statistics 2021).

gleaned from Figure 1.4.[27] It needs to be noted that English firmly established itself as the most prominent home language in the 2020 census, consolidating a trend started earlier.

Cavallaro and Ng (2021: 136) report figures from even further back in time. They state that the share of Chinese vernaculars was as high as 59.5 per cent in 1980 and 74.4 per cent in 1957. The corresponding figures for English are 11.6 per cent in 1980 and 1.8 per cent in 1957; those for Mandarin 10.2 per cent (1980) and 0.1 per cent (1957). The share of Tamil was 3.1 per cent in 1980 and 5.2 per cent in 1957; that of Malay 13.9 per cent in 1980 and 13.5 per cent in 1957. One may note that home language use of English exceeded all other languages for the first time in 2015.

Singapore is an apt example of a multilingual society that is largely based on individual bilingualism, namely Mandarin/English, Malay/English, and Tamil/English for the main ethnic groups. English enjoys a special position in this multilingual ecology, as it is the language known by everyone. In fact, there is another language in this multilingual ecology that does not surface in the official statistics: Colloquial Singapore English (Singlish). Although denounced as a

[27] I wish to thank the Singapore Department of Statistics for their assistance in reconstructing the data for 1990. The data for 1990, 2000, 2010, and 2020 come from the Census of Population. The data for 2005 and 2015 are based on the General Household Survey.

hybrid language ("broken English"), it is spoken practically by all Singaporeans and enjoys substantial covert prestige as a local solidarity code.

In an official capacity, Hong Kong is a trilingual (Cantonese, Putonghua,[28] English) and biliterate (Chinese, English) city (Special Administrative Region of the People's Republic of China). It is nevertheless clear that the city is substantially more multilingual (Bolton, Bacon-Shone & Lee 2021). According to the Thematic Household Survey Report No. 66 (Census and Statistics Department Hong Kong 2019: 88), 88.8 per cent of the population quote Cantonese as their mother tongue, while 3.9 per cent state that it is Putonghua. Other Chinese vernaculars (dialects) contribute to 3.3 per cent of the mother tongues. For 1.4 per cent of the Hong Kong population, English is the mother tongue, with other European languages contributing only 0.3 per cent. Filipino and Indonesian range at 0.3 and 0.1 per cent, respectively. Other Asian languages account for 1.9 per cent of the mother tongues. Concerning the usual spoken language, the 2016 Population By-Census lists Cantonese for 88.9 per cent of the population, though only 1.9 per cent with respect to Putonghua (Census and Statistics Department Hong Kong 2017). The figure for other Chinese vernaculars (dialects) is 3.1 per cent; that for English 4.3 per cent. Other languages represent the usual spoken language for 1.9 per cent of the Hong Kong population.

Dubai, which is one of the seven emirates tied together in the United Arab Emirates, experienced a relatively recent population increase growing into a global city of more than 3 million inhabitants within only a few decades. The lion's share of this population growth can be attributed to expatriates and foreign workers who in 2019 accounted for 92.1 per cent of Dubai's population (Dubai Statistics Center 2020; see Figure 1.5). In other words, not even 10 per cent of the city's population have Emirati roots.

The foreign population bears a host of nationalities, with Indians being the most populous group. Other countries represented in Dubai in sizeable numbers of people are Pakistan, Bangladesh, Egypt, Iran, the Philippines, China, as well as Great Britain, the United States, and several European countries. Figures available online represent non-official estimates and need to be interpreted with caution (Dubai Statistics Center 2020). There is no information on language use within or across these immigrant groups, although it is obvious that the city is extremely multilingual (see Chapter 6). The linguistic landscape is strongly dominated by English – especially all businesses and the education system – which is used as the lingua franca and the de facto official language (with Arabic being the de jure official language). In view of the fact that many foreign

[28] The term 'Putonghua' (common speech) is widely used in the context of Hong Kong. Within the People's Republic of China, it relates to the standardized spoken official form of Chinese. Putonghua is linguistically similar to Mandarin (see Mair 2013 for further discussion).

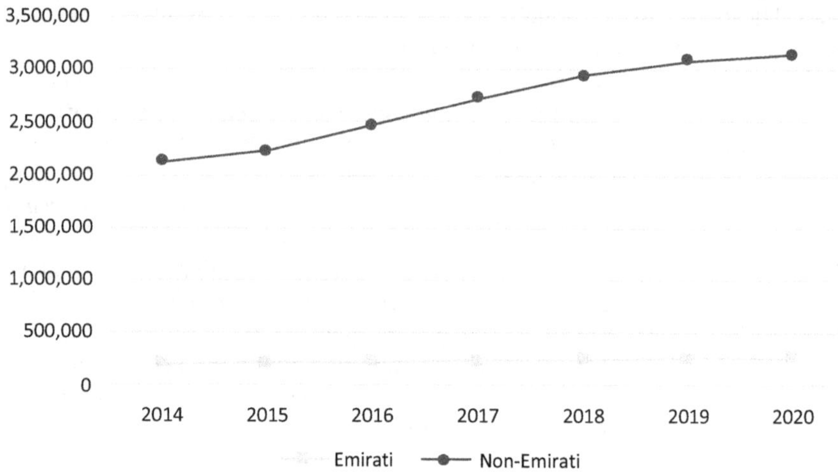

Figure 1.5 Foreign population of Dubai in relation to the local Emirati population (Dubai Statistics Center 2020).

workers hail from former British colonies where English is spoken as one of the postcolonial varieties of this language, Dubai also exemplifies a melting pot of international Englishes.

1.2.6 *Summary*

It is important to bear in mind that the outcomes of the migration processes sketched in the above urban areas are not the result of random or chaotic processes. Quite the opposite is the case. They are due to carefully monitored immigration policies, although not necessarily fully explicit language policies. Besides other criteria, the resulting mix of languages tends to be at least partially a function of territorial proximity. For example, Chinese and Austronesian languages are more prominently represented in Pacific Rim Cities. The relatively high number of Chinese immigrants in Italy must have different reasons (OECD 2019: 351, 371).

As we saw in Section 1.1, Canada and the United States permit lower annual inflows of immigration than Australia and New Zealand (averaging 0.4% vs. 1.1% of the population), where the share of foreign-born residents is higher (28.8% vs. 14.4% in 2018). Much of that inflow can be expected to concentrate on urban areas. Conspicuously, English has always remained the majority language in the urban areas surveyed above, in spite of massive multilingualism. The permissible immigration inflow is apparently low enough to maintain this balance. Generally, Central and Northern European countries permit more immigration than Southern European countries, with people mainly flowing in from Eastern Europe, Asia, and Northern Africa. With no doubt, the national languages continue to be the majority languages, that is, English and German for London and Hamburg, respectively. Singapore, Hong Kong, and Dubai stand out as former British colonies or protectorates. Their immigration histories and multilingual ecologies will be scrutinized in more detail in Chapter 6.

1.3 The Rediscovery of Multilingualism

The cline from monolingualism to bilingualism, multilingualism, and plurilingualism offers a spectrum of linguistic options that has been subject to tremendous change over time – both objectively and in terms of the respective attitudes, ideologies, and perceptions. Monolingualism used to be the preferred linguistic policy option (or ideology; see Philips 2015, Silverstein 1979) during the creation of the nation states in the eighteenth and nineteenth centuries when unity, homogeneity, a high degree of segregation, as well as the creation of national identities were top priorities (Aronin & Singleton 2012; Braunmüller 2019; Franceschini 2013; Gogolin 2020; Hobsbawm 1990).[29] German romanticism has been held responsible for the principle of "one nation, one language," but its origins are probably much older (Edwards 2009: 206–211; Wasserfall 2019: 24).[30] As language is an important symbol of identity, bilingualism, multilingualism, as well as dialect language came to be denounced as deficient, with languages across Europe becoming the target of standardization and purification (Baugh & Cable 2002; Curzan 2014). This monolingual orientation primarily concerned the masses, as bilingualism of the respective national languages with at least a lingua franca (especially Greek, Latin, and French) had always been an emblem of education in the upper classes. The history of Latin as the language of religious study, religious practice, and education is especially long. In contrast, earlier traditional and smaller clan-based societies must have embraced multilingualism or multi-dialectism – and hence intense language

[29] Ricento (2006b: 14–15) points out that this ideology was unchallenged in the decades after World War II: "Western-based academic language-planning and LP [language policy] approaches in the 1950s and 1960s often subsumed a number of ideologies about (1) the nature of language – that is, as a finite, stable, standardized, rule-governed instrument for communication; (2) monolingualism and cultural homogeneity as necessary requirements for social and economic progress, modernization, and national unity (with stable diglossia as a fall-back, compromise position); and (3) language selection as a matter of 'rational choice' in which all options are equally available to everyone, or could be made equally available."

[30] Wasserfall (2019: 24) argues that the concept was exported to Japan "during the Meiji period (1868–1912) when the country was rapidly reforming according to western models." Evans (2018b: 30) draws attention to the "one-clan one-language ideal" as attested in different parts of the world. This may be seen as the historical precursor to the principle of "one nation, one language."

contact – as the norm (Evans 2018a); it also seems to have been accepted as normal during the Roman and Habsburg Empires and thus cannot be regarded as a natural development following the creation of bigger polities (Franceschini 2013: 5–6).

Multilingualism is currently re-established and also rediscovered as a consequence of international migration, in spite of a (still) strong monolingual habitus (Gogolin 2008). Some countries and regions are officially bilingual (Canada, the Spanish part of the Basque Country), some trilingual (India), or quadrilingual (Singapore). Official, societal, and individual multilingualism need to be considered separately (Leimgruber, Siemund & Terassa 2018; Siemund, Al-Issa & Leimgruber 2021; Siemund, Schulz & Schweinberger 2014). There have perhaps always been changing beliefs and fashions about growing up and using one or several languages (see Aronin & Singleton 2012: 54–55 on shifting norms).[31] Bilingualism has by now been extensively researched and it seems clear that children can easily acquire and master two or three languages simultaneously (Meisel 2011: 248). They may even enjoy certain advantages over monolinguals (see Chapter 2). Even though the spoken registers may be highly multilingual, monolingualism remains enforced through various institutions in script-based societies, such as administration, education, and the legal system, amongst others. Linguistic purism strengthens monolingualism and stands in opposition to functional multilingualism. Recent technological developments foster linguistic homogenization, especially the use of English (as on the Web), but also allow diasporas to stay in contact with their linguistic communities back home.

1.3.1 Prehistoric Multilingualism

Social structure determines language use. Accordingly, the structure of social organization allows us to draw inferences regarding the use of language. Steering clear of the question of when, where, and under which circumstances human languages arose, hunter-gatherer societies count amongst the earliest forms of social organization. For lack of evidence, I can only offer speculation here. However, I believe that the main determinants of life (hunger, fear, envy, love, diseases, accidents, etc.) were the same as today. In principle, these small bands of people could have lived in isolation or interacted with other bands to varying degrees. Mostly, they will have led nomadic or quasi-nomadic lives, being pushed around by the vagaries of food supply, competing bands, natural disasters, and the weather. Provided that each such band spoke a separate

[31] According to Aronin and Singleton (2012: 55), these normative changes are also reflected in the emergence of new focal research issues such as the concept of language, the identification of native speakers, and the ownership of language, amongst others.

language, we can already see the potential for monolingualism, bilingualism, and multilingualism. Perhaps, bands speaking different languages joined for hunting and warfare. Perhaps, they regularly exchanged members of their communities due to shortages of men, women, or children. Perhaps, they split up and reunited in new constellations due to external crises and internal strife. Mountainous areas and islands tend to foster locational permanence and segregation, whereas life in the prairies, savannas, as well as along rivers and ocean shores promotes movement of people and language contact. The bottom line is that language diversity, language contact, and multilingualism should be considered a defining characteristic of the human species right from the start (see Evans 2018a; Romaine 2017: 542). Moreover, the term 'language' may not be fully appropriate for these early nomadic and volatile communication systems, as it conveys stability and certain territorial associations. We will explore the problem around defining the term 'language' in more detail in Chapter 7.

When people begin to settle down and pursue agricultural activities, social life comes to be organized around clan structures inhabiting small settlements and villages. As long as these have approximately the same size measured in terms of number of people and economic activity, they will be spread, more or less equidistantly, across a certain territory and yield a largely symmetric form of social organization in which each clan is about as powerful as the others. The individual clans speak their own languages or dialects and come to be identified by them. These languages would typically be confined to the spoken medium. The gain in stability means less movement, less spontaneous language contact, and more coherent and better identifiable communication systems. It is these communication systems that are now emblematic of the people speaking them and the territories they inhabit. Aronin (2005: 9) argues that the clan language "was essential for the development of each individual and society as a whole" suggesting an internally monolingual organization of the clans. In contrast, Evans (2018a: 913), especially in relation to Australia and New Guinea, draws attention to the various social and economic dependencies between clans culminating in the principle of exogamy in marriage (marriage outside one's social group).[32] To avoid incest and build up more distant social relations, partly as an insurance against times of hardship (plagues, droughts, wars), it was sensible and common to establish marriages across different clans. Exogamy in marriage is often tantamount to exogamy in language. This, however, meant that another language was placed into the nuclear family leading to bilingualism. If this happened on a large and systematic basis, the result would have been a primarily multilingual rather

[32] In addition, Evans (2018a: 906) views language as a social technology and multilingualism as an essential means to develop this technology.

than a monolingual society (which may, of course, contain monolingual members).[33] Moreover, the resulting multilingualism would have been rather egalitarian (Evans 2018a: 915) in contrast to that found in modern societies, where languages are associated with different functions and stark prestige differences.[34] Nevertheless, such egalitarian multilingualism requires a consensual basis, that is, an egalitarian linguistic ideology (Evans 2018b: 30). Exogamy may also be combined with a taboo system that forbids the use of the other clan's language in the clan married into.

1.3.2 Multilingual Kingdoms and Empires

Some form of institutional monolingualism, as I will argue here, is likely to arise as the domineering pattern when the power balance between clans becomes asymmetric. In other words, as soon as one clan begins to assume a superior position and to dominate other clans (economically, culturally, ethnically, and religiously), the arising hegemony will typically also be acted out linguistically, as languages are such powerful symbols of identity and highly apt tools for controlling other people. Language can now be used to demarcate the territorial boundaries of a kingdom in such a way that each individual within its realm is required to speak and understand the ruling clan's language, at least to a certain extent or with the help of translators. This new asymmetric power situation presupposes certain technological advancements necessary to manage large groups of people (a system of transportation, armed forces, a writing system, some kind of long-distance communication system). Language now also serves as a gatekeeper to the more prestigious positions of society.

At the social and individual level, such kingdoms or empires are not necessarily monolingual and they probably never were. The bigger they become, the more diverse will be the ethnic and linguistic groups harnessed within their political borders. Nevertheless, the language spoken by the ruling elite is decreed to be obligatory across the kingdom or empire's territory irrespective of the fact that many other languages and dialects exist. Privileged positions in society (administration, business, academia, religion, the legal system, and the medical profession) presuppose knowledge of this language. Most written communication will proceed in the language of the social elites; the other languages being primarily spoken languages. There may be special religious languages. Such must have been the situation in the

33 Gal (2007: 150) documents comparable evidence for South America.

34 Moreover, Evans (2011: 293) emphasizes the importance of multilingual discourse and multilingual narratives for understanding especially Australia's complex linguistic texture. Patterns of migration do not represent a sufficient explanans, as intricate social factors are involved. Multilingualism is analyzed as a means for "semiotic elaboration" (i.e. the enrichment of languages).

Greek,[35] Persian, Roman, Arab, Ottoman, Russian, Spanish, Habsburg, and British Empires (Biville 2018; Fortna 2002; Mairs 2016; Menocal 2002; Rochette 2012),[36] altogether ethnically and linguistically heavily diverse polities, as there was no technology to enforce a single language across the entire territory (like modern media and education systems) and apparently no (explicitly enacted) monolingual ideology driving linguistic homogeneity.[37] This extensive societal multilingualism likely translated into bi- and trilingualism at the individual level, but this does not exclude that some communities remained largely monolingual. There must have been great demand for interpreters and translators (see also de Swaan 2001: 176). The medieval Anglo-French kingdom furnishes another good example of a society in which the aristocracy spoke French and Latin while the lower classes continued to speak (Middle) English, with a certain level of bilingualism in both directions and extensive code-switching (Critten & Dutton 2020; Pahta, Skaffari & Wright 2018; Schendl & Wright 2011).

As societies become increasingly economically and socially stratified, languages identify distinct social groups rather than different clans. Urbanization helps to propel these processes, creating new economic centres that trade and engage in cultural exchange with other cities, as in the medieval Hanseatic League. This early common market involved extensive multilingualism, language contact, semi-communication, and Middle Low German as a widely accepted lingua franca (Braunmüller 1996). In particular, Braunmüller and Ferraresi (2003) show that language contact and multilingualism have been widespread throughout European history.

1.3.3 Nations and Nation States

Modern nation states represent the continuation of these centralization processes in which the ruling elites try to enforce a greater cultural homogeneity across their territories. Following industrialization, populations grow rapidly and flood into dense urban areas. Unless the upper strata of society take a vested interest in issues of diversity, ethnic and linguistic diversity always bears the danger of uprisings and territorial separation. Autocratic and despotic

[35] During the mass wedding at Susa, organized by Alexander the Great in 324 BC, thousands of Greek soldiers, officers, and noblemen were practically by decree married to Persian women to foster the unity of the Macedonian Empire. One can only speculate about the linguistic outcomes, but an increase in multilingualism is likely (Worthington 2005: 217–218).

[36] I am generalizing here across these contexts, but it should be clear that a systematic comparison of these polities would reveal many important differences. There is hardly literature detailing the multilingual practices in these empires.

[37] However, linguistic pressure from above in the Roman Empire must have been substantial. Otherwise, Vulgar Latin would not have given rise to the many Romance languages.

rulers, especially, may develop the idea that a culturally homogenous territory is easier to control than a heterogeneous one. Economic forces may also be involved. Such processes of centralization and homogenization presuppose new technologies and could only be turned into reality with the advent of printing, a fast transportation system like the railway, increasing industrialization, and a compulsory education system. These appear in the centuries after the middle ages. Moreover, nation states require the ideological construct of a nation that identifies groups of people by their cultural commonalities, above all their common language. Protestantism and the ensuing translation of the Bible into the vernaculars formed the basis of the subsequently developing national languages. The mushrooming of language academies across Europe (see Baugh & Cable 2002), like the *Accademia della Crusca* (1582), the *Académie Française* (1635), and the *Real Academia Española* (1713), in their endeavour to standardize and thus create national languages, qua corpus and status planning, are an important concomitant, if not driving force, of the nation building processes (see also Chapter 7). This new collective identity is independent of clan associations, with (rather artificially selected) national languages now serving as the main emblem of national identity. We need to bear in mind that nation states can be based on diverse forms of government, including central and federal democracies, monarchies, and dictatorships. Accordingly, there can be the acknowledgement of and peaceful coexistence with ethnic and linguistic minorities, but this is no necessity. Nevertheless, as the nation state defines itself in terms of cultural homogeneity and national identity, monolingualism inadvertently becomes the majority pattern.

Postcolonial nation states represent an interesting twist on this pattern. These are typically multi-ethnic and multilingual polities forged out of territories under former colonial rule. They were established when the colonial powers (Germany, Great Britain, France, the Netherlands, Portugal, Spain, the United States) receded. Subsequently, they faced the challenge of developing a national identity. Interestingly, these postcolonial states tend to be multilingual, in some cases extensively multilingual, with the former colonial languages often adopting the role of a nationwide lingua franca and being designated as one or even the only official language (see Chapter 5). India, Singapore, Nigeria, Ghana, and South Africa furnish compelling examples. India is officially bilingual (Hindi, English), but pursues a trilingual policy of Hindi and English in combination with another regional language. Given the strong ethnic and linguistic differences between Northern and Southern India, English – though the former colonial language – is perceived as more neutral than Hindi. Singapore is officially quadrilingual (English, Malay, Mandarin, Tamil) with English, again, being the language of interethnic communication. English is the only official language in both Ghana and Nigeria despite the fact that these countries harbour massive ethnic and linguistic diversity.

Finally, South Africa adopted a system of eleven national languages, including English. These examples make clear that the combination of nation states and monolingualism is by no means a necessity. However, language then becomes a less decisive emblem of national identity unless one of the languages assumes a privileged position.

The present post-modern Western nation state is characterized by a multi-ethnic and multilingual texture superimposed on the previously established monolingual structure. This new social layer arose as a consequence of globalization and immigration, propelled by demographic imbalances and shortage of labour. International migration concentrates on urban areas, as detailed in Section 1.2. Typically, these nation states are officially monolingual, but heavily multilingual in social and individual terms, especially in the areas of the cities with high levels of immigration. Arguably, traditional settlement countries like the United States, Canada, Australia, and New Zealand have been shaped by immigration, practically being defined by it, but they too have experienced a substantial increase in ethnic and linguistic diversity over the past decades.

1.3.4 Summary

Unlike Aronin (2005), I do not believe in a general trajectory from monolingual to multilingual forms of social organization in the course of human history.[38] Human societies possess the potential to arrange their communication exchange and communicative needs in different ways, and I think they always have. Monolingualism, bilingualism, and multilingualism represent alternative ways to organize societies. Different periods, locations, and their societies developed different preference patterns, for various reasons as explained above. The crucial question is what determines these differences.[39] Strong social asymmetries in language contact situations may produce monolingualism in the long run. Socially symmetric language contact encourages

[38] Aronin (2005: 9) equates tribal societies with "a language," nation states with "the language," and globalization with "languag*es*" (emphasis in the original). Aronin and Singleton (2012: 46) discuss seven dimensions that distinguish historical and contemporary multilingualism.

[39] Evans (2018b: 15) informs us that Vanuatu and Samoa, although comparable in size and population, differ drastically in terms of language diversity. While Vanuatu attests more than 135 languages, Samoa counts just 1. Contact with Papuan languages is suggested as an explanation for the diversity on Vanuatu. Ethnologue (Eberhard, Simons & Fennig 2022) lists Vanuatu as the country with the highest language density. I am wondering whether language ideologies could produce a similar outcome. For example, Europe currently cherishes multilingualism besides other forms of heterogeneity and diversity. In contrast, the People's Republic of China is rapidly disseminating Putonghua as its national language supplanting the other Sinitic languages (see Chapter 5). Almost 1.4 billion speakers are converging on a single language (retrieved from www.cia.gov/the-world-factbook/countries/china/, accessed on 02 May 2021). Arguably, China is taking the idea of the monolingual nation state to a whole new level.

multilingualism, evidently in combination with other factors. Ancient Rome must have been as linguistically diverse as modern Dubai, with cheap labour and tourists pouring in from all across the empire's provinces.[40] However, the dominant language was Latin. The modern nation state exhibits a historically unusual preference for widespread monolingualism over alternative forms of sociolinguistic organization.

1.4 Monolingual and Multilingual Upbringing and Education

I believe that other languages and language diversity – as other ethnic groups and ethnic diversity – have always been viewed with curiosity and apprehension. The unknown other is interesting and frightening at the same time, like two sides of the same coin. Language diversity can be conceptualized as an enrichment as well as an affliction. The story of the Tower of Babel emphasizes the latter perspective, as language dispersion is enacted as a punishment for megalomania. A corollary of this narrative is that successful collaboration presupposes a common language. This, in turn, offers an apt motivational basis for promoting monolingualism. A narrow communicative perspective furthers this presupposition, the problem, of course, being that language is not merely a tool for communication. Since the nation states created in the eighteenth and nineteenth centuries – a time of rapid industrialization and early globalization – were based on the smooth collaboration of hitherto unknown numbers of people, the plea for a common language appears understandable. Language diversity was primarily conceptualized as a problem, not as a resource or enrichment. The development of constructed languages like Volapük (1880) and Esperanto (1887) falls into the same period.[41] All of these attempts at creating a single global language failed. Ironically, the natural language English now assumes this position.

1.4.1 The Reassessment of Bilingualism and Multilingualism

During the past 150 or so years, the scientific assessment of bilingualism and multilingualism – also monolingualism – has undergone dramatic changes. While the initial discourse in the field (from the late 1800s until about 1950) was characterized by a strong rejection of bilingualism in favour of a monolingual model of life and education, much effort was subsequently dedicated to showing that bilingually raised children are not deficient and can acquire and separate their two languages just as well as monolingual children can

[40] In historical terms, of course, cheap labour and tourists translate into slaves and pilgrims.
[41] Retrieved from www.britannica.com/topic/Esperanto and www.britannica.com/topic/Volapuk, accessed on 19 February 2021.

(from around 1950 to 1990; see Peal & Lambert 1962). More recently, we witness a strong turn towards a positive assessment of bilingualism and multilingualism in that current research probes into, and is also able to identify, beneficial effects of bilingualism and multilingualism over monolingualism (Aronin 2005: 10; Bialystok 2018).

Tucker and d'Anglejan (1971) address a number of myths about bilingualism that must have enjoyed wide currency in the first half of the twentieth century (and earlier). They concern cognitive ability, educational attainment, language proficiency, and also linguistic identity. They read as follows:

1. Children who are instructed bilingually from an early age will suffer cognitive or intellectual retardation in comparison with their monolingually instructed counterparts.
2. They will not achieve the same level of content mastery as their monolingually instructed counterparts.
3. They will not acquire acceptable native language or target language skills.
4. The majority will become anomic individuals without affiliation to either ethnolinguistic contact group. (Tucker & d'Anglejan 1971: 491)

Taken together, they strongly devalue bilinguals in comparison to monolinguals. Moreover, they discourage bilingual models of education and advocate a monolingual organization of society. Evidence for the viewpoints expressed above is not difficult to find, even in respectable academic contributions. For example, Saer (1923: 38) – which is one of the earliest studies exploring the Welsh–English bilingual context[42] – argues for a superiority in intelligence of "monoglot children" over bilingual children that persists throughout their academic careers (especially rural children). In particular, these children suffer from a two years' delay in vocabulary acquisition, confusion regarding dextrality, and above all a general "mental confusion." The below extract expresses the gist of this study:

> It is suggested that the greatest influence on the mental confusion occurring in bilingualism is exerted by the language used by bilingual children in their play and in their free association with youthful companions when that language is not also that in which they are taught at school. (Saer 1923: 38)

To be fair, such studies must be assessed in their historical context. They convey a narrative written from the perspective of a technologically superior

[42] Hakuta (1989) offers a very readable and informative annotated bibliography on bilingualism and intelligence testing. He remarks, "I realized that the problem of bilingualism and intelligence actually had two identities: one as a genuine scholarly topic, and the other as a social issue related to the education of immigrants." (Hakuta 1989: 1). In a way, the present book also contains these two perspectives. Chapters 2, 3, and 4 scrutinize various theoretical problems (based on empirical data), whereas Chapters 5 and 6 address social, ideological, and language policy issues.

society that extends its scope of influence on other people as well as their languages and cultures (see Williams 1977: 739, 741 for the context of Wales). This strategy is acculturation by assimilation and marginalization (see Berry 1997). Similar strategies were also pursued in North America and Australia regarding the indigenous populations. But apart from these more general issues, it is my impression that the stereotypes and concerns voiced above can be encountered even today.

By the middle of the twentieth century, the evidence accumulated to support negative effects of bilingual upbringing was shattering. In the research overview part of their study, Peal and Lambert (1962: 2–5) discuss around ten studies in the section "Studies Supporting the Detrimental Effects of Bilingualism on Intelligence" that report better performance of monolinguals on "both verbal and nonverbal intelligence tests" (Peal & Lambert 1962: 2). About the same number of studies in their report found negative effects of bilingualism in verbal tests, although no effect or even a slight positive effect of bilingualism in non-verbal tests. "Favorable Effects of Bilingualism on Intelligence" could be detected by a mere two studies. Another large batch of studies was found to be inconclusive.

It is interesting to note that these early studies typically did not control for two parameters that are still widely discussed today, namely type of bilingualism and socio-economic status (amongst several others). These represent a more constructive approach to account for the observed differences. However, it also needs to be mentioned that the value of at least some of the early studies consists precisely in raising awareness of the importance of these additional factors (Jones 1960, as discussed in Peal & Lambert 1962: 2).

Against this background, the significance and value of Peal and Lambert's (1962) study become understandable. They were amongst the first to control systematically for type of bilingualism as well as socio-economic status. The study worked with ten-year-old children from Montréal (seventy-five monolinguals and eighty-nine bilinguals) and great pains were taken to create a subsample of balanced bilinguals (French, English) that was then compared to a subsample of monolingual (French) students. The study showed that bilinguals outperformed monolinguals on a number of cognitive tests. However, as Hakuta and Diaz (1985: 322–323) and also Peal and Lambert (1962: 15) themselves point out, the results need to be interpreted with a certain degree of caution, as they may have been skewed by the sampling procedure. Also, the authors are very cautious regarding the question of whether bilingualism augments cognitive development or whether high cognitive development encourages bilingualism. As Peal and Lambert (1962: 20) put it, "It is not possible to state from the present study whether the more intelligent child became bilingual or whether bilingualism aided his intellectual development, but there is no question about the fact that he is superior intellectually."

Nevertheless, in spite of these shortcomings, Peal and Lambert's (1962) study sparked an immensely industrious and successful strand of research. Moreover, the past decades have seen a substantial diversification of disciplines. The initial interest in the field seems to have been driven primarily by psychologists. Subsequently, education studies also began to develop a strong interest in all issues of bilingual and later multilingual education that established itself as a separate field of research. The interest then spread to applied and theoretical linguistics, more recently also to sociolinguistics and historical linguistics, and even medical studies. Chapter 2 explores these developments in detail.

The historical reassessment of monolingualism, bilingualism, and multilingualism evidently correlates with fundamental changes in Western societies. Whereas the time before and during the two World Wars was characterized by a strong emphasis on nationality, clear and firm territorial boundaries, as well as a single national language, we can witness a move towards more permeable political borders in post-war Europe and a general trajectory towards tighter European integration (political, economic, cultural). The settlement countries (United States, Canada, Australia, New Zealand) began to embrace their ethnic and linguistic diversity more strongly, although the negotiation of linguistic and ethnic diversity with all its inherent conflicting interests has never ceded, and probably never will (see Chapter 5). The fall of the Iron Curtain in 1989, fostered by affordable and reliable long-distance traffic, opened the scene for unprecedented global migration and movement of labour, inducing a sharp increase in societal and individual multilingualism. Evidently, the key word here is globalization.

1.4.2 *Monolingual and Multilingual Ideologies and Environments*

These external developments challenge long-established monolingual practices that different world regions (Europe, North America, Australia and New Zealand, Africa, Asia, the Middle East) respond to with new language policy approaches. It is, however, not the case that monolingual practices have generally been replaced by multilingual paradigms, even though the awareness of multilingualism has risen. We will discuss these problems in more detail in Chapters 4–6 (see also Bonnet & Siemund 2018b; Singleton & Aronin 2019). Traditionally non-English speaking areas, such as most European countries, face the additional challenge of developing English proficiencies, as this is the current world language. Bilingual students – both speakers of minority languages and heritage bilinguals – learn English as their third or additional language. 'Super-diversity' is currently a widely used term to capture the resulting linguistic, ethnic, and social complexity (Vertovec 2007).

As our lives have always been embedded in ideologies, and probably always will, research results also need to be interpreted within their ideological context. Studying monolingualism and multilingualism within adversative ideological settings carries the danger of producing self-fulfilling prophecies. The reality, however, is that early studies on cognitive differences between monolinguals and bilinguals were carried out precisely in a context that favours monolingualism. Moreover, there often is a noticeable difference in prestige between the language of the monolingual group (typically English) and the other language of the bilingual group (typically a minority or indigenous language). For example, the studies by Saer (1923) as well as Jones and Stewart (1951) involved bilingualism of English and Welsh. Harris (1948) drew on bilingual subjects from Montana and Pueblo native Americans, but there is no reference to the actual languages apart from English.[43] There are several studies conducted on immigrant groups in the United States (see Peal & Lambert 1962: 2–3 for references). Peal and Lambert's (1962) study was also special in that it focused on English and French, two languages of high and relatively equal prestige and considerable typological proximity.

It would appear, then, that apart from type of bilingualism and socio-economic status, there is reason to believe that the ideological setting as well as the social status (prestige) of the languages also matter and need to be controlled for (see Aronin & Singleton 2012: 111). It is perhaps no coincidence that the more recent studies reporting bilingual advantages – though not necessarily related to issues of intelligence – come from Canada, the Spanish part of the Basque Country, and the Spanish autonomous region of Catalunya. In these areas, the respective official languages (English and French) and the regional minority languages (Basque and Catalan) enjoy high social prestige, with Basque and Catalan being co-official languages besides Spanish in the relevant regions. Moreover, the ideological settings are favourable in regard to bilingualism. Canada officially became a bilingual country in 1969; the Basque Country in 1978. Catalan received official status in 1979 (see also Chapter 5).[44]

As far as I can see, the initial studies in the field primarily relied on tests for verbal and non-verbal intelligence. Such intelligence tests do not seem to figure prominently any longer (although they keep being used), perhaps as a consequence of a more critical perspective on these tests. After all, they typically measure highly specific types of symbolic intelligence.[45] The more

[43] It is stated that students speak "their native Indian language" and that English is frequently learnt as a second language (Harris 1948: 333).

[44] Retrieved from www.britannica.com/topic/Official-Languages-Act, www.britannica.com/topic/Basque-language, www.britannica.com/place/Catalonia, accessed on 19 February 2021.

[45] Any test determines its outcome. If one asks a student cohort to complete some progressive matrix, this will likely stratify the group. One may relate the emerging differences to intelligence, but this evidently is a far-reaching claim (for a recent discussion see van der Maas, Kan & Borsboom 2014). Bourdieu's (1991) critical work on language as a means to reproduce social power relations also needs to be considered in this context.

recent and current focus of psychologists interested in bilingual and multilingual advantages is executive control, which tends to be measured using reaction time experiments of various congruent and incongruent conditions (see Bialystok 2020). The 1970s saw a rising interest in metalinguistic awareness practically opening up a new research field that is still around (Cummins 1978). Educationists zoom in on the relationship of multilingualism and educational attainment. Language acquisition studies discover bilingualism as a distinct field of study, a major concern here being if and to what extent bilingual children are able to separate their languages (Meisel 2004, 2011). Applied linguistics and language didactics begin to pursue the question whether a bi- or multilingual experience positively impacts further language acquisition. Teaching and classroom ideologies arise as a matter of concern. We will explore these topics in detail in Chapter 2. However, it should be clear from these few observations that research questions and areas are by no means immune to the surrounding ideological setting, and to a certain extent perhaps even determined by it. On the whole, bilingualism and multilingualism have experienced an immense valorization. There remains, of course, the danger of turning them into ideologies themselves.

The increasingly common bilingualism (or multilingualism), with English as an additional language (national language plus English), is pushing the field to identify new research foci. While it used to be common to compare bilingual groups to monolingual controls, it is becoming more and more difficult to find "pure" monolingual speakers, especially outside the so-called 'inner circle' countries (Kachru 1985). In view of these developments, the search for bilingual advantages becomes a moving target. As this categorical distinction dissolves, research needs to focus more closely on a comparison of different bilingual and multilingual groups.

1.4.3 Homogenization and Convergence

Over the past decades, global migration has led to a sharp increase in linguistic diversity in specific world areas, certainly not all. Moreover, our perspectives on linguistic diversity and multilingualism have changed considerably. The diversity-as-a-problem perspective has generally been replaced by a more resource-oriented attitude – not only in academic circles. In no small degree, this is also due to a sharp increase in language deaths and endangered languages that alerted people (see Thomason 2015). As so often, assets are only recognized as such when they begin to disappear.

One may be wondering where the current developments are headed. My present and somewhat sobering assessment on this matter is that the observable increase in linguistic diversity in selected world regions is embedded in very strong forces of homogenization and convergence that are bound to curtail the current mosaic-like picture in the long run.[46] Moreover, unless external events such as diseases and natural disasters force us into greater isolation, language loss will continue to result in fewer languages with more speakers each (see Bromham et al. 2021; Romaine 2017: 553). Finally, the contemporary more positive assessment of linguistic diversity and multilingualism can easily be forfeited. Ideologies are subject to change.

An especially strong homogenizing force comes from the education systems, since these are largely organized monolingually (Aronin & Singleton 2012: 49–50; Gogolin 2008, 2020) and can be expected to remain largely monolingual[47] for practical and economic reasons – in spite of current efforts to enrich the curricula with multilingual elements (Bonnet & Siemund 2018a; Krulatz, Dahl & Flognfeldt 2018; Naqvi et al. 2013). The number of teachable subjects and resources in general are limited. Some common language is necessary. Not all languages can be included that invariably leads to frustration. Speakers of minority languages (especially parents) may prefer the majority language(s) for matters of social prestige. Homogeneity and heterogeneity are poles on a continuum and the education systems need to find a workable compromise. Similarly, administration, cultural institutions, the media, politics, as well as the judicial and medical systems exert strong homogenizing pressure.[48]

Another important force of homogenization and convergence is the current – even if deplorable – organization of languages into more and less prestigious languages in the so-called World Language System (de Swaan 2001; Mair 2013; Piller 2016). Languages reflect the social reality around them. They are strong markers of social identity and tend to be equated with the social groups that speak them. If a group is culturally and economically strong, their language is valorized. The opposite holds for weak and disadvantaged social groups.

A third force driving homogenization and convergence is global English, the hub language and international lingua franca. There is an interesting conflict here. Although higher levels of bilingualism develop due to the widespread use of English as an additional language and its increasingly lowered age of onset, this also curtails linguistic diversity and multilingualism. Smaller and less prestigious languages disappear following the development of bilingualism in the national majority languages and English. For practical purposes, for

[46] Braunmüller and House (2009) contains papers discussing various issues related to convergence and divergence in language contact.

[47] This refers to the medium of instruction in the content subjects. Language classes are different.

[48] I can only speculate about the effects of the economy and the labour market. Regarding the situation in Germany, Esser (2009: 84) argues that mother tongue knowledge in a heritage language does not produce positive effects on the German labour market. If at all, multiculturalism is associated with negative status effects. Young multilinguals entering the labour market can be expected to be sensitive to these demands and adjust accordingly. This, in turn, produces homogenization. Knowledge of German and English can be expected to reflect the demands of the labour market.

example, the European Union seems to be moving towards a bilingual model of national language and English, in spite of the officially encouraged – and celebrated – multilingualism and plurilingualism (Berthelheimer, Hufeisen & Montanari 2019; Council of Europe 2020; Jeffery & van Beuningen 2020: 177–178). Ironically, the widespread and early use of English promotes bilingualism, but curtails linguistic diversity.

Finally, although Western Europe and perhaps the Western World in general is currently rediscovering multilingualism, other parts of the world converge on bilingual or semi-bilingual models in which English in combination with a national language or a small number of heritage or indigenous languages dominate societies (China, Malaysia, Singapore, India, the United Arab Emirates, some African countries) – despite the fact that the official and public discourse often embraces multilingualism. We will return to these issues in more detail in Chapter 5.

1.4.4 Summary

In the same way as the linguistic organization of societies has been subject to tremendous changes over time, the evaluation of, as well as the attitudes towards monolingualism, bilingualism, multilingualism, and language diversity have been fluctuating. Language diversity has been conceptualized both as a burden and a blessing. It is difficult to tell whether linguistic reality determines attitudes, conversely, or reciprocally, as there is a complex interplay of external forces and cultural conventions. In strongly hierarchical societies, the individual preferences of the person in top position may come to be a major factor.

1.5 The Hierarchy of Languages and the Special Role of English

As already alluded to, there is a complex hierarchy and value system behind languages. Some languages enjoy higher prestige than others, contingent on the economic power of the relevant societies and their communicative potential (Bourdieu 1991; de Swaan 2001; Mair 2013). English is currently the most valued language along the status or power dimension, though smaller languages serve important identity maintaining functions in relation to the solidarity dimension.[49] In many postcolonial settings, English remains in use as the official language and apparently even helps to ease potential conflicts

[49] Here and elsewhere in this book I am using the terms 'status' and 'solidarity' in the sense of Ryan, Giles and Sebastian (1982). Status relates to prestige and power, whereas solidarity concerns the in-group value of languages. Solidarity is based on symmetry and reciprocity, while status pertains to social differences. (See also Brown & Gilman 1960 on the opposition of 'power' and 'solidarity'.)

Hyper-Central Language
English, the hub of the world language system

Super-Central Languages
French, Portuguese, Spanish, Russian, Hindi, Arabic, Mandarin, Malay

Central Languages
German, Dutch, Finnish, Korean, Wolof, Quechua, ...

Peripheral Languages
6,000+

Figure 1.6 The World Language System according to de Swaan (2001: 4–6) and Mair (2013: 259).

between smaller languages. The discourse on the role of English is divided between acknowledging its usefulness as a tool for global communication and drawing attention to the risks it poses for the survival of especially smaller languages (see also Aronin & Singleton 2012: 49).[50]

In much of linguistics, and for good reason, there is a consensus to disregard the different social assessments of languages and consider them equivalued. In fact, linguists currently tend to direct their scientific efforts towards the lesser valued and little researched languages. In the context of the present book, however, it is unavoidable to acknowledge that languages represent cultural capital that correlates with the prestige and power of the social groups using them. De Swaan's (2001) World Language System models the world's languages as a function of their associated cultural capital (see Figure 1.6), operationalized in terms of the number of speakers for whom they are relevant – socially, culturally, or economically. This system – not surprisingly – places English in top or central position as the current hub language of the world and acknowledges a number of super-central and central languages. The overwhelming majority of the world's languages have peripheral status only (see also Aronin & Singleton 2012: 137).

Individual – and perhaps also societal multilingualism – tends to be inversely related to de Swaan's (2001) World Language System in that speakers of less prestigious and peripheral languages, unless they live in complete isolation, can be expected to be more multilingual than native speakers of English and the super-central languages. As Mair (2013: 260) points out, "Monolingualism is a luxury which few speakers of a peripheral language can afford. Amongst

[50] The interested reader is referred to Ricento (2015a) for a topical selection of contributions on this matter.

speakers of the hyper-central language, on the other hand, it is widespread. Bilinguals will typically add a language from higher up to their repertoire, and only in exceptional circumstances from lower down." Hence, the language ecology[51] one grows up in is likely to affect one's views of monolingualism, bilingualism, and multilingualism, as speakers of smaller languages may find it essential for survival, while native speakers of English simply do not need it. We may also note that the extension of one's linguistic repertoire usually proceeds from bottom to top in de Swaan's (2001) hierarchy, with English being added to practically everyone's repertoire.

All linguistic areas accept English as the hub language of the world, even though not necessarily voluntarily, not to the same degree, and often simply for strategic reasons. In native English-speaking areas, the result typically is large-scale monolingualism, even though many minority groups in these societies are bilingual or multilingual. In non-native English-speaking areas, English tends to be the most privileged language besides the relevant national languages, leading to widespread bilingualism and a strong presence of English in the education systems. The national languages are symbolic of the nations that speak them. English is developing from a foreign language to an additional language in many territories. The Scandinavian countries furnish representative examples with English being allocated a special position in the curricula besides foreign languages (see Berthelheimer, Hufeisen & Montanari 2019: 63 on the situation in Norway). The status of English in the Netherlands has been likened to that in former British colonies, although its spread there is a consequence of globalization instead of colonialism (Edwards 2016). Generally, the status of English in Europe is different from that of the other languages of the Union (Jeffery & van Beuningen 2020).

To be sure, de Swaan's (2001) model offers a global perspective that, naturally, plays out differently in specific world areas. For instance, in the case of Europe, the current 'political' division of languages is that of English as a lingua franca, the national languages of the European countries, foreign languages as recognized and taught in the education systems, recognized regional and minority languages, and a wide variety of unrecognized immigrant

[51] The use of the term 'ecology' in linguistics originates in Haugen's (1972, 2001) work. He defined it as "the study of interactions between any given language and its environment" (Haugen 1972: 325) and envisioned several parameters to describe language ecologies more closely (see also Chapter 7): language classification, language users, domains of use, degree of multilingualism, varieties and variation, written traditions, standardization, institutional support, and language attitudes (Haugen 1972: 336–337). Most of these are also relevant in the context of the present book, but especially degree of multilingualism will be fanned out in several directions. One may note that acquisition patterns and migration do not surface as separate parameters in Haugen's typology.

languages (see Aronin & Singleton 2012: 137; Extra 2013: 139). Similar analyses may be proposed for North America, Australia, China, India, and other territories of high linguistic diversity. What unites them is some implicit social hierarchy and value system behind the languages.

Clyne's (1992) conception of pluricentrism represents a viable alternative to the strongly hierarchical systems outlined above. Languages may possess more than one centre that each come with their specific usage patterns and codifications. English possesses such centres in North America, Great Britain, and Oceania (with further subdivisions); Spanish in Spain and Latin America; French in France, Switzerland, and Canada; German in Germany, Austria, and Switzerland, and so on. This approach allows for a more detailed calibration of the mutual influences and prestige levels, as some languages are norm-providing while others are norm-receiving. The result is a complex network rather than a vertical hierarchy.

In sum, languages are never independent from their social context and reflect the social reality of their speakers. They manifest strong differences in their respective bases of speakers, and indicate the economic strength of the societies that use them, as well as their cultural importance and influence. As analysts, we can impose different ordering relations on them, but as de Swaan (2001: 1) states succinctly, it "is multilingualism that has kept humanity, separated by so many languages, together."

1.6 A Note on Terminology

Sound scholarly work presupposes clear, precise, and well-defined concepts and terminology. Nobody would rebuff this dictum. However, the present monograph pursues an interdisciplinary approach drawing on research from other fields besides linguistics. This necessitates some flexibility in the interpretation of the concepts and terms. And even within the bounds of linguistics proper, language has been interpreted in fundamentally different ways. Writing a monograph on multilingual development is reminiscent of building a complicated card house that is difficult to keep in balance and in danger of collapsing. Indeed, the process requires some artistic qualities, and I need to appeal to the reader to bear with my terminological imprecisions.

The difficulties begin with the term 'language' itself. There is no sound definition, and the term as such signifies no more than an intuitively plausible symbolic-interactive construct of group identity and belonging. It is based on various linguistic, social, and also political dimensions. Language labels typically identify a social group and their language. The label 'German' refers to the language and the people speaking it. I decided to postpone a more detailed discussion of this term until Section 7.3.1 of the final chapter. The reader will be more sensitive to the relevant issues after reading this book, not before.

Evidently, if the term 'language' evades a forthright definition, then all derivative terms must be equally problematic. This, first and foremost, concerns monolingualism, bilingualism, trilingualism, and multilingualism. All of these have been subject to extensive debate. The first three of these terms trivially relate to situations involving one, two, or three languages, respectively, both at the individual and social levels. Depending on the extension of the term 'language', their meaning, however, fluctuates. Multilingualism tends to be used as a cover term for bilingualism and trilingualism as well as situations that involve more than three languages.[52]

Another dimension in the scholarly debate concerns the question to what extent languages represent separate and distinguishable entities, both socially and cognitively. The terms 'monolingualism', 'bilingualism', 'trilingualism', as well as 'multilingualism' have frequently been used in a way that respects clear boundaries between languages. In an extreme – and somewhat implausible – interpretation, multilinguals come to be analyzed as a unification of several monolinguals with there being no cross-overs between languages and no surplus effects. Conversely, one may wish to emphasize the interrelations and mutual dependencies between the languages in a multilingual's repertoire and in multilingual societies. The term 'plurilingualism' has been suggested as an appropriate label for this perspective much as that of 'multilingual ecologies'.[53] This shift in perspective furthermore motivates the differences in the use of the terms 'code-switching' and 'translanguaging' (García & Wei 2014).

Different types of bilingualism and multilingualism need to be distinguished depending on the age when the relevant languages are acquired. Accordingly, there is early and late bilingualism as well as child and adult bilingualism, with various stages in between. Moreover, the acquisition process can result in balanced and unbalanced bilinguals (or multilinguals). One may also speak of stronger and weaker languages. The latter are highly complicated terms, as they necessitate means to assess one's knowledge of language in objective terms. They relate to language dominance, to be scrutinized in Chapter 3 in the context of heritage bilinguals. The terms 'acquisition' and 'learning' are frequently used to distinguish natural language development from that based on tutoring in dedicated social institutions. I here use these terms interchangeably except when referring to child language acquisition proper. I consider the difference gradual, not categorical. Moreover, both processes may work concurrently.

As this book considers multilingual development in the context of globalization, different immigrant groups will be discussed in their multilingual

[52] Berthele (2021: 84) writes that "[m]ultilingualism as a scholarly term can be used as contrasting with bilingualism (more than two languages) or as including bilingualism (two or more languages)."

[53] Cenoz and Gorter (2013) offer a thorough discussion of plurilingualism.

ecologies. Typically, heritage or ethnic languages come to be embedded in the context of a majority language, usually the national language of the territory. Heritage languages are often restricted to the home or family context. Heritage languages may also be referred to as 'minority languages', but the latter term is also employed for the languages that became marginalized when national languages arose.

Heritage bilinguals have often been described as subtractive bilinguals, as their first or heritage language may become relatively weaker over time, while the relevant majority language – which may technically be their second language – tends to become relatively stronger. Again, the metaphorical terms 'weak' and 'strong' need to be interpreted with caution, as they may simply relate to the fact that heritage bilinguals receive formal instruction in the majority language and develop academic abilities only in this language. Conversely, situations of additive bilingualism arise when consecutive language acquisition results in languages of equal strength. There also is the notoriously critical term of "semilingualism," which will be discussed in more detail in Chapter 2.

Finally, there are the concepts of 'nativeness' and 'native' languages. I learnt from many discussions with heritage bilinguals that they find it difficult to say what their native language is. I believe that most multilinguals share this problem. A native language is tied to a strongly monolingual environment and ideology where the boundary between 'self' and 'other' is clearly marked.

1.7 Target Audience and Structure of the Book

This book addresses the academic specialist and non-specialist alike. I am trying to reach out to students as much as to established researchers. Accordingly, the book oscillates between more narrative and more technical passages, with everyone being invited to extract the information that they find relevant and comprehensible. It is my hope that the book is accessible to everyone interested in multilingual development, although it is probably beyond what laypeople can absorb. The book does not exclusively target linguists, but also educationists, psychologists, and sociologists. Sometimes, in my discussion of historical and political issues, I deliberately remain a little vague. I am not an expert here and the devil is in the detail.

Regarding academic teaching, this book represents an up-to-date research monograph that is geared towards more advanced courses, and may be either used partially or completely. I have used the manuscript as a coursebook in several seminars on multilingual development. In my experience, one chapter provides sufficient information to cover two classes of ninety minutes each.

As we have seen, Chapter 1 introduces the reader to current globalization-induced migration processes and the concomitant increase in linguistic diversity and multilingualism, especially in densely populated urban areas.

Chapter 1 also draws attention to the relatively recent rediscovery of multilingualism in the Western World after a long period of predominantly monolingual ideologies. It also considers the history of multilingualism. Monolingual and multilingual approaches to organizing societies are introduced and compared. Furthermore, I explained that languages are associated with different functions, status, and prestige, and that English enjoys an extremely privileged status in today's world.

Chapter 2 focuses the discussion on various advantages (or effects) widely associated with individual and societal multilingualism. It introduces and evaluates research findings from psychology regarding executive function and cognitive reserve, from education studies in relation to cognitive development and educational attainment, and also from language learning and teaching especially with respect to metalinguistic awareness. Moreover, the chapter considers various controversial issues in this domain that are currently hotly debated, as certain results from previous studies prove difficult to replicate. All in all, Chapter 2 compiles support for the scaffolding effects of one's multilingual experience.

The elaboration of the theoretical underpinnings is continued in Chapter 3 with a discussion of cross-linguistic influence in the context of third or subsequent language acquisition, or, more generally, language acquisition in multilingual settings. After expounding the relevance and recent emergence of third language acquisition as a separate field, it is asked which of the previously acquired languages – first language (L1), second language (L2), both L1 and L2 – plays the most important role for subsequent language acquisition and which additional factors are involved. These questions are evaluated in relation to currently discussed models of cross-linguistic influence. An important finding emanating from Chapter 3 is that language dominance is a highly important factor for the selection of the language that becomes active for cross-linguistic influence. This factor appears especially relevant in heritage language contexts.

The discussion of multilingual advantages then zooms in on language acquisition and learning in Chapter 4 where potentially positive effects of multilingual upbringing for subsequent language acquisition in comparison to a monolingual socialization are explored and compared. Such learning advantages have been widely researched, but comparatively little attention has been paid to how they play out in different areas of language learning (spoken and written production and reception) as well as in different language domains (phonology, morphosyntax, lexical development). Curiously enough, while multilingual learning advantages tend to surface for more general proficiencies, they are much harder to identify for specimens of bona fide grammatical cross-linguistic influence. This paradoxical situation is explored in relation to third language acquisition and is based on numerous case studies from article usage, subject-verb agreement, tense and aspect, word order, and lexical transfer. Moreover, the exact type of multilingual upbringing as well as the languages involved turn out to be crucial to experience further language learning advantages. Chapter 4 also argues that current language didactics fails to make use of multilingual advantages such that initial benefits observable in younger learner cohorts tend to wither in more advanced learning stages.

Since it is becoming increasingly clear that potential multilingual advantages are strongly influenced by the specific situation of multilingual upbringing that an individual experiences, a study on multilingual development cannot be complete without reference to the relevant contextual determinants. Therefore, Chapter 5 ventures into a survey of language policy and identity issues, as these are largely responsible for the status and the prestige associated with different languages. Multilingual language policies in different parts of the world are compared with one another, asking how and to what extent they determine the linguistic identity of individuals and their motivation to invest into languages and the development of multilingual identities. It is argued that potential multilingual advantages may easily be forfeited in unfavourable ideological settings.

Chapter 6 applies the findings from the previous chapters to an analysis of the so-called 'New Englishes' in their respective multilingual ecologies. In the postcolonial territories of what is today India, Singapore, South Africa, Nigeria, and the Gulf Region (as well as others), English enjoys a highly privileged status while, at the same time, occurring in distinct localized or nativized forms (Indian English, Singapore English, etc.). These local varieties cannot be understood without an assessment of the wider multilingual ecologies to which English had been transplanted. Moreover, the chapter scrutinizes the different roles that English adopts in such multilingual ecologies, ranging from a first, second, or additional language to a foreign language and also a lingua franca. The discussion draws on extensive historical and contemporary evidence from Singapore, Hong Kong, and Dubai as urban centres where the relevant social and linguistic forces manifest especially strongly.

Chapter 7 works towards a typology of the patterns and limits of multilingualism. It offers a succinct summary of the factors involved in multilingual development, thus pulling together the various research strands explored in the monograph. Furthermore, it tries to identify the conditions under which multilingual upbringing can be successful and play out its inherent advantages best. Chapter 7 also offers some thoughts on the relevance and limits of statistical models and testing. Chapter 7 further argues for a continuum from monolingualism to multilingualism and tries to reconceptualize multilingualism in terms of homogeneity and heterogeneity. The space opened by these two dimensions identifies overlapping focal areas of monolingualism, bilingualism, trilingualism, multilingualism, and plurilingualism. In addition, Chapter 7 develops a typology of the various multilingual contexts in which English is used, paying particular attention to the dimension of migration. Finally, it develops ideas for future research, especially in relation to a principled comparison of multilingual urban areas in different parts of the world.

1.8 Chapter Summary

Chapter 1 has shown that migration is an omnipresent phenomenon, leaving its traces in different parts of the world, especially urban areas. Crucially, Western Europe needs to be considered just as much a target of immigration as the traditional settler countries (United States, Canada, Australia, New Zealand). Luxembourg and Switzerland stand out in regard to their immigrant populations.

Urban multilingualism in the cities surveyed here has fostered extensive bilingualism and multilingualism with at least 50 per cent of the populations speaking more than one language – especially amongst the younger strata. Multilingualism in Singapore, Hong Kong, and Dubai is much higher. Not least due to the status of English as a world language and lingua franca, Western Europe has developed into an extensively multilingual area. In addition, heritage bilingualism is widespread.

Multilingualism, as such, is not a new phenomenon and may be considered a defining condition of the human species. However, the speed with which it keeps spreading and the density that it developed in urban areas are relatively recent phenomena without historical precedents. These processes are not universal, though. While the Western World has rediscovered multilingualism after a long period of pervasive monolingualism, China currently appears on its ways towards a form of social organization in which monolingualism and homogeneity are of paramount importance.

Bilingualism and multilingualism used to be associated with various cognitive deficits, but this negative perspective has fortunately been replaced with a more nuanced assessment that allows for the recognition of the various benefits resulting from a multilingual experience. It is as such remarkable that knowledge of several languages can be mandated to be a problem at all. However, any language experience is a complex phenomenon that can easily be discredited in various directions given suitable ideologies and norms.

What is crucial to understanding deficit-based evaluations of multilingualism is the social pecking order behind languages. In the extreme case, this hierarchical arrangement of languages into 'valuable' and 'inferior' can produce a dynamics that practically forces speakers to forfeit their knowledge of language.

2 On Advantages and Effects of Multilingual Development

Countering traditional monolingual ideologies that associate multilingual development with various limitations, more recent research probes into potential advantages of this developmental experience. The deficit view of bilingualism was seriously questioned in the by now classic study by Peal and Lambert (1962), opening up a highly successful strand of research documenting the ability of children to successfully acquire two languages simultaneously and even certain positive effects of bilingualism. Section 2.1 explores the multilingual advantages (or effects) emanating from psychological studies, especially in terms of executive control and cognitive reserve. Research shows that bilinguals can outperform monolinguals in measures such as reaction time and inhibition control. Moreover, multilingualism may even help to boost cognitive reserve, slowing down dementia and other cognitive ageing processes. However, the field is currently going through a "replicability crisis (Bialystok 2020: 9)," as earlier research results fail to be corroborated.[1] A critical reassessment is necessary. Section 2.1 also ventures into the parameters that may account for the conflicting research results.

Section 2.2 extends the discussion of the advantages that multilingualism has on cognitive development and educational attainment. The hypothesis under scrutiny here is that previous multilingual experience can be associated with positive effects in these areas. These issues are quite critical, especially in the context of bilingual heritage children. Provided the existence of such positive effects can be corroborated, they are suggestive of the fact that if bilingual heritage children are able to maintain and develop their heritage language, they will also be more successful in the relevant majority language (typically the language of instruction in the education system) and show higher educational attainment. Cummins (1976, 1979, 1996, 2001) introduced far-reaching claims that the interdependence of languages is considered largely decoupled from cognitive ability – at least in his earlier publications. In addition, there is the idea of competence thresholds that need to be surpassed for the positive effects

[1] Apparently, this replicability crisis is more general and affects the field of psychology as a whole (Bialystok 2020: 9).

of previous multilingual experience to materialize. Again, earlier enthusiasm is currently giving way to a more nuanced view, as positive effects fail to be replicated consistently. Section 2.2 also addresses terminological problems regarding the notions of 'competence' and 'performance' that have led to various misunderstandings between linguistics and education studies.

More recently, bilingualism and multilingualism have been argued to carry additional positive effects in that they facilitate the acquisition of additional languages and foster metalinguistic awareness. Positive influences of a previous multilingual experience on subsequent language acquisition will be explored in detail in Chapter 4, but Section 2.3 paves the way into this discussion by exploring the accumulation of such conscious and unconscious knowledge about language. Different types of metalinguistic awareness that have been shown to correlate, in various ways, with language proficiencies need to be distinguished. Section 2.3 closes with an examination of the predictors of metalinguistic awareness and Chapter 2 ends by garnering the main insights and controversies.

2.1 Executive Function and Cognitive Reserve

While the research focus of the early studies on bilingual disadvantages – and later advantages – lay in testing verbal and non-verbal intelligence, this focus shifted in the final decades of the twentieth century towards studying executive function or control (see Bialystok, Craik & Luk 2012 for an overview). The relationship between bilingualism and executive function is still hotly debated. Perhaps as a concomitant with a more general awareness of behavioural consequences on the quality of life, as well as life expectancy (food and alcohol consumption, physical exercise, sleep, musical activities, playing chess, etc.), the beginning of the twenty-first century saw an increasing interest in issues of bilingualism and cognitive ageing. The only areas in which bilingual children's progress is perhaps somewhat delayed in comparison to their monolingual peers are lexical development and verbal fluency, but these disadvantages tend to disappear once the entire linguistic competence across all languages is considered (Bialystok, Craik & Luk 2012: 241; Bialystok et al. 2010; Ivanova & Costa 2008).[2]

2.1.1 Executive Function (Control)

Bialystok, Craik and Luk (2012: 241) describe executive control as "the set of cognitive skills based on limited cognitive resources for such functions as inhibition, switching attention, and working memory." Bilingualism has been

[2] Vocabulary differences between monolinguals and bilinguals apparently affect terms from the home context more strongly than terms from the school context (Bialystok et al. 2010: 530).

hypothesized to impact executive control positively, since bilinguals, when using one language, unconsciously need to inhibit the other. This follows from the assumption that the languages in the bilingual's mind are typically coactive (see Aronin & Singleton 2012: 85 for discussion). Accordingly, executive control experiences a training effect. The following quotation offers an apt summary of this connection (see also Bialystok 2018: 294):

> Frequent use of the inhibitory processes involved in language selection in bilinguals will result in more efficient inhibitory processes, which will confer general advantages on nonlinguistic interference tasks – that is, those requiring conflict resolution. These advantages will be reflected in reduced interference effects in bilinguals as compared to monolinguals. In other words, bilinguals should show an advantage over monolinguals on trials with response conflict. (Hilchey & Klein 2011: 628)[3]

Executive function is assessed using a variety of tasks, notably the Simon task, the flanker task, and the Stroop task (Hilchey & Klein 2011: 628). These comprise experiments involving congruent and incongruent conditions of certain stimuli (colours, shapes, letters, etc.) while gauging the performance (usually reaction times) of subjects when confronted with these conditions (Donnelly, Brooks & Homer 2015: 596). For example, when doing the Simon task, participants see differently coloured (red or green) shapes (circles, squares) on either the left or right half of a computer screen. The colours are associated with buttons equally positioned on the left- or right-hand side. Participants are then asked to press the button associated with the relevant colour as soon as the object appears on the screen. If the coloured object and its associated button match in position (both left or right in the congruent condition), the measured reaction time is typically lower than if they do not (one left and the other right in the incongruent condition). Inhibitory control is defined in terms of reaction time in the incongruent condition minus reaction time measured in the congruent condition (interference cost). Smaller differences are interpreted as greater inhibitory control. Global reaction time is calculated as the mean of both congruent and incongruent reaction times (Donnelly, Brooks & Homer 2015: 596; Paap, Johnson & Sawi 2015: 267). The flanker task and the Stroop task are variations on this experimental set-up. Arrows pointing in one direction are flanked by an arrow pointing in the same (congruent) or the opposite (incongruent) direction. The Stroop task is based on colour adjectives printed in matching and non-matching colours.

[3] Valian (2015) is quite critical of the special nature of this connection. She draws attention to the fact that there are many other activities that influence executive function, as, for instance, "active video game playing, education, musical training, and aerobic exercise" (Valian 2015: 3). She concludes that "[r]esearchers fail to find an advantage for bilingualism in part because there are many other cognitively enriching activities that monolinguals may engage in that are as potent as, or more potent than, bilingualism" (Valian 2015: 19).

It may be worth pointing out that these are standard psychological tests that have been used to examine the influences of a host of other factors on executive control, such as level of blood alcohol, tiredness, illnesses, and so on. In studies searching for multilingual advantages, a bilingual subject group is typically tested against a monolingual control group. The tests described earlier have been conducted with both children and adults. They tend to report faster (i.e. 'better') performance in bilinguals over monolinguals. There are interesting age differences such that, for example, young adults show the smallest differences across monolingual and bilingual groups or no differences at all (Bialystok 2018: 292–293).

2.1.2 Cognitive Reserve

More recently, it has also been hypothesized that bilingualism positively impacts cognitive reserve. This construct describes a cognitive buffer that shields against age-related symptoms of cognitive decline. It is widely accepted that physical, intellectual, and social engagement contribute to cognitive reserve (Bialystok, Craik & Luk 2012: 246–247). The impact of bilingualism on cognitive reserve was, inter alia, tested on a sample of 184 patients diagnosed with dementia (91 monolinguals and 93 bilinguals) by Bialystok, Craik and Freedman (2007). The study found that patients with a bilingual background showed a delayed onset in the symptoms of dementia, appearing approximately four years later than in monolingual patients. The analysis controlled for several confounding factors such as education and occupation status. Similarly, Craik, Bialystok and Freedman (2010) examined the effects of bilingualism on the onset of Alzheimer's disease (102 bilinguals and 109 monolinguals). They also reported a significant delay in the onset of the relevant symptoms in bilingual patients. Aveledo et al. (2021) offer an extension of this line of research into multiple sclerosis. In relation to age differences, Bialystok et al. (2004) encountered stronger processing advantages in older bilinguals relative to older monolinguals when comparing them to corresponding younger cohorts on the Simon task. In sum, it is argued that bilingualism can counterbalance age-related cognitive decline.

2.1.3 Controversial Issues

After substantial initial enthusiasm regarding bilingual boosting effects on executive control, usually measured in terms of higher inhibitory control and shorter general reaction times, the field has been going through a sobering period that started around 2010. As positive effects associated with bilingualism failed to replicate in follow-up studies, recent publications have called for a reorientation of the field (Leivada et al. 2020; Paap & Greenberg 2013; Paap, Johnson & Sawi 2016). The following paragraphs summarize the main points of criticism.

As it is impossible even to attempt to survey and discuss the plethora of studies on bilingualism and executive control, I here exclusively rely on the available meta-analyses. Even these need to be interpreted with caution, as they can only compare subsamples from the pool of potentially relevant studies, use diverging criteria for inclusion and exclusion, and focus on different phenomena.[4] For instance, Olusola et al. (2010: 211–213) considered no fewer than 5,185 articles for inclusion in their meta-analysis, but eventually confined the comparison to 63 studies from 39 articles involving 6,022 participants, since only these met their selection criteria.[5] Hilchey and Klein (2011) used 31 studies culled from 13 publications. Donnelly, Brooks and Homer (2015) reported from 39 studies with 73 comparisons and 5,538 participants. Paap, Johnson and Sawi (2015) restricted their meta-analysis to studies conducted after 2011. De Bruin, Treccani and Della Sala (2015) pursued the publication trajectory of 128 studies from conference presentation to final publication in print. Lehtonen et al. (2018) compared 152 studies, including unpublished theses.

Perhaps the most important points of concern are sample size and recruitment processes (see also Bialystok 2020: 13). It is not at all uncommon to find samples below 100 or even 50 participants. Given that these are meant to represent the totality of bilingual and monolingual speakers, some scepticism appears warranted. Moreover, it is well known that small samples can produce strong statistical cohort effects. Leivada et al. (2020: 8) report a recent small increase in average sample size. Paap, Johnson and Sawi (2015: 267, 271) argue that studies claiming bilingual advantages typically rely on small samples, whereas bigger samples tend to reveal no effects. The most common participants for studies are students. This, of course, is due to various practical considerations, but students are certainly not representative of society at large.

There may also be a problem of publication bias, as small studies reporting strong positive effects may stand higher chances of being accepted in journals. De Bruin, Treccani and Della Sala (2015: 99) make exactly this point. According to their survey of eventually published conference abstracts, "[s]tudies with results fully supporting the bilingual-advantage theory were most likely to be published, followed by studies with mixed results. Studies challenging the bilingual advantage were published the least." Lehtonen et al. (2018: 413) come to similar conclusions.[6] Paap, Johnson and Sawi (2015: 266) point out

[4] Bialystok (2020: 12) provides a rather critical assessment of meta-analyses, although this is arguably the best data type available (Leivada et al. 2020: 2).

[5] One criterion for selection was that "participants were reported to be equally (or almost equally) proficient in two languages" (Olusola et al. 2010: 211).

[6] These authors argue "that small studies with low precision and large, positive effect sizes might be overrepresented in the peer-reviewed literature, or that comparably small studies with large, negative effect sizes are underrepresented" (Lehtonen et al. 2018: 413).

that null findings may easily be interpreted as type II errors by reviewers, leading to a rejection of the studies.[7]

A third problem area relates to various confounding background variables, the most important of which is the distinction between monolinguals and bilinguals. Traditionally conceived as a categorical binary variable, more recent research has revealed that bilingualism is a continuum or rather spectrum of experiences (DeLuca et al. 2019; Leivada et al. 2020: 6–7).[8] Even the otherwise helpful distinction between balanced and unbalanced bilinguals represents more of a label for a problem instead of a solution. Speakers can be bilingual in many different ways and further studies would need to operationalize and assess this correctly and consistently. We will encounter many ways of being bilingual and multilingual in the later chapters of this book. Additional confounds include the languages involved and their social prestige, age, socio-economic status, cognitive development, research lab, task design, code-switching behaviour, and even cultural differences (Paap, Johnson & Sawi 2015: 268).[9] One may add that bilinguals may also maintain different individual conceptions of their bilingualism (double monolingualism versus one language system) that may tinker with the measurable effects. Finally, there remains the problem of causality (does bilingualism impact cognition or vice versa?) and the thorny issue of using appropriate statistics.

2.1.4 *Summary*

The scientific quest for bilingual disadvantages and advantages in relation to cognition has now been going on for more than a hundred years. Considering the entire time span, it is fair to say that it has produced mixed results with ups and downs, winners and losers (see also Section 1.4.1). In view of the research effort (manpower, lab time, etc.) spent, these inconclusive results are surprising. The quest is likely to continue for another hundred years, but my suspicion at this point is that there will be no conclusive outcome. It may therefore be wise to pause for a moment and ask what drives this endeavour and what additional complications there are. I can think of at least the following three points.

First, the issue of bilingual advantages and multilingualism in general is intimately tied to the allocation of resources. I am not aware of any exact calculations, but I presume that it is more costly to organize a society on

7 Type I errors relate to false positives, type II errors to false negatives.

8 Bialystok (2020: 15–16) points out that "no two bilingual samples can be identical, and different studies will capture details of the individual experiences of the participants. A systemic problem in the literature is that studies rarely report these details, and when they do, rarely report information that can be compared across studies."

9 Bialystok (2020: 17) argues that even the concept of executive function is not particularly well defined.

bilingual or multilingual principles in comparison to a simple monolingual form of organization. Central systems of society, such as education, administration, medical services, and so on, need to be able to respond to different language demands. A bitter technocrat may argue that this is simply too expensive. In the long run, however, it may turn out that such resources are well spent, as the devaluation and loss of linguistic identities represent social time bombs that can heftily backfire, taking societies to the brink of collapse (see Section 1.4.3). The Canadian model of integration stands out as one of the more far-sighted in this respect.

Second, scholars and their students may – consciously or unconsciously – participate in this ideological debate, which, in turn, may influence how studies are designed and hence their outcomes. For example, I have frequently noticed how sensitively students adjust to my points of view. Scholars who believe in multilingualism, bilingual advantages, and the beauty of linguistic diversity are likely to influence their students in this way, or they unconsciously attract students who harmonize with their views. Since study participants tend to be recruited from students, some ideological bias appears unavoidable. Bilingual students may be highly motivated in such an environment, whereas monolingual students may merely participate for the sake of the incentives.

Third, the very idea of what counts as an advantage is subject to various, partially conflicting interpretations. For example, although the aforementioned increase in cognitive reserve associated with bilingualism appears to be a marvel, Leivada et al. (2020: 4) argue that a delayed appearance of phenomena of neurodegeneration may be tantamount to a delayed diagnosis, as the patients simply compensate behaviourally.

2.2 Cognitive Development and Educational Attainment

Potentially positive effects of bilingualism and bilingual education have also been a prominent research topic in education studies. The question in this field asks in which ways bilingualism impacts cognitive development and educational attainment. Cummins (2000: 58–59) distinguishes between "cognitive academic language proficiency" (CALP) and "basic interpersonal communicative skills" (BICS), and strictly speaking, only the former academic language underlies the claims made in education studies.[10] Essentially, this is a register difference that has been referred to with different terms: restricted versus elaborated code (Bernstein 1971), conversational and academic language proficiency (Cummins 1991), and basic and higher language cognition

[10] Cummins (2000: 58) motivates the distinction between BICS and CALP by the observation that children may seem fluent in a language, but nevertheless fail in academic tests related to that language.

(Hulstijn 2015).[11] Both codes can be further structured and are probably better viewed along a continuum (Aronin & Singleton 2012: 112–114; Baker 2011: 169–172; Cummins 2000: 59; Kecskes & Papp 2000: xxiii).[12] Moreover, there is the term 'language competence' that is used in different ways and has caused considerable confusion (see below). In sum, education studies understand 'bilingualism' first and foremost as 'academic language bilingualism', typically in the written genre. Only this particular register is studied in its influence on cognitive development and educational attainment.

2.2.1 *Language, Competence, and Performance*

These terminological issues are quite critical, as the terms 'language' and 'competence' can be understood in fundamentally different ways. When linguists – especially in acquisition studies and bilingualism research – talk about language, they typically refer to the underlying mental capacity or what Chomsky (1986) defined as the "I-language" (in opposition to "E-language"). Except for certain clinical cases, all human beings are believed to possess the mental capacities necessary to develop languages (a language capacity).[13] These initial mental representations ("initial state") then further mature according to the linguistic input children receive from their environment. Input from different languages provokes different maturation processes, but the linguistic core is universal and remains the same. Crucially, all children – provided they receive the requisite input – develop into fully competent speakers (native speakers). There are no better or worse speakers.

The perspective of education studies, with their focus on academic language, is completely different, as academic language is a highly specific register systematically developed throughout our academic careers (Biber 2006). Some parents start this process even before the beginning of school. It appears to be a matter of debate how early, in which contexts, and in which quality and quantity even very young children acquiring their first language receive instructions related to academic language from their caretakers – and how they interpret them. Beginning at school, at the latest, children develop literacy and are explicitly taught the rules of written languages. They learn the differences between spoken and written as well as appropriate and inappropriate language. They begin to develop explicit grammatical knowledge and

[11] Hulstijn (2015: 21) explains the difference as follows: "Basic language cognition is the language cognition that all native speakers have in common; higher, extended language cognition is the domain where differences between native speakers can be observed."

[12] Kecskes and Papp (2000: xxiv) note that "middle-class children acquire the academic variety with ease because it is closer to their vernacular."

[13] This capacity has been referred to as the "Language Acquisition Device" or the "Language Making Capacity" (see Meisel 2011: 2 for discussion).

metalinguistic awareness, and they are penalized for using the wrong code in the wrong context. Moreover, the academic world encourages spoken language according to the principles of written languages ("Speak in full sentences!").[14] There is substantial prescriptivism, of which children and also many educators are unaware, working in the background. Opposing language "fluent surface skills" to "complex cognitive operations" (Cummins 1979: 227), the educational perspective implies a devaluation of basic interpersonal communicative skills and a concomitant valorization of cognitive academic language proficiency.[15] In this world, people are sorted into more and less educated according to their language use. Part of the mission of the education system is to produce people with different levels of education. Here, we do find better and worse speakers or language users.

Similar observations are relevant for the term 'competence', as linguists use this term for the knowledge system behind languages that cannot be observed directly. In education studies, the same term is widely used to gauge performance, that is, the observable output of language processing. Whereas (mature) native speakers of a language are, by definition, equally competent from a linguistic perspective, the educational approach imposes a finely differentiated grid of competence levels on the language users. Our naturally acquired language competence is different from the culturally developed language competence – especially that found in the education system. Needless to say, these differences in perspective offer endless opportunities for misunderstandings and fruitless controversial discussions.

In several successive publications, Cummins (1976, 1979, amongst others) developed two hypotheses on academic language competence in the bilingual speaker, namely the "threshold hypothesis" and the "interdependence hypothesis" (see also Baker 2011). They both concern the level of academic language competence of the languages in the bilingual mind. They will be briefly discussed in what follows.

2.2.2 *Language Competence Levels (Thresholds)*

Bilingual education programmes revealed that minority language children tend to underperform regarding educational attainment and academic language competence, whereas majority language children appear to benefit from bilingualism (Cummins 1979). Minority language children are members of indigenous

[14] See Kaltenböck, Heine and Kuteva (2011) on the distinction between sentence grammar and thetical grammar.

[15] Cummins (2001), however, offers a well-argued defence of the distinction between "basic interpersonal communicative skills" (BICS) and "cognitive academic language proficiency" (CALP); see also Cummins (2000: Ch. 4).

communities, prominently in the United States, Canada, and Australia, who were raised in their community language and then entered English-medium educational programmes. Alternatively, the label is used for immigrant children – no matter whether foreign-born or not – who equally start educational programmes conducted in the majority language English. Immigrant children in other contexts (such as Europe) face similar problems in other majority language situations (German, French, Swedish, etc.). In contrast, bilingual majority language children acquire another language in addition to the language of their environment, as in the context of English–French bilingualism in Canada, but also majority language children in Europe learning English at an early age.

Various additional conditions correlate with this distinction. Minority language children typically go through transitional bilingual submersion programmes or simply majority language submersion programmes. They are considered to develop subtractive bilingualism or even "semilingualism" (see below). Subtractive bilingualism can lead to dominant bilingualism where high academic competence is only achieved in one language, while the other language remains at a lower competence level. Bilingual majority language children attend immersion programmes, enjoy maintenance bilingualism, and become additive bilinguals. The outcome of additive bilingualism is high levels of (academic) competence in both languages (balanced bilingualism). Moreover, the two groups tend to differ strongly in terms of social background and socio-economic status. Finally, the languages involved carry very different levels of social prestige, with minority languages, typically, being devalued in the respective majority language contexts. Minority languages may be oral languages without a writing system.

The threshold hypothesis (Cummins 1979: 230) claims that situations of additive bilingualism produce positive cognitive effects, whereas such positive effects cannot be expected in situations of dominant bilingualism (in which one language is stronger than the other). In other words, a certain level of academic language competence needs to be surpassed in both languages before any "positive cognitive effects" of bilingualism can be detected. As Cummins explains,

> [. . .] the level of competence bilingual children achieve in their two languages acts as an intervening variable in mediating the effects of their bilingual learning experiences on cognition. Specifically, there may be threshold levels of linguistic competence which bilingual children must attain both in order to avoid cognitive deficits and to allow the potentially beneficial aspects of becoming bilingual to influence their cognitive growth. (Cummins 1979: 229)

Cummins thus postulates a relationship between linguistic competence in first and second language and cognitive growth. The definition of "positive cognitive effects" remains somewhat unclear, but they can be expected to relate to higher educational attainment or better school grades (see also Lasagabaster 1998, 2001). Put differently, additive bilingualism is associated with higher intelligence. As this is a far-reaching proposition, some scepticism appears to be in order. As for bilingual children with low academic language competence in both languages, Cummins (1979: 230) even assumes negative cognitive effects or intellectual disability (retardation). This is the widely discussed condition of "semilingualism" (Swedish *halvspråkighet*; Hansegard 1968). It justly attracted considerable criticism due to its pejorative implications. Although semilingualism as such defines a condition of low academic language competence in the two languages of the bilingual child, there is the danger of mistaking it for language ability in general, thus creating linguistically deficient children. As MacSwan warns us,

> Prescriptivism and semilingualism are both doctrines that attribute a linguistic deficit to some population of children, creating a climate for academic failure by assigning these students to "low-ability groups." (MacSwan 2000: 8)

The conditions outlined above produce a lower and a higher threshold of bilingual competence that can vary from child to child and cannot be defined in absolute terms (Cummins 1979: 230). This makes it difficult to operationalize them and produce empirical support for them. Berthele and Vanhove (2020: 553) point out that "no one so far has shown empirically that there is a non-linear developmental slope whose shape would be evidence for such thresholds."

2.2.3 Language Interdependence

Furthermore, Cummins (1979) hypothesized a relationship of interdependence between the languages in the bilingual mind such that academic competence in the one language positively influences academic competence in the other. This interdependence hypothesis, provided it is valid, has important practical implications. For example, heritage language speaking children could benefit from developing their heritage language academically inasmuch as this could be advantageous for academic development in the majority language. As Cummins explains,

> The developmental interdependence hypothesis proposes that the level of L2 competence which a bilingual child attains is partially a function of the type of competence the child has developed in L1 at the time when intensive exposure to L2 begins. (Cummins 1979: 233)

The interdependence of languages in the sense of Cummins (1979; see also 1976) can be viewed as a special case of facilitative cross-linguistic influence in which proficiency in one language is assumed to boost proficiency in another (Berthele & Vanhove 2020: 550–551; Lechner & Siemund 2014). It concerns largely unspecified higher-order cognitive abilities to the exclusion of the more specific linguistic properties that are the traditional focus of studies charting cross-linguistic influence (see Chapter 3).[16] Although interdependence was originally conceptualized in the context of bilingualism proper, it was more recently extended to multilingual situations, especially the acquisition of English as a third language on a previous bilingual experience (see Chapter 4).

As with thresholds, it remains challenging to operationalize and measure the interdependence between languages. As Berthele and Vanhove (2020: 553–554) point out, several in principle observable data sets measuring academic competence in heritage and majority language are compatible with language interdependence, especially under the assumption of thresholds. What is more, language interdependence is also consistent with several alternative principles such as language giftedness or more general cognitive skills (working memory, general intelligence, world knowledge, test-wiseness; Berthele & Vanhove 2020: 562).

2.2.4 *Summary*

Language acquisition and language development are two different pairs of shoes, although the latter term may encompass the former (as in this book). To use an analogy, their relationship is comparable to that of walking and dancing. Children learn to walk without instruction, and this is what also happens with language during first language acquisition. Dancing is a social activity that requires instruction and training – similar to the development of academic language in the education system. Evidently, walking is a prerequisite for dancing and the more fundamental psycho-motoric activity. It appears plausible that previous dancing experience facilitates the mastering of novel dances, much like knowledge of the academic conventions in one language facilitates the learning of the relevant conventions in another. Talent for dancing corresponds to verbal intelligence. Viewed from this perspective, language interdependence is not at all unexpected.

Moreover, learning the conventions of academic language is not the same as learning an additional language, as they relate to different, albeit partially

[16] Cummins (2009: 267) operationalizes transfer as that of "conceptual knowledge," "metacognitive and metalinguistic strategies," "pragmatic aspects of language use," "specific linguistic elements," and "phonological awareness." Berthele and Vanhove (2020: 551) criticize that these attributes mostly relate to general cognition: "The main problem in extending the notion of transfer to cognitive attributes in general is that in that case the theory should no longer be considered one of linguistic interdependence, but of general cognition. Therefore, correlational patterns of measures of linguistic skills would be mere epiphenomena of general cognitive effects and the educational discussion should no longer be about language promotion but about promotion of cognitive skills." I concur.

overlapping knowledge systems. This explains (part of) the struggle experienced by minority language children during their early school careers. They are faced with a double challenge, while majority language children can focus on the academic content. Transitional bilingual programmes provide children with the necessary time to learn the majority language:

> [. . .] language minority children benefit from native language instruction not because they suffer from semilingualism, but because it allows them to keep up academically while learning English. (MacSwan 2000: 32)

However, neither language interdependence nor bilingual programmes will be able to counterbalance low language prestige and the concomitant loss of motivation to invest into minority languages. The reasons behind these problems are entirely social. They do not arise with prestigious languages. Across the world, English is learnt as an additional language with a continuously decreasing age of onset. The result is widespread bilingualism of the relevant national language and English. In the Scandinavian countries, the Netherlands, and increasingly also Germany, it is becoming more and more difficult to find monolingual speakers. To the best of my knowledge, no one has ever associated this situation of bilingualism with cognitive effects, neither in terms of retardation or advancement. Learning English is simply a social requirement, there being no room to assess its potentially negative or positive consequences. In addition, it would be practically impossible to recruit the necessary monolingual controls to drive any such comparison.

On a similar note, bilingualism across Europe – involving a vernacular in combination with the highly prestigious lingua francas of Latin, French, and now English – has always been considered an emblem of high education largely restricted to the elites. If at all, there is a narrative of high education corresponding to cognitive advancement in an educational sense. No one ever suspected this condition to produce mental retardation. As education is a hallmark of contemporary knowledge-based societies, this type of bilingualism (national language plus English) is now disseminating through societies all over the world.

2.3 Metalinguistic Awareness

Apart from language professionals, most people use their (native) languages without extensive explicit knowledge of them. It is one of the striking facts about language that we can use it without having to think about it. Language use thus shares important characteristics with other unconsciously used bodily functions like walking, seeing, hearing, digesting, and the like. Language use is quasi-automatic and possible without any awareness of language.

Nevertheless, some people develop language awareness by themselves and most people – often obligatorily – participate in educational programmes that develop such awareness. This concerns metalinguistic abilities that allow one to reflect on notions like language, dialects, accents, nativeness, proficiency, grammar, dictionary, sounds, words, sentences, meaning, letters or characters, as well as the relationship of language to social constructs like gender, ethnicity, politeness, and age. In the words of Jessner (2006: 42), metalinguistic awareness relates to the "ability to focus attention on language as an object in itself or to think abstractly about language and, consequently, to play with or manipulate language" or "the ability to focus on linguistic form and to switch focus between form and meaning [. . .] to categorize words into parts of speech; [to] switch focus between form, function, and meaning; and [to] explain why a word has a particular function" (Jessner 2008: 277). Evidently, metalinguistic awareness is a prerequisite for being a language professional.

People who develop metalinguistic awareness spontaneously can perhaps be considered natural linguists. However, in this modern world with compulsory, early, prolonged, and extremely reflective education systems, the training of metalinguistic awareness starts already during childhood. Phonological awareness training including the relationship of sounds and their graphic representations can be found as early as kindergarten and preschool. Elementary schools introduce and train word classes, form–meaning relationships, orthography, clause structure including hypotaxis and parataxis, and the properties of written academic language by means of an explicit meta-language. By the age of eleven or twelve, children can be assumed to have acquired extensive metalinguistic awareness.

Bilingualism and multilingualism are widely assumed to foster metalinguistic awareness (Bialystok 2001; De Angelis 2007; Franceschini 2016; García 2008; Jessner 1999, 2006, 2008; Kecskes & Papp 2000; Sanz 2012; see also Cook & Wei 2016 on multi-competence). Conversely, metalinguistic awareness can be expected to impact positively on the acquisition of additional languages. Folk wisdom has it that language learning is, at least partially, a function of the languages learnt earlier. There is indeed scientific support for the assumption that previous language knowledge facilitates the learning of new languages (see Chapter 4). Herdina and Jessner (2002: 130) view metalinguistic awareness as an essential component of multilingual proficiency that itself involves knowledge of several language systems, cross-linguistic influence, and the multilingualism factor.[17]

[17] Herdina and Jessner (2002: 130) explain that the "multilingualism factor expresses an essential difference between multilingual and monolingual speakers." In particular, they argue that the multilingual system "contains components the monolingual system lacks" and "that even those components the multilingual system shares with the monolingual system have a different significance within the system."

One of the earliest studies on metalinguistic awareness and bilingualism is that of Cummins (1978). The study tested metalinguistic abilities in Irish–English bilingual school children and corresponding English monolingual control groups. It revealed that the bilingual students scored higher on certain tests, though not on all. The arbitrary relationship between words and their referents could be established as an area where bilingual children outperform their monolingual peers (Cummins 1978: 141–143).[18] Reder et al. (2013), Kopečková (2018), as well as Hofer and Jessner (2019), represent more recent studies in this research paradigm, arguing along the same lines.

2.3.1 *Types of Metalinguistic Awareness*

Gombert (1992) introduced the very useful opposition of epilinguistic and metalinguistic awareness, with epilinguistic awareness referring to unconscious, spontaneous, and contextualized manifestations of language reflection as self-repair in speech (see also Wrembel 2013: 120). Self-repair of slips of the tongue would fall into this domain. Metalinguistic awareness proper, in contrast, is decontextualized, conscious, and intentional, a typical example being language analysis in the classroom or conscious reflection on language properties. Most work on metalinguistic awareness concerns this conscious type.

Metalinguistic awareness as such may concern all levels of linguistic analysis. It can be developed and tested in relation to graphemes, phonemes, morphemes, words, phrases, clauses, sentences, registers, and text types – essentially any linguistic unit that is amenable to conscious inspection (see Sanz 2012 for an overview). To be sure, professional linguists develop further types of metalinguistic awareness, but this is subject to more extensive theorizing and also speech technology. Metalinguistic awareness typically reveals itself by subjects' comments on and analyses of the above language domains. Such comments and analyses may be induced by metalinguistic awareness tests (such as Pinto, Titone & Trusso 1999). During second and further language acquisition, metalinguistic awareness may follow the recognition of errors, divergent hypotheses about the target language, as well as conscious comparisons with earlier acquired languages. One may further distinguish metapragmatic awareness (Safont Jordà 2003, 2005) that reveals conventions about language use unconsciously adhered to (as, for example, concerning the use of the imperative; see Siemund 2018b).

[18] The children were asked the following question: "Suppose you were making up names for things, could you then call the sun 'the moon' and the moon 'the sun'?" Nearly 70 per cent of the bilingual children agreed, compared to less than 30 per cent of the monolingual children (Cummins 1978: 141). I believe that such a question is outside the scope of experience of a monolingual child. If it were to be used as a measure of intelligence, the monolingual child would fail.

2.3.2 *Metalinguistic Awareness and Language Proficiency*

Multilingualism, metalinguistic awareness, and language proficiency (in an academic sense) are highly interrelated. This would not appear to be entirely unexpected. The acquisition and development of languages in the education system proceeds on the basis of reflective pedagogies that themselves are based on complex linguistic concepts and theorizing – although this theorizing and the concepts are hardly ever questioned in the school system. One may suspect that students performing well on language proficiency tasks (oral and written production and reception) also acquired the underlying linguistic concepts and are able to reflect on them (and vice versa). In multilingual situations – especially those embedded in the education system – substantial time is devoted to teaching languages including the requisite linguistic concepts. Here, too, it would appear reasonable to surmise a positive relationship between (educational) multilingualism, metalinguistic awareness, and language proficiency.

Such positive correlations have been documented in several studies. For example, in a comprehensive study carried out in the Basque Country with 252 bilingual students (Basque, Spanish) who studied English as a foreign language, Lasagabaster (1998, 2001) identifies significant correlations between metalinguistic awareness, language proficiency, and various skills in English (listening, reading, speaking, grammar, and writing). In particular, Lasagabaster (1998) demonstrates a monotonic increase of metalinguistic awareness contingent on the proficiency of students in one, two, or three languages. Those highly proficient in three languages achieve the highest metalinguistic awareness scores. Furthermore, Lasagabaster (2001) examines the impact of students' metalinguistic awareness in their first language (Basque or Spanish) on different skills in English. Interestingly enough, metalinguistic awareness positively influences English reading, grammar, writing, and speaking skills in a statistically significant way, though not listening skills.[19] It is one of the few studies where these skills are distinguished. Hofer and Jessner (2019) compare South Tyrolian (Northern Italy) primary school students in multilingual streams (where instruction proceeds in German and Italian) and traditional Italian-medium programmes and report better results of the former group in regard to proficiency in English and German as well as metalinguistic awareness (tested for Italian). They conclude that early multilingualism fosters language proficiency and metalinguistic awareness.

Again, we need to bear in mind that the above studies were carried out in contexts of additive multilingualism involving languages of high social

[19] Listening skills, nevertheless, show positive correlations with metalinguistic awareness (Lasagabaster 2001: 320–321).

prestige. Spellerberg (2016) offers an interesting point of comparison in this respect (see also El Euch 2010). This study – placed in Denmark – involved 219 students aged 14–16 of which 106 were classified as monolingual and 113 as bi-/multilingual. The majority of the bi-/multilingual students came from immigrant families speaking a great variety of home languages. The study distinguished three language groups, namely monolingual Danish students, bi-/multilinguals who speak the majority language Danish at home, and bi-/multilingual who do not speak Danish at home (but one of the heritage languages, which are less prestigious in the context of Denmark). The measurement of metalinguistic awareness in this sample revealed a monotonic increase from the last group to the first. Monolingual Danish students scored highest.[20] Moreover, metalinguistic awareness and school leaving exam results were shown to be strongly related. What needs to be borne in mind in the interpretation of these findings is that metalinguistic awareness also depends on socio-economic status and that the metalinguistic awareness test was administered in the majority language, Danish. In particular the latter fact may have skewed the results considerably (recall the discussion of Saer 1923 in Chapter 1), as some heritage students may have found it difficult to complete the test. Nevertheless, the study serves as a warning that a simple equation of multilingualism, metalinguistic awareness, and proficiencies (academic achievement) falls short of reality.

2.3.3 *Predictors of Metalinguistic Awareness*

Given that metalinguistic awareness is a complex cognitive measure, it is influenced by a host of different parameters. Moreover, as metalinguistic awareness needs to be measured by some kind of test, the task design including its comprehensibility will determine the outcome. This is not different from other complex cognitive measures, such as intelligence or executive function.

It would appear intuitively plausible to claim that metalinguistic awareness is a function of the languages that one knows, but this cannot be more than a very rough estimate, since knowledge of language is difficult to define. For each language in a speaker's repertoire, we need to determine age of onset, type of acquisition, length of exposure or instruction, the type of instruction (if applicable), the proficiency levels reached, frequency and domains of use, as well as the development of literacy. Some of these parameters predict language dominance (see Chapter 3). I consider explicit linguistic instruction an extremely important parameter, as it requires hard work to lay open the systemic properties of languages (see also De Angelis 2007: 122–123). Uninstructed

[20] Interestingly, speaking Danish at home turned out to be the crucial factor (Spellerberg 2016: 30).

contemplation may lead to folk linguistic generalizations that perhaps reveal more about a speaker's underlying stereotypes and cultural biases than metalinguistic awareness proper.

I wish to remain agnostic about which of the above parameters exerts the strongest effects, but it would appear that the influence of literacy should not be underestimated (De Angelis 2007: 118–120). Literacy development practically forces the language user into developing metalinguistic awareness, as graphemes need to be related to sounds and meanings in a systematic way. It is usually taken for granted that phoneme awareness drives literacy, but there may just as well be a path in the opposite direction (Phillips, Clancy-Menchetti & Lonigan 2008).[21]

Finally, the kind of pedagogical approach used within the classroom matters for the development of metalinguistic awareness (see Chapter 4). Pedagogies explicitly addressing multilingualism and language diversity can be expected to give a boost to metalinguistic awareness. Allowing for the use of multiple languages in the (language) classroom rather than enforcing a monolingual habitat will be beneficial for the development of metalinguistic awareness. The traditional monolingual classroom valorizes and devalues languages according to their alleged classroom relevance and social prestige (see Fuller 2020: 171 on "normative monolingualism"). It then becomes difficult to discuss and draw on the devalued languages, even though they could be helpful and relevant.

2.3.4 *Summary*

In comparison to executive function and cognitive development, the positive impact of multilingualism on metalinguistic awareness appears intuitively more plausible. Evidently, there is a closer relationship between the latter two concepts as they both relate to language proper. One may compare the development of metalinguistic awareness to that of meta-cultural awareness as a consequence of (conscious) travelling and cultural immersion. This also leads to the identification of similarities and differences between one's own culture and the foreign culture as well as conscious reflection of it. If not done in an informed way, there looms the danger of forming cultural misconceptions (stereotypes) much as with folk linguistic generalizations.

There are several questions about metalinguistic awareness that remain unanswered by current research. First, it remains somewhat unclear whether bilingual and multilingual language users per se show higher levels of metalinguistic awareness in comparison to their monolingual counterparts. It appears evident that metalinguistic awareness increases in instructed language acquisition

[21] Not surprisingly, syllable awareness and morphological awareness impact literacy development in Chinese (Pan et al. 2015).

and perhaps during formal education in general. It is, however, less clear if multilingualism positively impacts metalinguistic awareness if there is no education system and hence no formal instruction. There is an important methodological problem here, as this would need to be measured with either very young children who did not receive formal education or in cultures without an education system. The very concept of metalinguistic awareness may be meaningless outside the education system.

Second, as argued above, monolingually raised children usually receive extensive grammatical tuition in their first language, starting already in elementary school, perhaps earlier. It can be taken for granted that this raises their metalinguistic awareness. However, if and to what extent this also facilitates subsequent language acquisition remains difficult to answer, but I suppose it does. In fact, even for bilingual children learning additional languages, the evidence is far from unanimous (see Rutgers & Evans 2017).

Third, if it is the case that metalinguistic awareness facilitates the acquisition of additional languages, one may hypothesize that this also affects the scope and direction of cross-linguistic influence. For example, it could be the case that learners with higher levels of metalinguistic awareness show less cross-linguistic influence of the non-facilitating type, and perhaps higher degrees of facilitating influence. In addition, metalinguistic awareness may produce different effects of cross-linguistic influence in production and reception, speaking and writing. Such studies presuppose sophisticated research designs. Another problem concerns the specific domains of language learning where positive effects of metalinguistic awareness can be expected. The development of phonology and morphology may profit to a lesser (or perhaps higher) extent than lexical or syntactic development. The phonology of a foreign language is a well-known area of imperfect acquisition. Current research is suggestive of the fact that bilingual and multilingual learners indeed show certain advantages in this domain, perhaps as a consequence of heightened metalinguistic awareness. These issues will be followed up in Chapters 3 and 4.

2.4 Chapter Summary

The discussion about putative multilingual advantages remains highly controversial and also emotional, as it affects far-reaching policy decisions. Chapter 2 attempted to provide an objective state-of-the-art report, discussing research findings on executive function, cognitive reserve, cognitive development, educational attainment, and metalinguistic awareness. It furthermore tried to identify the boundary conditions that help to explain why some studies report positive results while others do not. Current research suggests that the characteristics of the speaker groups sampled, especially in terms of their type of bilingualism and multilingualism (balanced, unbalanced, heritage speakers, etc.), offer important clues for a better understanding of this domain (Hamann, Rinke & Genevska-Hanke 2019). Moreover, the social prestige associated with the languages studied appears to influence the results considerably. Language users are not deterministic machines, but react to social pressure in intelligent ways.

With regard to executive control, several recent replication studies and meta-analyses fail to corroborate any simple bilingual advantage hypothesis (Duñabeitia & Carreiras 2015; Leivada et al. 2020; Paap, Johnson & Sawi 2016). Lehtonen et al. (2018: 394), using a meta-analytic comparison, came to the conclusion that "healthy bilingual adults do not have such a cognitive control advantage. The synthesis of 152 studies and 891 comparisons and several moderator variables does not show systematic advantages across the analysed cognitive domains, tasks, or bilingual populations." Much work remains to be done to unravel this paradox and explore why different research camps come to contradictory results, that is, identify the relevant boundary conditions (Titone et al. 2017).

Moreover, even though the interdependence between languages in bilingual and multilingual speakers has been successfully documented, there seems to be no convincing evidence for thresholds in the sense of Cummins (1976, 1979), neither in language nor literacy development (Berthele & Lambelet 2018; Berthele & Vanhove 2020). Furthermore, even with respect to language interdependence there remains the suspicion that more general cognitive factors or simply language giftedness drive the observable correlations rather than language itself (Berthele & Vanhove 2020).

The only area where advantages of bilingual and multilingual upbringing have not been seriously questioned appears to be metalinguistic awareness. I concur, even though I find it difficult to disentangle the influence of multilingualism itself from the influence of explicit language instruction in the educational context. As more time is devoted to explicit language instruction, a concomitant increase in metalinguistic awareness appears expectable. It would be quite deplorable if this did not happen. Be that as it may, El Euch (2010) and Spellerberg (2016) also offer some contradictory evidence in this domain.

3 Cross-Linguistic Influence

This chapter explores cross-linguistic influence and various theories thereof in multilingual settings in which more than two languages interact with one another. It is specifically interested in the direction and strength of such influence, contingent on parameters like age of onset, proficiency, typological proximity, recency of use, language dominance, as well as various others.

The chapter begins with some general definitional remarks on transfer, cross-linguistic influence, and language contact in Section 3.1, motivating the relevance of the term 'cross-linguistic influence' as a cover term that subsumes different types of language interaction in the multilingual mind. It further separates cross-linguistic influence from the related notion of language interdependence used in education studies. Chapter 3 considers additional language acquisition as a special language contact scenario, necessitating some background information from language contact studies.

Section 3.2 scrutinizes the special case of cross-linguistic influence on third language acquisition. It argues for a principled distinction between second and third language acquisition regarding type and direction of cross-linguistic influence. Moreover, the acquisition of a third language against the background of two already existing languages gives rise to four distinct scenarios of cross-linguistic influence whose plausibility is assessed. However, these must be relativized against the specific acquisition trajectories during which the background languages were formed. Adult and child language acquisition simply produce different results, but they only form the extreme poles on a continuum with many intermediate cases.

Chapter 3 continues with a careful assessment of current models of cross-linguistic influence, the most prominent of which being based on absolute L1 transfer, the L2 status factor, typological proximity, linguistic proximity, as well as cumulative enhancement. Section 3.3 assesses their plausibility and discusses the predictions they make. Here, the discussion reveals that the models in fact capture different acquisition scenarios and are, in that sense, difficult to compare. Complete cumulative enhancement, however, is ruled out as an unrealistically optimistic model.

Section 3.4 extends the discussion of cross-linguistic influence to third or additional language acquisition in situations of heritage bilingualism. This type of bilingualism typically arises in immigrant contexts that are themselves a consequence of international migration, as evidenced in Chapter 1. Language acquisition in heritage contexts produces different types of unbalanced bilingualism that can be described in terms of language dominance. This is a complex concept that needs to be operationalized by means of various linguistic and extra-linguistic factors. Crucially, language dominance can be used to predict patterns of cross-linguistic influence in subsequent language acquisition. Chapter 3 closes with the observation that no model of cross-linguistic influence proposed so far uses language dominance as the main explanatory dimension.

3.1 Conceptions of Cross-Linguistic Influence

As cross-linguistic influence has been discussed in separate fields, the following sections circumscribe the concept from the perspective of bilingualism studies, multilingualism, second language acquisition, education studies, and language contact. They differ in their explanans and explananda, but, are jointly interested in the impact that languages exert on one another in bi- or multilingual situations.

3.1.1 Transfer and Cross-Linguistic Influence

It is inevitable to have interaction between the languages in the multilingual mind. The terms ‘transfer’, ‘cross-linguistic influence’, and ‘cross-linguistic interaction’ have been used to describe these mutual dependencies. As they arose in different contexts and periods, their extensions diverge.

Transfer is perhaps the term with the longest history and is also used most widely. It originates in language contact and second language acquisition studies (Odlin 1989, 2010; Weinreich 1953). Broadly speaking, transfer describes the impact of previous language experience (as a first or native language) on subsequent language learning processes or the mutual influence of the languages in the multilingual’s mind. For the most part, transfer is tantamount to interference, that is, aberrant manifestations of previous linguistic knowledge in newly acquired knowledge or of one language in another. Weinreich (1953: 1) defined interference as “instances of deviation from the norms of either language which occur in the speech of bilinguals as a result of their familiarity with more than one language.” This is also known as ‘negative transfer’.

Transfer may also make itself apparent in terms of facilitation effects when previous knowledge helps with the acquisition of new linguistic structures or, the languages in the multilingual’s mind support one another. Such phenomena have also been referred to as positive transfer of reinforcement. Odlin (1989: 27) writes that "[t]ransfer is the influence resulting from similarities and differences between the target language and any other language that has been previously (and perhaps imperfectly) acquired." Evidently, interference is much easier to recognize and measure than facilitation.[1] Moreover, it has been vastly documented in the research literature (Puig-Mayenco, Gonzáles Alonso & Rothman 2020; Rothman, Gonzáles Alonso & Puig-Mayenco 2019: 221–223).[2]

Such transfer or cross-linguistic influence has been extensively described and investigated in second language acquisition research (Odlin 1989, 2003, 2010) on the more practical side, leading to didactic methods of how to suppress negative transfer while exploiting positive transfer (contrastive analysis, error analysis). It also led to the formulation of scales of learning difficulty depending on the degree of similarities and differences between first and second language in a particular grammatical domain (Stockwell, Bowen & Martin 1965).[3]

Interference and facilitation effects can be observed on all levels of linguistic analysis: phonology, morphology, syntax, semantics, lexicon, pragmatics, and in orthography. For example, German learners of English as a foreign language tend to transfer final devoicing, fail to produce adverbs from adjectives by adding *-ly*, use verb-second word order, overgeneralize the progressive aspect, use the verb *give* in the meaning of 'exist', are more likely to employ the imperative than a native speaker of English, and may capitalize nouns. Such interference phenomena are not at all difficult to detect and can be classified into omissions, substitutions, calques, overproductions, underproductions, and the like. Conversely, substantial overlap in the vocabulary due to cognates, the orthography, and the inventory of grammatical categories can be assumed to facilitate the acquisition process, although the criss-crossing of forms and functions also poses severe learning problems.[4] Still, for a German native speaker, learning English arguably involves fewer barriers than learning Chinese.

1 Routinized cognitive processes can be expected to exhibit latency. When operating in a novel normative system, interference is thus expected.

2 These authors provide a quasi-meta-analysis of ninety-two recent studies in the area of third language acquisition with a focus on morphosyntactic phenomena. No fewer than eighty-two out of these ninety-two studies report non-facilitative transfer. Rothman, Gonzáles Alonso and Puig-Mayenco (2019: 235) conclude that "[w]hen a trend is as ubiquitous as nonfacilitative transfer was in the data, it is likely easier to understand what the explicit and even implicit implications are."

3 The hierarchy of difficulty proposed in Stockwell, Bowen and Martin (1965: Ch. 11) predicts that learning difficulties are strongest if the second language contains an obligatory category that the first language lacks. Learning a second language becomes easiest when both first and second language share an obligatory category.

4 For that reason, the English present perfect is a notorious troublemaker for German learners of English.

The notion of interference is inherently dependent on certain norms. Without norms, there would be no interference or negative transfer. We need to recognize the first and second language as separate and coherent systems in order to detect deviations from them. In a world without norms, the interference phenomena introduced above would hardly matter and probably go unnoticed as they are not likely to produce misunderstandings. Crucially, norm-deviations could also be conceptualized as an enrichment.[5]

Each linguistic community unconsciously produces norms, however subtle, since languages serve as markers of identity. This process is known as 'enregisterment' (see Johnstone, Andrus & Danielson 2006). Norm-conformity translates into higher levels of group identity. Standardized (written) languages offer means to produce such identity effects across large numbers of speakers. They help to identify nations and form national identities. Contingent on a group's level of tolerance, linguistic norm-deviations can be associated with different degrees of out-group status. For example, in spite of (still) massive dialectal differences observable across the British Isles, people self-identify as English-speaking. Certain interference effects may even be associated with high prestige, as, for instance, speaking German with an American accent (especially after World War II).[6]

Grading within the school system is based on norms, too. Here, linguistic (and other) in-group behaviour is a prerequisite for educational success, giving rise to 'correct' and 'incorrect' language (errors). For instance, code-switching as one prominent form of interference may serve as a style marker amongst adolescents, but is frowned upon in the classroom and penalized. The spoken German of adolescents is replete with English lexical items such as *lost*, *cringe*, *no front*, *random*, *loot*, *down*, *drop*, *ready*, *smooth*, *secret*, etc.[7] The precise demarcation of languages and dialects as well as 'correct' and 'incorrect' language is highly important in this context, as the grading system otherwise breaks down. The identification of first or native languages as well as second languages, including their association with different values, is partially a consequence of this.[8]

[5] It is difficult to avoid the normative associations inherent in the terms 'facilitative' and 'non-facilitative' transfer, but perhaps 'covert' and 'overt' cross-linguistic influence would be more neutral. Non-facilitative transfer is usually overt in the sense that it can be recognized, while facilitative transfer stays under the radar, as it were.

[6] I vividly remember listening to American radio broadcaster Rik De Lisle before the fall of the Iron Curtain in what was then East Berlin. Rik used to broadcast in German with a strong American accent, but this interference was intended and served as a marker of prestige. In fact, Rik was still on air at the time of writing.

[7] I owe these observations to our children and their peers. In the context of Germany, the English lexical item *lost* was selected as the *Jugendwort* (youth word) in 2020 (www.zdf.de/nachrichten/panorama/jugendwort-2020-lost-100.html, accessed on 7 February 2021).

[8] The field of error analysis researches the systematic aspects of 'errors', but the field would not exist without the assumption of norms and norm-deviations.

Second language acquisition studies have long been concerned with such normative issues, on the practical side trying to produce speakers of a second language who can count as 'native-like'. In the ideal case, they are indistinguishable from native speaker norm models. Crucially, 'native-like' relates to such norm models and does not include all the speakers of a language who learnt it as a first language. Dialect speakers typically do not serve as norm models. I have frequently met speakers of International English as a second (or additional) language who I experienced as more comprehensible (i.e. more norm-conforming) than native dialectal speakers.

We need to be aware of these normative issues for the subsequent discussion of cross-linguistic influence, as there are these highly evaluative and ideological concepts lurking in the background. For example, the assumption of neatly delineated linguistic systems representing different languages in our minds (multiple monolingualism) is often taken for granted, but definitely open to debate (see Rothman, Gonzáles Alonso & Puig-Mayenco 2019: 76). The discourse is based on many spatial metaphors ('capacity', 'device', 'storage', 'system', 'architecture') and it stands to reason if there are really neural correlates directly corresponding to them. A conceptualization of multilingual repertoires in terms of complex and highly interrelated systems appears closer to reality (multi-competence in the sense of Cook & Wei 2016; dynamic systems according to Herdina & Jessner 2002).

As a matter of fact, the term 'cross-linguistic influence' was partly introduced to provide a more neutral and also more encompassing cover for all phenomena arising from the interaction between languages (Cenoz, Hufeisen & Jessner 2001b: 1; Kecskes & Papp 2000: xvi; Sharwood Smith & Kellerman 1986: 1). In comparison to transfer, with its focus on the influence of the first language on second language acquisition, cross-linguistic influence also subsumes influence in the opposite direction (forward and backward transfer; Pavlenko & Jarvis 2002), the mutual influence in constellations involving more than two languages, as well as avoidance phenomena and language attrition. Herdina and Jessner (2002: 29) propose the term 'cross-linguistic interaction' as an alternative umbrella term for all observable transfer phenomena. Whatever the most appropriate term may be, it is essential to be aware of and avoid the normative and evaluative associations that the early discourse introduced. This is due to its valorization of the first or native language and the concomitant denigration of all additionally acquired languages. The perspective offered here is one of a multilingual repertoire in which the languages are equivalued with the aim to study their mutual and multifarious interactions. Needless to say, I vigorously embrace a beneficial conception of all language experience.

3.1.2 Cross-Linguistic Influence and Language Interdependence

As all interactions between the languages in the multilingual's mind are covered by the term 'cross-linguistic influence', the interdependence between languages observed in education studies can be viewed as a special instance of it (Berthele & Vanhove 2020: 550–551). Recall that the competencies in a multilingual's language repertoire are assumed to be interrelated such that the languages support one another (scaffolding). Cross-linguistic influence in this special sense is always facilitative and taken to boost language and also cognitive development. Again, competence in the relevant studies relates to academic language competence and not to language ability in general.

In regard to the broader or typical understanding of cross-linguistic influence, there now arises an intriguing paradox since cross-linguistic influence can be both facilitative and inhibitory (aka positive and negative transfer). Many, if not most studies on the acquisition of additional languages (here focused on third language acquisition) document ample cross-linguistic influence of a non-facilitating kind. This is because previously acquired languages evidently interfere with subsequent language learning processes (see Note 2). We will scrutinize many examples later in this chapter and also in Chapter 4. Practically all currently discussed models (absolute L1 transfer, Na Ranong & Leung 2009; L2 status factor, Hammarberg 2018; Williams & Hammarberg 1998; typological primacy, Rothman 2011; linguistic proximity, Westergaard et al. 2017) document extensive non-facilitative influence, though they usually struggle to record broad positive effects. Apparently, educationists and psychologists, on the one hand, and linguists, on the other, measure and analyze very different effects (Lorenz & Siemund 2019; Siemund & Lechner 2015).

One way to accommodate this paradox is to draw a distinction between cross-linguistic influence at the level of specific linguistic categories (realization of phonemes, morphemes, word order, grammatical categories, lexical items, etc.) in contrast to the more general language skills of reading, writing, listening, and speaking (interdependence).[9] The latter group of skills may be broadly subsumed under verbal intelligence, but great care needs to be exercised in the use of this term. Cross-linguistic influence at the specific grammatical and lexical level can be both facilitative and inhibitory, while it appears more or less consistently facilitative at the general language skills level. I find this intuitively plausible as language experience of any kind is

[9] Lexical items are crucial for the assessment of reading, writing, listening, and speaking skills. Measures of language interdependence typically rely on lexical items. They also give rise to lexical transfer. In other words, one type of exponent realizes different types of cross-linguistic-influence.

likely to increase one's general language abilities (including metalinguistic awareness). Rothman, Gonzáles Alonso and Puig-Mayenco (2019: 24, 147) restrict the term 'transfer' to the level of linguistic representations and consider the above general language skills as performance variables. However, this perspective ignores the fact that the latter are based on sophisticated knowledge systems, too. It may be more adequate to phrase the distinction in terms of naturally acquired versus culturally developed linguistic knowledge. Distinguishing between language knowledge and language skills conceals the performance (including performative) aspects of the former and the knowledge base necessary for the latter.

To be sure, much depends on how one tests and measures specific and general language knowledge/abilities. Whereas the identification of grammatical and lexical cross-linguistic influence appears like a relatively straightforward and objective procedure, the assessment of reading, writing, listening, and speaking skills is heavily dependent on suitable tests. These skills are latent measures dependent on plausible proxies.[10] Someone who speaks and writes a lot may be considered more proficient than a less verbose person, but this is certainly open to debate. Shyness, in the same vein, may easily be mistaken for inability. Assessing specific and general knowledge/abilities in tandem produces results different from focusing on just one domain. Counting 'errors' or non-target-like realizations against some normative plane and assessing verbal expressiveness, flexibility, or metalinguistic awareness tap into different knowledge domains.

We may draw on the analogy of dancing again. If I know several dances and can perform them well, I will probably count as a more competent and experienced dancer in comparison to someone who knows just one dance – however well they can perform it. Crucially, my impression of an experienced dancer will not be hampered by the fact that they, here and there, include elements from one dance into another (negative transfer or interference). Unless the dances have to be performed in a competition, such occasional transfer will hardly be noticed. Moreover, in other contexts such negative transfer of dancing elements may be interpreted as expressiveness or creativity, resulting in innovative forms or changes of traditional dance styles or even entirely new dance styles. Reverting to the linguistic context, such considerations show that more opportunity for, and also more attestations of cross-linguistic influence do not contradict higher levels of language experience and proficiency. Certain normative contexts simply enforce a focus on norm-deviations, while other contexts may consider cross-linguistic influence (for example, in terms of code-switching or the use of a foreign accent) as a

[10] For example, a reading comprehension test or a written production task based on a picture stimulus.

mark of high verbosity. The bottom line is that cross-linguistic influence and language interdependence should be considered related, but different concepts.

3.1.3 Additional Language Acquisition as Language Contact

Already Weinreich (1953: 1) pointed out that the "language-using individuals are [. . .] the locus of [. . .] contact." Language contact and all cross-linguistic influence first and foremost happen in the minds of the bilingual and multilingual speakers. They are individual phenomena that may – given the right social conditions – advance through a community and establish themselves as a new norm.

As the acquisition of additional languages in instructed settings works towards some target norm, the goal is to suppress and relinquish all instances of cross-linguistic influence and thus contact-induced change. They are more likely to be maintained in non-instructed acquisition or contact settings, since the normative forces of stigmatization and penalization do not operate there. Outcomes of cross-linguistic influence may even come to be used as novel in-group markers.

From the perspective of language contact in the individual, then, foreign language acquisition in a classroom and the development of a pidgin in intense language contact situations are, at least qualitatively, not fundamentally different. Similar phenomena will be observable at the individual level, although the social outcomes are very different.

Since the focus of the present chapter lies on additional language acquisition, I will primarily draw on work in this domain. However, many concepts are reminiscent of or equal to those developed in language contact studies. The two fields have largely been working side by side without extensive cross-pollination, but they definitely meet in the study of postcolonial Englishes (see Chapter 6). I will therefore introduce a few important concepts at this point.

Language contact studies have been primarily interested in three issues, namely (i) the relationship between the social parameters of the contact situations and their resulting outcomes, (ii) the mechanisms underlying contact-induced language change, and (iii) the linguistic features targeted by language contact processes as well as their likelihood of being targeted (Siemund 2008). How exactly specimens of contact-induced change percolate through and stabilize in communities is a largely unresolved issue. Socially influential personalities as well as social networks are likely to play a prominent role. These processes are difficult to observe; their outcomes, however, are not.

Regarding the social parameters of language contact situations, the main parameters determining their outcome are the size of the populations speaking the relevant contact languages, the duration of language contact, the relative social prestige and power of the groups and languages involved, the number of bilinguals including their acquisition trajectories and modes of acquisition, the number and type of bilingual encounters, various territorial parameters (adjacency, inclusion), as well as whether the language contact situation is stable or whether one community is shifting to the language of the other. They may loosely be described as predictors of contact-induced change (Thomason 2001: 60), although this label can hardly do justice to the underlying complexities and mutual interactions. Intensity of contact appears crucial, but this concept is difficult to define (Thomason 2001: 66).[11] Increased contact intensity typically results in more opportunity for contact-induced change. The history of English furnishes a good number of examples of different social contact settings, notably contact with Latin and Celtic as well as the Scandinavian invasion during Old English times, the Anglo-French contact period in the Middle Ages, colonialism and concomitant language shift and death practically all over the world, language contact on slave plantations giving rise to English-based pidgins and creoles, English as a lingua franca, as well as English media consumption and the Internet in modern times.

As far as the mechanisms of contact-induced change are concerned, the literature knows a plethora of labels which, however, essentially describe two fundamentally different situations. The relevant studies usually assume (explicitly or implicitly) that one language is stronger than the other, that is, the language contact situation involves unbalanced bilinguals. On the one hand, then, the stronger language may incorporate elements of the weaker language, as, for example, during lexical borrowing. In this scenario, the speakers use their stronger language and occasionally draw on their weaker language. Lexical borrowings from English into German may serve as illustration (e.g. *flirten*, *downloaden*, *chillen*, *Gangster*, *trendy*). On the other hand, unbalanced bilinguals may extensively communicate in their weaker language – as in many minority language situations – thereby imposing various elements of their stronger language onto their weaker language. In the extreme case, they speak the grammar of their stronger language with lexical material of their weaker language. A prominent example of that type of substratum influence or shift-induced interference is the *after*-perfect in Irish English (*I'm after eating.* 'I have eaten.') or the *already*-perfect in Colloquial Singapore English (*I eat already.* 'I have eaten.'). Table 3.1 provides a summary of the most widely used terms for these two scenarios.[12]

[11] Thomason (2001: 66) explains intensity of contact in terms of "the amount of cultural pressure exerted by one group of speakers on another." The borrowing scale, which helps to predict under which conditions which linguistic items can be exchanged from one language to another, relates to intensity of contact (Thomason 2001: 70–71).

[12] Crucially, the two situations can be identified by the presence or absence of imperfect learning (Thomason 2001: 66).

Table 3.1. *Terminology used in language contact studies (adapted from Li 2021: 84).*

	Weak > strong	Strong > weak
van Coetsem (1988); Winford (2005)	Borrowing under recipient language agentivity	Imposition under source language agentivity
Heine and Kuteva (2005)	Transfer involving phonetic substance; transfer of form-function units	Grammatical replication
Johanson (2002)	Copying: code adoption	Copying: code imposition
Matras (2009)	Matter replication	Pattern replication
Ross (1991)	Exo-borrowing (adoption)	Substrate (shift-induced interference)
Thomason and Kaufman (1991)	Borrowing	Shift-induced interference, substratum interference
Weinreich (1953)	Borrowing	Transfer, interference

The third area of language contact studies concerns the linguistic structures and elements that can be exchanged from one language to another. Thomason (2001: 63, 70–71) holds that in principle all linguistic levels can serve as sources and targets of contact-induced change, but that some are more likely to be affected than others. The crucial condition, according to her, is intensity of contact, with casual contact primarily affecting the lexicon while intense contact may impact the grammatical system. A fundamental generalization, according to Thomason (2001: 69), is that "vocabulary is borrowed before structure." Lexical borrowing – in the situations of borrowing described in Table 3.1 – typically proceeds along the following scale of word classes:[13]

(1) nouns > adjectives > verbs > adverbs > others (based on Onysko 2007: 131)

Similar formulations can be found in Haugen (1950: 224) and Matras (2009: 157). Concerning shift-induced interference or substratum interference, the hierarchy shown in (2) may be assumed (see Thomason 2001: 75–77 for discussion). In other words, interference is especially prominent in phonology and syntax. This hierarchy can also be taken to be relevant for the early stages of second and third language acquisition.

(2) phonology > syntax > lexicon > morphology

[13] The frequency of occurrence of the borrowed items mainly motivates this hierarchy. Nouns outnumber the other word classes by a wide margin. The difference between adjectives and verbs is rather insignificant. Content words are generally easier to borrow than function words (Thomason 2001: 70).

Language contact studies have also developed the more specific theories of systemic transfer (Bao 2015), replica grammaticalization (Heine & Kuteva 2005), and recapitulation (Ziegeler 2014). They have been discussed in relation to the analysis of postcolonial Englishes (see Chapter 6).

3.1.4 Summary

Cross-linguistic influence or transfer cannot be diagnosed without the recognition of separate languages. As languages are partially fluid and also overlapping systems that exist in different degrees of crystallization, the identification of their mutual influences represents a great challenge. The clear differentiation of languages in educational contexts is at least partially a consequence of the strong norm-orientation in this field and certainly not representative of the world at large. Studying pidginization processes against standard written language norms would be a completely fruitless exercise. Accordingly, the various fields interested in cross-linguistic influence have developed different foci of research, methodologies, and models.

In language contact studies, interestingly enough, nearly all models that have been put forward to describe the mechanisms of contact-induced change and predict their outcomes have primarily considered the scenario of two languages in contact. Variably, these have been described as source, donor, or model language and target, recipient, or replica language. With the exception of perhaps Mufwene (2001), models of language contact for multilingual situations have yet to be developed, yet these currently seem to constitute the more prominent scenario. Language acquisition studies with their recently developed focus on third or additional language acquisition is more advanced in this respect. Third language acquisition essentially takes place in multilingual constellations. This will be the topic of the next section.

3.2 Third Language Acquisition

For a long time, third (L3) or subsequent (L*n*) language acquisition was simply considered a special case of second (L2) language acquisition and assumed to be governed by the same principles. It was believed that L3 learners go through the same developmental stages as L2 learners and that transfer or cross-linguistic influence could be predicted by the same parameters as in L2 acquisition. Around the year 2000, we could witness an increasing interest in L3 acquisition driven by the observation that L3 learners behave differently from L2 learners in that such learners acquire their third language on a bilingual substrate (of different types) and are influenced in their acquisition process by all previously acquired languages and their mutual interactions (Cabrelli Amaro, Flynn & Rothman 2012a; Cenoz & Jessner 2001a; Cenoz,

Hufeisen & Jessner 2001a; De Angelis 2007). This can also be taken as a response to an increasingly multilingual environment that became incompatible with the traditional division between first and second language acquisition. Without any doubt, there is considerable overlap between second and third language acquisition, but there are also noticeable differences that will be discussed in the following sections.

3.2.1 Differences and Similarities between Second and Third Language Acquisition

The most important difference between second and third language acquisition is that the latter proceeds against the substrate of two previously acquired languages, whereas the former process merely encounters one earlier acquired language. In other words, third language acquisition is defined by its interaction with two languages, not just one (Cenoz, Hufeisen & Jessner 2001b: 2). Cenoz (2003: 71) defines it as "the acquisition of a non-native language by learners who have previously acquired or are acquiring two other languages." Using a different terminology, one can say that the L3 initial state is different from the L2 initial state as both L1 and L2 influence L3 development (Leung 2005). Third language acquisition may be generalized to additional language acquisition, meaning that all previously acquired languages are taken to interact with subsequent acquisition processes.

One could surmise, alternatively, that since first language acquisition is driven by universal grammar (human's innate language ability) and since a second language is largely learnt through first language experience (at least during the initial stages), third language acquisition is primarily a function of one's second language. Generally, one could hypothesize that L*n* acquisition is determined by L(*n*-1) acquisition. However, such a straightforward conception of third or additional language acquisition falls short of reality, as will be explained in this section. Crucially, the definition of a third language lacks precision since the observable acquisition trajectories are quite heterogeneous (see also Chapter 7).

Generally speaking, third or additional language acquisition offers more opportunity for cross-linguistic interaction than second language acquisition. The more languages there are, the more mutual interaction is, in principle, feasible. Provided this is correct, the question arises as to which parameters select the direction and strength of influence from one language onto another. Having said that, there is no reason to believe that cross-linguistic influence in third or additional language acquisition is qualitatively different from that observable in second language acquisition. The surface manifestations of cross-linguistic influence look similar and can be categorized as omissions, overuse, underuse, word order changes, and the like. Moreover, if first and second language strongly overlap structurally, interference and facilitation effects in the third language may play out more forcefully than in the second language.

Language acquisition studies have invested much effort into defining the boundary between first and second language acquisition, although the relative weight of cognitive and cultural factors remains a matter of much debate (Rothman, Gonzáles Alonso & Puig-Mayenco 2019: 14–15).[14] It is widely believed that there is a window or critical period of several years during infancy that allows languages to be acquired in a native-like way. This window has been variably described to close approximately between the age of six and the beginning of puberty (Meisel 2013: 72). To complicate things further, the critical period may terminate even earlier for certain grammatical subsystems ('sensitive phases'), such as phonology and syntax (Friedmann & Rusou 2015; Meisel 2013). There appears to be no critical period for lexical development, as we keep learning new lexical items throughout our lives. By definition, third language acquisition compares to second language acquisition as regards the critical period, as both are acquired after it. Infant trilingualism is outside third language acquisition proper and represents a special case of first language acquisition (Stavans & Hoffmann 2015). We will consider different acquisition trajectories in Section 3.2.3.

In classic second language acquisition, the status of the first language as the native language or mother tongue can be taken for granted. Disregarding clinical cases and given sufficient input, children cannot but acquire a language (like walking, seeing, and hearing). If they grow up in an environment with an education system, they will normally also develop written language, but this is not a natural process. It is irrelevant whether the first language carries high or low prestige, as this does not matter in the family or immediate community. In third language acquisition, the status of the second language can be quite different. It can be a foreign language, a late first or early second language, a language with low or high prestige, and a written and/or spoken language. One may also consider the acquisition of additional languages by bilingually raised children as a special case of third language acquisition, but I believe that this proposition is not uncontroversial.

If another language is learnt after the critical period, its status as a second language (rather than a second first language) is undisputed. Once additional languages are acquired, they may become stronger than the original second language. The numbering L2, L3, L*n* then becomes rather meaningless, other

[14] These authors point out that children in the process of L1 acquisition receive abundant input, do not encounter cross-linguistic influence, and are in need of a language. Adult L2 learners, in contrast, often lack sufficient input, receive non-native input, experience cross-linguistic influence, and have less of a need for the second language.

than describing a chronological relation.[15] Such problems do not normally arise in first and second language acquisition, apart from the very special case of first language attrition. But even if I emigrate to another country as a young adult where I consistently use a second language for the rest of my life, I will normally not lose my first language entirely (Schmid 2002).[16]

Since bi- and multilingualism, in comparison to monolingualism, are associated with higher levels of metalinguistic awareness (see Chapter 2), third or additional language acquisition can be expected to benefit from this greater experience with languages. This is something the child, in monolingual acquisition, has to do without as there is no other language to compare their language with. The level of metalinguistic awareness can further be used as a diagnostic to distinguish between second and additional language acquisition. It goes without saying that this presupposes a meaningful amount of (instructed) input in these languages.

3.2.2 *Influences and Interactions across and between Languages*

In principle, constellations involving three languages offer ample opportunity for cross-linguistic influence, though some paths of influence are more likely than others. Focusing on the impact of the previously acquired languages on third language acquisition, the following four scenarios arise:

1. There is no influence from the background languages.
2. There is exclusive influence from the first language.
3. There is exclusive influence from the second language.
4. There is influence from both the first and the second language.

The assumption of no influence from the background languages means that the third language is acquired like a first language, perhaps even with full access to our innate language learning abilities. One would need to discard all obvious and ubiquitous interference of the background languages on the third language as performance problems to maintain this view. I do not consider this plausible (see Section 3.1.1). Exclusive influence from the first language is tantamount to saying that the third language is acquired like a new second language. Third language acquisition comes to be a special case of second language acquisition. Given the distinct status of the first language as one's native language acquired during the critical period, this view deserves some attention. The third scenario of exclusive influence from the second language builds on a strongly sequential acquisition order in which each previously

15 The use of terms like 'L1', 'L2', and 'L3' frequently implies differences in proficiency such that L1 is the strongest language and L3 the weakest.

16 Schmid (2002) draws attention to various issues of identity and attitude for language attrition.

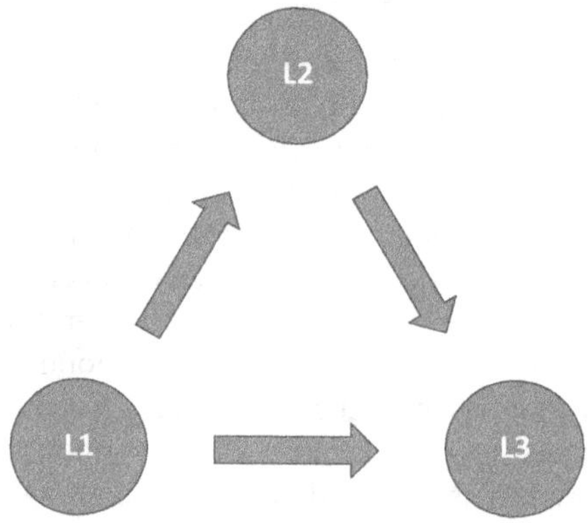

Figure 3.1 Unidirectional cross-linguistic influence among three languages.

acquired language influences the newly acquired language. This option also merits further discussion, as we will see. Finally, there is the possibility that all previously acquired languages interact with the language to be acquired. It will transpire in the course of this chapter that this is the most realistic assumption, although the quality and quantity of the influence from the background languages are contingent upon a host of additional parameters. Figure 3.1 illustrates these scenarios of cross-linguistic influence, except for the case of no influence.

It appears worth pointing out that there is furthermore the possibility of influence from the first language on the third language, mediated through the second language. The process of acquiring the second language may have resulted in the retention of structures of the first language in the second language – known as fossilizations or incomplete acquisition. These may come to be passed onto the third language. I am not aware of any research into such effects.[17]

The paths of cross-linguistic influence depicted in Figure 3.1 form the central interest of the present chapter. However, we need to be aware that there also is the possibility of influence in the opposite direction. The second language may exert influence on the first language, and so may the third on the second and the first. Such cases of backward transfer or bidirectional transfer have scarcely been explored. They may be facilitative and non-facilitative

[17] For example, L1 German learners of L2 English are known to transfer German final devoicing to English, which does not have final devoicing. When such learners continue to learn another language without final devoicing, such as L3 Norwegian or Swedish (Hans-Olav Enger, personal communication), final devoicing may be transferred to L3 Swedish from L2 English, and not L1 German.

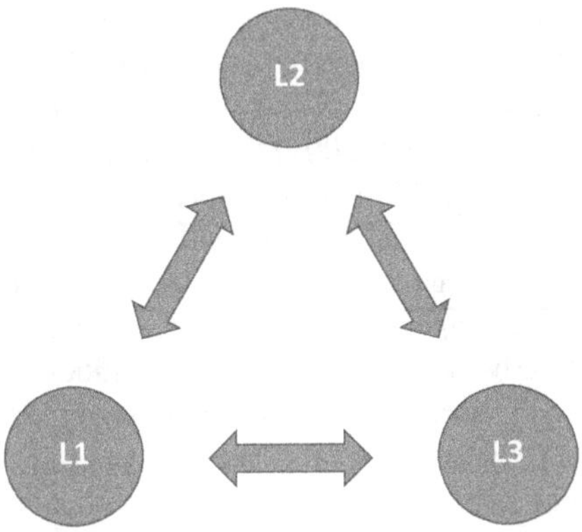

Figure 3.2 Bidirectional cross-linguistic influence among three languages.

(see Kecskes & Papp 2000; Pavlenko & Jarvis 2002). These additional paths of influence are captured in Figure 3.2.[18]

The representation in Figure 3.2 is more symmetric and also more systemic. The understanding is that every new language that is added to one's language repertoire invariably begins to interact with the previously acquired languages causing a reorganization of the entire linguistic system. Theories adopting this perspective include Herdina and Jessner's (2002) Dynamic Model of Multilingualism as well as Dynamic Systems Theory (see Kopečková et al. 2016). These approaches are reminiscent of structuralist assumptions inasmuch as additions to a semiotic field enforce an internal reorganization of that field.

Provided that it is the case that all background languages can influence the acquisition of further languages, the question then arises as to which parameters control the selection of the languages, the strength as well as the target domain of their influence. The literature has accumulated a wide array of potential parameters, although their impact and interaction remain a matter of much debate. De Angelis (2007: Ch. 2) considers language distance, proficiencies in the languages involved, recency of use, length of residence in the relevant language environments, exposure, order of acquisition, as well as contextual parameters like formality. None of these are easy to measure and there are certainly additional parameters.

Language distance may be operationalized in terms of genealogical relatedness and typological, as well as psychotypological, proximity (Kellerman 1983).

[18] Generally, the number of paths of potential cross-linguistic influence increases with the number of languages according to the following series: 2, 6, 12, 20, 30, 42, etc. The formula is $n*(n\text{-}1)$.

Being a close family member, however, is no guarantee of similarity. English, for example, counts as a Germanic language, but is – in structural and lexical terms – definitely on the fringes of the Germanic phylum and also a non-central member of Standard Average European (Haspelmath 2001).[19] Typological proximity is highly domain-dependent. English and Mandarin Chinese share the order of Subject-Verb-Object in basic declarative clauses and tend towards the isolating morphological type, but sharply diverge in phonology and, of course, lexis. Europeans tend to perceive Chinese, Japanese, Vietnamese, Malay, and Korean as Asian languages, but they effectively belong to different families.

Regarding proficiency we need to distinguish between spoken and written production as well as listening and reading comprehension. Interview and corpus data are likely to produce results different from experimental data and data elicited by picture stimuli. The format of these tests influences the results. Highly competent language users may hide their proficiencies due to motivational issues. One may be highly proficient in only certain domains of use. Measuring proficiency is highly complicated, as this is a typical latent variable often based on proxies (in contrast to directly observable variables).

Similar considerations apply to recency of use, length of residence, exposure, and formality. We need to decide if listening to a song on the radio counts as recency of use. People travel and migrate so that residency becomes a moving target. Exposure is a quantitative variable, but it is a truism to say that the quality of input is more important for language acquisition than its quantity. Formality is only one amongst other contextual parameters and certainly not a binary variable.

As far as further parameters interacting with cross-linguistic influence are concerned, we need at least to mention age of onset, language status in the community, norm expectations, as well as the social prestige associated with a language. Age of onset is important as it decides if a language counts as a first language, a late first or early second language, or a second language. We will look into this more closely in the next section. A language can be a majority or minority language in a community, a home language, used in the education system, or restricted to other functional domains. It may also have the status of a lingua franca. Languages may be associated with different norm expectations. I can easily use English words in German without breaking norms, but a German student in an English classroom would be penalized for using German words. Cross-linguistic influence gains prestige in one context, but leads to sanctions in another. A prestigious language likely exerts more and different influence than a non-prestigious language.

[19] For example, English lacks dative external possessors and uses the same expression to encode reflexive markers and *self*-intensifiers.

Finally, cross-linguistic influence may play out differently in phonology, morphology, syntax, semantics, the lexicon, and pragmatics. We will discuss many specific examples later in this chapter and also in Chapter 4. Moreover, there may be variation over time such that linguistic domains vulnerable to influence at some point in time prove more resilient at another.

3.2.3 Acquisition Trajectories

Depending on the actual acquisition scenario, third or subsequent language acquisition can mean very different things (Cabrelli Amaro, Flynn & Rothman 2012b: 3–4). The classic third language acquisition studies focused on speakers who had acquired a first language as a child (monolingual acquisition), moved on to studying a second language in instructed contexts (second or foreign language acquisition), and then started to learn yet another language during tertiary education. Here, the labels L1, L2, and L3 designate a chronological order and it is easy to decide which of the languages is first, second, and third. Evidently, these labels come to mean very different things in other situations of language acquisition. Regarding the specific case of studying English as a third language, the three main scenarios listed below can be distinguished (see also Aronin & Singleton 2012: 122–123; Cenoz & Jessner 2001b: viii–ix; Hammarberg 2018; Hoffmann 2001: 3).

1. Native speakers of a national language who study another language as a foreign language before studying English.
2. Speakers of regional minority languages and the relevant majority language studying English.
3. Immigrants who speak a heritage language, learn the majority language of their target country, and then continue to study English.

Besides the first scenario already discussed above, the world knows many areas where recognized and unrecognized regional minority languages are spoken within the boundaries of national borders (see Chapter 5). In Europe, this inter alia concerns Basque, Breton, Catalan, Frisian, Low German, Sardinian, Sami, Scots, Sorbian, and Welsh. There are large numbers of autochthonous ethnic minority languages across the Americas (indigenous languages) where the former colonial languages are now used as the official majority languages. The label ‘Chinese’ covers many other Sinitic languages besides being used for Mandarin and Putonghua, that is, the national standard language. The African continent, in particular, bears witness to arbitrary political borders that criss-cross ethnic and linguistic boundaries and where English and other former colonial languages have been maintained as official or co-official languages. There is widespread bi- and multilingualism of different types: balanced, unbalanced, early and late first and second languages, trilingualism, diglossia, triglossia, etc.[20] English frequently happens to be learnt and studied as a third language in these areas.

Accordingly, when studying third or additional language acquisition, individual acquisition trajectories need to be scrutinized very carefully. It would scarcely be admissible to compare adult L2/L3 learners with heritage bilinguals studying English in the school context. Bilingual speakers of regional minority languages can be assumed to be quite heterogeneous. Age of onset matters, as does proficiency in the background languages, their contexts of use, and their social status. Classic second languages are by definition acquired after the critical period and do not normally reach ultimate attainment. Speakers of regional minority languages as well as heritage speakers, besides their first language, acquire a majority language at varying ages of onset – typically when they begin kindergarten or at the time of immigration. These can be considered late first or early second languages. Not infrequently, the majority language develops into their dominant language, due to the education system, matters of prestige, peer group pressure, and frequency of use, although the respective regional minority and heritage languages are chronologically their first languages. Having said that, regional minority languages especially may also be acquired as late first or early second languages, perhaps also as regular second languages.[21]

Given current global mobility levels, language acquisition trajectories may pass through different locations. A child may be born in India to a Hindi-speaking father and a Bengali-speaking mother. The family may move to the Gulf region when the child is three where they frequently speak English as a lingua franca besides some Arabic. When the child is ten years of age, the couple is hired by a Chinese IT company in Shenzhen where they spend another five years before moving to the South of India. This additionally brings them into contact with Cantonese, Putonghua, and perhaps Kannada. Such multilingual acquisition trajectories are by no means infrequent, with English often having the status of a third language.

3.2.4 Summary

Third or additional language acquisition is different from second language acquisition. The more languages that have been acquired, the more influence is in principle feasible from the background languages. The languages may

[20] Here and elsewhere in the present book I follow Fishman's (1967: 34) assumption that "bilingualism is essentially a characterization of individual linguistic behavior whereas diglossia is a characterization of linguistic organization at the socio-cultural level."

[21] I have met several students from Low German and North Frisian areas whose university studies sparked an interest in them to learn the regional minority languages of the areas they were born into, that is, often the language of their forefathers.

influence one another in all directions, although some paths of influence are more likely than others. Important moderator variables include age of acquisition, proficiency, recency of use, and language distance. In addition, the more languages there are in the multilingual's repertoire, the higher their level of metalinguistic awareness. Studies of third language acquisition need to control closely for the acquisition trajectories of the subjects, as they otherwise run the risk of comparing incompatible cohorts of learners.

3.3 Models of Cross-Linguistic Influence

The influence of previous experience on subsequent language experience during third language acquisition has been modelled in different ways. However, all models have been designed to capture one of the three viable theoretical scenarios, namely exclusive influence from the first language, exclusive influence from the second language, and models that assume both influence from the first and second language. The unlikely case of no influence from the previously acquired background languages has so far not given rise to explicit research. Moreover, the models partially diverge in their recognition of non-facilitative cross-linguistic influence.

As we will see, some caution needs to be exercised in the juxtaposition of the models, as they typically result from empirical studies that are difficult to compare. The cohorts of participants differ in size, in their age of onset, their proficiency levels, their learning stage (initial vs. later; early, intermediate, advanced learners), as well as the languages involved. The different acquisition trajectories described above may at least partially be responsible for the emergence of competing models. Regarding third language acquisition in the context of minority and heritage language bilingualism, it appears more appropriate to refer to the background languages in terms of 'minority' and 'majority' language. The labels 'first' and 'second' language are quite misleading in these contexts.

3.3.1 Transfer from the First Language

The idea of exclusive or predominant transfer from the first language is based on its privileged status as a native language. Amongst the studies arguing in favour of such L1 effects are Hermas (2010, 2014) and Na Ranong and Leung (2009). These accounts are consistent with the 'Full Transfer/Full Access Hypothesis' (FT/FA; Schwartz & Sprouse 1996) that postulates complete transfer of the L1 grammar at the initial state of L2 (here L3) acquisition, though with an option to reset syntactic parameters at a later stage based on universal grammar.

The two studies by Hermas investigate L3 acquisition of English in the context of adult bilinguals of (Moroccan) Arabic and French. They employ acceptability judgement tests and preference tests on null subjects and word order (placement of adverbs and negation, placement of subject and verb). The Arabic–French bilinguals are tested against monolingual Arabic, French, and English native controls. The experimental cohorts comprise twenty (Hermas 2010) and fourteen speakers (Hermas 2014), complemented by different control groups (native speakers of Arabic, English, and French). French and English are non-null subject languages, while Arabic can be analyzed as a null subject language. English places frequency adverbs before the verb, whereas French and Arabic do not. According to typological accounts, Arabic is a Verb-Subject-Object (VSO) language, but English and French are Subject-Verb-Object (SVO) languages. Capitalizing on these differences, Hermas (2010, 2014) makes a convincing case for predominant influence from Arabic in the English of the L3 learners.[22] For example, Hermas (2014: 15) shows that negative transfer in null subjects amounts to as much as 52 per cent, indicating strong interference effects from Arabic. These results are the more surprising as the L2 French of the participants is not different from the monolingual French controls on this parameter. What needs to be borne in mind is that the subjects in these studies are learners of English in their initial stages. The studies may produce different result with advanced learners. Crucially, Arabic is the more distant language in this setting, showing that cross-linguistic influence does not necessarily seize the typologically closest language.

Another study that we will briefly consider here is Na Ranong and Leung (2009), in which twenty native speakers of Thai (L1), who had learnt English in late childhood (L2), studied Chinese as an L3 at university. The empirical domain of the study concerns null objects, which are permissible in Thai and Chinese, though not in English. There are two control groups, namely a native British English group learning Chinese (*n*=7) and a native Chinese group learning English (*n*=20). The test instrument was an "offline written interpretation task that consisted of single bi-clausal sentences without context involving embedded null or overt objects" (Na Ranong & Leung 2009: 172). The authors find that L1 Thai speakers learning Chinese as a L3 perform similarly to L1 speakers of Chinese. This is taken to suggest a privileged role of the L1 in the acquisition of a third language. One potential problem in this account is that the native British English learners of L2 Chinese equally showed a performance similar to Chinese L1 speakers.

[22] Hermas (2010: 343) states that "[t]he results of acceptability judgement tests and preference tests show that the initial state of L3 English is influenced exclusively by the final state of L1 Arabic."

3.3.2 L2 Status Factor

On a personal note, I quite clearly recall the following incident during my language learning experience as a student back in the 1990s. When I started to learn Swedish after German (my native tongue), Russian, English, French, and Spanish, I consistently failed to produce Swedish verb-second structures, although this should have been very easy for me to master. After all, German is a verb-second language much as Swedish. Apparently, the other languages with their SVO structures blocked access to my verb-second knowledge – which still must have been in place, since I continued speaking German with verb-second syntax. I am certain that I am not alone in having had this experience.

Hammarberg (2001: 37) describes this phenomenon as "[a] desire to suppress L1 as being 'non-foreign' and to rely rather on an orientation towards a prior L2 as a strategy to approach the L3" and named it the "L2 status factor" (see also De Angelis & Selinker 2001; Williams & Hammarberg 1998). The idea is that the status of a language as a second language promotes it to being the main source of influence in third language acquisition. This proposal has been explored in several subsequent publications, inter alia Bardel and Falk (2007, 2012), Falk and Bardel (2011), Falk, Lindqvist and Bardel (2015) in relation to metalinguistic awareness, as well as Hammarberg (2010, 2018). Here, I will comment on some of these studies, as they nicely illustrate my own experience with more objective data.

The L2 status factor arose from acquisition trajectories in which first, second, and third language can be clearly distinguished both in terms of acquisition process and chronological order. The first and the second language are separated by the upper boundary of the critical period, while the third language usually comes in during tertiary education. For example, Bardel and Falk (2007) studied five learners of L3 Swedish (L1: Dutch, English, or Hungarian; L2: Dutch, English, or German) as well as four learners of L3 Dutch or Swedish (L1: Albanian, Italian, or Swedish; L2: Dutch, English, or German). The empirical domain is the placement of negation that can appear pre- or post-verbally, depending on the language. The study is based on observational data (audio and video recordings). The results strongly support the L2 status factor. The authors do not find evidence for L1 transfer. They conclude that "in L3 acquisition, the L2 acts like a filter, making the L1 inaccessible" (Bardel & Falk 2007: 480).

Additional support for the L2 status factor can be drawn from Falk and Bardel (2011). This study explores the placement of object pronouns in L3 learners of German. The overall sample (n=44) is divided into two cohorts of equal size (n=22) of which one has French as their L1 and English as their L2, whereas English serves as the L1 and French as the L2 in the other cohort.

Object pronoun placement varies between pre- and post-verbal position according to language as well as main and subordinate clauses. The study uses a grammaticality judgement and correction task. The authors again predominantly detect influence from the second language, both positive and negative.

In view of the prominence widely ascribed to one's first language, the L2 status factor is in need of explanation. Hammarberg (2018: 143), drawing on Williams and Hammarberg (1998), argues that the mechanism underlying L2 acquisition is different from that relevant for L1 acquisition. During L3 acquisition, one can witness "a reactivation of the L2 type mechanism" (see also Hammarberg 2001: 36). Furthermore, he argues that the L2 and the L3 are conceptualized as "foreign" in contrast to one's first language. Therefore, the L1 is suppressed during L3 acquisition. Similarly, Bardel and Falk (2012: 68) maintain that the "L2 status factor is an outcome of the higher degree of similarity between L2 and L3 than between L1 and L3, regarding age of onset, outcome, learning situation, degree of metalinguistic knowledge, learning strategies and degree of awareness in the process of language appropriation."

3.3.3 Typological Proximity

I will begin this section with another personal anecdote. When I started to study Spanish, I noticed that my previously acquired French frequently intervened in lexicon, morphology, and syntax – perhaps also phonology. This surprised me, as I concurrently studied English according to a dense syllabus and expected interference from this far more active language. Such observations, of which I presume there are many, form the basis for models of cross-linguistic influence that consider language distance as the most important factor.

Language distance as the determining factor underlying the selection of the first or second language as the source of influence in third language acquisition has been most prominently argued for within the Typological Primacy Model (Rothman 2011; Rothman & Cabrelli Amaro 2010; Rothman, Gonzáles Alonso & Puig-Mayenco 2019). To illustrate, the idea here is that languages like Russian and Bulgarian are more closely related than, say, English and Tagalog, and that such differences and similarities drive cross-linguistic influence in the L3. Empirical support for this position is available through Rothman (2011), where a cohort of speakers with L1 Italian, L2 English, and L3 Spanish (*n*=12) is contrasted with another cohort of speakers of L1 English, L2 Spanish, and L3 Brazilian Portuguese (*n*=15). Native speakers of Spanish (*n*=17) and Brazilian Portuguese (*n*=16) served as controls. The grammatical domain studied concerns the placement of adjectives in Spanish, which can occur before the noun they modify in a non-restrictive interpretation and after the noun in a restrictive interpretation (*el valiente león* 'the brave lion' vs. *el léon valiente* 'the lion that is brave'). The subjects were asked to interpret and complete sentences. Both L3 groups performed like the native controls on all tasks, giving rise to the conclusion that the requisite knowledge was taken from either the L1 Italian or the L2 Spanish. Accordingly, a case for typological primacy or proximity is made as the decisive factor governing cross-linguistic influence in third language acquisition. The data offered in Rothman and Cabrelli Amaro (2010) can be used to make a similar point (based on realized and unrealized pronominal subjects), but the results of this study equally offer support for the L2 status factor.

A number of interesting questions arise in the context of the Typological Primacy Model that are discussed in detail in Rothman, Gonzáles Alonso and Puig-Mayenco (2019). One relates to the very concept of language distance that, as argued in Section 3.2.2, can be operationalized in terms of genealogical, structural (typological), or psychotypological proximity. Speakers of Norwegian will consider Swedish a closely related language, and this judgement makes sense along all three dimensions. However, the three parameters may easily diverge, as when Hungarian and Finnish are considered unrelated due to their territorial detachment, or when Chinese and Vietnamese are lumped together genealogically. The latter represent erroneous assumptions, motivated by psychotypology (i.e. perceived language distance). Whereas Rothman (2011: 112) conceived typological primacy in terms of Kellerman's (1983) notion of psychotypology, Rothman, Gonzáles Alonso and Puig-Mayenco (2019: 160) distance themselves from any allusions to a conscious assessment of language distance that this term may evoke. They insist on a completely unconscious and structure-based evaluation of language distance. Once structural similarity is identified as primary, the question arises as to which layer of linguistic analysis is used by learners to determine typological proximity. Rothman, Gonzáles Alonso and Puig-Mayenco (2019: 162–163) argue for an "implicational hierarchical approach" that views lexical similarities as primary, followed by those in phonology/phonotactics, functional morphology, and finally syntactic structure.[23] One is reminded of the various hierarchies proposed in language contact studies and it needs to be determined to what extent they are related (see Section 3.1.3). Another issue concerns the question of whether cross-linguistic influence from the typologically closest language is complete (i.e. systemic) or whether it can only be partial. Although Rothman, Gonzáles Alonso and Puig-Mayenco (2019: 155–156) stipulate holistic transfer, at least at the initial stages, they do not completely rule out influence from the other background language at later stages. This point can be considered open to further investigation.

[23] The idea is that the human parser traverses sequentially through this implicational hierarchy searching for similarities between the languages involved.

3.3.4 Linguistic Proximity

The problem with the Typological Primacy Model just discussed is that cross-linguistic influence in third language acquisition has also been observed to emanate from the language that is not typologically closest to the L3. The studies by Hermas (2010, 2014) are in fact sufficient to falsify this model, as they show the L1 Arabic to influence the L3 English in the presence of the L2 French. Westergaard et al. (2017) conducted another study on the potential sources of cross-linguistic influence in third language acquisition, focusing on the acquisition of English word order by Norwegian–Russian bilinguals. This study used three cohorts of participants, contrasting Norwegian–Russian bilinguals (n=22) with Norwegian monolinguals (n=46) and Russian monolinguals (n=31). The two latter groups represent classic second language learners of English. Participants were confronted with grammaticality judgement tasks regarding adverb placements (pre-verbal vs. post-verbal) as well as subject-auxiliary inversion. Regarding the placement of adverbs, Russian and English are patterned to position the adverb before the verb (*Emma often eats sweets*), whereas such adverbs occur post-verbally in Norwegian. The results here show that learners of English with a monolingual Russian background experience facilitation, whereas those with a monolingual Norwegian background encounter interference. Crucially, learners with a Norwegian–Russian bilingual background scored intermediate results. This pattern is reversed in the condition involving subject-auxiliary inversion, as here English patterns with Norwegian in contrast to Russian (*What will the little girl read?*). The authors conclude that cross-linguistic influence can, in principle, take its origin in either of the background languages depending on the phenomenon considered (see Siemund & Lechner 2015 for a similar point of view).

Westergaard et al. (2017: 670) account for the observable cross-linguistic influence in terms of what they call "linguistic proximity," itself defined as "abstract structural similarity" between linguistic properties of the third language and the respective background languages (see also Slabakova 2017). One can analyze the concept of linguistic proximity as a continuation and application of Weinreich's (1953: 7) work on "interlingual identification" to trilingual and multilingual contexts (instead of just bilingual contexts). Interlingual identification represents the cognitive process of matching phonological and grammatical structures between languages so that they can begin to enhance or interfere with one another. Still, linguistic proximity does not explain which factors select the one over the other background language as the source of cross-linguistic influence.

Similarly, Siemund, Schröter and Rahbari (2018) as well as Lorenz et al. (2019) document influence from all previously acquired languages on the acquisition of English demonstrative pronouns and the sequential order of object pronouns in double object constructions. However, in the latter study, cross-linguistic influence manifests itself primarily in terms of distributional skewings. Apparently, the frequency of the relevant patterns in the source languages at least partially determine what surfaces as cross-linguistic influence in the L3. Siemund, Schröter and Rahbari (2018) identify language dominance as the crucial condition. We will explore this condition in detail in Section 3.4.

The perspective from linguistic proximity on third language acquisition produces interesting insights on putative learning advantages in such situations, especially their relative character. For example, in Westergaard et al.'s (2017) study, the Norwegian–Russian bilingual learners of English manifest both interference from Norwegian and facilitation from Russian in regard to English adverb placement. From the perspective of a monolingual Norwegian learner of English, they experience learning advantages. However, from the perspective of a monolingual Russian learner, this looks like a disadvantage. Provided it is correct that the source and quality of cross-linguistic influence depend on the phenomenon considered, as argued by Siemund and Lechner (2015), the L3 learner will experience a mix of facilitation and interference effects whose source can be reconstructed in either of the background languages. Crucially, these are contingent on a host of additional factors (recency of use, proficiency, length of exposure, language dominance, etc.). Such situations of tension resulting from the properties of the background languages will be discussed in more detail in Chapter 4.

3.3.5 Cumulative Enhancement

Although I consider it overly optimistic to privilege facilitation effects during third language acquisition, or to assume that interference does not occur at all, this position has indeed been argued for in the research literature, especially by Flynn, Foley and Vinnitskaya (2004).[24] The proposal needs to be evaluated in the context of the general discussion on bilingual or multilingual advantages, where such positive effects have been claimed for various cognitive domains (intelligence, cognitive control, educational attainment, language learning, metalinguistic awareness, a delay in the onset of mental illnesses, etc.; see Chapter 2). As the field currently goes through a replicability crisis, some caution appears advisable. While I do see some support for multilingually induced proficiency gains and concomitant boosts of metalinguistic awareness, there is too much evidence of grammatical cross-linguistic influence of a non-facilitating type to warrant the assumption of exclusively positive effects of a previous multilingual experience.

24 See Berkes and Flynn (2012) for another study on cumulative enhancement.

Flynn, Foley and Vinnitskaya (2004) study the acquisition of English relative clauses in two cohorts of Kazakh–Russian bilinguals, namely a cohort of adult learners (*n*=33) and one of child learners (*n*=30).[25] Relative clauses in English and Russian are both head-initial, whereas they are head-final in Kazakh (i.e. the relative clause precedes its nominal head). The study uses an elicited imitation task. At least as far as the cohort of adult learners is concerned, the authors find high percentages of correctly formed English relative clauses in the data, which they interpret as facilitative influence from Russian. Apparently, Kazakh as the first language does not interfere with the learning of English. Given the other models discussed so far, it becomes apparent that these results are also consistent with typological primacy and the L2 status factor. Moreover, the share of target-like English relative clauses barely reaches 70 per cent for adults in the data and is much lower for the children studied.

3.3.6 *Summary*

The preceding discussion has shown that the existing models of cross-linguistic influence in contexts of third language acquisition differ along a number of dimensions. First, they can be discriminated in relation to whether they allow influence from both/all background languages or privilege the first or second language, respectively. Second, they evoke disagreement regarding the question of whether cross-linguistic influence is holistic or occurs in relation to specific phenomena, sometimes selecting the one, sometimes the other language. Third, the models contain disagreement as to whether early, intermediate, and advanced learners are subject to the same type of cross-linguistic influence. Fourth, there is the issue of cumulative enhancement. Here, I adopt the position that cross-linguistic influence can emanate from all background languages, contingent on additional parameters. It can be facilitative or non-facilitative, bearing in mind that cases of non-facilitative transfer simply represent norm-violations. There is nothing inherently deficient about interference. Language dominance is one of the most salient parameters determining the source of cross-linguistic influence, to be explored in the following section.

3.4 Heritage Bilingualism and Language Dominance

More recent research has extended the field of third language acquisition to bilingual heritage speakers learning English (or other languages) as an

[25] Kazakh is described as the subjects' first language; Russian as their second language.

additional language. This scenario is considerably different from traditional third language acquisition where the second and third language have the status of adult second languages. For bilingual heritage speakers, in contrast, the background languages may have the status of two first languages (balanced or unbalanced), or one first language in combination with a late first or early second language. There arise substantial difficulties in the application of the concepts of L1 and L2 in these contexts, apart from perhaps the chronological ordering (Montrul 2016).[26] Heritage bilingualism may be additive or subtractive; the speakers may be early or late bilinguals. Heritage bilingualism is commonly unbalanced, with the majority language of the surrounding society frequently being stronger than the heritage language or developing into the stronger language over time. Heritage speakers often experience language shift from their heritage language to the respective majority language so that they eventually consider the majority language as their native tongue. Literacy development characteristically focuses on the majority language and may not occur in the heritage language. Any additional languages – mostly English in non-native English-speaking areas – typically come to be learnt as early second or regular second languages (or third languages, depending on one's definition of these concepts). Nevertheless, the question after the influence of the previously acquired languages arises in the same way, though the theoretical implications are different. Current research suggests that the majority language impacts the subsequent language learning processes more strongly than the heritage language (Hopp 2019; Hopp et al. 2018; Fallah & Jabbari 2018; Lorenz 2019; Lorenz & Siemund 2020; Lorenz, Toprak & Siemund 2021; Lorenz et al. 2020; Siemund & Lechner 2015; Siemund, Schröter & Rahbari 2018).

Although there is certainly some overlap, discussing third language acquisition in heritage contexts – where mostly children and young adolescents serve as subjects – and adult third language acquisition without further differentiation amounts to comparing apples and oranges. The acquisition scenarios are simply too different. As a matter of fact, some of the diverging results discussed in Section 3.3 that gave rise to the five competing models of cross-linguistic influence may be due to such contextual factors. The L2 status factor, especially, is rooted in adult third language acquisition of speakers for whom the first and second language can be clearly distinguished.

As for third language acquisition in heritage speaker contexts, one important or perhaps even the most prominent predictor of cross-linguistic influence

[26] Montrul (2016: 251–252) operationalizes the similarities and differences between heritage speakers and second language learners in terms of order of acquisition, the socio-political status of the languages, functional differences, language dominance, time and mode of acquisition, as well as the contextual setting.

appears to be language dominance. It represents a substantially complex construct that can be operationalized in different ways (Grosjean & Byers-Heinlein 2018: 9–10; Hamann, Rinke & Genevska-Hanke 2019; Silva-Corvalán & Treffers-Daller 2016). In what follows, I will distinguish between linguistic and extra-linguistic factors for defining language dominance, briefly describing them. Crucially, language dominance is not a static concept, but one that can change in the course of one's lifetime – perhaps even several times. It is possible for a second or third language to become one's dominant language, thus significantly changing the status of one's first or native language.

3.4.1 *Linguistic Factors*

Amongst the most important linguistic factors indexing language dominance are proficiency, exposure, and use (see Franceschini 2016: 103–105). They all hide various additional dimensions and, crucially, as such describe factors related to performance. They only permit restricted conclusions regarding underlying linguistic knowledge. Limited performance may point to unbalanced bilingualism, incomplete acquisition, and attrition, but subjects may easily be misjudged by their performance.

Proficiency needs to be further broken down into productive and receptive abilities along the dimensions of speaking, writing, listening, and reading. This further includes fluency and accuracy, but it is easy to see that a timid and introverted – or merely unmotivated – person runs the danger of being underestimated when solely assessed along these dimensions. Some subjects may wish to hide their language knowledge for whatever reasons. Proficiency can be assessed for different areas of language separately, that is, for pronunciation, morphosyntax, lexical comprehension and production, lexical diversity, and perhaps even pragmatic knowledge. Moreover, proficiency as measured by self-assessments and objective tests is known to produce different results (although often correlated). Degree of exposure can be assumed to correlate positively with language dominance. It needs to be considered in combination with age of onset. Nevertheless, although placing young children in front of mono-directional media such as the television yields substantial exposure, the effect on language dominance – not to mention language acquisition – can be expected to be low. What matters is exposure in terms of meaningful social interaction, although passive participation apparently does not impact acquisition success negatively (Franceschini 2016: 104). Moreover, restricted albeit highly meaningful exposure may yield substantial knowledge gains (Grosjean & Byers-Heinlein 2018: 15–17). Language use, finally, can relate to both active and passive command, include considerations of frequency, domains of use, as well as people interacted with. Speakers who use a language actively, frequently, in many social domains, and with a high number of interlocutors are likely to be dominant in that language.

3.4.2 *Extra-Linguistic Factors*

Grosjean and Byers-Heinlein (2018) convincingly argue that the languages available in a multilingual community are typically used for different social domains and topics. Moreover, multilinguals show strong preferences regarding which languages they use in communication with which interlocutors. Also, some languages may be restricted to oral use, others to writing, yet others may be used for both. Considering myself, I use German with my family, but in the academic context I largely use English – both in speaking and writing. I believe that my language proficiency in relation to academic topics is higher in English than German. I read and write much more in English than I do in German. For the home domain, this pattern is reversed. Here, German (including my local dialect) serves as an important identity marker. Grosjean and Byers-Heinlein (2018: 8) describe such patterns in terms of what they call the 'complementarity principle'.[27]

In heritage contexts, we typically find a duality of majority language and home language. Immigrant families prefer to speak their heritage language in the family, but need to use the language of the environment (often the respective national language) outside the home context – for shopping, in administrative and official communication, in the education system, at work, etc. Quite often, the younger generation prefers to speak the majority language with their peers so that the heritage language comes to be restricted for communication with their parents and grandparents. Due to peer group pressure and matters of social prestige, adolescents may refuse to speak their heritage language. While the older generation is dominant in the heritage language (and sometimes exclusively speak the heritage language), the younger generation typically becomes dominant in the majority language. Here, we can witness language shift in real time, as it were. We will encounter illustrative data from Singapore in Chapter 6. Interestingly, English as the current global lingua franca is usually part of the respective language repertoires and may come to compete with the majority language, particularly in smaller countries with relatively low numbers of majority language speakers (as in the Scandinavian countries and the Netherlands). Some heritage speakers in such countries may even experience English as their most dominant language, especially so if English enjoys official status in their country of origin.

All in all, these extra-linguistic factors determine what Aronin and Singleton (2012: 59) refer to as the Dominant Language Constellation, that is, the "set of

[27] The complementarity principle ultimately goes back to Grosjean (1997: 165), there called "complementary principle" and defined as follows: "Bilinguals usually acquire and use their languages for different purposes, in different domains of life, with different people. Different aspects of life require different languages."

languages on which the life of an individual or a society is dependent" (see also Lo Bianco & Aronin 2020). It is easy to see how such constellations influence the performance factors addressed in the previous section and how they may ultimately rebound on the cognitive status of the languages.

3.4.3 Summary

As is true so often, what appears like a well-defined and intuitively plausible concept can and needs to be fanned out into various directions. Language dominance supports this pattern, obeying various linguistic and extra-linguistic dimensions. Establishing a mono-dimensional measure is impossible. Crucially, although the rationale for operationalizing language dominance is to assess its impact on cross-linguistic influence, we need to bear in mind that we could equally use cross-linguistic influence as a predictor for language dominance. More cross-linguistic influence in one direction is tantamount to greater language dominance or imbalance of the languages in the multilingual's mind. Such observations underline the systemic nature of the domain at hand where mono-directional paths of influence are rare.

3.5 Chapter Summary

Chapter 3 explored cross-linguistic influence focusing on constellations of three languages, as they frequently arise in multilingual situations. It identified cross-linguistic influence as the more encompassing concept in comparison to the traditional notion of transfer widely used in second language acquisition studies. It also discussed the relationship between cross-linguistic influence and language interdependence, as proposed in education studies. While language interdependence builds on the proficiency-enhancing qualities of multilingualism (qua metalinguistic awareness), cross-linguistic influence can be both facilitative and inhibitory, the latter manifesting itself as interference. Crucially, non-facilitative transfer only arises within a normative system. Moreover, the mechanisms underlying cross-linguistic influence show important parallels to those identified in language contact studies with its focus on contact-induced language change.

The third chapter went on to examine the differences and similarities between second and third language acquisition. Before third or additional language acquisition emerged as a separate research field, it was widely assumed that the principles of second language acquisition could simply be generalized to third language acquisition. The current consensus is that all previous language experience impacts on the acquisition of further languages and needs to be factored in appropriately. Moreover, three or more languages offer considerably more paths of mutual influence among languages than merely two languages. What complicates the study of cross-linguistic influence immensely is the diverse and heterogeneous set of acquisition trajectories that one encounters in today's globalized world. A host of parameters, relating both to the acquisition processes as well as the multilingual contexts, need to be controlled for to allow comparability of the data and results.

Chapter 3 furthermore showed that there arc several competing approaches trying to model cross-linguistic influence in third language acquisition. They differ in their assumptions concerning possible influence from the background languages (only one vs. both/all languages) as well as additional parameters determining their selection (language distance or typological proximity, status as a first or second language). Whereas most models acknowledge facilitative as well as non-facilitative influence from the background languages, the cumulative enhancement model stands out in assuming only facilitation effects.

Interestingly, there is as yet no model that would formulate language dominance as the most important predictor, although it evidently impacts the strength and direction of cross-linguistic influence in important ways. The problem here is that language dominance itself represents a multidimensional concept that can be dissected along several parameters, both linguistic and extra-linguistic. Language dominance as an influencing factor is especially important in minority and heritage language contexts as well as heterogeneous multilingual settings.

4 Language Development in Multilingual Settings

This chapter enquires into potential advantages of multilingual upbringing in relation to further language development. Importantly, Chapter 4 does not target natural (spontaneous, untutored) language acquisition typical of babies, toddlers, and young children, but focuses on language development in educational institutions and settings. Following Cenoz (2003), it argues that any such advantages play out more forcefully and are easier to identify in regard to general proficiencies rather than specific grammatical phenomena.

Section 4.1 defines the areas of language development in relation to different knowledge domains and skills. It explains different types of proficiencies in opposition to grammatical knowledge, and elaborates on how type of bilingualism interacts with knowledge of language. Crucially, it argues that measuring general proficiencies in situations of balanced bilingualism can yield the strongest positive effects. However, balanced bilingualism does not safeguard against non-facilitative grammatical cross-linguistic influence. Again, cumulative enhancement proves an overly optimistic scenario.

Section 4.2 surveys important studies documenting proficiency advantages of learners of English with a multilingual background, both based on objective and self-assessed measures. The majority of these studies was conducted in the officially bilingual areas of the Spanish part of the Basque Country as well as Catalunya, typically relying on objective measures. These are then contrasted with studies based on self-assessments that, nevertheless, point to the same direction.

Section 4.3 continues with a discussion of several case studies of rather specific grammatical areas where such advantages are much harder to identify, while both facilitative and non-facilitative cross-linguistic influence become generally visible. Learners of English with a multilingual background experience influence from all their previously acquired languages. Some language constellations produce enhancing effects in some grammatical domains, others produce inhibition. Case studies are drawn from morphosyntax, phonology, as well as lexical development.

Following that, Section 4.4 focuses on the special scenario of bilingual heritage speakers and whether their experience of multilingual upbringing entails advantages for subsequent language development. Various grammatical subsystems will be explored in detail, focusing on determiners, subject-verb agreement, tense and aspect, word order, and lexical transfer. Again, it proves crucial to distinguish between general proficiencies and specific grammatical knowledge. Language dominance arises as a crucial predictor of cross-linguistic influence such that principally available enhancing effects of the background languages can be forfeited due to their weaker status and the overriding influence of the stronger language – usually the majority language. Moreover, the discussion reveals that bilingual heritage speakers typically experience learning advantages at an earlier age that subsequently disappear or are levelled out. Section 4.4 also raises the question of whether advantages seen in younger age cohorts disappear due to monolingually biased forms of language pedagogies.

The last point leads over to Section 4.5 where different language learning pedagogies are critically evaluated in relation to their relevance for language development in multilingual settings. Monolingual pedagogies are contrasted with multilingually aware pedagogies and their respective strong and weak points are assessed.

4.1 Objectives of Language Development

The goal of language development in educational institutions – from kindergarten to university – consists in the formation of grammatical and lexical knowledge, the development of literacy and language awareness, as well as the conditioning of language-related proficiencies, such as spoken and written production as well as listening and reading comprehension. This process typically includes the development of pragmatic and cultural knowledge. Kindergarten and early school years represent contexts where natural language acquisition still occurs, but already these childhood institutions contribute substantially to our culturally based language socialization in terms of norms.[1]

4.1.1 Language Proficiencies versus Grammatical and Lexical Knowledge

In linguistics, we find the widely accepted distinction between competence and performance, first introduced by Chomsky (1965) into the scientific discourse (see also Chapter 2). The two constructs are not at all uncontroversial.

[1] It goes without saying that the dividing line between nature and nurture is notoriously difficult to define, if it can be defined at all. The point here is that the influence of cultural institutions on language development begins very early and becomes stronger with increasing age until we exit the education system. Some people enjoy the privilege of continuing systematic language development thereafter.

Competence relates to grammatical knowledge and the relevant mental representations. It is about grammar as a rather abstract rule-based system originating in the innate human language capacity. Performance concerns the actual language use emanating from these mental representations. Performance yields an insufficient and always different reproduction of the underlying competence and is subject to all kinds of limitations and influences (memory, time, tiredness, distractions, mental decline, alcohol, drugs, etc.). Usage-based linguistics has criticized the dichotomy intensely and argued for a continuum of grammaticity and lexicality – or function and content – instead (Hopper & Traugott 2003; Tomasello 2003). Grammar and usage (competence and performance) are here viewed as essentially coextensive, with the latter feeding into the former over time (qua grammaticalization).[2]

Regarding the perspective of language development adopted in the present context, it is useful to distinguish between grammatical and lexical knowledge, on the one hand, as well as language proficiencies, on the other. Here, grammatical knowledge is used in a sense similar to competence, albeit less idealized and more explicit.[3] However, language proficiencies are not the same as performance, although both terms concern language use. While performance in the Chomskyan sense is inherently deficient and considered subordinate to competence, language proficiencies describe complex skills developed as a result of intense and often laborious training in educational contexts. They characterize the development of language according to certain social norms and can thus also be explicated in terms of rules, dos and don'ts. Speaking in an educated manner, academic writing and reading, but also listening while extracting the relevant information represent complex skills that need to be acquired. Some of the norms relate to grammatical phenomena, as in the prohibition of split infinitives or the concern about ending sentences with a preposition (pied piping) in English. Others cover the use of contextually appropriate lexical items (including political correctness and taboos), register differences, the internal organization of academic texts and speech, and orthographical issues. The interface and exact boundary between competence including our innate linguistic abilities and social norms relating to language use have been a matter of debate for a long time and it remains controversial if and to what extent the latter impacts the former or vice versa.

Lexical development forms the essential substance for both the development of grammatical knowledge and that of proficiencies. Grammatical knowledge

[2] Grammaticalization theory assumes that certain lexical items develop into grammatical markers over time. Moreover, discourse structure condenses into syntax diachronically and thereafter into morphology (see Hopper & Traugott 2003 for details).

[3] I use the term 'grammar' here in a traditional sense that encompasses phonology, not just morphosyntax.

without lexical items remains empty. More advanced lexical development typically correlates with higher proficiencies or is considered symptomatic of it. Moreover, it is viewed as a sign of education and intellectual growth. Lexical development does not figure prominently in the present chapter, with the exception of a discussion of lexical transfer as observed in bilingual heritage speakers learning English in Section 4.4.6.

There are many schemes to assess language proficiencies, one of the most prominent being the Common European Framework of Reference for Languages (CEFR). Apart from distinguishing six proficiency levels grouped under the three broader labels "basic user," "independent user," and "proficient user," the CEFR assumes five kinds of language activities or skills. These are listening, reading, spoken interaction, spoken production, and writing (Council of Europe 2020). Alternatively, these could be arranged as reception (listening and reading), production (spoken and written), and spoken interaction. Notably, the CEFR operationalizes the proficiency levels in terms of "can-do" descriptors that facilitate assessment purposes. They can be used by both instructors and learners. Furthermore, language proficiencies can be assessed with a wide array of instruments measuring reading speed (including eye tracking), speaking fluency, listening and reading comprehension, verbosity, lexical diversity, accuracy and correctness, coherence, style, register awareness, and also metalinguistic awareness (see Chapter 2). Again, the subsequent sections will offer ample illustration.

Grammatical knowledge, as we will see, can be assessed with a variety of instruments accumulating correctness scores or degrees of target-like usage. It is always measured against certain rules, norms, or standards – whatever their precise epistemological basis. Students can easily be tested as grammatically deficient, even though they are highly competent language users. The rating scores can be derived from grammaticality judgement tasks, C-tests or related gap filling exercises, sentence construction tasks from arrays of words, or the evaluation of corpus data. Type/token ratios offer a good diagnostic of lexical diversity. Many examples of data resulting from the use of such instruments will be discussed in the later sections.

If it is the case, as widely assumed in the research literature, that multilingual experience impacts additional language acquisition positively, such performance gains should be revealed by the above instruments. Cenoz (2003: 80) argues that "[g]eneral aspects of L3 proficiency show more favorable to bilinguals than those studies in which very specific aspects of language proficiency were analyzed" (see also Cenoz, Hufeisen & Jessner 2001b: 5; Kopečková 2016: 410). Accordingly, one is led to expect clearer results for the more general CEFR proficiencies (reception and production) in comparison to grammatical and lexical correctness scores where cross-linguistic influence can trigger interference effects.

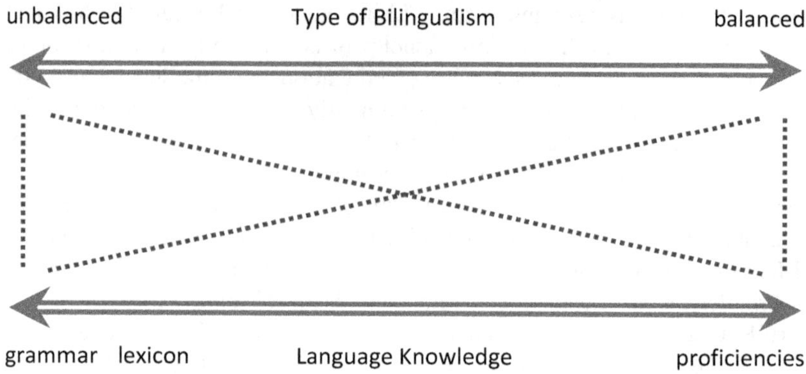

Figure 4.1 Type of bilingualism and language knowledge (Siemund & Lorenz 2023).

4.1.2 Type of Bilingualism and Language Knowledge

The hypothesis just formulated, however, is too simplistic and cannot be developed into a realistic model, as learning advantages resulting from previous multilingual experience heavily depend on the type of bi- or multilingualism. A recurrent theme encountered in Chapters 2 and 3 was that balanced or additive bilingualism is associated with clearer positive cognitive effects than unbalanced or subtractive bilingualism. Crucially, this concerns both the discussion of language interdependence in the sense of Cummins (1976, 1979) as well as cross-linguistic influence when understood in terms of cumulative enhancement (Siemund & Lorenz 2023). Strongly unbalanced bilinguals primarily experience cross-linguistic influence from their dominant language. There is only one source for facilitation effects (though only one source for interference as well). The relationship between language knowledge and type of bilingualism is captured in the model shown in Figure 4.1.

In this model, the continuous variable "type of bilingualism" ranges from unbalanced to balanced, while "language knowledge" opens up a scale from grammatical and lexical knowledge to proficiencies (reception and production). The latter is tantamount to establishing a continuum from declarative – and also encyclopaedic – knowledge (*about*) to procedural knowledge (*how-to*).[4]

[4] Proficiencies or skills necessitate grammatical and lexical knowledge, while the latter remain silent without the former. In addition, proficiencies or skills presuppose extensive content knowledge. They are content-oriented. In simple pidgins, grammar, lexicon, and proficiencies are more or less collapsed and not clearly distinguishable. Sprachausbau leads to a sharper differentiation between grammar, lexicon, and proficiencies (see Kloss 1978 on Sprachausbau).

Type of bilingualism builds on the conception of language dominance developed in Chapter 3.[5]

As for the acquisition of additional languages by learners with bi- or multilingual backgrounds, the model predicts proficiency gains for balanced bi-/multilinguals (the rightmost vertical line), but not for learners with unbalanced language backgrounds (the diagonal line from top left to bottom right). The latter – especially those who are strongly unbalanced – are expected to perform like learners with a monolingual background. In other words, learners of additional languages with a bi- or multilingual background are expected to outperform those with a monolingual background, with the additional caveat that this holds on average and provided that further cognitive, social, attitudinal, and motivational background variables are controlled for.[6]

Regarding grammatical and lexical knowledge, it is predicted that type of bilingualism does not privilege facilitative over non-facilitative cross-linguistic influence, although balanced bilinguals may be better at inhibiting non-facilitative cross-linguistic influence (qua executive control; see Chapter 2). Both balanced and unbalanced bi-/multilinguals are expected to experience both types of cross-linguistic influence during the acquisition of additional languages. However, whereas unbalanced bi-/multilinguals primarily encounter cross-linguistic influence from their dominant language (the leftmost vertical line), balanced bi-/multilinguals can expect evidence from all their background languages in the currently acquired language (the diagonal line from top right to bottom left). Regarding facilitation and interference, learners with prior unbalanced bi-/multilingual experience behave like learners who underwent a monolingual socialization. All in all, the model predicts an increase in multilingual learning advantages on both scales from left to right.

Needless to say, the model in Figure 4.1 interacts with additional variables such as language distance. Learning Portuguese as a third language against the background of Italian and Spanish is likely to produce substantial interference, but there will also be huge facilitation effects (especially regarding lexical knowledge).[7] Conversely, a bilingual speaker of Swedish and German, in

[5] Berthele (2021: 86) operationalizes the opposition of balanced versus unbalanced bilingualism in terms of proficiency or mastery. Balanced bilinguals are assumed to possess "native-like control of 2 'proper' languages."

[6] Especially the relationship between additive/balanced bilingualism and cognition is a tricky one and may easily lead to circularity in the argumentation (see Chapter 1).

[7] Moreover, known subject matter can provide substantial facilitation effects seemingly supporting interdependence. For example, if a German–Greek bilingual learning English is tested on reading comprehension based on Homer's sagas (or epic poems) of Ulysses, and these sagas had previously been studied in German and Greek, English comprehension difficulties will be compensated by subject knowledge. Such scenarios trivially confirm the idea of multilingual advantages.

acquiring Chinese as a third language, may experience as much facilitation and interference as a monolingual speaker of Swedish or German.

4.1.3 Summary

This section argued to draw a distinction between language proficiencies as well as grammatical and lexical expertise, as these types of language knowledge apparently respond differently in regard to the acquisition of additional languages in multilingual settings. While there is an expectation of generally positive effects on language proficiencies, grammatical and lexical knowledge can be subject to both facilitative and non-facilitative cross-linguistic influence from the background languages (see also Chapter 3). I furthermore reasoned that language proficiencies represent sophisticated knowledge systems that cannot be relegated to mere performance. The CEFR was introduced as one prominent scheme to measure proficiencies.

4.2 Development of Language Proficiencies

The following sections underpin the previous more general observations with evidence drawn from a selection of rather insightful studies. We will first consider studies based on objective measures, followed by those relying on self-assessments. We need to bear in mind that no study is directly comparable to another, as they typically rely on different participants, language backgrounds, test instruments and designs, measures, data, and statistics. Nevertheless, they seem to point in the same direction.

4.2.1 Objective Measures

There are several studies documenting a positive effect of bilingualism on the acquisition of additional languages, especially English (Cenoz & Valencia 1994; Safont Jordà 2003, 2005; Sagasta Errasti 2003; Sanz 2000), mostly carried out in the Spanish part of the Basque Country and Catalunya. (See also Cenoz 2013a, 2013b; Cenoz & Jessner 2001a, 2001b; Cenoz, Hufeisen & Jessner 2001a, 2001b.) Notably, these are areas of additive bilingualism (as in the Canadian French–English context) in which the regional and co-official languages Basque and Catalan are held in high esteem by the local populations and serve as emblems of their identity (after several decades of oppression). The national language is (Castilian) Spanish with which Catalan stands in close typological proximity. Basque, in contrast, is an isolate language of unknown ancestry unrelated to Spanish.[8] It currently remains unclear which

[8] Vennemann (2003) offers a thought-provoking, though not uncontroversial, reconstruction of the origin of the Basque language and its position in prehistoric Europe.

aspects of language learning (listening, reading, speaking, writing, grammar) profit most from bilingual or multilingual upbringing.

Cenoz and Valencia (1994) studied 320 bilingual (Basque–Spanish, 52%) and monolingual (Spanish, 48%) secondary school students acquiring English as a third language in the Basque Country. Both Basque and Spanish are used as languages of instruction and they are also taught as separate school subjects. Levels of Basque and Spanish are high in the bilingual population. Sixty-eight per cent of the bilingual students were first language speakers of Basque; for the remaining 32 per cent this was Spanish.[9] Cenoz and Valencia (1994) found a significant relationship between bilingualism and English language achievement, though they do not detail which CEFR domain benefitted most. Even though different CEFR domains are distinguished in principle, an aggregate value was calculated for the statistical analysis (Cenoz & Valencia 1994: 201). Confounding factors such as socio-economic status, exposure to English, general intelligence, attitudes, and motivation had been controlled for (Cenoz & Valencia 1994: 199–200; see also Cenoz 2003: 75). Cenoz and Valencia (1994: 204) conclude that "bilingualism has a positive mediating effect on third language learning." They explain the observed advantages by taking recourse to metalinguistic awareness (Cenoz & Valencia 1994: 205; see Chapter 2 and the subsequent studies by Lasagabaster 1998, 2001).

The study by Sanz (2000) was conducted in Catalunya where Catalan and (Castilian) Spanish serve as co-official languages. It sampled 124 Catalan–Spanish bilingual high school students learning English and compared their results with seventy-seven Spanish-speaking subjects (recruited from two private schools that differ in their language of instruction, i.e. Catalan vs. Spanish). The students completed English grammar and vocabulary tests. In other words, the main CEFR domains were not tested. The bilingual students obtained higher scores in English compared to their monolingual peers for which Sanz (2000: 36), inter alia, also offers metalinguistic awareness as an explanation. Factors such as general intelligence, exposure to English, attitudes, motivation, and socio-economic status were controlled for. The main instruments were Raven's Progressive Matrices Test (Foulds & Raven 1950) and the CELT English proficiency test (Harris & Palmer 1970), though only the structure and vocabulary sections of the latter were used. English proficiency was calculated as an aggregate score (Sanz 2000: 31). It remains unclear, however, whether the positive findings carry over to the main CEFR domains. Sanz (2000: 33–34) concludes that "students in the Catalan immersion program showed an advantage as L3 learners compared with students in a monolingual school. Catalan

[9] All bilingual students in this study had Basque as the language of instruction (Cenoz & Valencia 1994: 199).

bilingualism, like Basque bilingualism, explains superior English achievement independently from other variables."

The writing skills of a sample of 155 secondary school students, again in the Basque Country, are investigated in Sagasta Errasti (2003). All students were Basque–Spanish bilinguals learning English, but seventy-eight had Basque as their home language while this was Spanish for seventy-seven students. Accordingly, the students differ in terms of language dominance.[10] All students followed a school model in which instruction proceeds in Basque and Spanish is taught as a regular subject.[11] This means that the Basque-dominant group followed a maintenance programme, while the Spanish-dominant group went through an immersion programme. The students were asked to write an informal letter and a recipe in three languages (Basque, Spanish, English). They also completed a background questionnaire. The texts were assessed according to fluency, grammatical complexity, lexical complexity, and accuracy (Sagasta Errasti 2003: 32–33). The study shows that students with Basque as their dominant language have higher written production skills in English than their peers with Spanish as their main L1 (maintenance vs. immersion), although this primarily applies to the overall production measure. Moreover, students with the highest bilingual competence also achieved the highest score in English, again measured in terms of overall production.[12]

There have also been attempts to identify positive effects of bilingualism for the processing of indirectness and politeness. For instance, Safont Jordà (2003) studied the realization of requestive speech acts by eighty monolingual (Castilian Spanish) and eighty bilingual (Catalan and Castilian Spanish) female learners of English as a foreign language. The assessment was carried out for situations of requesting using discourse completion tests, role-playing tasks, as well as discourse evaluation tests. In the latter test, the subjects were asked to evaluate the appropriateness of certain request verbalizations in given contexts. The study found rather striking advantages in bilinguals over monolinguals in this particular domain. Bilingual subjects in this study evaluated the verbalization of request situations more appropriately and used a higher number of conventionally indirect forms, that is, they proved more sensitive to issues of politeness. Safont Jordà (2003: 59) explains these findings in terms of a heightened metapragmatic awareness of the bilingual subjects.[13]

[10] Language dominance was operationalized as language use at home, in social contexts, and at school (Sagasta Errasti 2003: 32).

[11] This is Model D in the Basque school system. Modal A uses Spanish as the language of instruction, while Model B is a bilingual programme in which Basque and Spanish are used side by side (Sagasta Errasti 2003: 29).

[12] This study, however, did not control for social background variables.

[13] Although this study did not include social background variables, it relied on a relatively homogenous sample of university students.

4.2.2 Self-Assessed Measures

Mueller (2018) and Siemund and Mueller (2021) also offer support for the assumption of certain advantages in relation to multilingually raised users of English as an additional language. In a large-scale survey amongst 1,454 students and 341 instructors regarding their self-assessed proficiencies in English as an academic language, sampled at a university in a non-English speaking country (Hamburg, Germany), multilingually raised students and instructors quite consistently provide higher English assessments in comparison to their monolingually raised peers. The most common background languages amongst monolingually raised students and instructors were German, Russian, Chinese, Polish, French, Turkish, Spanish, and Italian. The multilingually raised students and instructors attested Russian, Polish, Italian, Spanish, Dutch, Turkish, Persian, and several other languages in combination with German, but also in combination with other languages such as Armenian, Ukrainian, and Catalan. Languages from farther away included Korean, Tamil, Hindi, Kannada, and Twi. The study excluded students and instructors raised in English.

Figure 4.2 provides the relevant comparison in the student cohort of this study, with the five proficiencies distinguished (listening comprehension, reading comprehension, spoken interaction, spoken production, written expression) accumulated into an aggregate value (composite score).

As can be gleaned from Figure 4.2, multilingually raised students (*M*=25.37; *SD*=4.2) self-assessed their English-language abilities with greater confidence in

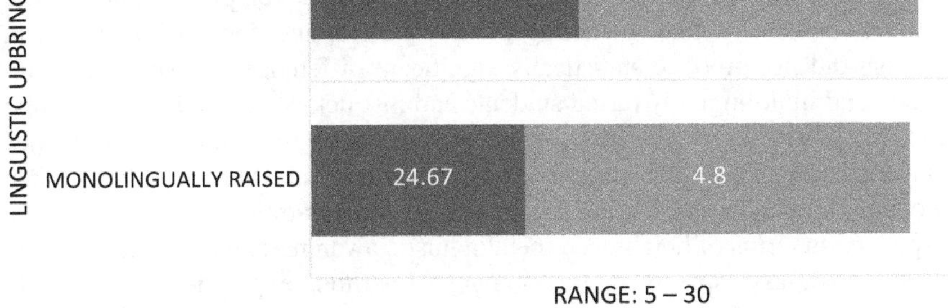

Figure 4.2 Monolingually raised versus multilingually raised students' average self-assessed proficiency levels (Siemund & Mueller 2021: 251).

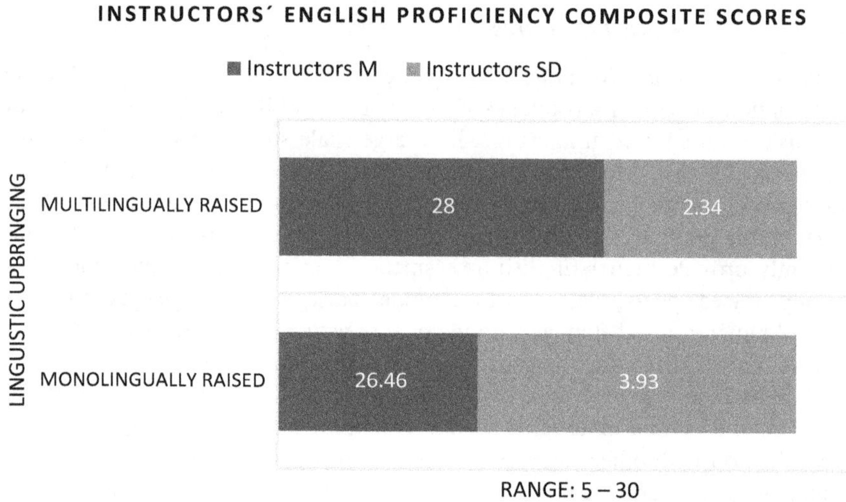

Figure 4.3 Monolingually raised versus multilingually raised instructors' average self-assessed proficiency levels (Siemund & Mueller 2021: 252).

comparison to monolingually raised students [M=24.67; SD=4.8; Levene-Test for Homogeneity of Variance: F=2.84; p=0.09; t(289.12)=−2.00; p<0.05]. Figure 4.3 depicts the corresponding comparison for the instructors in the sample, again based on aggregate values combining the different proficiencies.

Contrasting monolingually raised instructors (M=26.46; SD=3.93) with multilingually raised instructors attests significantly higher English proficiencies in the latter cohort [M=28; SD=2.34; Levene-Test for Homogeneity of Variance: F=5.56; p=0.02; t(250)=−2.02; p<0.05].

However, although the aggregate differences are statistically significant, they are driven by specific CEFR domains, namely reading comprehension for students, written expression for instructors, and spoken production for both students and instructors. Listening comprehension and spoken interaction in English did not produce statistically significant differences between monolingually and multilingually raised students and instructors, respectively. Siemund and Mueller (2021: 258–259) argue that previous multilingual experience may reduce one's anxiety in using new languages and that therefore spoken production benefits most. The higher reading scores amongst students may be explained in terms of heightened metalinguistic awareness, whereas instructors' stronger self-assessments in the domain of written expression may simply indicate a greater familiarity with composing English academic texts. The study concludes that multilingual learning advantages are restricted to certain domains and obey specific boundary conditions.

The study just described used a design previously employed to explore the sociolinguistics of Singaporean multilingualism (Leimgruber, Siemund & Terassa 2018; Siemund, Schulz & Schweinberger 2014), where Malay, Mandarin, and various Chinese vernaculars (Cantonese, Hainanese, Hakka, Hokkien, and Teochew), as well as Tamil and other Indian languages compete in the linguistic space (see also Chapter 6). Interestingly enough, in this context too, students with a multilingual background (three or more languages) tended to assess their language proficiencies more favourably than bilingual students.[14]

4.2.3 *Summary*

The studies discussed in the previous paragraphs document impressive proficiency advantages by speakers with bi-/multilingual backgrounds in relation to English as a third or additional language. However, one needs to be cautious and should bear in mind that the studies from the Basque Country and Catalunya involve balanced bilinguals with high proficiencies in their background languages. These represent favourable conditions. Moreover, all languages (Basque, Catalan, Spanish) carry high prestige and are actively promoted. The multilingual ideological climate is rather positive in the relevant regions. Furthermore, the studies relying on self-assessments may contain a certain ideological bias due to the largely positive associations with multilingualism in academia and particularly in the city state of Singapore. There is a certain danger of over-reporting positive results.

4.3 Development of Grammatical and Lexical Knowledge

The results of the studies surveyed in the preceding section are impressive, but they are considerably more difficult to replicate in the context of bilingual heritage speakers, as will be detailed in Section 4.4. Moreover, it is rather difficult to demonstrate consistent facilitation effects in the development of grammatical and lexical knowledge, as specific grammatical and lexical phenomena – like article usage, subject-verb agreement, tense and aspect, double object constructions, negation, word order, gender marking, expletive subjects, code-switching, semantic extensions, calques, and others – respond differently to the multifarious contextual parameters. Some illustration will be provided in Sections 4.3.1 and 4.3.2. Part of the problem is a difference in focus, as such grammatical and lexical studies are typically interested in the direction and

[14] Like Sagasta Errasti (2003), none of the above studies controlled for social background variables, but achieved comparability through their focus on relatively homogenous student samples.

strength of cross-linguistic influence (see Chapter 3) and to a much lesser degree in bilingual or multilingual learning advantages. Moreover, early research (Cenoz 2001) suggested that there are no differences between different bilingual groups in relation to cross-linguistic influence.[15] It is only recently that we are beginning to find an explicit research interest here. Many other phenomena could be and partially have been investigated for positive effects, including phonological ones (intonation, realization of specific phonemes, final devoicing, voice onset time), alphabetization including spelling issues and the learning of scripts (faster learning of new scripts, familiarity with scripts, understanding of script basis). I will briefly address phonological issues in Section 4.3.2, but will disregard alphabetization and scripts. Lorenz (2019) offers a topical overview.

Positive effects in the above areas of language development (here focusing on English) can be identified in terms of higher target-like realizations (or less non-facilitative cross-linguistic influence) in the linguistic behaviour of learners with a multilingual background in relation to those learners who grew up in a monolingual environment. Another possibility could be that multilingually raised learners do not differ from monolingually raised ones in regard to the number of non-target-like realizations, but rather regarding their type or quality. For example, multilingually raised learners could perhaps produce higher numbers of non-target-like realizations that do not greatly impede comprehensibility and intelligibility, though lower numbers of communicatively crucial ones. This would likewise illustrate a positive effect of multilingual upbringing. If, in contrast, multilingual learners merely show different target-like realizations from monolingual learners, but produce more or less the same number of non-target-like realizations of the same type or quality, this would not demonstrate facilitative effects, but merely different types of cross-linguistic influence. One could further hypothesize that learners with a multilingual background invariably draw on facilitative structures in their background languages (cumulative enhancement), but this position appears overly optimistic (see Chapter 3).

The studies to be surveyed in what follows assume, either explicitly or implicitly, the principles for the identification of cross-linguistic influence developed in Jarvis (2000) and Jarvis and Pavlenko (2008), that is, "intragroup

[15] This study contrasted three Basque–Spanish bilingual groups of English learners (L1 Basque, L1 Spanish, L1 Basque and Spanish) and found no differences in the quantity of cross-linguistic influence across these groups (Cenoz 2001: 15). Spanish turned out to produce stronger effects than Basque (Cenoz 2001: 14).

Table 4.1. *Evidence for cross-linguistic influence (Jarvis & Pavlenko 2008: 35).*

Type of evidence	Description
Intragroup homogeneity	Evidence that the behaviour in question is not an isolated incident, but is instead a common tendency of individuals who know the same combination of languages.
Intergroup heterogeneity	Evidence that the behaviour in question is not something that all language users do regardless of the combinations of L1s and L2s that they know.
Cross-linguistic performance congruity	Evidence that a language user's behaviour in one language really is motivated by her use (i.e. the way she demonstrates her knowledge) of another language.

homogeneity," "intergroup heterogeneity," and "cross-linguistic performance congruity." These are described in Table 4.1.

Intragroup homogeneity provides evidence that different groups of language learners in particular language combinations manifest common learning trajectories (and not chaotic behaviour). Intergroup heterogeneity furnishes evidence that the observable behaviour is not due to general learning strategies and trajectories, but originates in the different language backgrounds of the speakers. Finally, cross-linguistic performance congruity harks back to Weinreich's (1953: 7) concept of "interlingual identification" and allows one to analyze an observable feature in one language as originating in another. Needless to say, interference provides stronger evidence than facilitation, as it can be detected more easily.

4.3.1 Morphosyntax

Recent and ongoing research is suggestive of the fact that any bilingual or multilingual learning advantage can only be identified with respect to specific grammatical, lexical, and phonological phenomena as well as specific language constellations. Moreover, what manifests itself as an advantage (cumulative enhancement) in one constellation can be a disadvantage (cumulative inhibition) in another.

For example, for L1 Spanish–L2 Basque and L1 Basque–L2 Spanish learners of English, García Mayo and Slabakova (2015) primarily find influence from Spanish with respect to the realization of null objects, even though Spanish is the L1 in the first group and the L2 in the second. Basque allows null objects across the board, Spanish only with generic nouns, and English not at all. The examples in (1) and (2) illustrate the grammatical facts in Spanish.[16]

(1) Spanish (García Mayo & Slabakova 2015: 484–485)

a.	¿Compr-ó	Inés	el	libro	para	su	hija?
	buy-3SG.PST	Inés	the	book	for	her	daughter

‘Did Inés buy the book for her daughter?’

b.	√	Sí,	lo	compr-ó.
		yes,	CL.ACC.3SG.M	buy-3SG.PST

‘Yes, she bought it.’

c.	*	Sí,	Ø	compr-ó.
		yes	Ø	buy-3SG.PST

‘Yes, she bought it.’

(2) Spanish (García Mayo & Slabakova 2015: 485)

a.	¿Traj-eron	café	para	la	cena?
	bring-3PL.PST	coffee	for	the	dinner

‘Did they bring coffee for dinner?’

b.	√	Sí,	lo	traj-eron.
		yes,	CL.ACC.3SG.M	bring-3PL.PST

‘Yes, they brought some.’

c.	√	Sí,	Ø	traj-eron.
		yes	Ø	bring-3PL.PST

‘Yes, they brought some.’

The realization of arguments in Basque can be gleaned from examples (3) and (4). In this language, basically all arguments can be left unexpressed, as in example (4), contingent on contextual parameters.[17]

(3) Basque (García Mayo & Slabakova 2015: 485; Duguine 2008: 312)

Ni-k	Jon-i	artikulu-a-k	eman	d-i-zki-o-t
I-ERG	Jon-DAT	papers-ABS-PL	give	PRS-root-3PL.ABS-3SG.DAT-1SG.ERG

‘I gave the papers to John.’

(4) Basque (García Mayo & Slabakova 2015: 486; Duguine 2008: 312)

[e ERG]	[e DAT]	[e ABS]	eman	d-i-zki-o-t
			give	PRS-root-3PL.ABS-3SG.DAT-1SG.ERG

‘I gave them to him/her/it.’

[16] The following glosses are used in examples in (1) and (2): 3 = third person; ACC = accusative; CL = clitic; M = masculine; PL = plural; PST = past tense; SG = singular.

[17] The following glosses are used in examples (3) and (4): 1 = first person; 3 = third person; ABS = absolutive; DAT = dative; [e] = phonologically silent argument; ERG = ergative; PL = plural; PRS = present; SG = singular.

Table 4.2. *Possibility of null objects in English, Spanish, and Basque (García Mayo & Slabakova 2015: 487).*

	Specific sentences	Generic sentences
English	No	No
Spanish	No	Yes
Basque	Yes	Yes

As is well known, English does not permit null objects and therefore remains unillustrated. Table 4.2 summarizes the response of the three languages to null objects.

The study involved 119 participants distributed across the three language groups as follows: L1 Basque–L2 Spanish–L3 English (*n*=23), L1 Spanish–L2 Basque–L3 English (*n*=25), L1 Spanish–L2 English (*n*=47), and an English native control group (*n*=24).[18] The participants were confronted with a grammaticality judgement task. The results show that L1 Spanish learners of L2 English deliver very similar test performance when compared to the trilingual groups. In fact, the only significant differences arise between the English native control group and the other groups. All Spanish groups experience cross-linguistic influence from Spanish in their L2 or L3 English. Crucially, influence from Spanish can be considered an advantage when viewed from the Basque side (as it reduces the number of non-target-like null objects) and a disadvantage from the English perspective (as it produces non-target-like null objects in generic contexts). We may note in passing that the results are also compatible with the idea of typological proximity as the driving force behind cross-linguistic influence, since English and Spanish are more closely related than either is to Basque (an isolate language).

Similarly, Slabakova and García Mayo (2015), in a parallel study involving 110 participants, find stronger influence from Spanish in the acquisition of English by L1 Spanish–L2 Basque (*n*=24) and L1 Basque–L2 Spanish (*n*=23) bilingual groups that plays out differently in left dislocation, topicalization, and focus fronting (cumulative enhancement vs. inhibition). There is also a monolingual Spanish group learning English (*n*=39) as well as an English native speaker control group (*n*=24). The three languages differ in their requirement to take up the topicalized, left-dislocated, or focus-fronted constituent by a pronoun or clitic. The relevant language-specific facts are shown in Table 4.3.

[18] The learners of English differed somewhat regarding their level of English proficiency (García Mayo & Slabakova 2015: 491).

Table 4.3. *Topicalization, left dislocation, and focus fronting in English, Spanish, and Basque. Adapted from Slabakova and García Mayo (2015: 214).*

	Topicalization	Left dislocation	Focus fronting
English	No pronoun	Pronoun	No pronoun
Spanish	Clitic	Clitic/pronoun	No clitic
Basque	No pronoun	No pronoun	No pronoun

As for topicalization, the English native group responds to the stimuli differently than the Spanish groups. Inhibition (or interference) from Spanish becomes visible in English, but no enhancement (facilitation) originating in Basque. Under left dislocation, the English native and Spanish groups respond similarly. Apparently, there is facilitation from Spanish, but no interference related to influence from Basque. In the third condition (i.e. focus fronting), the four language groups show largely similar behaviour. In other words, bilingual advantages or facilitation effects are structure-dependent.[19] Slabakova and García Mayo (2015: 222) conclude that "cumulative enhancement as well as cumulative inhibition are possible processes in L3 acquisition."

The two studies just surveyed offer a representative snapshot of the current discussion. Again, it needs to be borne in mind that they were conducted in a region with widespread additive bilingualism, languages enjoying high social prestige, and a generally favourable multilingual climate. Imaz Agirre and García Mayo (2017) make a similar point for the L3 acquisition of English double object constructions, again testing Spanish–Basque bilinguals. They report inhibition effects originating in Basque, arguing against cumulative enhancement and typological proximity. For the acquisition of gender agreement in L3 English, Imaz Agirre and García Mayo (2018) report strong non-facilitative transfer from Basque. Moreover, non-target-like structures were more prominent amongst L3 in comparison to L2 learners. In sum, previous multilingual experience does not predict general advantages for subsequent grammatical development, as one encounters both enhancement and inhibition.

4.3.2 *Vocabulary*

A number of studies have investigated lexical cross-linguistic influence in third language acquisition (Bardel 2015; Ringbom 1987, 2001, 2007). Research questions here typically pertain to the relative influence of the background

[19] Generally, the influence of Spanish appears stronger than that of Basque in either of the trilingual groups (Slabakova & García Mayo 2015: 221–222).

languages as well as the relative weight of transfer of form and transfer of meaning, also over time using longitudinal designs. Learning advantages as a result of a previous multilingual experience are usually not addressed. Agustín-Llach (2019) studied lexical knowledge, lexical fluency, and (lexical) cross-linguistic influence in eighty-six Spanish monolingual and eighty-seven Spanish–Basque bilingual learners of English as an L2 and L3, respectively. However, this study largely failed to detect significant differences between the two cohorts of students, although slightly positive tendencies could be attested for the bilingual group in the area of lexical cross-linguistic influence.[20] Apart from Agustín-Llach (2019), I am not aware of any studies discussing lexical cross-linguistic influence in connection with multilingual learning advantages. One could surmise, for instance, that learners with a multilingual background are more sensitized to the occurrence of lexical transfer and can control it more consciously due to their averaged higher metalinguistic awareness. We will explore such issues in more detail in Section 4.4.6 in the context of bilingual heritage speakers.

4.3.3 *Phonology*

Various studies in the morphosyntactic domain have shown that cross-linguistic influence in situations of third language acquisition is domain-specific, occurs property-by-property, can be due to L1 and/or L2 activity, and is not necessarily facilitative (though it can be). These conclusions follow from the discussion of cross-linguistic influence in Chapter 3, with the studies surveyed in Section 4.3.1 providing additional support.

Similar results have also been reported from recent studies on the acquisition of L3 phonological features (see Cabrelli Amaro & Wrembel 2016 for an overview). For example, Kopečková (2016) studied the acquisition of the Spanish and English rhotic sounds in nineteen students in Germany (aged 11–12) over a period of three years. Four of the students had a bi-/multilingual background, speaking Croatian, Israeli Hebrew, Polish and Italian, and Russian alongside German. Another student was a heritage speaker of Spanish. These five bi-/multilinguals were contrasted with fourteen monolingual German speakers studying English and Spanish as foreign languages. The realization of rhotic sounds varies, with German and Israeli Hebrew selecting the uvular

[20] Monolingual students produced more lexical tokens and types in comparison to the bilingual students (Agustín-Llach 2019: 893). On average, bilingual students produced slightly fewer instances of lexical cross-linguistic influence. However, with the exception of literal translations, these differences did not reach statistical significance (Agustín-Llach 2019: 895). This author concludes that "the impact of schooling and similar EFL learning experiences are strong enough to discard any possible advantages gained from bilingualism" (Agustín-Llach 2019: 898).

variant, while the other languages in the sample exhibit dental or alveolar variants. The study found that bilinguals with the relevant phoneme already in their inventory (i.e. in the background languages) acquired it faster than bilinguals lacking it. Nevertheless, the latter group of bilinguals still outperformed foreign language learners.[21] Interestingly enough, the Spanish heritage speaker performed basically like the monolingual German learners. We will come back to this issue in Section 4.4.

Antoniou, Liang, Ettlinger and Wong (2015) studied the phonetic acquisition of vocabulary items in artificial languages resembling English, Mandarin, and Korean. They tested cohorts of English monolinguals as well as Mandarin–English and Korean–English bilinguals. The authors hypothesized that bilingual learners outperform monolingual ones and that the Mandarin–English and Korean–English bilinguals would be better at learning the phonetic features of lexical items in Mandarin-like and Korean-like languages, respectively. As expected, the bilingual groups generally outperformed the monolingual groups. Moreover, Mandarin–English bilinguals found it easier to learn Mandarin-like words in comparison to English monolinguals. Also, the Korean–English bilinguals achieved the highest number of target-like realizations of the artificial items resembling Korean. The authors conclude that general bilingual learning advantages are "modulated first by whether the contrast in question is 'easy' or 'difficult', and then by how similar these contrasts are to those in the learners' native language(s)" (Antoniou et al. 2015: 690).

4.3.4 Summary

In comparison to general proficiencies, learning advantages due to previous multilingual experience are more difficult to substantiate in relation to specific grammatical areas and vocabulary. Cross-linguistic influence is not generally enhancing, as there are also inhibitory effects. The direction and strength of cross-linguistic influence depend on the actual language contact or learning situation, again with factors like language distance, proficiency, and – above all – the particular grammatical and lexical facts determining the results. Cross-linguistic influence is not holistic, but structure-dependent. Apparently, general language proficiencies as well as specific grammatical and lexical knowledge rely on different cognitive mechanisms and strategies.[22]

[21] These statements represent broad generalizations. There is substantial individual variation, also over time (see Kopečková 2016: 418–421).

[22] I find it remarkable that the linguistically oriented studies on cross-linguistic influence usually do not control for social background variables. The studies on interdependence and general proficiencies typically do, especially the more recent ones. The latter frequently originate in education departments. It would seem that linguists and educationists hold different views regarding the role of these social background factors.

4.4 Bilingual Heritage Speakers

As the preceding sections have revealed, studies involving (more or less) balanced bilinguals acquiring English as a third language tend to find positive influences of bilingualism when compared to monolingual control groups (Agustín-Llach 2019; Cenoz 2003, 2013b; Cenoz & Valencia 1994; Lasagabaster 1998, 2001; Safont Jordà 2003; Sagasta Errasti 2003; Sanz 2000). An important caveat, however, is that the research focus of these studies concerned general proficiencies, and not domain-specific grammatical and lexical cross-linguistic influence.

In comparison, early research investigating unbalanced bilingual heritage speakers did not report differences between bilingual speakers and monolingual controls, or even identified disadvantages of such bilingual speakers (Cenoz 2003: 77; Sanders & Meijers 1995; Van Gelderen et al. 2003). Such conflicting results are in need of clarification. In view of the increasing number of heritage speakers in the Western World learning English as an additional language, this specific learner group deserves special attention.

This section examines the language development of bilingual heritage speakers in multilingual settings, trying to identify advantages for subsequent language learning in this particular group. Again, the additional or third language is typically English, learnt as part of the school curriculum subsequently to or concurrently with the heritage language and the respective majority language. We begin the discussion with a review of a number of studies testing general language proficiencies (Section 4.4.1). This will be followed by an evaluation of several case studies taken from different grammatical domains (Sections 4.4.2–4.4.6). Here, I take the liberty of drawing on a range of studies that I have supervised or contributed to. Other relevant studies will of course not be forgotten.

4.4.1 English Language Proficiencies

Sanders and Meijers (1995) studied thirty-one Turkish–Dutch bilingual students, fifteen Moroccan Arabic–Dutch bilingual students, and monolingual Dutch students learning English as a second or third language in the Netherlands.[23] They tested the students for grammatical judgement, spontaneous language use, word comprehension, word production, and word recognition. Bilingual and monolingual students were matched with respect to intelligence and socio-economic status. No differences in achievement between bilinguals and monolinguals were found (Sanders & Meijers 1995:

[23] Students were selected in a way that favoured balanced bilinguals. However, the Moroccan Arabic students were not literate in that language (Sanders & Meijers 1995: 63).

74).[24] Similarly, Van Gelderen et al. (2003), again in the context of the Netherlands, analyzed the L2/L3 English reading skills of 338 students of whom 281 were monolingual Dutch speakers and 57 bilingual speakers with Turkish, Moroccan, or Surinam family backgrounds. The study reports significantly lower reading comprehension skills in the bilingual L3 group, but since it did not control for cognitive and socio-economic background factors, the results need to be interpreted with a grain of salt.

More recent studies tend to control for cognitive, linguistic, social, and socio-economic background variables. They sometimes do detect positive effects in the multilingual speaker groups, but also report strong differences contingent on the above factors. For instance, Edele, Kempert and Schotte (2018) studied German monolingual (n=7,964) learners of English as a second language as well as Russian–German (n=352) and Turkish–German (n=436) bilingual learners for whom English is an additional language. The bilingual learners were placed into four groups and two different proficiency bands, namely balanced speakers at a high level, L1 dominant and L2 dominant speakers, as well as balanced bilingual speakers at a low level. They found that high level bilinguals in both groups outperformed average monolingual students while such advantages could only be confirmed for the Russian–German L2 dominant bilinguals. Bilingual students in the low proficiency band as well as L1 dominant students scored significantly below the German monolingual control group. Further analyses identified the language of instruction (German) as the main explanatory variable behind English proficiency. The studies carried out by Maluch and Kempert (2019), Maluch et al. (2015), and Maluch, Neumann and Kempert (2016) equally report positive effects of bilingual heritage upbringing on learning English, but the observable enhancing effects are typically contingent on additional factors. Maluch and Kempert (2019: 879) point out that formal instruction in the home language, simultaneous versus sequential bilingualism, and code-switching behaviour influence the learning outcome in English. Maluch et al. (2015: 82) attest positive influences of their bilingual heritage for students with Chinese–German and Polish–German backgrounds, but less positive and even negative effects for other bilingual heritage groups. Moreover, being bilingual contributes only little to explaining the observable variance, with proficiency in the language of instruction (German) having a much greater effect. Finally, Maluch, Neumann and Kempert (2016: 115) identify age as an important factor inasmuch as younger cohorts of bilingual heritage students show stronger positive effects of their previous language experience on English

[24] Nevertheless, Sanders and Meijers (1995: 75) do note that the different first languages of the children impact grammatical cross-linguistic influence such that group-specific learning patterns arise. They consider this an issue for language pedagogies (see Section 4.5).

proficiency than older students. Similar age effects of previous bilingual experience also figure prominently in Hopp et al. (2019) in relation to the acquisition of vocabulary and grammar. In this study, too, advantages related to bilingualism surface in the younger age cohort and evaporate in the older ones, while the influence of the majority language (German) becomes stronger with increasing age. Similar observations and generalizations can be gleaned from Fleckenstein, Möller and Baumert (2018), Göbel, Rauch and Vieluf (2011), Hirosh and Degani (2018), Klieme et al. (2006), and Schwartz et al. (2007).

Lorenz et al. (2020) analyzed the data from the first wave of a four-year longitudinal project that followed the learning trajectories of students across Germany at four measuring points (*Multilingual Development: A Longitudinal Perspective,* University of Hamburg, 2014–2019; www.mez.uni-hamburg.de). Students were recruited from school year seven (twelve and thirteen years of age) and year nine (fourteen and fifteen years of age). The study is based on a sample of 1,718 participants, of whom n=914 have a monolingual German background, while n=319 are Russian–German and n=485 Turkish–German bilingual heritage speakers.[25] In these age groups, students can be regarded as beginners or intermediate learners of English. The study assessed reading fluency and comprehension in German and the background languages, and relied on C-tests to measure proficiency in English.[26] It further collected data on the students' self-concepts on language learning in general, their motivation to learn English, and their self-assessments on learning English. Crucially, the study also determined the students' cognitive abilities, their socio-economic backgrounds, gender, as well as school type and school year. The authors fitted two regression models shown in Table 4.4, with the second model factoring in the influence of heritage language proficiency. The second model only includes the heritage speakers, as it is only here that heritage language proficiency is relevant. The models explain approximately 70 per cent of variance.[27]

As in the studies surveyed before, the results underline the strong influence of the majority and instructional language German on English proficiency, especially reading comprehension in German. There is also a slight effect of

[25] The bilingual heritage students are dominant in German. Average proficiencies in the heritage languages are significantly below those in German. Moreover, the heritage languages are largely confined to the home context and mainly used in communication with parents (Lorenz et al. 2020: 190–191, 195).

[26] Four short gapped texts were used that the students had to complete within twenty minutes (Lorenz et al. 2020: 192).

[27] Variables that did not add substantially to the explanatory power of the models were excluded. Model 1 uses eight predictor variables, while there are seven in model 2 (Lorenz et al. 2020: 198–199).

Table 4.4. *English proficiency as a response variable in a multiple linear regression analysis (Lorenz et al. 2020: 198).*

Parameter	Regression model 1	Regression model 2
Intercept	−45.22*** (2.65)	−32.134*** (4.06)
Reading comprehension German	0.35*** (0.03)	0.37*** (0.05)
Reading fluency German		
Reading comprehension heritage language	–	0.10* (0.05)
Reading fluency heritage language	–	−0.01** (0.00)
Group: Russian–German	-0.22^{ns} (0.68)	
Group: Turkish–German	−1.60* (0.63)	
Cognitive ability test	0.53*** (0.05)	0.40*** (0.08)
Gender: male	−1.59** (0.52)	
School: other	−11.89*** (0.58)	−12.76*** (0.95)
School year	6.47*** (0.26)	5.68*** (0.43)
Socio-economic status		
Self-concept		
Motivation	1.13* (0.55)	
Self-assessment	7.09*** (0.36)	6.81*** (0.58)
No. of observations	1,661	648
R^2	0.71	0.68
p-value	< .001	< .001

Note: Significance codes: ns = not significant; ns p > .05, * .05 >= p > .01, ** .01 >= p > .001, *** .001 >= p > 0. *Model 1 includes 57 missings and model 2 includes 156 missings.*

bilingual heritage group membership. Being of Turkish–German belonging impacts English proficiently negatively when all other variables are kept constant, albeit only weakly. Cognitive ability, gender, school type, and school year manifest strong predictors, especially school type and school year. Interestingly enough, socio-economic status did not prove statistically significant in the context of the other variables in this sample. Motivation and especially self-assessment in English show strong effects. In model 2, the impact of heritage language proficiency on English proficiency is rather weak, but measurable.

A similar data set from the same research project is used in Lorenz, Toprak and Siemund (2021) to fit two structural equation models assessing the interplay and mutual effects of the different variables. Disregarding partially incomplete data sets, the study analyzes a total of *n*=1,409 students distributed across German monolingual students (*n*=852), Russian–German students (*n*=237), and Turkish–German students (*n*=320). Proficiency in German and English is defined as latent variables measured in terms of reading comprehension and C-tests, respectively. The study further defines the students' background as a

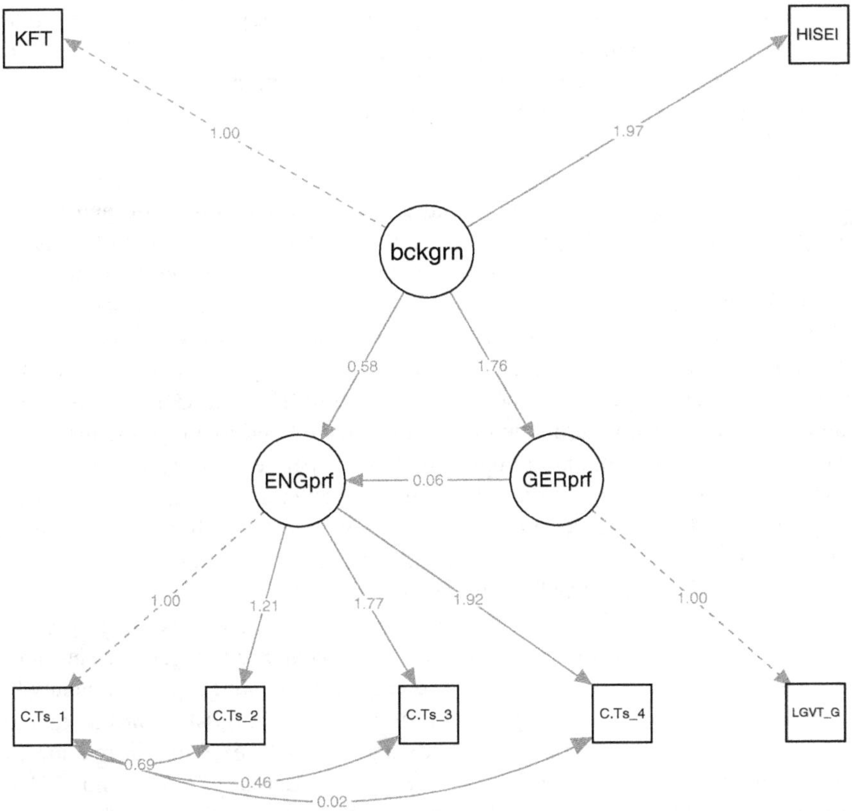

Figure 4.4 The base model of English proficiency and (unstandardized) path estimates (Lorenz, Toprak & Siemund 2021: 282).
Note: KFT = cognitive ability, HISEI = socio-economic status, bckgrn = background variables, ENGprf = English proficiency, GERprf = German proficiency, C.Ts_1/2/3/4 = English C-Tests, LGVT_G = German reading comprehension.

latent variable measured through cognitive ability and socio-economic status. The structural equation model (base model without heritage language proficiency) is depicted in Figure 4.4.

An examination of the statistical output again reveals a strong effect of the instructional language German on English proficiency, although statistical significance is lost in the subsamples of monolingual and bilingual students as well as Russian–German students (the model could not be fitted for the Turkish–German students due to multicollinearity). There remain positive tendencies, however. Socio-economic status and especially cognitive ability turn out to be strong predictors of English proficiency in these models that are statistically significant across groups (disregarding Turkish–German students).[28] Lorenz, Toprak and Siemund (2021: 293) conclude that "any observable multilingual boost is highly group specific, and closely interacts with general cognitive ability."

In a follow-up study using a largely similar student body, Lorenz, Toprak and Siemund (2022) examined the predictive power of linguistic and extra-linguistic variables on English proficiency. A total of 849 German monolingual learners of English were tested against 236 Russian–German and 318 Turkish–German bilingual learners. Altogether, 1,403 secondary school students were involved. The extra-linguistic variables included cognitive ability, school type, gender, socio-economic status, self-concept, motivation, and self-assessment. Language proficiency was assessed for English, German, Russian, and Turkish. Two structural equation models were fitted to gauge the interplay of these variables, explaining approximately 90 per cent of the variance. The model that includes the heritage languages Russian and Turkish is shown in Figure 4.5. Most variables turned out to influence English proficiency in a statistically significant way, albeit with varying effect sizes. Moreover, the models revealed only small differences across the three language groups. Lorenz, Toprak and Siemund (2022) argue that "the three language groups are more similar than different and that the heritage languages Russian and Turkish add comparatively little to predicting English language proficiency."

The above studies relate to general proficiencies in English. Third language acquisition in bilingual heritage contexts has also been explored in relation to cross-linguistic influence (Lorenz 2018, 2019; Lorenz & Siemund 2019; Lorenz et al. 2019; Siemund & Lechner 2015; Siemund, Schröter & Rahbari 2018). These studies show that all background languages can be active, that language dominance is a strong predictor of cross-linguistic influence, that cross-linguistic influence works on a property-by-property basis, and that one can observe cumulative enhancement and/or cumulative inhibition depending on the specific language constellation and the phenomena investigated. The following sections summarize the results from a variety of studies focusing on different grammatical phenomena.

4.4.2 *Determiners*

The label 'determiners' here subsumes definite and indefinite articles as well as demonstrative pronouns. English evidently possesses all these expressions in

[28] This study excludes several of the background variables factored in by Lorenz et al. (2020).

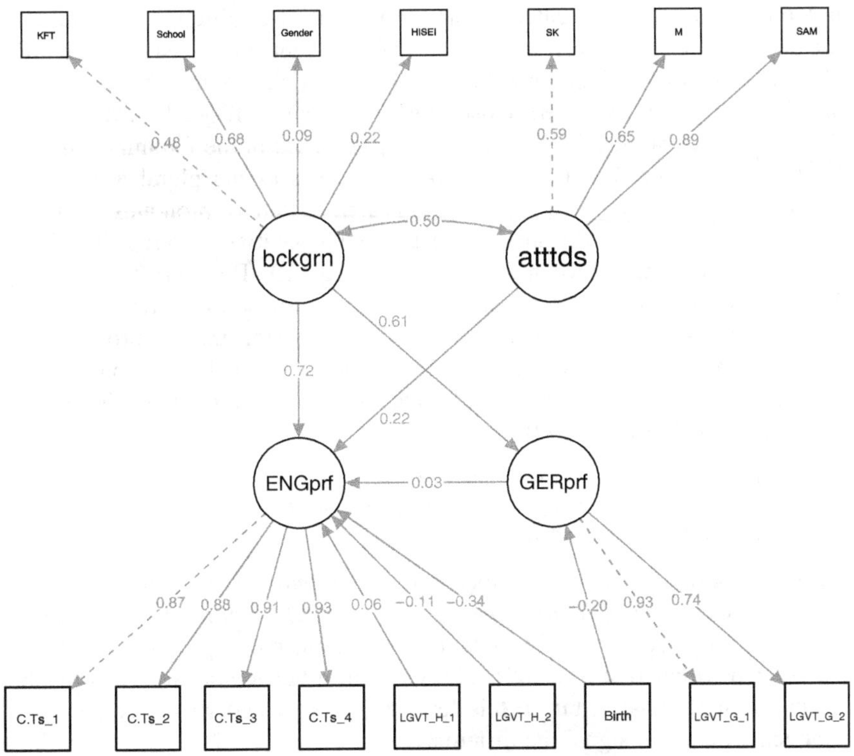

Figure 4.5 Structural equation model 2 to explain proficiency in English with standardized path coefficients (Lorenz, Toprak & Siemund 2022).
Note: KFT = cognitive ability subtest, HISEI = socio-economic status, SK = self-concept, M = motivation, SAM = self-assessment, bckgrn = background variables, atttds = attitudes, ENGprf = English proficiency, GERprf = German proficiency, C.Ts_1/2/3/4 = English C-Tests, LGVT_H_1 = heritage language reading comprehension, LGVT_H_2 = heritage language reading fluency, LGVT_G_1 = German reading comprehension, LGVT_G_2 = German reading fluency.

its grammatical inventory, additionally drawing distinctions between proximal and distal forms in the singular (*this* vs. *that*) and plural (*these* vs. *those*) demonstrative pronouns. Definite (*the*) and indefinite (*a*, *an*) articles do not exhibit further differentiations.

These distinctions give rise to important cross-linguistic parameters of variation, here briefly illustrated by German, English, Russian, Turkish, and Vietnamese. These languages serve as the empirical basis of the studies discussed below. Russian and Vietnamese do not encode definiteness and indefiniteness with dedicated expressions, but use different grammatical means (e.g. word order) to encode the relevant functional distinctions. Turkish possesses an indefinite, but no definite article. German boasts definite and indefinite articles superimposed by a (complicated) gender system. The definite articles are *der* in the masculine gender, *die* in the feminine, and *das* in the neuter. The feminine form *die* also serves as the plural article. The German articles can also be used as demonstrative pronouns and can express distance contrasts in combination with locative adverbs like 'here' and 'there' (German proximal *hier* and distal *da*). Russian, Turkish, and Vietnamese all possess demonstrative pronouns encoding different remoteness contrasts. The two main functions of demonstrative pronouns of relevance here are deictic (5a) and anaphoric (5b). In their anaphoric use, demonstrative pronouns can also refer back to situational entities (Huddleston & Pullum 2002: 1505–1509).

(5) a. This apple looks riper than that one.
  b. I raised some money by hocking the good clothes I had left, but when *that* was gone I didn't have a cent.

Furthermore, the English demonstrative form *that* is also used to introduce subordinate clauses (*He told me that he cannot come*). This function is historically related to the use of *that* as a demonstrative pronoun (Siemund, Schröter & Rahbari 2018: 385). The German article/demonstrative *das* also occurs as subordinator, but in this function, it is spelled with a double <s> grapheme (*dass*) to signal the difference.

Siemund and Lechner (2015) studied the use of English definite and indefinite articles in a sample of sixty students from two age groups (twelve and sixteen years of age) and four language backgrounds, namely German monolinguals as well as Russian–German, Turkish–German, and Vietnamese–German bilingual heritage speakers. They all acquired English in instructed settings in German schools. The cross-sectional data were gathered within the research cluster *Linguistic Diversity Management in Urban Areas* (Cluster of Excellence, 2009–2013). However, it was decided to exclude the Turkish–German bilingual students from specific grammatical analyses, as they differed too strongly from the other groups in terms of socio-economic status, educational background, and level of schooling (Siemund & Lechner 2015: 151).

The students produced spoken and written English in response to picture story stimuli. Figure 4.6 shows the realization of articles in their written productions. There are no differences across groups (in a statistically significant sense), even though Russian and Vietnamese do not possess articles. In other words, Russian and Vietnamese are not active, as otherwise – and due to interference – there would be lower rates of target-like article productions in the Russian and Vietnamese

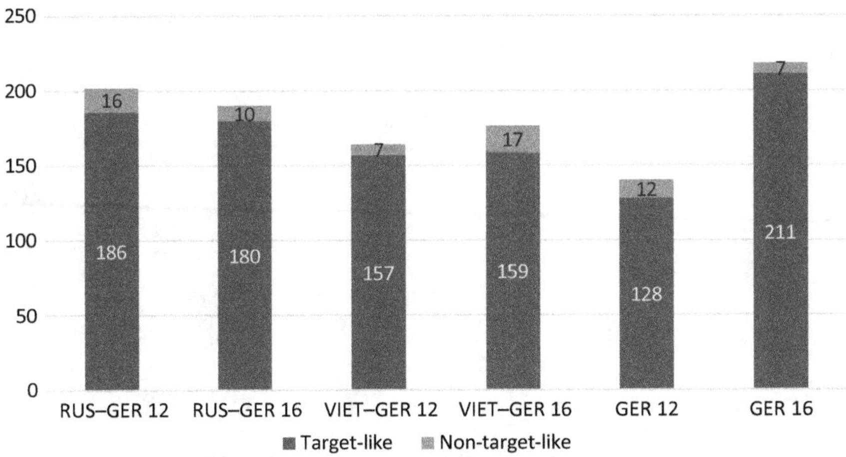

Figure 4.6 Absolute frequencies of article use (Siemund & Lechner 2015: 155).

groups in comparison to the German monolinguals.[29] It appears plausible that the acquisition process of English is facilitated by German, as its article system is very similar to that of English (see also Kupisch, Snape & Stangen 2013).

The results from this particular grammatical domain make clear that the bilinguals' knowledge of German facilitates the acquisition of the English article system. They are practically indistinguishable from the learners with a monolingual German background.

In a related and extended study based on 172 informants taken from the same data pool as the previous study, Siemund, Schröter and Rahbari (2018) explore the use of demonstrative pronouns in four learner groups. These are German monolinguals (*n*=40), Russian–German bilinguals (*n*=40), Turkish–German bilinguals (*n*=44), and Vietnamese–German bilinguals (*n*=48), again split across the two age groups of 12- and 16-year-olds. Both oral and written performance was assessed. The distribution of the forms *this* and *that* across the four learner groups can be gleaned from Figure 4.7, here restricted to the oral data.

The noteworthy difference in Figure 4.7 concerns the peaks in the Russian–German group in relation to the identifying (anaphoric) and subordinating function of *this*. Siemund, Schröter and Rahbari (2018: 398–399) argue that the overuse of *this* in the identifying function can be motivated by transfer from

[29] L1 Russian and L1 Turkish are known to influence article production in L2 English negatively (Ionin, Ko & Wexler 2004; Snape, García Mayo & Gürel 2013).

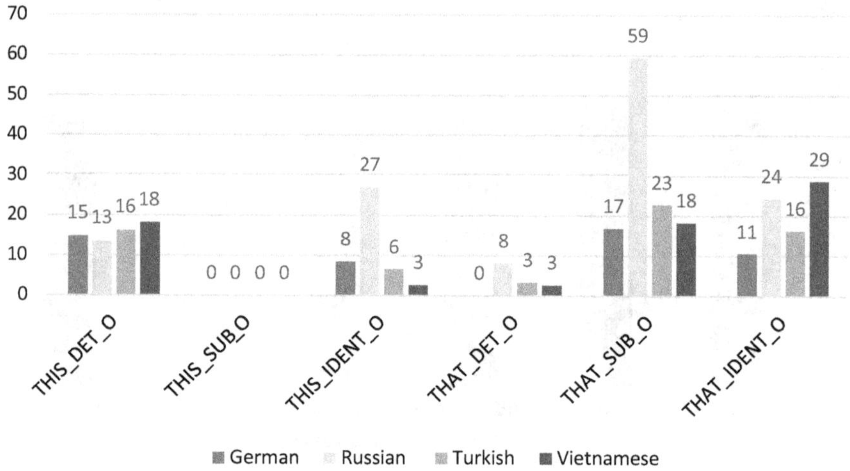

Figure 4.7 The distribution of *this* and *that* in the oral data in relation to background languages and function (Siemund, Schröter & Rahbari 2018: 395).
Note: DET = determinative, SUB = subordinating, IDENT = identifying.

Russian, since the simple personal pronouns of Russian are not available in this function and the demonstrative pronouns come to be used instead. The high ratio of subordinating uses in this group of bilinguals, in contrast, appears to be an indicator of their familiarity with academic language (qua hypotaxis).[30] As far as I can see, this particular grammatical domain in this specific language constellation eschews an interpretation in terms of multilingual learning advantages or disadvantages.

4.4.3 *Subject-Verb Agreement*

The study by Siemund and Lechner (2015) further explored the realization of English subject-verb agreement in the German monolingual as well as the Russian–German and Vietnamese–German student cohorts (as described above). Verbal agreement in English is rather exceptional from a cross-linguistic point of view inasmuch as it is only marked in the third person singular non-past with the exception of the verb *be* (Siemund 2013: Ch. 10). It represents a common learning problem for German students of English. German

[30] The Russian–German bilingual students produced the highest number of words in the written task, which can be taken as an indicator of high academic performance (Siemund, Schröter & Rahbari 2018: 397–398).

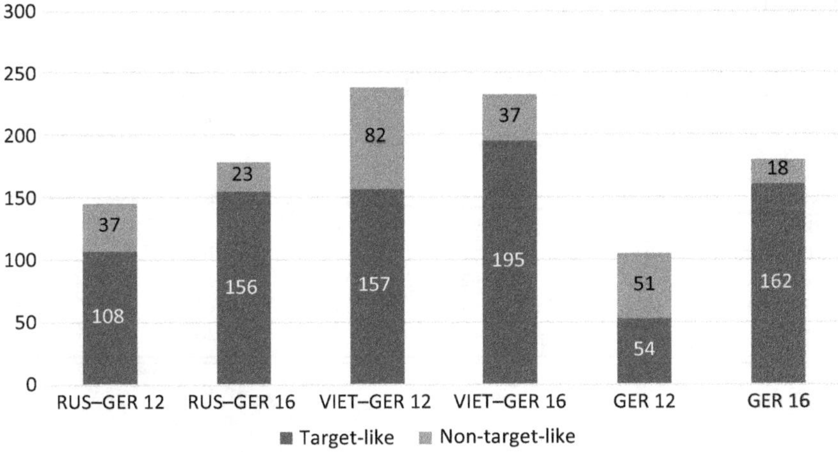

Figure 4.8 Absolute frequencies of subject-verb agreement (Siemund & Lechner 2015: 152).
Note: RUS–GER 12 versus GER 12: X-squared=13.19, df=1, p-value < .001; VIET–GER 12 versus GER 12: X-squared = 5.67, df=1, p-value=.017.

and Russian are synthetic languages possessing extensive verbal morphology (Russian more so than German), while Vietnamese is strongly isolating. Provided that the heritage languages influence the acquisition of subject-verb agreement in English, one could hypothesize advantages for the Russian–German and German monolingual learners, and certain disadvantages for the Vietnamese–German learners.

The results on subject-verb agreement displayed in Figure 4.8 do not confirm these expectations. The German monolingual group shows the lowest target-like realization in the younger cohort and performs significantly worse than the two bilingual groups. The younger Russian–German students turn out to be most target-like, followed by the younger Vietnamese–German group of learners. The non-target-like verb forms here include cases of lexical transfer.

With increasing age, the three cohorts become more similar. Testing for statistical significance reveals meaningful differences between the younger bilingual cohorts and the monolingual students. The differences are not statistically significant in the older cohorts, apparently due to similar learning progress. The results allow for the tentative conclusion that the younger bilingual groups can activate certain learning advantages, perhaps related to their bilingualism. We may recall that similar age-related effects are also reported in Maluch, Neumann and Kempert (2016: 115) and Hopp et al. (2019: 107). However, since Siemund and Lechner (2015) did not control for additional background variables, this conclusion can only be provisional.

Table 4.5. *The complete data set of Lorenz's study (2019: 199).*

Language group	12-year-old students	16-year-old students	Total
Russian–German	15	23	38
Turkish–German	20	21	41
Vietnamese–German	26	22	48
Russian monolingual	10	10	20
Turkish monolingual	7	5	12
Vietnamese monolingual	10	10	20
German monolingual	20	20	40
English native	15	15	30
Total	123	126	249

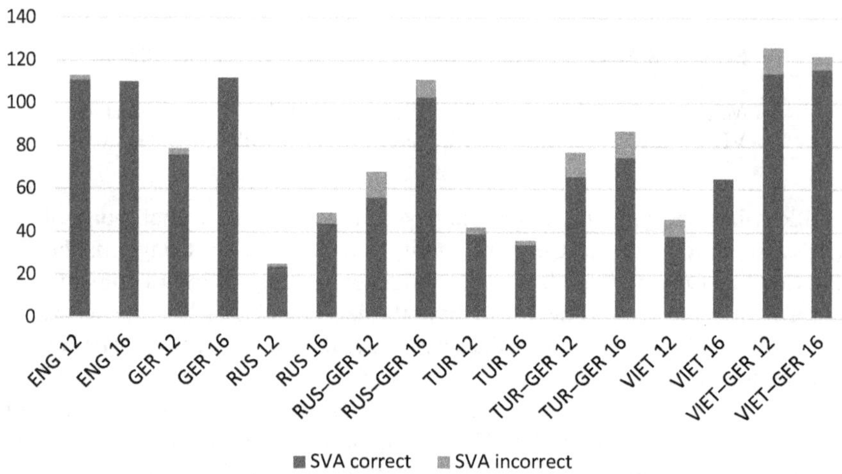

Figure 4.9 Subject-verb agreement of the verb *be* (Lorenz 2019: 231). Reproduced with permission.

Lorenz (2019) offers another assessment of subject-verb agreement of the previously discussed sample of students, but for her study she used the entire sample of 173 students that she additionally extended with monolingual native English and Vietnamese speakers. This augmented sample comprises 249 students, as detailed in Table 4.5.

Lorenz (2019) carefully distinguishes between occurrences of the verb *be*, as its paradigm is highly idiosyncratic, and other verbs that take the third person *s*-suffix regularly. Figure 4.9 shows that students do not generally encounter problems in learning the relevant forms of *be* and their usage.

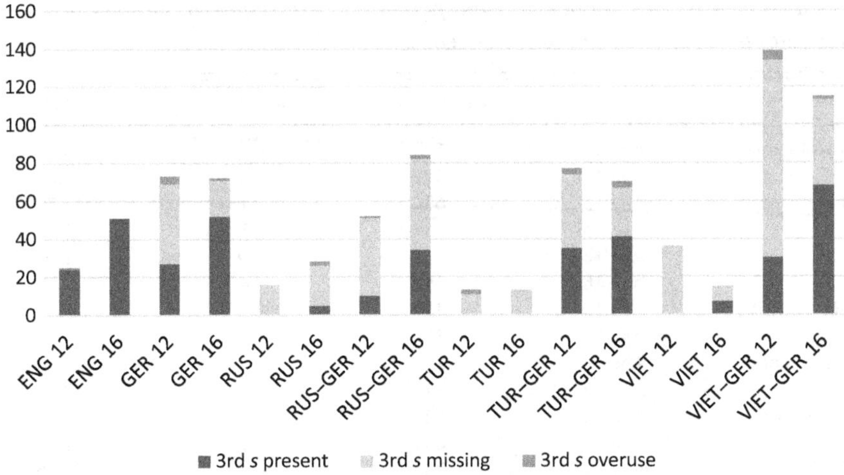

Figure 4.10 Presence/absence/overuse of 3rd person singular {-s} (Lorenz 2019: 231). Reproduced with permission.

The number of non-target-like forms is low, arguably due to the high frequency of these forms and the pedagogical effort dedicated to them. Linear regression modelling shows that Russian–German and Turkish–German group membership are the only significant predictors (Lorenz 2019: 235). They influence the target-like realization of *be* in a negative way.

The results for the other verbs look very different, as summarized in Figure 4.10. Non-target-like occurrences of verb forms are pervasive and can be encountered in all groups, except for the English native speakers. The younger cohorts generally exhibit higher ratios of non-target-like occurrences.

Figure 4.10 furthermore shows that most non-target-like occurrences are due to missing *s*-suffixes and not their overuse. Such overgeneralizations appear more prominent in the younger age cohorts. A linear regression model reveals that age as well as group membership in the English, Russian, Turkish, and Vietnamese monolingual groups are amongst the strongest predictors of third person *s*-suffix omission ratios (Lorenz 2019: 234). Needless to say, the direction of influence in the case of the English monolingual group is the opposite to that found in the other groups. Membership in the Russian–German bilingual group influences the realization of target-like forms negatively.[31]

[31] Overuse of subject-verb agreement can be illustrated as follows: *The Father will this Fish cuts.* (TUR-GER 12); *Son and Father goes at home and son looks in the bucket with the Fish.* (TUR-GER 16), both taken from Lorenz (2019: 231).

Table 4.6. *Absolute frequencies and percentages of required and missing copulative verbs (adapted from Lorenz 2019: 239).*

		Required *be*	Absent *be*	% of absent
ENG mono	Age 12	60	0	0.00
	Age 16	47	0	0.00
GER mono	Age 12	63	1	1.59
	Age 16	68	1	1.47
RUS mono	Age 12	32	10	31.25
	Age 16	35	8	22.86
RUS–GER	Age 12	47	0	0.00
	Age 16	85	1	1.18
TUR mono	Age 12	32	8	25.00
	Age 16	24	3	12.50
TUR–GER	Age 12	52	0	0.00
	Age 16	60	1	1.67
VIET mono	Age 12	22	8	36.36
	Age 16	38	1	2.63
VIET–GER	Age 12	84	1	1.19
	Age 16	72	0	0.00
Total		821	43	5.24

The numbers in Figure 4.10 display an age-related increase in target-like forms, but it appears impossible to diagnose learning advantages for the bilingual groups. This once again underlines the importance of cohort composition as well as influence of the actual analysis on all such putative effects.

In relation to the verb *be*, Lorenz (2019: 234) furthermore considered its realization as a copulative verb across the different learner groups. Much like the use of articles for the expression of definiteness, the occurrence of copulative verbs is an established cross-linguistic parameter of variation. Russian, Turkish, and Vietnamese count amongst the languages without copulas, whereas German and English use 'be' as a copulative verb. Accordingly, monolingual learners of English with a Russian, Turkish, or Vietnamese background can be expected to show substantial interference effects in this domain of grammar.[32] Table 4.6 confirms these expectations, especially for the younger age groups where the differences are statistically significant throughout.

Interestingly, the bilingual groups behave like the German monolinguals with regard to the acquisition of this grammatical parameter. Apparently, they experience facilitation from German rather than interference from Russian,

[32] Typical examples include *They Ø very happy* and *Fish Ø in net* produced by a 12-year-old and a 16-year-old Russian monolingual student, respectively (Lorenz 2019: 239).

Turkish, or Vietnamese. This could be considered a bilingual learning advantage qua cumulative enhancement. Again, the perspective matters, as this bilingual learning advantage holds in relation to Russian, Turkish, and Vietnamese monolingual learners, but not in comparison to learners with a German monolingual background.

4.4.4 Tense and Aspect

The above sample of 249 monolingual and bilingual students studying English, as used by Lorenz (2019), also offers important insights into the development of tense and aspect. As far as aspectual distinctions are concerned, the background languages Russian and Turkish grammatically encode an opposition between perfective and imperfective using verbal morphology. The largely fusional language Russian possesses semi-systematic pairs of verbs encoding this aspectual distinction, differentiated by both prefixes and suffixes (*chitat'* 'read' imperfective; *prochitat'* 'read' perfective). Turkish is an agglutinating language with the suffix *-(I)yor* expressing the imperfective aspect. In both languages, the imperfective aspect includes uses as a progressive. German lacks grammatical aspect, but adverbs (and other means of expression) can be used to signal ongoing situations. As an isolating language, Vietnamese does not mark grammatical distinctions morphologically. Progressiveness can be expressed using the non-obligatory element *đang*. The target language English periphrastically encodes a contrast between progressive and non-progressive situations in all tenses, with speakers needing to decide for each utterance whether it is to be portrayed as ongoing/unbounded or bounded/habitual. The English progressive aspect yields different interpretations depending on the tense used and in combination with verbs encoding aktionsarten such as states, activities, accomplishments, and achievements (Vendler 1957). It represents a well-known learning problem that especially students with a German background find difficult to master.[33]

In her analysis of the progressive aspect, Lorenz (2019) distinguishes carefully between formal correctness (accuracy) and semantic adequacy in the analysis of the English acquisition data. In other words, she assessed separately whether the periphrastic construction of *be* + *-ing* was produced accurately and whether the use of the progressive aspect – independently of its formal correctness – matched the necessary contextual requirements.

[33] This learning situation nicely illustrates a learning problem that corresponds to the most complex scenario on the hierarchy of difficulty proposed in Stockwell, Bowen and Martin (1965: Ch. 11). The language to be acquired contains an obligatory category that the first language lacks (see Chapter 3).

Table 4.7. *Formal correctness, target-like usage, and absence of auxiliary (adapted from Lorenz 2019: 255).*

Language group		Form correct		Meaning target-like		Auxiliary missing	
		Abs. freq.	%	Abs. freq.	%	Abs. freq.	%
ENG	Age 12	19	95.00	19	95.00	–	0.00
	Age 16	34	91.89	37	100.00	2	5.41
GER	Age 12	8	42.11	17	89.47	11	57.89
	Age 16	25	62.50	33	82.50	8	20.00
RUS	Age 12	2	33.33	6	100.00	4	66.67
	Age 16	11	50.00	21	95.45	8	36.36
RUS–GER	Age 12	8	44.44	14	77.78	8	44.44
	Age 16	10	52.63	18	94.74	8	42.11
TUR	Age 12	6	46.15	13	100.00	7	53.85
	Age 16	5	100.00	5	100.00	–	0.00
TUR–GER	Age 12	8	40.00	15	75.00	12	60.00
	Age 16	13	40.63	27	84.38	16	50.00
VIET	Age 12	7	43.75	14	87.50	6	37.50
	Age 16	7	53.85	12	92.31	1	7.69
VIET–GER	Age 12	18	52.94	30	88.24	14	41.18
	Age 16	31	73.81	37	88.10	7	16.67
Total		212		318		112	

Interestingly enough, the analysis reveals that monolingual Russian and Turkish learners of English achieved nearly complete target-like realizations of the progressive aspect in relation to meaning (no non-target-like realizations), although their performance is comparatively low when considering formal accuracy of the progressive.[34] Russian–German and Turkish–German bilinguals, in contrast, behave like monolingual German learners both in terms of formal and functional correctness. These findings are summarized in Table 4.7. Not surprisingly, the native speakers of English scored highest in terms of accuracy, both regarding form and meaning.

Figure 4.11 displays the proportions of formal accuracy in the realization of the English progressive aspect as a function of the different student cohorts. With the exception of the English native speakers, we can see a general increase in formal accuracy from the younger to the older cohorts. Given the instructed learning context, this increase is certainly expected.

[34] It needs to be mentioned, though, that the absolute numbers are relatively low.

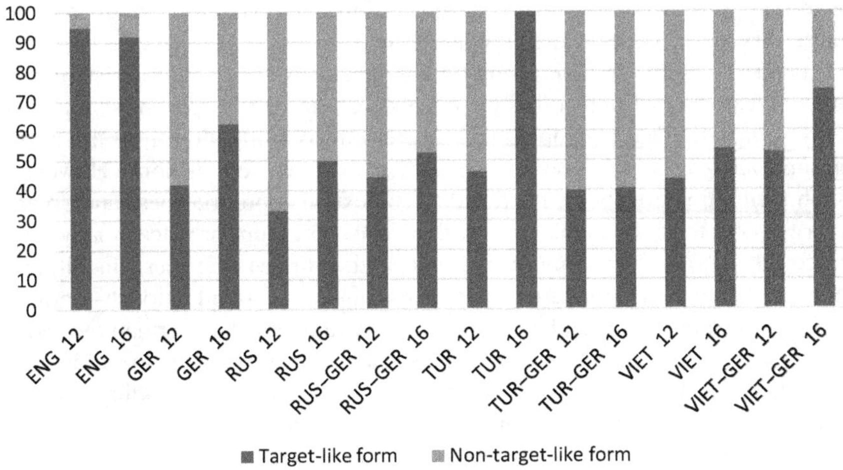

Figure 4.11 Target-like form versus non-target-like form of progressives (proportions).
Adapted from Lorenz (2019: 256). Reproduced with permission.

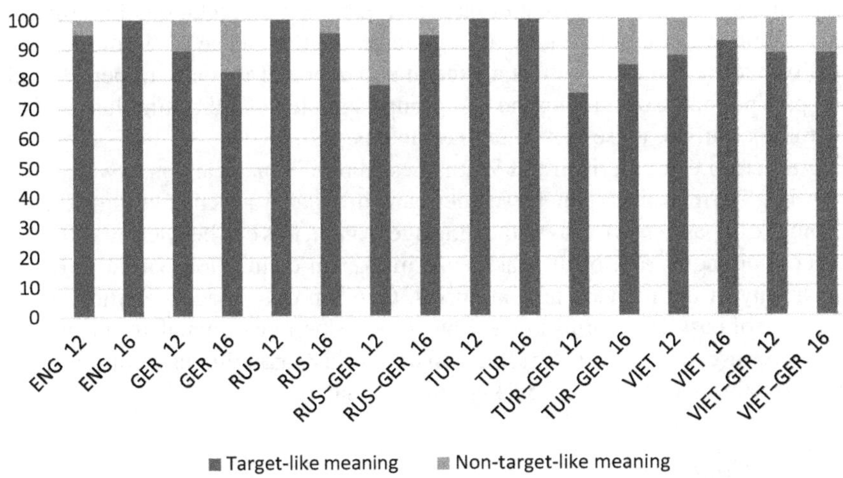

Figure 4.12 Target-like meaning versus non-target-like meaning of progressives (proportions).
Adapted from Lorenz (2019: 256). Reproduced with permission.

The corresponding graphic representation for functional accuracy can be found in Figure 4.12, depicting target-like meanings in relation to non-target-like meanings across the different cohorts of speakers. There is no unanimous learning progress observable with increasing age, but the average rate of target-like occurrences is much higher than in Figure 4.11.[35]

It appears like a very interesting finding that the Russian and Turkish monolingual learners of English find the contexts of the English progressive aspect easy to master. One is tempted to interpret this as facilitation from the background languages, as these encode similar aspectual oppositions. However, such facilitation effects are restricted to contextual appropriateness and do not carry over to formal accuracy, where these speaker groups produced many non-target-like forms. Furthermore, it is interesting to see that these facilitation effects cannot be encountered in the Russian–German and Turkish–German bilingual groups. This can be interpreted in such a way that German overrides any potentially facilitating effects of Russian and Turkish. Here, the additional knowledge of German appears to result in inhibition. These findings do not support the idea of cumulative enhancement and show that bilingualism cannot generally be considered an advantage. This lends further support to the argument made earlier that advantages related to bi-/multilingualism are contingent on specific conditions. Moreover, general proficiencies need to be considered separately from cross-linguistic influence in specific grammatical domains.

This cautious perspective leads over to the grammatical domain of tense marking where the learner data practically eschew interpretations in terms of facilitation or inhibition. Figure 4.13 indicates a prominence of simple present and past tense forms as well as a general avoidance of the present perfect and the past perfect. Considering the age groups sampled and the stimulus used (a picture narrative), these results are not unexpected.

Furthermore, the German and Vietnamese monolingual learners as well as the Russian–German and Vietnamese–German bilingual groups display an increase in the use of past tense forms with rising age. Again, this can be interpreted as the successful acquisition of the past tense marker in connection with a growing sensitivity of the relevant textual norms. One can only speculate whether the high use of past tense forms in the younger Russian monolingual group and the exclusive use of simple present forms in the Turkish monolingual groups can be related to influence from the background languages.

4.4.5 *Word Order*

The influence of the background languages on the acquisition of English in bilingual heritage contexts has also been explored in relation to word order.

[35] An example of a non-target-like form is the following: *The man and child walking*, written by a Turkish monolingual student. The next example illustrates a correct form used in an inadequate context: *They were feeling very good [. . .]* and was produced by a Russian–German student (Lorenz 2019: 254).

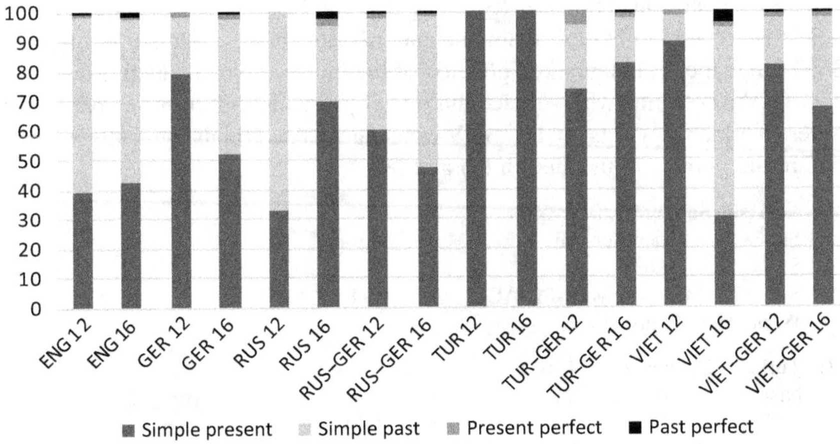

Figure 4.13 Tense overview (proportions): simple present/past, present/past perfect.
Adapted from Lorenz (2019: 275). Reproduced with permission.

This section considers the order of the basic constituents (subject, object, verb) and furthermore discusses the patterning of pronominal objects in double object constructions.

As for the basic order of constituents, Şahingöz (2014) searched for influences of the background languages Turkish and German in the English productions of bilingual students culled from secondary schools (*Gymnasium*) in and around the city of Hamburg, Germany (see also Sağın-Şimşek 2005; Siemund 2022). The corpus was compiled from elicited written and spoken utterances sampling twenty-six Turkish–German bilingual students around the age of sixteen. This student cohort was flanked by two control groups, namely twenty-six German monolingual students and eighteen Russian–German heritage speakers. The study did not control for social background variables, but all participants were recruited from the same school type.

German, Turkish, and English crucially differ in regard to the basic order of constituents. German belongs to the cross-linguistically rare type of verb-second languages that, however, places the verb in clause-final position in embedded clauses. This is illustrated in (6).

(6) German
a. Hastig aß Paul seine Suppe mit dem Löffel.
hastily ate Paul his soup with the spoon
'Hastily Paul ate his soup with the spoon.'
b. weil Paul seine Suppe hastig mit dem Löffel aß.
because Paul his soup hastily with the spoon ate
'because Paul ate his soup hastily with the spoon.'

The English translations in (6) show that the basic order of subject-verb-object is adhered to in both main and subordinate clauses. English is a typical SVO-language. The unmarked position of the finite verb in Turkish is the right edge of the sentence with subject and object placed before it in this particular order. Turkish belongs to the SOV-languages. Adverbials typically appear before the verb, as illustrated in (7) and (8).[36]

(7) Turkish (Şahingöz 2014: 53)

Soner	ders-ler-i-ni	yap-tı.
SBJ	OBJ	V
Soner.NOM	homework-PL-ACC-POSS	do.PST.3SG

'Soner did his homework.'

(8) Turkish (Şahingöz 2014: 63)

Nisa	ders-ler-i-ni	hızlı	yap-ıyor.
SBJ	OBJ	ADV	V
Nisa.NOM	homework-PL-ACC-POSS	quickly	do-PRS.3SG

'Nisa does her homework quickly.'

Şahingöz (2014: 120) reports that the Turkish–German bilingual students produced utterances that are in principle compatible with the word order patterns of Turkish and German. For instance, the non-target-like pattern shown in (9) mirrors the word order of both background languages, when compared to examples (10) and (11). Such patterns can be interpreted in terms of interference from both Turkish and German or inhibitory reinforcement. However, in view of the obvious parallels between examples (9) and (10), influence from German appears the least costly assumption.[37]

(9) I spoke with my friends German [. . .] (Turkish–German student)

(10) German

Ich	sprach	mit meinen Freunden	Deutsch.
I	spoke	with my friends	German

'I spoke German with my friends.'

(11) Turkish

Ben	arkadaş-lar-ım-la	Almanca	konuş-t-um
I	friend-PL-POSS-DAT	German	speak-PST-1SG

'I spoke German with my friends.'

Similar results surface in the analysis of the placement of adverbials, where non-target-like realizations like (12) are common (Şahingöz 2014: 125). Here again, one can establish parallels in both Turkish and German, as illustrated in

[36] The following abbreviations are used in examples (7) and (8): 3 = third person; ACC = accusative; NOM = nominative; OBJ = object; PL = plural; POSS = possessive; PST = past tense; SG = singular; SBJ = subject; V = verb.

[37] Example (11) contains the following abbreviations: 1 = first person; DAT = dative; PL = plural; POSS = possessive; PST = past tense; SG = singular.

(13) and (14). However, since (12) is practically a congruent translation from German, the assumption of influence from this language appears the most convincing interpretation.[38]

(12) my mother spoke most of the times Turkish [. . .] (Turkish–German student)

(13) German

Meine Mutter	sprach	die meiste Zeit	Türkisch.
my mother	spoke	most of the time	Turkish

'My mother spoke Turkish most of the time.'

(14) Turkish

Anne-m	çoğu zaman	Türkçe	konuş-ur-du
mother-POSS.1SG	most of the time	Turkish	speak-AOR-PST

'My mother spoke Turkish most of the time.'

Although for the above learner productions influence from both Turkish and German can be plausibly reconstructed, examples like (15) below tip the balance into the direction of the majority language German (Şahingöz 2014: 134). This example manifests verb-second word order that finds no equivalent in Turkish, only in German.

(15) In the town where i live are many afghan people [. . .] (Turkish–German student)

Şahingöz (2014: 140–143) further points out that the Turkish–German students produced considerably more non-target-like utterances in comparison to their monolingual peers. Their English skills as measured by C-tests are generally lower, which may be due to uncontrolled for language external factors (Şahingöz 2014: 110). In the written productions of the Turkish–German group, Şahingöz (2014: 140–142) establishes an error index of 2.90 – measured in terms of transfer-induced word order deviations per 1,000 characters. The corresponding error index for the German monolingual group is 1.08. In the spoken productions, the error indices are 3.32 for the bilingual and 1.89 for the monolingual students. Most of the non-target-like realizations concern the placement of adverbials and verb-second word order. The relative share of these non-target-like realizations does not differ across the two groups, further strengthening the hypothesis of influence mainly coming from German. What is also interesting is that the Russian–German group of heritage speakers behaves more or less like the Turkish–German cohort in regard to non-target-like word order patterns. Accordingly, Şahingöz (2014: 185–186) concludes that her study cannot attest qualitative differences in the realization of non-target-like word order patterns depending on language background. In other words, monolingual and bilingual learners of English are by and large indistinguishable in relation to cross-linguistic influence.

[38] The abbreviations used in example (14) are: 1 = first person; AOR = aorist; POSS = possessive; PST = past tense; SG = singular.

Let us now turn to the relative order of pronominal objects in double object constructions, as examined by Lorenz et al. (2019). The study is based on 195 participants in 2 age groups (school years seven and nine) differentiated into 3 learner cohorts, namely German monolinguals (*n*=111), Russian–German (*n*=49) as well as Turkish–German (*n*=35) bilingual heritage speakers. A total of 85 participants are in school year seven; 110 in school year nine. They acquire English as an L2 or L3, respectively. The study focuses on the acquisition of the pronominal object patterns shown in (16).[39]

(16) a. She sold me it. (IO>DO)
b. She sold it to me. (prepositional DO>IO)
c. She sold it me. (DO>IO)

Example (16a) is known as the canonical double object construction, while (16b) represents the prepositional construction (see Siemund 2013: Ch. 11). Moreover, there is a dialectal variant of (16a) in which the order of direct and indirect object is reversed (16c) – known as the alternative double object construction (Gast 2007). The study uses a sentence assembly task during which subjects have to construct grammatical sentences from randomly ordered arrays of words (*sell – me – she – it*).[40] The background languages have different preferences for ordering pronominal objects that can be exploited to diagnose influence from the background languages on English. The dominant patterns in German, Russian, and Turkish are exemplified in (17) – (19), but there is substantial language internal variation (Lorenz et al. 2019: 1416).[41] These dominant patterns were confirmed in an online word order test with seventy-five native speakers of German, Russian, Turkish, and English.

(17) German (Lorenz et al. 2019: 1417)

Ich	gab	es	ihnen	gestern.
1SG	give.1SG.PST	3SG.N	3PL.DAT	yesterday.

'I gave it to them yesterday.'

(18) Russian (Lorenz et al. 2019: 1417)

Ona	proda-ët	mne	ėto.
3SG.F	sell-3SG.PRS	3SG.DAT	DEM.SG.N

'She sells me it.'

(19) Turkish (Lorenz et al. 2019: 1417)

O	bu-nu	bana	gönder-iyor.
3SG	DEM-ACC	1SG.DAT	send-3SG.PRS

'He sends it to me.'

[39] The abbreviations are as follows: DO = direct object; IO = indirect object.

[40] The following five patterns were used for the elicitation task: *sell – me – she – it*; *them – yesterday – give – it – I*; *it – he – me – give*; *send – it – he – me*; *us – it – they – buy – yesterday* (Lorenz et al. 2019: 1415).

[41] Examples (17) – (19) contain the following abbreviations: 1 = first person; 3 = third person; ACC = accusative; DAT = dative; DEM = demonstrative; F = feminine; N = neuter; PL = plural; PRS = present tense; PST = past tense; SG = singular.

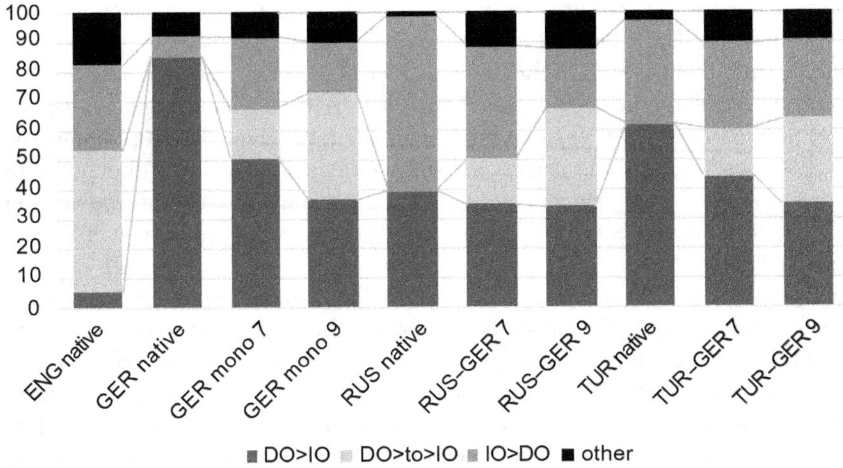

Figure 4.14 Monolingual and bilingual students in comparison with native speakers' responses (proportions).
Adapted from Lorenz et al. (2019: 1419).

The study reports influence from all background languages on English that is especially prominent in the case of Russian. Both English and Russian position the indirect object before the direct one in double object constructions. Apparently, the Russian–German students experience this as facilitation in the acquisition of English. In contrast, the students with a German monolingual background as well as the Turkish–German heritage bilinguals face inhibitory effects. All learner groups progress towards the English native patterns from school year seven to school year nine. Figure 4.14 provides an overview of all responses.

Even though influence from all background languages on English is in principle possible, Lorenz et al. (2019: 1425–1426) conclude that the majority language German, due to its privileged status in society and the education system, exerts a disproportionately strong influence. In this respect, the results from this study match the findings from the studies surveyed previously. In addition, the authors draw attention to the importance of frequency effects, as some combinations of pronouns in double object constructions are vastly more frequent than others (for example *me it* vs. *us it*; Lorenz et al. 2019: 1425). These frequency differences, in turn, have repercussions on the observable cross-linguistic influence.

4.4.6 *Lexical Cross-Linguistic Influence*

Especially during the initial stages of acquisition, learners of additional languages produce substantial lexical transfer. This can hardly come as a surprise, since the learners' vocabularies in the newly acquired language are still small and lexical transfer can hence be analyzed as a strategy to increase their expressive power. Foreign language teaching tends to frown upon lexical transfer, as the reigning pedagogical ideology dictates a monolingual development targeting native speaker models and norms (Fuller 2020; Malabarba 2019). Language mixing carries the stigma of incompetence. Although there are several studies on lexical transfer in third language acquisition (see Section 4.3.2), this phenomenon has hardly been addressed in relation to bilingual heritage contexts.

Lexical transfer as a special type of cross-linguistic influence has been made the subject of enquiry in the study by Lorenz, Hasai and Siemund (2021). The authors analyzed the written productions of altogether sixty monolingual German (n=20) as well as Russian–German (n=20) and Turkish–German (n=20) bilingual heritage learners of English in the German school system. The longitudinal study followed the students over a period of two years and collected data at four measuring points. A total of 240 texts was thus collected and scrutinized for instances of lexical transfer. The students were in school year seven (age 12/13) at the beginning of data collection. Lexical transfer is related to various additional parameters, like gender, school type, socio-economic status, proficiency in English, as well as attitudinal variables.[42]

The analysis distinguishes between types and tokens of lexical transfer, there being 1,553 tokens and 1,295 types altogether. Lexical transfer proper is categorized as either form-based or meaning-based, with additional parameters capturing loan translations, false and real cognates, as well as morphological and orthographic integration. Crucially, form-based and meaning-based transfer can occur concurrently. Table 4.8 provides a summary of the descriptive statistics.

There is an expectable decrease in the means of types and tokens over time (not strictly monotonic). German proves to be the main source language underlying lexical transfer. There are also instances due to cross-linguistic influence from Russian, but hardly any cases that could be related to Turkish (n=6 or 1.6 per cent). German accounts for 77.1 per cent of lexical transfer types in the Russian–German group, and for 91.0 per cent in the Turkish–German group. Figure 4.15 summarizes the details in relation to lexical transfer types, aggregated across the four measuring points (T1–T4). The hybrid categories capture cases where lexical transfer can be attributed to either language (e.g. Russian or German). These amount to 22.29 per cent in

[42] The data were collected within the project *Multilingual Development: A Longitudinal Perspective*, University of Hamburg, 2014–2019; www.mez.uni-hamburg.de. See also Section 4.4.1.

Table 4.8. *Frequency overview (absolute frequency, mean frequency per 100 words) of lexical transfer types and tokens per language group. Adapted from Lorenz, Hasai and Siemund (2021: 801).*

		German monolingual		Russian–German bilingual		Turkish–German bilingual		Total	
		Types	Tokens	Types	Tokens	Types	Tokens	Types	Tokens
T 1	Absolute	121	145	139	161	119	142	379	448
	Mean per 100	5.31	6.33	6.33	7.32	4.44	5.31	5.33	6.28
T 2	Absolute	94	120	129	169	100	131	323	420
	Mean per 100	4.03	5.10	6.39	8.22	4.40	5.66	4.93	6.31
T 3	Absolute	112	126	125	146	80	88	317	360
	Mean per 100	4.34	4.81	4.54	5.32	3.12	3.41	3.99	4.50
T 4	Absolute	83	97	105	129	88	99	276	325
	Mean per 100	3.53	4.06	4.46	5.40	3.60	3.99	3.86	4.48
All	Absolute	410	488	498	605	387	460	1,295	1,553
	Mean per 100	4.26	5.01	5.40	6.53	3.89	4.59	4.51	5.36

Note: T1–T4 refer to the four measuring points of this longitudinal study.

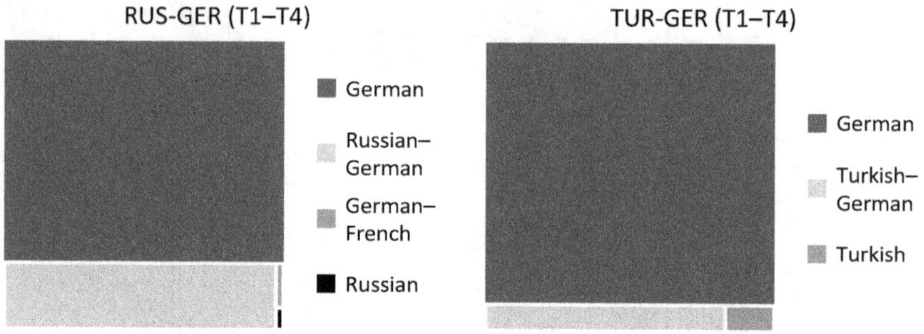

Figure 4.15 Source language of lexical transfer types of the Russian–German and Turkish–German bilingual students, in per cent.
Adapted from Lorenz, Hasai and Siemund (2021: 802).

the Russian–German group, and 7.49 per cent in the Turkish–German group. Two cases produced by the Russian–German group can be attributed to influence from German or French.

The authors explain these findings with the dominant status of German and the closer typological proximity between Russian, German, and English in comparison to Turkish. The Turkish–German group produced the lowest token ratios in three out of the four measuring points. It stands to reason that this particular learner group possesses exceptionally high levels of awareness for lexical transfer due to widespread code-switching in the Turkish–German community. A multiple regression analysis reveals the statistically significant negative impact that proficiency in English, belonging to the Turkish–German group of students, socio-economic status, and the four measuring points have on lexical transfer.

4.4.7 *Summary*

The preceding sections focused the discussion of multilingual learning advantages on the specific context of bilingual heritage speakers acquiring English as an additional language, especially in Germany. This context witnesses a dominance of the majority language due to its prominent status in society, high social prestige, and its role as the language of instruction in the education system. Heritage speakers are typically unbalanced bilinguals with the heritage language not infrequently being restricted to the spoken domain and the home context. Moreover, in the host countries, the social value of the heritage languages does not usually extend beyond the immediate communities speaking them.

The assessment of research on heritage bilinguals has demonstrated that a previous multilingual experience does not produce consistent proficiency gains when acquiring additional languages. Moreover, the consideration of general language proficiencies, on the one hand, and specific grammatical knowledge, on the other, produces different results. There is both inhibitory and enhancing cross-linguistic influence, but potentially enhancing cross-linguistic influence from the heritage languages is typically suppressed as a result of the dominant status of the majority language. Crucially, the majority language accounts for the lion's share of observable cross-linguistic influence. As argued earlier, the assumption of cumulative enhancement represents an overly optimistic scenario.[43]

The situation remains controversial, as research results are influenced by a host of factors. Besides type of bilingualism and the type of language knowledge investigated, the various heritage communities do not behave alike. This could be due to the different languages involved, but also perhaps cultural differences. Knowledge of different writing systems may be a further factor (see Usanova 2019). The studies discussed here were all conducted in the educational context. It is to be expected that the home or family context produces diverging results (see also Hirosh & Degani 2018: 899). Finally, there are indications that younger heritage learners can profit to a greater extent from their multilingual upbringing than older learners. To the extent that such findings replicate, current language pedagogies need to be reconsidered. This will be the topic of the next section.

4.5 Language Pedagogies

The tentative bottom line of the preceding sections is that type of bilingualism (balanced vs. unbalanced) and type of language knowledge (general proficiencies vs. specific grammatical and lexical knowledge) are useful predictors for the success of learning additional languages against prior multilingual experience. Balanced bilingualism can be associated with certain learning advantages especially in relation to general proficiencies, plausibly owing to heightened metalinguistic awareness. Grammatical and lexical cross-linguistic influence can be enhancing or inhibitory depending on the actual language constellation. As far as the specific case of heritage bilingualism is concerned, age as well as influence from the majority language have proved crucial. Grammatical and lexical cross-linguistic influence primarily originates in the (dominant) majority language, and especially so for older students. I consider the interplay

[43] Brehmer, Steinbach and Arifulin (2021), in the context of bilingual Polish–German and Russian–German heritage speakers, recently studied the interlingual correspondence recognition abilities in relation to a monolingual German control group. The bilingual groups did not show superior performance.

of these factors plausible, as younger heritage students can on average be assumed to be the more balanced bilinguals in comparison to their peers in the upper grades for whom the majority language has developed into their dominant language.

It appears as if learning advantages emanating from prior multilingual experience can materialize as long as the background languages remain equally active. If one language is promoted while the other background languages fall into disuse,[44] multilingual learners come to be indistinguishable from monolingual learners. To use an analogy, if I play several musical instruments, learning speed and success in another one will at least partially be a function of my activeness in my current instruments – the more so if they all belong to the same genetic group, that is, string instruments or brass instruments. Learning to play the viola against the background of playing the violin and the cello seems like learning Norwegian in the context of already speaking Danish and Swedish. Moreover, staying active in all these instruments is likely to offer mutual support, although one can plausibly also expect a certain amount of interference.

4.5.1 *Monolingual Pedagogies*

The languages in one's multilingual repertoire provide support for one another rather than producing conflict and friction. However, in spite of convincing evidence to the contrary, the language learning environments widely encountered in present secondary and tertiary education (still) manifest a strong monolingual orientation inasmuch as other languages besides the actual target language need to be inhibited. This is known as the "monolingual principle," as discussed in Cummins (2007: 223).[45] In the English foreign language classroom in Germany, for instance, the use of German and other languages carries the stigma of incompetence and everybody strives to avoid it (Fuller 2020: 173). The apparent assumption is that other languages would interfere with the acquisition of English and that spending time on these languages or just allowing them in would waste valuable classroom time that would better be devoted to English. (See Malabarba 2019: 244–246 for a reconstruction of

[44] Disuse does not mean language loss. Nevertheless, it is not untypical in bilingual heritage contexts that the heritage language becomes less active over time and dominated by the majority language. I wish to emphasize that the yardstick against which language proficiency – and hence dominance – is measured commonly relates to academic written language. It must not be confused with general language ability (see Chapter 2).

[45] The monolingual principle "emphasizes instructional use of the target language (TL) to the exclusion of students' L1, with the goal of enabling learners to think in the TL with minimal interference from L1" (Cummins 2007: 223). In fact, Cummins (2007: 223) attributes the formulation of this principle to Howatt (1984).

this philosophy as Krashen's 1985 legacy.) Especially for bilingual heritage speakers, however, German can be a very useful bridging language assisting the acquisition of English. Language teaching pedagogies enforcing such a monolingual environment prioritize a time-on-task approach and force students into a monolingual mode of thinking (Berthele & Vanhove 2020: 553; Piller 2016: 99–103). There is a growing suspicion in the field that crucial language learning resources are squandered this way.

Students in a monolingual language classroom experience extensive normative pressure and the general situation can hardly be understood without taking into consideration decades of monolingual habituation in the context of forging the European nation states out of a complex mosaic of feudal centres all speaking their own dialects and languages (Gogolin 2008, 2020; see also Chapter 1). Surprisingly, this monolingual conditioning happens in a linguistic habitat where the majority language German – and other majority languages in other countries for that matter – experiences heavy lexical and partially other influences from the global language English and people happily code-switch from German, Dutch, Swedish, Italian, and many other languages into English in their conversations. Apparently, the monolingual orientation is heavily context-dependent with especially strong forces being at play in the education system.[46] School curricula by virtue of naming and identifying specific languages and language classes impose walls that are difficult to penetrate.

Primary and secondary school teachers of English play an important role in perpetuating the monolingual orientation in language education. Typically being raised in the country where they teach English and being native speakers of the language of that country, they are expected to serve as near-native role models for their students. Consequently, they experience extensive pressure and will try as much as they can to fulfil these expectations. One strategy, amongst others, is to behave like a monolingual English native speaker and avoid the use of other languages. Studies investigating teachers' beliefs and classroom practices tend to reveal a persistent monolingual orientation in the classroom in spite of generally positive attitudes towards language diversity and multilingualism (Gorter & Arocena 2020: 3–5; Haukås 2016; Woll 2020: 1). In addition, it appears that teachers remain strongly committed to using the target language only in class so as to ensure a maximum of exposure and opportunity to use that language. Using other languages is expected to remain the exception, discounting perhaps primary education.

As far as English tertiary language education is concerned, as in English university language classes, the problem is aggravated by the fact that the native instructors of English are typically recruited from inner circle countries

[46] Interestingly, speakers adapt to these contextual requirements. At some level, they must be aware of them.

dominated by widespread monolingualism. More often than not, they only speak English. As students in expanding circle countries are habitualized into striving for native speaker norms and to talk to native English speakers as much as possible, native instructors of English develop little incentive to learn the language of the country where they teach.[47] Moreover, since the English language represents a global business of considerable magnitude, there may even be resentment to watering it down, so to speak, with other languages, even though this could benefit the learner in developing their communicative competence. Evidently, such observations tie in with issues of language policy and planning as well as the use of English as a world language. These will be the topics of Chapters 5 and 6.

Crucially, advantages of multilingualism principally available may remain inaccessible due to didactic approaches that had been designed for monolingual students (Bonnet & Siemund 2018a; Cenoz & Gorter 2017; Hopp et al. 2020; Hu 2018; Melo-Pfeifer 2018). Traditional monolingual didactics falls short of taking into consideration multilingual classrooms and students with heterogeneous backgrounds. Cross-linguistic influence and interaction tend to be suppressed. Languages other than the target language are silenced. Crucial resources remain unused. Norton (2018: 245) states that "the extent to which teachers are able to recognize the value of the linguistic or cultural capital learners bring to the classroom – their prior knowledge, home literacies, and mother tongues – will impact the extent to which learners will invest in the language and literacy practices of their classrooms." Current monolingual ideologies discriminate against multilingual speakers, especially when they speak non-prestigious languages (see Chapter 1).

4.5.2 Multilingually Aware Pedagogies

It should be noted that the monolingual approach prioritizing the target language based on the so-called direct method (Cummins 2007: 222), as sketched out and criticized above, cannot be entirely misguided. After all, it has produced and continues to produce good results. My own language training mostly followed the direct method, but I also believe that conscious language reflection provoked by contrastive linguistics and language typology aided my language skills. Accordingly, I do not wish to make a plea here for language pedagogies that are dominated by translation exercises and textual work, as in traditional Latin classes, and that are far removed from the

[47] The terms 'inner' and 'expanding' circle are used in the sense of Kachru (1985) and correlate with the use of English as a native and foreign language. English is widely used as a second language in so-called 'outer' circle countries.

demands of interpersonal communication. Still, one can ask if it is really necessary to silence one's background languages entirely or if there are ways to employ them usefully for one's language learning success. Current research emphasizes the fact that the languages in the multilingual's mind are strongly interconnected and amount to more than just the sum of the individual languages (Cook & Wei 2016; Herdina & Jessner 2002; Kecskes 2010). Silencing one or more to the exclusion of the target language appears like an unnecessary act of self-mutilation.

There are two concepts that currently figure prominently in language pedagogies. These are metalinguistic awareness and pedagogical translanguaging (Cenoz & Gorter 2017, 2020; García & Wei 2014; see also Berthele 2021). Metalinguistic awareness, as discussed in Chapter 2, refers to the ability to reflect on and analyze language. Multilingualism is generally believed to enhance metalinguistic awareness. Pedagogical translanguaging describes a set of didactic strategies to involve the entire learner's linguistic repertoire for the purpose of further language learning. Generally, this approach conceives of a speaker's entire multilingual repertoire as one interconnected space without the need to compartmentalize it into different languages that live their lives in isolation. Students are allowed to draw on all semiotic resources available. Pedagogical translanguaging can be expected to boost metalinguistic awareness and students learn that languages are not in conflict, but support one another (Cenoz & Santos 2020: 7).

The research literature offers relatively diverse ideas on how to operationalize translanguaging, concerning language proper, but also related issues pertaining to identity formation and language policy (see Chapter 5). Cenoz and Gorter (2017: 910), for example, mention the importance of discussing cognates to foster vocabulary development, the comparison of compounding strategies and derivational morphology, the formation of writing skills in different languages, and translation exercises. Texts could be read and listened to in one language and summarized in another. Such strategies and activities focus on the activation of cross-linguistic parallels and provoke students to think abstractly about languages and linguistic categories. They help to keep all languages active. Hopp et al. (2020) demonstrate the beneficial effects of such strategies in a recent intervention study. These authors, inter alia, implemented activities fostering vocabulary expansion, raising phonological awareness, and triggering language or grammatical comparisons (Hopp et al. 2020: 154). Furthermore, the study of English could go beyond the standard varieties and involve samples of other world Englishes (Siemund, Davydova & Maier 2012). Needless to say, allowing diversity into the language classroom poses great challenges for testing and grading. Moreover, it may stir anxieties in the teaching personnel, as normative boundaries are crossed, and students may be using languages that the instructors do not understand.

The available background languages could further be incorporated drawing on dual language books, multilingual books, the Internet, as well as the linguistic and cultural identity of learners, thus increasing motivation and investment into learning. Modern textbook design would benefit from reflecting current multilingual realities and should offer exercises related to translanguaging. The overall objective would be to create a multilingual learning environment, avoiding the creation of a double or triple monolingual habitus.

4.5.3 Summary

The preceding paragraphs opposed and discussed language pedagogies that silence previously acquired languages with those that actively involve them. I argued for an approach that considers previous language experience as a resource for further language learning, rather than a problem that needs to be suppressed. On the whole, the benefits appear to outweigh the problems. Knowledge of language should not be conceived of as a deficit. Pedagogical translanguaging defines a set of strategies to turn previous language experience into an advantage for the acquisition of new languages.

4.6 Chapter Summary

The main goal of Chapter 4 was to explore potentially positive effects of a previous multilingual experience for subsequent language learning processes. It contrasted the learning of additional languages, especially English, from the opposition of a multilingual in comparison to a monolingual upbringing of the relevant language learners. The studies surveyed typically compared multilingual learner groups with monolingual controls in the context of educational institutions.

Chapter 4 argued that type of bilingualism, as operationalized in terms of language dominance, and the type of language knowledge investigated play a pivotal role for understanding language learning processes against a multilingual substrate. More specifically, I argued that situations of balanced bilingualism and a focus on general language proficiencies are most likely to expose enhancing effects for learning additional languages. However, we still know relatively little about the extent to which different CEFR domains are impacted. Cross-linguistic influence, as observable in different grammatical domains and the lexicon, can aid additional language acquisition by means of cumulative enhancement, but certain constellations also produce inhibitory effects. The assumption of universally facilitating effects has turned out to be overly optimistic and needs to be tempered.

Moreover, Chapter 4 discussed the acquisition of English as an additional language in bilingual heritage contexts. Building on results from recent and ongoing project work, I argued for the critical influence of age and the majority language, due to the latter's rather dominant status in many bilingual heritage speakers. Positive effects of multilingual upbringing are more likely to present in younger age cohorts when the dominance of the majority language is lower or the students' multilingual repertoire is more balanced. In addition, such effects depend on the heritage context considered, the specific languages involved, as well as a host of further background variables. Grammatical and lexical cross-linguistic influence mainly finds its origin in the majority language and can be both enhancing and inhibitory. To complicate things further, it currently remains unclear if observable multilingual advantages are causally related to language development proper or are contingent on more general cognitive skills (Berthele & Udry 2022; Berthele & Vanhove 2020; Lorenz, Toprak & Siemund 2021).

Finally, Chapter 4 also touched upon recent advances in language pedagogies that try to cater for a multilingual clientele. Although the teaching and learning of English (and other languages) as an additional language still widely follows a largely monolingual approach in which the other languages in the students' repertoires remain silent and unused, pedagogical translanguaging offers an approach to involve these background languages actively. It remains to be seen to what extent this approach can find its way into current curricula and, of course, teacher education programmes. Evidently, language pedagogies are a function of the surrounding language policies and constrained by them. Accordingly, language policy issues in multilingual contexts will be the topic of the next chapter.

5 Multilingual Language Policies, Identities, and Attitudes

This chapter is based on the conviction that the problems dealt with in the preceding chapters need to be embedded into the larger multilingual ecologies in which they occur. Since language dominance has proven an important predictor of cross-linguistic influence, which, in turn, determines the acquisition of additional languages, including expectable benefits of previous multilingual experience, we now need to follow-up on the factors that are responsible for language dominance (see Chapter 3). This includes the limiting case of monolingualism. Evidently, these factors are related to or the result of various issues of language policy and planning – both explicit and implicit – that shape the language ecology encountered in a particular region, even down to the nuclear family.

Some crucial fundamentals of language policy and planning will be introduced in Section 5.1. These will also be relevant for understanding Chapter 6. The discussion reflects on the ideologies underlying all decisions of language policy and planning, arguing that multilingualism itself represents a form of ideology that needs continuous critical assessment.

A selection of important language policy and planning issues as well as the resulting multilingual language ecologies are then compared focusing on Europe, North America, and Australasia in Section 5.2 as well as Africa, Asia, and the Middle East in Section 5.3. Needless to say, this survey must be selective and cannot be exhaustive. Nevertheless, it reveals the continuing tension produced by traditional Western monolingual ideologies in their penetration into the still rather complex linguistic fabrics in other parts of the world. Ironically, global migration has brought this conflict home where it is now forcefully being negotiated within the very borders of officially monolingual Western countries. Contemporary language policy and planning cannot be understood without acknowledging the special status of English.

Since language policies are highly consequential for identity issues, cultural and social capital, as well as investment into languages, there follows a discussion of these relationships in Section 5.4. Darvin and Norton's (2015) model of identity and investment offers an apt theoretical frame. Although this section also introduces fundamental issues relating to language and identity, its main focus lies on the problem of how these issues play out in multilingual societies. It helps to understand why existing cultural and social capital related to language can be lost, in spite of being principally valuable and beneficial to further language learning.

The chapter concludes with a discussion of multilingual identities and language attitudes in Section 5.5. It addresses the development of hybrid identities and the association of different types of attitudes (status and solidarity) with the languages in people's multilingual repertoires. Special consideration is given to the role of English regarding all processes of identity formation in modern societies.

Chapter 5 offers an overview of competing linguistic models and policy options underlying the linguistic organization of societies in different areas of the world. It does not wish to give policy recommendations, however, but rather tries to describe in most objective terms how different societies have found practical solutions to organizing their linguistic reality. It further tries to assess to what extent current research on multilingualism can impact language policy and planning (Berthele 2019). Ironically, we will see that policy and identity issues outrank questions related to multilingual advantages per se. Interests and emotions beat purely functional considerations.

5.1 Language Ideologies, Policy, and Planning

Contingent on particular world areas, we find very different language policies, including approaches that leave language development to itself (Bonnet & Siemund 2018b; Ricento 2006a, 2006b, 2015a; Ricento, Peled & Ives 2015; Ruíz 1984; Shohamy 2006; Spolsky 2004). More often than not, these policies are based on explicit or implicit language ideologies that Silverstein (1979: 193) defines as the "sets of beliefs about language articulated by users as a rationalization or justification of perceived language structure and use." Such beliefs may be explicated through narratives, rules, and laws, but often they remain implicit and are then only accessible through language-related practices.[1] Although it is quite common to believe that such rationalizations correspond to the *real* structure of the world and form a valid picture of it, they typically lag behind the actual developments, are used to maintain established power relations, or simply represent misconstructions. For example, language change tends to be more advanced than our research on it makes us believe it is – not to mention laypeople's beliefs of it. Moreover, rationalizations and justifications are quite regularly influenced by personal interests and

[1] Ricento (2006b: 11–12) notes that although "language behavior and social policy are ideologically encumbered, simply exposing these ideological formations is insufficient to justify enactment of particular policies." Language policies need to be based on sound research.

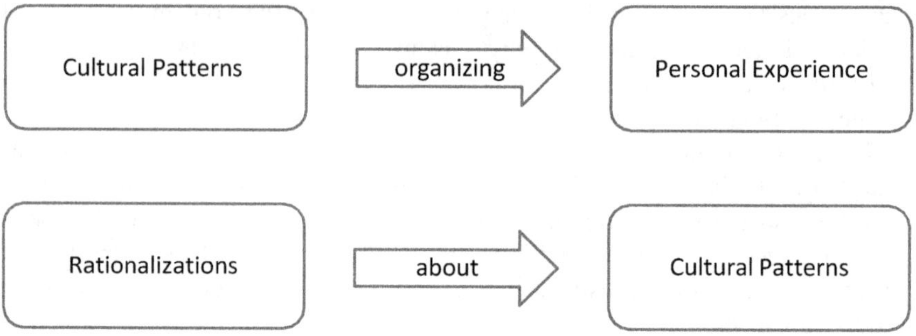

Figure 5.1 Primary phenomena and secondary interpretations.
Adapted from Silverstein (1979: 195).

various emotional biases (Kahnemann 2012), so that there may arise a rather large disconnect between our ideologies or assumptions about the world and the actual cultural patterns. Revolutions mark stages when the disconnect becomes untenable. Building on Boas' (1911) influential work, Silverstein (1979: 195) describes the relationship between cultural patterns, personal experience, and our subsequent rationalizations as in Figure 5.1.

The manifestation of cultural patterns in terms of personal experience are considered "primary" ethnological phenomena that progress through history without our conscious awareness. They become accessible through a system of "secondary" interpretations and explanations. These can be explicated and thus made the subject of conscious reflections. According to Boas (1911: 70–71), as cited in Silverstein (1979: 195), the distinction between primary and secondary phenomena is particularly pronounced in language, as linguistic categories are for the most part not available to immediate conscious reflection. It takes substantial linguistic training to reflect adequately on language and formulate the primary phenomena in terms of an explicit grammar. The grammatical domain of reflexivity, for example, as formulated in Chomsky's (1981) "Binding Conditions," is not accessible to the uninitiated. In other words, linguistic categories are relatively independent of secondary rationalizations, there being comparatively little influence from the latter on the former. Folk grammar is a far cry from an academically sound grammar.

For good reason, professional linguists tend to be quite careful and cautious about issues of standardization and politically enforced language change, knowing that all such endeavours barely scratch the surface of the architecture of language. The influence of secondary rationalizations on the deep structure of language is relatively low. In other words, such undertakings can be taken to pursue objectives that have little to do with language proper, language being exploited for other purposes that are largely symbolic in nature. For example, when English became the subject of standardization efforts in the seventeenth and eighteenth centuries, the main focus rested on the lexicon and orthography – often by appeal to the classical languages Latin and Greek as well as romantic ideals of regularity, purity, and harmony (Baugh & Cable 2002). Grammatical structure was targeted to a lesser extent. A notable example of grammatical engineering is negative concord (double negation) that blatantly contradicted the belief in the logical structure of language.[2] Standardization is always driven by ideology (see also Chapter 7).

Regarding the current discourse on multilingualism including the various advantages widely associated with it, as epitomized by the present book, I cannot resist the temptation to ask what the relationship between the observable cultural patterns, our personal experience, and the resulting rationalizations and interpretations is. As already argued in Chapter 1, the currently observable interest in all matters multilingual can at least partially be reconstructed as a response to globalization processes that developed an unprecedented dynamism after the fall of the Iron Curtain in 1989. The resulting scientific interest in the newly emerging linguistic diversity in Western urban areas is – especially in education studies – in no small portion driven by an interest to identify levers in this new multilingual texture that can be used to foster social cohesion, encourage participation, and counterbalance social segregation. The quest for multilingual advantages can be viewed as an attempt to define the conditions that help to organize this new social reality as efficiently and effectively as possible. There remains, of course, the danger of turning multilingualism into an ideology itself. This happens when the discourse on multilingualism begins to disconnect from the observable cultural and scientific reality. The current replicability crisis and the ensuing re-evaluation of the data as well as the recalibration of the theoretical discourse can be interpreted as a clear sign of it (see Chapter 2). As an illustration, we may just recall the proposal put forward in Leivada et al. (2020: 4) to reconsider bilingual advantages in term of merely "bilingual effects." This may be interpreted in such a way that the research results were overinterpreted in one particular direction and need to be adjusted.

The subsequent sections need to be read with these caveats in mind. Societies can be based on monolingual, bilingual, multilingual, plurilingual ideologies and promote monoglossia, diglossia, and polyglossia by means of their language policies (Ferguson 1959; Fishman 1967; Snow 2013). Most of these concepts may also result from spontaneous developments that arise without the intervention of an explicit language policy (policies from above and from below). However, there appear to be practical limitations regarding

[2] The idea was that two negative expressions necessarily produce an overall positive meaning, perhaps following mathematical logic (Baugh & Cable 2002: 248, 279, 314). Nevalainen (2006: 264) holds that negative concord had already lost ground amongst the educated elite before the prescriptive movement began. At any rate, it used to be a widespread dialectal feature.

how many languages an individual or a society can handle, especially in script-based societies running complex education systems. Multilingualism comes at a price, but certainly also offers many benefits. We need to be aware of the various political and economic interests lurking in the background. Much as specific dialects were – and still are – elevated to languages and appropriated for nation-building projects, multilingualism can be viewed as an endeavour to make a globalized society work. This touches political convictions.[3]

I consider multilingual language policies as inherently more complex than monolingual ones, as more stakeholders with diverging interests need to be involved. Canada, for example, maintains a special office – the Commissioner of Official Languages – to calibrate the influence and availability of its two official languages English and French. Chapter 1 revealed that modern urban areas easily harbour scores of different languages and linguistic communities. Such multilingual societies offer substantial challenges for status planning and corpus planning (Kaplan & Baldauf 1997: 30–50), as it is practically impossible to devote the same resources to all languages. However, countries as political entities do not necessarily have to be consistent in adopting these concepts and may use different approaches in different areas.

Language policies can also be identified in smaller social units, such as the home or family, the school, or the workplace (Curdt-Christiansen 2018; Ricento 2006b: 21; Spolsky 2009: 10–30). Individual language development is necessarily embedded within larger policy approaches and cannot be understood without them. Bilingual families need to decide between monolingual or bilingual upbringing for their children and, in the case of the latter, agree on a strategy to implement bilingualism or multilingualism. This boils down to a language policy decision in the home. Transnational families and diasporic communities especially are confronted with diverging language ideologies and practices. The education system is faced with the notorious question of the medium of instruction that tends to be answered in different ways at primary, secondary, and tertiary levels. We will encounter many illuminating cases in the following sections. Finally, global business cooperation – including academia – leads to the creation of multilingual work groups, and such teams need to agree on a common language with English typically being the preferred choice.

5.2 Europe, North America, and Australasia

This section explores multilingual language policy and planning issues in Europe, North America, Australia, and New Zealand. The rationale behind discussing these territories together is that they form a cultural unit commonly referred to as "Western."

[3] Ricento (2006b: 19) warns us that the researcher needs to be counted in as a potentially "interested" party.

5.2.1 *Europe*

Europe has been a mosaic of languages for millennia that represent extremely valuable cultural capital. This diversity continues to be an important international attraction. With the exception of Basque as an isolate and the Finno-Ugric languages, its present indigenous languages are of Indo-European ancestry (Albanian, Armenian, Balto-Slavic, Celtic, Germanic, Hellenic, Romance). Celtic used to be a very prominent language family but needs to be considered endangered today (see Vennemann 2003: 21).[4] The Roman Empire disseminated descendants of Latin over vast parts of the continent, especially Central Europe and the Southwest. The Central European and Northern Germanic languages border on the Balto-Slavic family in the East.

The continent at large is practically de jure monolingual at the national level, the current political organization being relatively recent.[5] Since the national citizens enjoy mobility freedom within the European Union, there is an impressive degree of multilingualism observable at the societal level. The European Union counts twenty-four official languages, these being the national languages of their currently twenty-seven member states. The education systems are primarily run in the national/official languages. Some member states have more than one official language, such as Belgium (Dutch, French, German), Finland (Finnish, Swedish), Luxembourg (French, German, Luxembourgish), Ireland (English, Irish), and Malta (English, Maltese). Switzerland, although not a European Union member state, represents another officially multilingual country where German, French, Italian, and Romansh are recognized as official languages. These are multilingual countries in an official sense in which the relevant languages dominate in specific territories or are used for specific functions.

According to the website europa.eu,[6] the European Union furthermore harbours over 60 indigenous regional minority languages that are spoken by approximately 40 million people. They are defined and explicated in the European Charter for Regional or Minority Languages.[7] The regional minority languages include Basque, Catalan, Frisian, Galician, Low German, Romani, Sami, Sorbian, Welsh, and Yiddish, amongst others. These languages lost the competition for national languages during the state formation processes in the

[4] The European prehistory after the last ice age is, of course, much more complex with more ethnolinguistic groups involved. Vennemann (2003) provides a very readable and informative reconstruction, especially regarding the influence of Vasconic and Semitic.

[5] The present European borders are an outcome of World War II and the political reorganization after the fall of the Iron Curtain in 1989.

[6] This is the official website of the European Union. Information related to language can be found at europa.eu/european-union/about-eu/eu-languages_en, accessed on 24 April 2021.

[7] The relevant documents are available online at www.coe.int/en/web/european-charter-regional-or-minority-languages, accessed on 24 April 2021.

eighteenth and nineteenth centuries (see Chapter 1). However, many regional minority languages are coextensive with one of the national languages, but are also spoken outside the relevant national territories. For example, Danish is a regional minority language in Germany, and German has the same status in Denmark. Croatian (Burgenlandcroatian), Slovenian, Hungarian, Czech, and Slovakian enjoy this status in Austria. Each of the Balkan states hosts numerous regional minority languages. German and Romani are the most widely recognized regional minority languages (in thirteen and sixteen countries, respectively). Speakers of regional minority languages are typically bilingual in the minority language and the relevant national language.

Protecting languages by charters and laws, however, does not guarantee their survival. While the development of Basque and Catalan in Spain can be considered success stories (see also Tabouret-Keller 2006: 679), the fate of Low German and North Frisian in Germany is less certain, in spite of serious efforts to protect and maintain them. Basque and Catalan are co-official languages in the autonomous communities of Catalunya and in the Basque Country. The situation of Basque in Spain is considerably more optimistic than in France where it is not recognized as a regional minority language. Cenoz and Gorter (2017: 902) point out that the proportion of Basque speakers increased in the Basque Autonomous Community and Navarre from 1991 to 2011, whereas it declined in the French part of the Basque Country within the same period.[8] Legislation may have indeed played a role here. Regarding the situation in Germany, however, Århammar (2008) soberly concludes that the language shift from North Frisian and Low German to High German in Northern Germany is practically complete and irreversible, although there remains a small pocket of active North Frisian speakers in the Western part of the rather small island of Föhr (speaking the local dialect of Fering).

In spite of being the indigenous languages of the British Isles and strong efforts for maintenance and revival, the Celtic languages remain under strong pressure from English. Sizeable numbers of speakers can still be found for Irish, Scottish Gaelic, and Welsh – less so for Cornish and Manx. Besides English, Irish is the co-official language of the Republic of Ireland and a recognized regional minority language in Northern Ireland. Although Irish is a compulsory subject in the Irish education system, the number of active

[8] These authors summarize the developments as follows: "A comparison of survey data from 1991 and 2011 indicates that the percentage of Basque speakers in the Basque Autonomous Community has increased from 24% to 32% and in Navarre from 9.5% to 11.7% (Basque Government 2012) due to policies designed to support the language. However, a lack of such policies in the French part of the Basque Country resulted in a decline in the number of speakers (from 33% to 21.4%) during the same period" (Cenoz & Gorter 2017: 902).

speakers remains low outside the Gaeltacht regions in the West, where Irish is still learnt as a first or native language (see Tabouret-Keller 2006: 680). According to Wilson and Deuchar (2017: 49), Welsh–English bilingualism hovers at around 19 per cent, with higher values found along the Western coastal areas. The figures for bilingualism in Wales are generally much higher than in Scotland, where only 57,600 inhabitants (about 1 per cent of the Scottish population) reported ability to speak Scottish Gaelic according to the 2011 census (MacQuarrie & Lyon 2017: 35). Again, these speakers mostly inhabit the Western parts of Scotland, especially the Hebrides. The ability to speak Scots is considerably more widely attested than that of Scottish Gaelic (Scotland's Census 2011).

Interestingly enough, there are only very few studies probing into potentially positive effects of bilingual upbringing and education in the European bilingual areas other than the Basque Country and Catalunya. I am aware of merely two studies investigating cognitive advantages (qua executive function) related to multilingual experience carried out in Wales and Ireland on the one hand and the Frisian-speaking part of the Netherlands on the other (Bosma, Blom & Versloot 2017; Young et al. 2017). The results are largely mixed being strongly contingent on several background variables. What comes out as a clear result, however, is that minority language education has no negative effects. The Basque Country and Catalunya evidently stand out in regard to the number of studies reporting facilitating effects (see Chapter 4). One could surmise that the relatively greater share of active and balanced bilinguals drives these effects, as explained in the preceding chapters. What is more, the social prestige associated with Basque and Catalan in Spain including their prominence in the relevant education systems appears higher than that of other regional minority languages (see Gorter & Cenoz 2011 for a comparison of Basque and Frisian).

The Council of the European Union invites its member states to teach "at least two languages in addition to the main language(s) of instruction from an early age" (Council of the European Union 2014). This recommendation can be understood as trilingualism (probably of a functional kind) involving one's respective national language, another language of the Union, and English. Other language constellations are in principle feasible, including quadrilingualism in officially bilingual areas. As far as I can see, reality widely boils down to bilingualism of national language plus English. Mollin (2020) reports considerable differences in the knowledge and use of English across the European member states, there being a strong cline from Northern to Southern and Eastern countries. There are exceptions to this general trend, of course. The Netherlands, Denmark, and Sweden achieve remarkably high scores, followed by Austria, Cyprus, and Finland. The extensive knowledge of English in the Nordic Countries and the Netherlands is in no small proportion driven by its widespread use in higher education, with many degree programmes taught exclusively in English.[9] This is by no means uncontroversial.

Immigrant languages typically have no official status and are in the responsibility of the relevant communities (Byram 2018; Extra & Yağmur 2004: 90). Although some municipalities support heritage language tuition,[10] immigrant bilingualism tends to be of a transitional type with individuals and heritage communities shifting towards the majority language within a few generations. At least in regard to the Netherlands and Germany, studies exploring advantages associated with multilingual experience have mainly been carried out in different groups of heritage speakers, but hardly in bilinguals speaking regional minority languages.

5.2.2 North America

Although North America – here understood as the part of the continent to the North of the Mexican border comprising the United States and Canada – possesses an extremely rich indigenous linguistic heritage, this is practically invisible in the current public sphere (see Ricento 2019a). One needs to travel to the native American reserves to appreciate what has remained of the expansive territories once populated by speakers of Algonquian, Athabascan, Eskimo-Aleut, Iroquoian, Penutian, Siouan, and many other families, depending on the scheme of classification (Mithun 1999: 6–7). Most of the continent is English-speaking, perpetuating the linguistic dominance of the Anglo-Saxon settlers. There also is an extensive superimposed layer of immigrant languages that continues to be fuelled by international migration and immigration. We discussed a few examples of multilingual conurbations in Chapter 1. The new immigrant languages are considerably more visible than the indigenous languages. This finds a parallel in the comparatively low visibility of most European regional minority languages other than those that also serve as national languages.

As we saw in the preceding section, the European nation states largely follow monolingual policies in administration, judiciary, and education, in spite of massive societal multilingualism across the continent. The United States adopts a similar policy in that monolingualism in English represents the socially

[9] Mollin (2020: 43) notes that the Netherlands "offers a large number of English-taught Master's degree programmes with 80% of all such programmes at Dutch universities taught entirely in English."

[10] For example, in 2021 in the Free and Hanseatic City of Hamburg, the following languages were in principle available for heritage language tuition: Albanian, Bosnian, Dari, Farsi, Greek, Italian, Croatian, Kurdish, Polish, Portuguese, Romani, Russian, Spanish, and Turkish. Attendance is voluntary (Behörde für Schule und Berufsbildung, Hamburg 2021; Landesinstitut für Lehrerbildung und Schulentwicklung, Hamburg 2021a, 2021b).

accepted default pattern. Speaking English only is not considered a deficit but is associated with overt prestige. There is, however, no explicit language policy at the federal level proscribing the use of other languages. Instead we find a widely diverging array of policy approaches at the levels of states and municipalities (King, Liu & Schwedhelm 2018; Ricento 2019a, 2019b: 1). As in Europe, this monolingual orientation is confronted with an enormous level of linguistic diversity at the societal and individual level, stemming both from the indigenous linguistic heritage and the many immigrant languages.

One of the important differences in relation to Europe is that the national language of the United States – that in fact was never officially declared as such – serves as the currently accepted global lingua franca.[11] Whereas students all over Europe (with the exception of Great Britain) invest a considerable time of their lives on learning English as a foreign language, second language, or lingua franca, US nationals enjoy the privilege of learning this language as their first language or as one of their first languages. One is reminded of the Roman Empire where subjects in the provinces had to learn Latin (and subsequently moulded their own languages out of it). As a consequence, the interest in learning foreign languages is low. Moreover, and again as in Europe, heritage bilingualism is widely considered transitional, meaning that these bilingual communities converge on the monolingual model over a few generations (King, Liu & Schwedhelm 2018: 79). There are, of course, no official measures to prevent heritage speakers from speaking their heritage languages, but the combined forces exerted by the majority language English, its social and international prestige, the English-based education system, economic pressure, the peer groups, and the desire to belong to the mainstream society inadvertently produce this language shift in the long run. Linguistic assimilation proceeds rapidly. As we saw in Chapter 2, this situation produced many studies of cognitive advantages or disadvantages related to transitional bilingualism, first focusing on the indigenous and later on the immigrant communities. Not surprisingly, it produced no studies on potential learning advantages of previous multilingual experience for additional languages.

The Official Languages Act of 1969 declared Canada a bilingual country in which English and French have co-official and equal status.[12] This, however,

[11] King, Liu and Schwedhelm (2018: 78–79) describe the situation as follows: "While English serves as the *de facto* language of the government and society, and 31 states have passed 'Official English' laws, language policy in general, and educational language policy in particular, is not guided by federal legislation. This is the case despite years of lobbying and unsuccessful attempts by organizations such as U.S. English to establish English as the official language of the U.S."

[12] Retrieved from www.britannica.com/topic/Official-Languages-Act, accessed on 27 April 2021. The Official Languages Act declared that English and French "enjoy equality of status and equal rights and privileges as to their use in all the institutions of the Parliament and Government of Canada."

does not mean that all Canadian citizens are English–French bilinguals, nor does it mean that the two languages have the same distribution and are offered for the same set of services across Canada's ten provinces. There are substantial regional differences. For example, the province of Quebec only recognizes French as an official language, following the Charter of the French Language (Bill 101) passed in 1977, although specific services are offered in both English and French.[13] In fact, New Brunswick is the only officially French–English bilingual province, that is, bilingualism here is regulated in the provincial law, not just by federal law.[14] The other provinces, especially in the Western parts of Canada, are primarily English-speaking, although the federal law requires many public and partially also private services to be offered in both languages. In other words, Canada's bilingual policy concerns specific contexts (federal agencies, courts, legislature) and does not generalize to all services or social contexts. Financial considerations, the number of eligible recipients, and issues of feasibility matter.

The United States and Canada differ quite emphatically in the extent to which they promote and employ transitional and maintenance bilingualism (Dicks & Genesee 2017; Gándara & Escamilla 2017). There could be no better example to illustrate the impact of language policy on the linguistic landscape. Whereas the United States widely implement transitional bilingualism (as well as English-only programmes), the Canadian approach is largely characterized by maintenance bilingualism. One can only speculate about the various historical and cultural reasons behind this rather fundamental difference, but there is probably no denying the fact that the prolonged and rather demanding coexistence of two highly prestigious and powerful languages (i.e. English and French) in Canada has a stake in it. Moreover, there is the widely held belief that additive bilingualism represents an achievement that "brings personal, social, cognitive and economic advantage without negative effects on first language or academic development" (Dicks & Genesee 2017: 454). Chapter 2 provided an overview of the research literature on which these assumptions are based. Originating in French immersion programmes, maintenance bilingualism has been extended so as to cover a wide range of heritage languages. The actual languages offered in such bilingual heritage programmes depend on the province considered (Wright & Chan 2019: 94–95).[15]

[13] Retrieved from www.britannica.com/place/Quebec-province, accessed on 27 April 2021.

[14] Retrieved from www.britannica.com/place/New-Brunswick-province, accessed on 27 April 2021.

[15] These authors mention "the Mandarin/English program in British Columbia (Vancouver School Board 2018), the American Sign Language/English, Arabic/English, Mandarin/English, German/English, and Hebrew/English programs in Alberta (Edmonton Public Schools 2018), the Ukrainian/English program in Saskatchewan (Government of Saskatchewan Education 2018), and the Ukrainian/English, German/English, Hebrew/English, and Cree/English bilingual education programs in Manitoba (Government of Manitoba Education 2018)."

Bilingual policies and education programmes are strongly subject to political developments. For several decades, especially the US states along the Mexican border – which used to belong to Mexico until they were practically annexed in the nineteenth century – pursued or tolerated a bilingual education policy (English + immigrant language, particularly Spanish), but in 1998 and 2000 California and Arizona reverted to an English-only policy (Propositions 227 and 203, thus connecting to policies in place before the 1970s; Wright & Chan 2019: 89), subject to ongoing debate. For instance, California Proposition 58 passed in 2016 revoked the restrictions imposed by Proposition 227 allowing public schools to decide on the teaching methods that they consider appropriate (Wiley 2019; Wright & Chan 2019: 90). As King, Liu and Schwedhelm (2018: 81) point out, for students with a Spanish background English-only instruction typically means to learn Spanish at home in the family, switch to predominantly using English with the beginning of formal education, only to relearn Spanish as a second language during secondary education. In other words, Spanish heritage students first revert to English to then study Spanish again.[16] This is perhaps not the most efficient approach, especially as policies and attitudes may quickly be overtaken by reality. For example, Lynch (2018: 15) states that "[i]n less than a decade, the ideological construction of Spanish in Miami transformed from a cultural liability of sorts into a valuable asset in the city's job market and the region's economic infrastructure."

Besides Spanish, Chinese represents a major heritage language in the United States and also Canada, especially along the West Coast (see Chapter 1). The label Chinese typically stands for Mandarin, Cantonese, and other Chinese languages. What is interesting about this heritage group is the long tradition of organizing Chinese language education as well as Chinese medium of instruction education within the community (King, Liu & Schwedhelm 2018: 87–91). It is not at all uncommon for children to spend extensive extra time in these community schools on weekends. Moreover, this educational policy approach can generally be found in Chinese diasporic communities and enjoys a long history, as Bao (2021) nicely documents for the context of Singapore. I can also witness this in my current home town, the Free and Hanseatic City of Hamburg. It is driven by a strong belief in the importance of Chinese ancestry and heritage, including the character-based script. We will take up this issue again in Chapter 6.

[16] King, Liu and Schwedhelm (2018: 80) write that "the U.S. approach to language study systematically squanders the myriad heritage linguistic resources present in our student body and then, often ineffectively and with minimal investment, teaches 'foreign' languages a decade later to those same students."

Neither in the United States nor in Canada do we find sizeable official language policies for the native American languages (Fettes 2019; King, Liu & Schwedhelm 2018; McCarty 2019; Patrick 2019), although there are specific local exceptions. For example, indigenous languages are officially recognized in the Northwest Territories of Canada and Nunavut, there also being initiatives to install immersion programmes (Dicks & Genesee 2017: 457). The survival of indigenous languages at large, however, depends on local initiatives in the relevant communities that can assume a wide variety of forms. Such language maintenance and reclamation programmes can be integrated into the school system or extracurricular activities.[17]

5.2.3 Australia and New Zealand

Just as along the North American West Coast, the presently perhaps most visible diasporic community in Australia and New Zealand is composed of Chinese (and other Asian) immigrants. This finds a ready explanation in Australia and New Zealand's participation in the Pacific Rim – a vast geographic area characterized by common economic interests and labour migration. Chinese immigration to the United States and Canada enjoys considerable time depth and proceeded in several waves. For example, the Western Rocky Mountain segment of the Canadian Pacific Railway, built in the latter half of the nineteenth century, could not have been completed without cheap labour contracted from China. Generally, and this equally applies to Canada, the United States, Australia, and New Zealand, there is an increase in immigration from Asia over time, while immigration from Europe becomes less important (Lo Bianco & Slaughter 2017b; Wright & Chan 2019).

Apart from English as the national and practically official language, language policy and planning in Australia has been concerned with the Australian indigenous languages, the various immigrant languages, and foreign languages (Lo Bianco & Slaughter 2017a, 2017b). As in other English-speaking countries, a major language policy concern regards English literacy levels. Similar to the European and Canadian model, Australia is promoting a profoundly multicultural and multilingual image, both nationally and internationally. This is especially perceptible in the affluent urban centres along the East Coast (Brisbane, Sydney, Melbourne) where community life is characterized by diverse immigrant groups and considerable linguistic diversity. Both the municipalities as well as the more recent immigrant groups share an interest in maintaining this linguistic diversity for reasons of identity formation, but also out of economic interests. Languages like Japanese, Korean, and Mandarin Chinese are associated

[17] King, Liu and Schwedhelm (2018: 86–87) provide a very readable account of Ojibwe language reclamation efforts in the US state of Minnesota.

with economic opportunities, especially in the Pacific area. Moreover, cultural and linguistic diversity have been identified as tourist attractions that entice people from all over the world. Accordingly, one finds a considerable variety of bilingual programmes in Queensland, New South Wales, and Victoria, both of the transitional and maintenance type. However, as Lo Bianco and Slaughter (2017b: 356) point out, the "overall number of bilingual programs across Australia has decreased significantly since 2000." It appears that bilingual programmes involving English and another high prestige language (notably French, German, Italian, Japanese, Korean, Mandarin) stand greater chances of continuity. Bissoonauth (2018: 62) shows for the Indian community that home language use of English amongst primary school students is as high as 80 per cent, suggesting an ongoing shift towards English. The use of English is highest with parents and siblings; it is lower with grandparents.

The bilingual programmes for the indigenous Australian communities remain a thorny area for language policy and planning, especially in the Northern Territories. After some enthusiasm in the 1970s, perhaps as a response to the developments in Canada, bilingual programmes slid into an ongoing erosion process fuelled by "inadequate program costing, high non-Indigenous staff turnover (up to 100 % annually) and regular absenteeism among Indigenous support workers" (Lo Bianco & Slaughter 2017b: 351). Literacy in English and also the indigenous languages remains low, aggravated by the fact that indigenous students frequently cannot understand the tests used to assess their English skills (Lo Bianco & Slaughter 2017b: 354). More often than not, they do not speak standard English, frustrating the communication between students and their standard English teachers who typically do not possess the requisite training to teach in such contexts (Lo Bianco & Slaughter 2017b: 352). The situation is reminiscent of the North American native and African-American contexts, but also harks back to the former colonial contexts of Wales and Ireland (and many other colonial contexts, for that matter). Evidently, the deep social divide between the Australian indigenous communities and mainstream Australian society can hardly be mended with bilingual programmes. We may note that testing for multilingual advantages under such conditions would be a completely fruitless and entirely misplaced exercise. Quite likely, the results would be similar to those obtained by Saer (1923) in the context of Wales. The Australian bilingual immigrant communities would here offer a more suitable testing ground, as the relevant languages entered Australia after English and not before. Moreover, they often carry high social prestige.

Australia's 2016 census reports a total of 64,762 speakers of Australian indigenous languages, contrasting with approximately 17 million English-only speakers (Australian Bureau of Statistics 2016c). Given a then population of around 23 million, only about 0.3 per cent of the population speak an indigenous language. This is lower than the percentage of Gaelic speakers in Scotland. In contrast, New Zealand's 2018 census reveals 185,955 speakers of Māori, New Zealand's indigenous language, in a total population of nearly 5 million (about 4 per cent). Moreover, the number of Māori speakers has been rising over the past years (Statistics New Zealand 2018). We may note in passing that the figures for ethnic belonging are generally higher. After some considerable loss in speakers in the 1970s and 1980s, Māori language rights activism successfully claimed greater support for their language, leading to the introduction of pre-school language programmes (1982) as well as Māori immersion elementary schools (1985). Most notably, Māori was elevated to the status of an official language in 1987, besides English (de facto) and New Zealand Sign Language (Hill 2017: 331–332; RSNZ 2013). Language revitalization here appears to be moving in the right direction.[18] Needless to say, there are numerous recent and not so recent immigrant groups and languages in New Zealand (see Chapter 1 on the situation in Auckland), but it is probably fair to say that Māori receives the greatest institutional support besides, of course, English.

5.2.4 Summary

In spite of considerable rhetoric to the contrary, monolingualism remains the official majority pattern across the Western World. The European nation states function primarily in their national languages and so do the United States and Australia. Canada, Belgium, Finland, Luxembourg, Ireland, Malta, New Zealand, and Switzerland pursue officially bilingual or multilingual policies, but the different languages typically correlate with specific territories. There is extensive functional bilingualism of the respective national languages and English across Europe. The most important factors driving the currently observable cultural and linguistic diversity in urban areas are global migration and immigration. The indigenous regional and minority languages tend to be backgrounded, with the exception of Catalan and Basque in Spain, Welsh in the United Kingdom, and Māori in New Zealand. Evidently, without dedicated action in their favour and equipping languages with specific rights and domains of use, they can quickly be lost.

5.3 Africa, Asia, and the Middle East

The motivation behind discussing Africa, Asia, and the Middle East in one section lies in the colonial history of many of their present polities. As a

[18] Notably, New Zealand has implemented a strategy called "Maihi Karauna" and their goals are, that by 2040, "85 per cent of New Zealanders (or more) will value te reo Māori as a key part of their national identity," "one million New Zealanders (or more) will have the ability and confidence to talk about at least basic things in te reo Māori," and that "150,000 Māori aged 15 and over will use te reo Māori as much as English" (Te Puni Kōkiri 2019: 11–14).

consequence, they share many problems and also manifest overlap in their approaches to language policy and planning.

5.3.1 Africa

Mirroring its colonial past, Africa is broadly divided between francophone and anglophone regions. Angola, Cape Verde, Guinea-Bissau, Mozambique, as well as São Tomé and Príncipe are officially Portuguese-speaking, while Equatorial Guinea is officially Spanish-speaking.[19] In what follows, I will mainly be elaborating on issues of language policy and planning in the anglophone parts. The anglophone countries in Africa include Botswana, Cameroon, The Gambia, Ghana, Kenya, Lesotho, Liberia, Malawi, Namibia, Nigeria, Sierra Leone, Tanzania, South Africa, Eswatini (Swaziland), Uganda, Zambia, and Zimbabwe.[20] In these countries, English serves as the sole official or co-official language in tandem with one or more African languages. In Cameroon, English shares the status as an official language with French. South Africa boasts eleven official languages, one of which is English (Mesthrie 2002). The others are Afrikaans, Ndebele, Sepedi or Northern Sotho, Sesotho or Southern Sotho, Swazi, Tsonga, Tswana, Venda, Xhosa, and Zulu. There are also several smaller languages.

In spite of being the only or one of the official languages, English is not typically learnt as a first language in the above anglophone countries. Naturally, first language acquisition and home language use are the domains of the numerous African languages spoken as the indigenous languages of these countries. In Nigeria, for example, Hausa, Yoruba, Igbo, and Fula represent major African languages besides hundreds of other languages with smaller speaker bases. Tanzania is home to numerous Niger-Kongo and Nilo-Saharan languages besides English and Kiswahili (Niger-Kongo, Bantu) as official languages, much as in neighbouring Kenya and Uganda.[21] Without any doubt, the above African countries are highly multilingual, both along the individual and social dimensions. In view of this impressive linguistic diversity, it makes sense to distinguish between home languages, regional, national, and official languages as well as lingua francas.

Language policies on the African continent are diverse, but English as a former colonial language and present global language enjoys high prestige and is widely adopted in the education systems (Chimbutane 2018). It also represents an important ethnically neutral language in countries where many

[19] Retrieved from www.britannica.com/, accessed on 28 April 2021.

[20] Retrieved from www.britannica.com/topic/English-language, accessed on 28 April 2021.

[21] Retrieved from www.britannica.com/place/Nigeria, www.britannica.com/place/Tanzania, accessed on 28 April 2021.

languages and ethnicities coexist (Nigeria, Ghana), in spite of being a former colonial language. Chimbutane (2018: 61) states that the former colonial languages "were perceived as the neutral languages of national integration, modernization and access to global development" in regard to projects of nation building. English in Africa is spoken as one of the standard varieties (British, American), but also occurs in many localized forms (Black South African English, Ghanaian English, Nigerian English, Nigerian Pidgin, etc.). Again, the situation is reminiscent of the various varieties of Latin that remained in the provinces of the Roman Empire after the empire collapsed.

Since English plays such a prominent role in the education systems of the anglophone African countries, it is frequently designated the sole language of instruction. Igboanusi (2014) reports for The Gambia that the language of instruction is exclusively English, in spite of the availability of language policies that could base education on the students' first language. Chimbutane (2018: 58) states a general "mismatch between policy and actual implementation, which results in the maintenance of the colonial legacy." The study by Igboanusi (2014: 558) discusses the consequences of this educational monolingualism and sourly concludes that since "English is the weakest language of the pupils, schools witness high drop-out rates, limited access to education, inability to read with understanding in the early grades, a lack of understanding of the content of the subject taught, and more seriously, high rate of illiteracy." Interestingly, this situation is not only in the responsibility of the governments that – as so often – impede the introduction of African languages as means of instruction due to a lack of resources, but also the parents and teachers who believe that the African languages are deficient, underdeveloped, and should not replace English in the education system (see also Bunyi & Schroeder 2017: 324). Opoku-Amankwa (2009) provides a rather sobering account of a similar situation in Ghana in which the local school policies as well as the African teachers apparently actively participate in cementing the English-only policy in education. This is more surprising as Ghana used to allow African languages as media of instruction in primary schools (Chimbutane 2018: 61). As Opoku-Amankwa (2009: 128) explains, drawing on a case study conducted at Tomso Primary School in Kumasi (Ghana), the "school insists that pupils speak English at all times and it is one of the ten-point classroom norms pasted in each classroom which states: *Speak English both inside and outside the classroom.*" One needs to bear in mind that the students in this particular school frequently do not come from the local area and are highly multilingual, a situation quite reminiscent of Western urban socially deprivileged neighbourhoods.

Some African countries have promoted the use of native languages in administration and education. For example, Kiswahili has gained substantial prestige and prominence in East Africa, with, for example, Tanzania having restructured its education system so that Kiswahili is given a more pronounced status in the curriculum (Tibategeza & du Plessis 2012), apparently also beyond elementary level (Chimbutane 2018: 64). However, as Chimbutane (2018: 61) points out, this typically involves backgrounding the other African languages.[22] One is reminded of Haugen's dictum who holds that to "choose any one vernacular as a norm means to favor the group of people speaking that variety and to disfavor others. It gives one group of speakers prestige as norm-bearers and a headstart in the race for power and position" (Haugen 1966: 932, as cited in Klöter 2020: 106). Generally, however, there seems to be a revalorization of African languages.

5.3.2 Asia

As it is impossible to discuss language policy and planning issues across all Asian countries, this section focuses on countries and regions formerly under British and American influence, notably Hong Kong, India, Malaysia, Pakistan, the Philippines, and Singapore. Here I cannot elaborate on the situation in Japan, Kazakhstan, Korea, or Russia, although there would be no scarcity of interesting observations. Historically, at least some Asian countries (Japan, China, Korea) appear to have imported the concept of a national language from Europe (Heinrich 2012: 59–70; Klöter 2020: 104).[23] Many Asian countries pursue a strong bilingual language policy with an emphasis on English in combination with a national language (Leimgruber, Siemund & Terassa 2018; Siemund, Al-Issa & Leimgruber 2021; Siemund, Schulz & Schweinberger 2014; Sun & Rong 2018). The status of English is special, as it often is a former colonial language and enjoys tremendous prestige. Tuition in English usually starts very early and some countries have made English the only or one language of instruction in the education system.

Language policy and planning issues in the People's Republic of China and Taiwan could easily fill a separate monograph (see Klöter & Söderblom Saarela 2020). The current importance of Mandarin – referred to as Putonghua[24] (common speech, national language) in the People's Republic of China – in Singapore and Taiwan cannot be understood without an

[22] Chimbutane (2018: 61) states that even in relation to "the case of Tanzania, which has been championed as a successful example of development and promotion of indigenous languages to high functions, it turns out that the promotion of Kiswahili, which is the first language of a tiny minority (mostly Zanzibari in origin), came at the price of exclusion of other local languages and their speakers."

[23] In Japan, the standardization of Japanese gained momentum during the final decades of the Meiji period (1868–1912) and is inextricably connected to the intellectual figure of Ueda Kazutoshi (Heinrich 2012: 59).

[24] The correct rendering in Pinyin (Pīnyīn) is Pǔtōnghuà 普通话. Here and elsewhere in the book I omit the tone marks on Pǔtōnghuà for the sake of simplicity.

appreciation of the developments in Mainland China since at least the foundation of the Republic of China in 1912 (Klöter 2020). Besides Beijing-based Mandarin, China is home to various other Sinitic languages or topolects ("dialects") of Mǐn, Wú, or Yuè – collectively referred to as Hànyǔ 汉语 'language of the Hàn people' – as well as a great number of ethnic minority languages (Klöter 2020: 102–103). Both the topolects and the ethnic minority languages are under immense pressure from Putonghua, in spite of officially sanctioned bilingual programmes for the ethnic minority languages (Gao & Wang 2017). Mandarin or Putonghua dominate linguistically and, as Klöter (2020: 101) remarks, "[w]henever this position is challenged nowadays, the competitor is not a Sinitic alternative but English as the most important international language." The ongoing language shift from the topolects to Putonghua is especially perceptible in major conurbations like Shanghai or Guangzhou, as a consequence of strong internal migration in China as well as the official promotion of Putonghua.[25] The latter city including the surrounding Guangdong Province used to be primarily Cantonese-speaking, but there now appears to be a rapid shift to Putonghua (Liang 2020). This contrasts with Hong Kong, a former British colony and present Special Administrative Region of China (SAR), where Cantonese is spoken by the majority of the population and represents an important marker of local identity (see also Chapter 6).

The most perceptible component of current language policy and planning in Hong Kong is its strategy of trilingualism in combination with biliteracy (BT policy; see Bolton, Bacon-Shone & Lee 2021; Poon 2021). Introduced immediately after the transferral of Hong Kong sovereignty to China in 1997, it stipulates spoken proficiency in Cantonese, English, and Putonghua as well as written competence in Chinese and English. This involves considerable tension, as Cantonese and Putonghua are associated with very different values and attitudes. Whereas Cantonese is the local indigenous language with which Hong Kongers strongly identify, Putonghua is the language of the political centre in faraway Beijing superimposed on Hong Kong after 1997. What is more, Cantonese is written using traditional Chinese characters, while the simplified system devised in the People's Republic of China is used to write Putonghua. English as a global and former colonial language is another important player in Hong Kong's linguistic arena. One can easily imagine that this situation produces conflict for policymakers, educationists, schools, teachers, parents, and students alike, as decisions need to be taken regarding the medium of instruction as well as the orthographies (see Wang & Kirkpatrick 2021).

[25] According to Ricento (2006b: 15), such language shift can be taken to reflect asymmetrical power relations rather than natural outcomes of language contact. The discussion of Hong Kong, Singapore, and the United Arab Emirates in Chapter 6 furnishes poignant case studies.

Equally a former British colony, Singapore assumed national independence in 1965, inheriting a complex ethnic and linguistic situation that posed considerable challenges to the subsequent nation building process (Siemund & Li 2020). Located at the Southern tip of the Malay peninsula, the indigenous language of the territory is Malay. However, due to large-scale immigration during British colonial rule, the current population is 76.0 per cent ethnic Chinese, 7.5 per cent of Indian descent, and 15.0 per cent Malay (1.5 per cent others, Singapore Department of Statistics 2021, 2019 figures). Evidently, the languages spoken by these populations belong to very different families. Bazaar Malay used to be the prominent lingua franca employed for interethnic communication during the colonial period (Bao 2021; Lim 2007). Today, English plays a prominent role as the language of the former colonial power and the current global language. It is one of the four official languages of Singapore besides Malay, Mandarin, and Tamil. In comparison to Hong Kong, English is more widely used in Singapore, especially as a home language, and there is a clearly distinct localized or nativized variety known as Colloquial Singapore English that accrues substantial covert prestige. As in Hong Kong and Mainland China, the moniker Chinese hides extensive linguistic diversity. In Singapore, historically attracting Chinese immigrants primarily from the Southern provinces of China, this translates into a Chinese substrate of Hokkien, Teochew, and Cantonese, amongst others (Bao 2021: 19). These vernaculars are now dominated (or have practically been replaced) by Mandarin due to strong activism within the Speak Mandarin Campaign started in 1979 that promoted Mandarin to the status of official mother tongue of all Chinese speakers – even though they in fact spoke a different Chinese at home. However, as Bao (2021: 32) argues, the roots of Mandarin in Singapore are much older and can be reconstructed in the education reforms following the Chinese 1911 revolution (see Klöter 2020 for a similar perspective on Taiwan). The mother tongues for ethnic Malays is Malay and so is Tamil for the Indian population, in spite of the fact that especially the latter group is linguistically more diverse. Since 1987, the medium of instruction in the entire education system has been English so that the mother tongue effectively come to be learnt as second languages, especially so as home language use of English is high (Siemund, Schulz & Schweinberger 2014: 361). In sum, Singapore has developed from an extensively multilingual society into one of officially enshrined individual bilingualism.

Interestingly, neighbouring Malaysia took a completely different direction by developing Malay (Bahasa Malaysia) into its national and sole official language. Before Malaysia gained independence in 1957, it had been under British control since the early nineteenth century, with Malacca and Penang being important trading posts that had also been used by other colonial powers. Much as in Singapore, labour was attracted from Southern China and India forming important diasporic communities (Gill 2014: 1).[26] Accordingly, Southern Chinese vernaculars as well as Tamil and other Indian languages are important minority languages.[27] English is widely used as a second language. Gill (2014) impressively documents the tension between Malay and English, especially in the education system, where the two languages have frequently alternated as media of instruction over the past decades.

Complex patterns in the choice of language of instruction have also been reported from the Philippines where both English and Filipino (a standardized form of Tagalog) are recognized as official languages (Tupas & Pefianco Martin 2017). As the Philippines form a huge archipelago comprising several thousands of smaller and bigger islands (7,107 islands according to UNESCO 2016b), it harbours impressive ethnic and linguistic diversity. The Philippines is a mosaic of several Malayo-Polynesian languages (Tagalog, Cebuano, Ilocano, etc.) and immigrant languages (Cantonese, Hokkien, Mandarin, Spanish) that – due to the movement of labour – come together in densely populated conurbations like Manila, Cebu, and Davao where they strongly interact with English. Tagalog, Cebuano, Ilokano, Hiligaynon, and Waray-Waray count amongst the strongest native languages in numbers of speakers (Ethnologue, Eberhard, Simons & Fennig 2022).[28] Like in other postcolonial countries, English – the language of the US American colonizers – remained even after independence was achieved in 1946 (Tupas & Pefianco Martin 2017: 250). The Philippines look back on a long history of bilingual education in which both Filipino and English serve as languages of instruction (the latter for mathematics and science; see Tupas & Pefianco Martin 2017: 250–251). Interestingly, in 2009 the Philippines implemented what is known as "Mother Tongue-Based Multilingual Education" (MTB-MLE), thus granting greater prominence to the various local languages (Tupas & Pefianco Martin 2017: 248). This programme identifies nineteen local languages for mother tongue education, namely Aklanon, Bikol, Cebuano, Chabacano, Hiligaynon, Iloko, Ivatan, Kapampangan, Kinaray-a, Maguindanaoan, Maranao, Pangasinense, Sambal, Surigaonon, Tagalog, Tausug, Waray, Yakan, and Ybanag (Tupas & Pefianco Martin 2017: 254–255). Needless to say, this sparked controversies regarding the inclusion and exclusion of languages, complex decisions in

[26] According to 2017 figures, 20.8 per cent of the Malaysian population identified as Chinese and 6.2 per cent as Indian (retrieved from www.britannica.com/place/Malaysia, accessed on 12 May 2021.)

[27] As for peninsular Malaysia, Gill (2014: 2) mentions Cantonese, Foochow, Hainanese, Hakka, Mandarin, and Teochew for the Chinese diaspora and Gujarati, Hindi, Malayalam, Punjabi, Tamil, and Telugu for the Indian community. There are many other linguistic groups in other parts of Malaysia.

[28] Additional useful information can be retrieved from www.britannica.com/place/Philippines, accessed on 28 April 2021.

relation to the development of orthographies, and discussions about the position of English. Whatever the impact on the students' educational success and their future careers, this move will help to preserve linguistic diversity in the Philippines.

India officially adopts a trilingual policy of Hindi, a regional or local language (like Tamil or Malayalam), and English, with English gaining in strength after a strong rejection after independence in 1947. Each Indian state determines their own official language besides English and Hindi as the nationally recognized official languages. Altogether, there are twenty-two officially recognized languages in India (Mahboob & Jain 2017). Pakistan, which until its independence in 1947 was part of British India, recognizes both English and Urdu as official languages as well as Balochi, Pashto, Punjabi, and Sindhi as regional languages. Both India and Pakistan have large populations and accommodate extensive linguistic diversity.[29] Not surprisingly, many problems and difficulties in the use and recognition of these languages find parallels in the situations of Malaysia and the Philippines discussed above, and also the African countries explored in Section 5.3.1. The education systems need to negotiate the conflict between the local or regional languages, the official languages, and English. More often than not, there is a strong social divide between English-medium schools and schools using the indigenous languages as media of instruction (Mahboob & Jain 2017: 242). English dominates tertiary education. Many different forms of bilingualism, trilingualism, and multilingualism coexist. Parents unconsciously perpetuate the status of English in their aim of giving the best education to their children. Some smaller local (tribal) languages only exist in oral forms and face extinction as they are not included in formal education programmes (Mohanty 2013). There is a "double divide" between English and the officially recognized Indian languages as well as the latter and the numerous smaller languages (see also Mahboob & Jain 2017: 242). It appears almost impossible to design a unified education system catering for all these diverging linguistic needs, necessitating local solutions.[30]

[29] Further information can be retrieved from www.britannica.com/place/India and www.britannica.com/place/Pakistan, accessed on 28 April 2021.

[30] Ricento (2006b: 12–13) traces the origin of this conflict to nation building projects in post-colonial territories following World War II. Then, Western language policy advisors typically recommended the creation of diglossic societies in which the former colonial languages (English and French) offered access to Western technology and education. The indigenous languages were meant to serve more local functions. This, however, inadvertently lowered the status of the indigenous languages.

5.3.3 *Middle East*

Although the Middle East belongs to Asia, it is here discussed separately with an emphasis on the Gulf Region and the United Arab Emirates. There hardly is another area in the world that has seen a similar economic expansion over the past decades, first driven by the discovery and export of oil, later by tourism and services (Siemund & Leimgruber 2021; Siemund, Al-Issa & Leimgruber 2021; Siemund et al. 2021). Since the Arabic Gulf coast is basically a desert whose economy was traditionally based on fishing and pearling,[31] population density used to be low. Dubai was a rather small fishing village in the nineteenth century. The newly arising economy required human labour and expertise, to be recruited from all over the world. As the brief excursion to Dubai in Chapter 1 showed, the population there is composed of no less than 90 per cent of foreigners. This makes Dubai one of the most multi-ethnic and multilingual cities in the world. The English language occupies a firm position in the United Arab Emirates, as in other Gulf countries, since it functions as the undisputed lingua franca already brought to the area when what is the United Arab Emirates today used to be a loose array of sheikdoms under British protectorate.

The social structure in the United Arab Emirates has been referred to as an "ethnocracy" (Longva 2005; Piller 2018), since it is strongly stratified according to ethnic belonging with a small group of local Emiratis, who practically own the area, at the top of the social hierarchy (Hopkyns 2021: 252). Furthermore, ethnic stratification can be found amongst the many groups of immigrants who are employed in different sectors of the economy. The numerically strongest immigrant groups in Dubai come from India, Pakistan, Bangladesh, and the Philippines (Siemund, Al-Issa & Leimgruber 2021).

Although Arabic is the official language of the United Arab Emirates, explicitly added to the constitution in 2008, the language most widely used is English. This is the language in which business proceeds and all tertiary education is conducted in. Local Emiratis frequently speak English in the public sphere, since shops, malls, and taxis are staffed by foreigners who do not speak Arabic. As a global language, English enjoys tremendous social prestige in the area so that the education system – even down to primary level – has increasingly adopted English as the medium of instruction (Zakharia 2017: 287–288). The position of English has grown so strong that serious concerns are being voiced over the decline of Arabic. The overwhelming use of English as the medium of instruction means that some students find it hard to follow the curriculum (Al-Issa & Dahan 2011; Siemund, Al-Issa & Leimgruber 2021; Siemund et al. 2021).

[31] Agriculture was practically restricted to the oases and the more fertile area along the East coast of the United Arab Emirates.

There now is a host of languages in the area, the most important of which are Gulf Arabic (Khaleeji), Modern Standard Arabic, English, Hindi, Urdu, Malayalam, Persian, Bengali, and Tagalog (Siemund, Al-Issa & Leimgruber 2021). Moreover, the lion's share of workers is recruited from former colonial areas under British or American control, such as India, Pakistan, and the Philippines. In these countries, English is still widely used and, what is more, occurs in local nativized forms. Accordingly, Dubai and the entire United Arab Emirates have developed into an important dialect laboratory where different varieties of English interact and are perhaps in the process of convergence.

5.3.4 Summary

No matter whether good or bad, English still plays an important role in many postcolonial countries in Africa and Asia. It typically serves amongst the official languages, is vital for inter-ethnic communication, and tends to be used as one or even the sole medium of instruction in the education system. Its position as a highly prestigious global language often makes it difficult for the local languages to find their proper place, if not to survive. Africa and Asia still enjoy impressive levels of linguistic diversity that are in stark contrast to the few language labels officially representing the relevant polities.

Countries keep experimenting with English and the local languages as media of instruction, oscillating in their implementation according to the age of the students as well as the subjects. By the end of primary education at the latest, instruction generally proceeds on the basis of English. There is a tendency to use English for science and mathematics. Tertiary as well as expensive private education is nearly exclusively English-based.

African and Asian countries' educational language policies keep shifting between English immersion programmes and transitional bilingualism. Elite programmes tend to be English-only. Some countries have implemented education in the mother tongues, with English coming in at a later stage. The People's Republic of China as a world region, comprising nearly 1.4 billion speakers in 2021,[32] appears to be moving towards a monolingual form of social organization with functional bilingualism in English.

Chapters 2, 3, and 4 unravelled many determinants of language development, but they did not consider the larger political and ideological contexts. Given the highly diverse array of language policies and learning contexts discussed in the previous sections, the question arises as to which factors promote investment into languages and which inhibit it. This will be the topic of the next section.

[32] Retrieved from www.cia.gov/the-world-factbook/countries/china/, accessed on 2 May 2021.

5.4 Identity, Ideology, Capital, and Investment

Current research on multilingual development is suggestive of the fact that additive, balanced bilingualism or multilingualism together with an equivalorization of languages represents the ideal and most beneficial state for the individual and perhaps also for humankind. Moreover, there is a consensus in the scientific community, and perhaps also in the wider population, that linguistic diversity is an asset not to be squandered. Languages represent important cultural goods. They offer windows into our human condition. Reality teaches a different lesson there being extensive (officially decreed) monolingualism, sharp deltas in language dominance, also over time, and harsh social value systems superimposed on the languages coexisting in a habitat. A common theme emanating from the preceding survey of language policy and planning issues was that most, perhaps all, world regions keep promoting English as well as a few other highly valued languages. These are reserved for the more prestigious and script-based domains of language (academia, administration, business, education, jurisdiction, politics, etc.), while the autochthonous languages are being relegated to the home and oral domains. As a consequence, they risk being devalued, run out of use, and disappear, opening the door for monolingualism to become the majority pattern.

Although I am sceptical that this situation can easily be amended, if at all, we can at least try to understand it. After all, the linguistic problems are to a large extent symptomatic of deeper social inequalities. As far as I can see, the model of identity and investment developed by Darvin and Norton (2015) goes a long way towards explaining the observable language conflicts, gains, and losses. It encourages an understanding for empowerment from below by foregrounding the relevance of individual decisions on language use. However, as individuals are highly sensitive to reigning ideologies, the latter need to be taken into consideration, too.

In general terms, Norton (2018: 241) defines identity as “the way a person understands his or her relationship to the world, how that relationship is structured across time and space, and how the person understands possibilities for the future” (see also Darvin & Norton 2015: 36). Regarding their linguistic identities, speakers are often drawn between considerations of power (status) and solidarity (Brown & Gilman 1960; see Duchêne & Heller 2012 on pride and profit). If, as a concomitant of my education process and my career aspirations, I give up my home dialect and replace it with the corresponding high code, I lose or at least loosen ties with my autochthonous community in favour of a community with which I associate a higher social status, prestige, and more economic power (Bourdieu 1991; Joseph 2004). I am projecting an imagined identity into a community that I wish to be part of. Considerations of power – typically perceived economic opportunity and social prestige – override

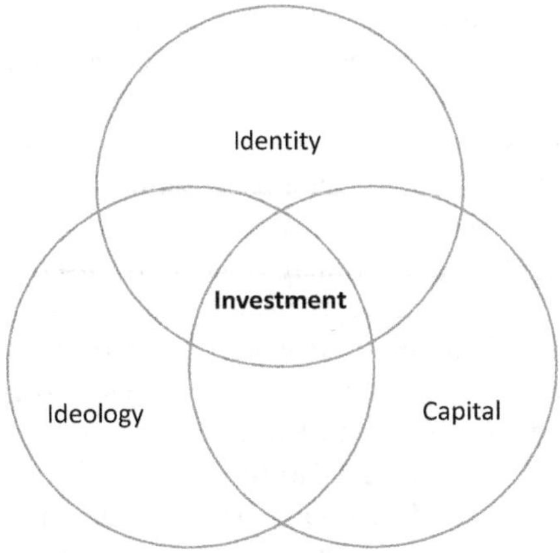

Figure 5.2 Darvin and Norton's (2015: 42) model of identity and investment. Annual Review of Applied Linguistics. Cambridge University Press. Adapted and reproduced with permission.

considerations of solidarity. For example, after the fall of the Iron Curtain and German reunification many East German speakers began to adapt to the German of their new West German compatriots, as this variety was established as the new standard. The Low German dialect spoken as the then standard in East Berlin was devalued in a matter of weeks and months and developed swiftly into a marker of lower social class membership (see also Dittmar & Paul 2019). High German was effectively learnt as another language. Arguably, this changed the speakers' identity.[33]

Besides individual identities and the surrounding ideologies, Darvin and Norton (2015) consider the relevance of one's capital for language learning decisions. Following Bourdieu (1991), capital is conceived of as a more encompassing term. It is not restricted to the material world, but also comprises social and cultural values. Academic knowledge, social networks, as well as experience about "how things work" represent invaluable cultural and social capital. The interactions between identity, ideology, and capital are depicted in Figure 5.2.

The model of investment shown in Figure 5.2 captures the observation that investment into languages and language learning only happens if the

[33] In the words of Darvin and Norton (2015: 45), identity can be conceptualized as "multiple, a site of struggle, and continually changing over time and space," and, moreover, as "a struggle of habitus and desire, of competing ideologies and imagined identities."

relationships between identity and ideology ("positioning"), identity and capital ("affordances/perceived benefits"), as well as ideology and capital ("systemic patterns of control") are in tune, as it were. For example, my personal construction of identity needs to overlap with the ideology around me, as I would opt out otherwise. Investment presupposes capital as well as the expectation that the investment increases one's capital. Finally, the capital must be compatible with the system in which it is to be used. Systemic ideologies impose barriers on the currencies that can be used within them.

In view of this investment model, the strong valorization of and emphasis on English in postcolonial countries becomes clear. It is viewed as a good investment, whereas little returns are expected from learning and maintaining the many indigenous languages. Darvin and Norton (2015: 37) explain that "if learners invest in a language, they do so with the understanding that they will acquire a wider range of symbolic and material resources, which will in turn increase the value of their cultural capital and social power." The high status of English is cemented by two facts. First, it functions as a gatekeeper and gate opener to the global world, and second, the indigenous languages are often too fragmented for any of them to achieve relevance at the national level (unlike French, German, and Spanish, which are strong national languages). This truly is a vicious circle. The model also explains the stronger investments into English in countries with smaller populations, like the Netherlands and the Scandinavian countries. Moreover, it suggests a strong overlap in the individual identity constructions and the reigning ideologies in the officially bilingual or multilingual countries that have achieved high levels of balanced bilingualism/multilingualism and a peaceful coexistence of the relevant languages. The model furthermore accounts for the intergenerational loss of heritage languages, unless these are backed up by strong national languages in the source countries (such as Chinese or Russian) or enticed by religious bonds (Arabic, Turkish). It even predicts the widespread confinement of heritage languages to the oral domain, since an investment in orality is sufficient for maintaining family relations qua the solidarity dimension.

Accordingly, individual investment into languages is a fragile phenomenon. In what used to be East Germany, students spent excessive amounts of time on what today one would call learning Russian as a second language. This exercise was largely unsuccessful for most students. Learning Russian was not considered a viable investment, but everyone had to. Moreover, Russian and the intense learning of Russian aroused somewhat undesirable political associations. This heavily curtailed any serious cognitive investment into Russian, in spite of the many hours spent on memorizing its vocabulary, grammar, and orthography, and in spite of the fact that a more profound knowledge of Russian would have been quite useful.

5.5 Multilingual Identities, Hybridity, and Language Attitudes

Transnational migration proffers new identity options and forces people into new identities. Globalization produces new ways to commodify language and identity (Heller 2003; Piller 2017).[34] Code-switching, code-mixing, code-crossing, language choice as well as other linguistic practices represent means to construe or negotiate identities, or to express multiple identities (Rampton 1995; Stavans & Hoffmann 2015). Status, power, and solidarity come to be associated with different languages in multilingual speakers, especially multilingual heritage speakers. The heritage language usually serves as the solidarity code, while the majority language is imbued with power and prestige. They both contribute to a multilingual speaker's social and cultural identity.[35] Having said that, considerations of solidarity (with a spouse, children, parents, a community, sodalities) may also override status even to an extent that principally available linguistic options are denied. Considerations of solidarity may also give preference to certain communities and their linguistic requirements (e.g. peer group vs. parents). Of course, status and solidarity may also go hand in hand, and status can easily come to dominate solidarity, as described in Section 5.4.

People may develop hybrid identities, index different identities according to contextual requirements, and construct as well as negotiate their identity with others (Eckert 2012; Johnstone 2010; Pavlenko & Blackledge 2004a). Identities are constructed through communication, as using language represents a social practice (Stavans & Hoffmann 2015). In this sense, identities tend to be unstable and dynamic. Contemporary multilingual urban areas provide ample illustration, as Wee (2021) shows for Singapore and Al-Issa (2021) as well as Hopkyns (2021) for Dubai, especially in the use of *Arabizi* and widespread translanguaging. Interestingly, elements of a solidarity code may come to be used as emblems of local identity by speakers who otherwise use the high code, as, for example, in Colloquial Singapore English (see Chapter 6), Kiezdeutsch, Ghanian Student Pidgin, Jamaican Creole, and Multicultural London English (Cheshire et al. 2011; Corum 2015; Leimgruber, Siemund & Terassa 2018; Mair 2013; Siemund, Schulz & Schweinberger

[34] Petrovic (2019), however, recently argued that language cannot be regarded as a commodity in the way other material products can. If at all, it is a "fictitious commodity." Graphic representations of languages, qua orthography and pictographic characters, add a material dimension to language. These can easily be commodified, in my view.

[35] Pavlenko and Blackledge (2004b: 16) hold "that identities are constructed at the interstices of multiple axes, such as age, race, class, ethnicity, gender, generation, sexual orientation, geopolitical locale, institutional affiliation, and social status, whereby each aspect of identity redefines and modifies all others." The languages in one's multilingual repertoire then offer additional dimensions.

2014; Wiese 2012).[36] Expatriate communities represent another promising field of research in which identity shifts and hybridization can be studied (Starr & Hiramoto 2019).

Issues of language and identity can be revealed by the attitudes that speakers hold towards the languages in their repertoires, using questionnaires, interviews, or visualizations (language portraits, Hu 2018: 162). Linguistic landscaping also represents a valuable approach to make such attitudes explicit (Shohamy & Gorter 2008). Language attitudes can be very positive, but also outright negative so that speakers practically reject using a language that they can in principle speak (see also Schmid 2002 on the factors underlying language attrition). If this happens, they intentionally curtail their linguistic and cultural capital – for which, of course, there may be very good reasons. There may be identity issues amongst adolescents, previous traumatic experiences, even life-threatening reasons (Piller 2016: 85–89). The heritage languages of multilingual speakers are often not regarded as valuable cultural capital and tend to be shadowed by the majority language and English. The latter are deemed to enhance a learner's social, cultural, and economic capital, thus offering a more promising future (see Section 5.4). English is especially strongly valued due to extensive anglophone networks in the world. Ironically, it even serves to construct new national identities in postcolonial countries that developed from former British colonies (Ghana, India, Nigeria, Singapore, etc.; see the discussion in Sections 5.3.1 and 5.3.2).

The value of a language is a function of the shared attitudes towards that language in a particular social group. Speakers will invest in languages, social ties, and cultural experience of what they consider a good investment from both the status and solidarity perspective. If, say, heritage languages are devalued by the majority society or in specific peer groups like adolescents, they will attract little investment and be lost in the long run. Heritage communities that value their own culture and language tend to invest in the respective languages, thus building up stable diasporas (Wei 1994). They develop a strong collective identity. Interestingly, identity and proficiency do not necessarily correlate (Pavlenko & Blackledge 2004b: 6).[37] Since English is generally associated with social upward mobility, it attracts tremendous investments in terms of language learning efforts, time spent in English-speaking countries, learning materials,

[36] Reference may here be made to Muysken's (2013: 709) four bilingual optimization strategies: "maximize structural coherence of the first language (L1); maximize structural coherence of the second language (L2); match between L1 and L2 patterns where possible; and rely on universal principles of language processing." Muysken (2013) describes how these strategies play out in different language contact situations, including ethnolects.

[37] These authors argue that low levels of identity with a target culture do not necessarily impede high proficiency in the target language, and that, conversely, high levels of identity do not automatically produce high levels of proficiency.

and the like. Multipliers in society, such as politicians, the media, and educators, can strongly influence the attitudes towards languages and thus the investment people are willing to make with respect to these languages.

Finally, it also matters how open societies are in regard to newcomers and to acknowledging other identities. A positive perception of other identities leads to more inclusive societies, which in turn is likely to boost motivation and participation. This follows from the strong relationship between investment and identity, ideology, and capital (Norton 2013, 2018: 244). Strongly othering societies are likely to marginalize, exclude, and lose members. Such considerations are relevant for societies at large, but also for smaller contexts such as classrooms, neighbourhoods, and work contexts.

5.6 Chapter Summary

Chapter 5 argued that multilingual advantages, language development, and also cross-linguistic influence cannot be understood without taking into consideration the wider multilingual ecologies in which one operates. It makes a difference whether one studies these issues in traditional European monolingual ecologies where other languages are learnt as classic second or foreign languages, in de jure monolingual ecologies with high numbers of immigrant speakers of other languages, in bilingual territories where the two languages enjoy the same status, coexist peacefully, and where the number of balanced bilinguals is high, in bilingual or multilingual areas with minority languages or stigmatized languages, or in highly multilingual ecologies with a common lingua franca. These constellations may arise due to various language-external conditions such as migration, imperial expansion and colonization, population displacement, famines, wars, diseases, natural catastrophes, climate change, amongst others, but also through explicit and implicit language policies, planning, and ideologies. These, in turn, strongly determine issues of identity and attitudes towards languages. All in all, the resulting language ecologies impact type of bilingualism as well as language dominance, determining cross-linguistic influence, language acquisition processes, and the way multilingual advantages can play out.

Most of the Western World has traditionally been characterized by linguistic homogeneity within its national boundaries, but is currently experiencing and rediscovering multilingualism due to global migration. Ironically, this happens after much of the autochthonous linguistic diversity has been forfeited. The territories under former colonial rule or influence are still extensively multilingual, but they are losing linguistic diversity at an alarming pace. The Western World's ideological stance is one of monolingualism in combination with certain concessions for linguistic minorities and, of course, elite bilingualism. Postcolonial anglophone countries in Africa and Asia tend to be officially bilingual or trilingual, with English being co-official. Some countries solely recognize English as their official language. Sadly, extensive linguistic diversity within the national boundaries of postcolonial countries favours English as a neutral choice, inducing a slow but steady shift towards it (for a comparison of English and Spanish as former colonial languages see Perez et al. 2021).

Regarding educational policies, it appears as if policymakers often face Hobson's choice, as there is no ideal approach that harmonizes pedagogical practice and constraints with individual linguistic (and other) diversity. The following four attested policy approaches yield different results. First, students with diverse language backgrounds can be instructed in the majority or global language beginning in primary school. Since many students will not be able to follow classroom discourse, this will be a frustrating experience for all parties involved. Second, instruction in the majority/global language can already start in preschool or kindergarten, effectively turning it into a second first language of the children. This will probably increase educational success, but devalue their home languages, lead to unbalanced bilingualism (unless the parents are actively involved), causing language shift and loss in the long run. Third, one may implement transitional bilingual programmes where instruction starts in the home language and gradually leads over to instruction in the majority language. This approach fetches students from where they are, but is also likely to produce language shift and loss over time. Finally, there is additive or maintenance bilingualism, which appears to be the preferred choice from a scientific perspective. This can work well in regions with two equivalued languages, but strongly multilingual settings again require decisions about which languages to promote. The Spanish part of the Basque Country, Catalunya, Canada, New Zealand, and Singapore illustrate the success of this approach, but the above discussion also revealed problems. Translanguaging and the enrichment of the curricula with material from all the students' background languages, as explained in Chapter 4, can be viewed as further refinements.

Very few areas in the world enjoy the privilege of developing additive bilingualism or even multilingualism for a broad range of people. Much of the world converges on functional bilingualism or multilingualism, especially when literacy is included as a criterion. Additive bilingualism – or even multilingualism – requires resources, political clout, and motivation of the people involved – essentially all three dimensions in the model of Darvin and Norton (2015). While Chapters 2 and 4 tried to identify the ideal setting for multilingual advantages to surface, the truth is that the world offers very many areas that are less than ideal.

6 The New Englishes in Their Multilingual Ecologies

This chapter extends the discussion of multilingual development to the so-called New Englishes as symbolic systems that developed in the former colonial territories and continued to develop after the collapse of the British Empire – or the withdrawal of the United States in the case of the Philippines – in the newly created independent polities. More precisely, the focus here lies on outer circle Englishes in the sense of Kachru (1985), thus excluding the inner circle countries where English is extensively used as a first language and where monolingualism in English is extant (Australia, Canada, New Zealand, United Kingdom, United States). The New Englishes will be analyzed from the perspective of their surrounding multilingual ecologies and not, as is more customary, in terms of hermetically delineated national varieties of English such as Indian English, Malaysian English, Singapore English, and the like. On that account, the chapter focuses on recent – and also more historical – multilingual outcomes of globalization where English plays a prominent role, has been incorporated into the local ecologies, interacts with many other languages, and shows or is beginning to show traces of localization or nativization. The chapter thus brings together the key issues discussed in the preceding chapters – globalization, migration, urban areas, multilingual advantages or effects, cross-linguistic influence, language acquisition and learning, language policies, identities, and attitudes – and pivots them on contexts of particular prominence.

Chapter 6 also affords additional perspectives: besides individual and societal multilingualism, it probes into multilingual interaction including intercultural communication. Detailed information will be presented from Singapore, Hong Kong, and the Gulf Region (especially the United Arab Emirates), as these have formed the research interest of the author for several years (Leimgruber, Siemund & Terassa 2018; Siemund 2018a; Siemund & Leimgruber 2021; Siemund & Li 2017, 2020; Siemund, Al-Issa & Leimgruber 2021; Siemund, Schulz & Schweinberger 2014; Siemund et al. 2021). Following an overview of the multilingual ecologies that English is embedded into (Section 6.1), the Dynamic Model of Postcolonial Englishes (Schneider 2003, 2007) as well as the World System of Varieties of English (Mair 2013) are discussed in relation to migration, multilingual language ecologies, and continuing language contact (Section 6.2).

Sections 6.3, 6.4, and 6.5 then scrutinize the multilingual ecologies of Singapore, Hong Kong, and Dubai in more detail, bringing together aspects of historical and current societal multilingualism. They all define the Englishes encountered in these locales, but crucially also the other languages. Recent data from Singapore, Hong Kong, and the United Arab Emirates help to appreciate the relevant multilingual ecologies and the role that English plays within them. The Gulf Region in particular offers a context where English – including the New Englishes – continues to be transplanted into. In the resulting language ecologies, these varieties of English interact in an unforeseen intensity and have now come together in what can be called a global dialect laboratory. Relatively newly developed contexts such as the Gulf Region mirror Singapore and Hong Kong in their early colonial stages when English came to be used as a lingua franca in a multilingual setting. The internal complexities of the new multilingual ecologies, however, are significantly higher with many more languages interacting in relatively small territories such as the United Arab Emirates. The fundamental principles, nonetheless, can be taken to be similar, so that the current situation in the United Arab Emirates provides important clues to the multilingual ecologies in Singapore and Hong Kong during the early colonial decades. All in all, Chapter 6 offers a systemic view of multilingual ecologies and works towards an operationalization of the factors that define them.

6.1 The Multilingual Ecologies Embedding the New Englishes

Besides Singapore, Hong Kong, and the Gulf Region, which represent the primary interest of this chapter, New Englishes that meet the present definition can be found in several African countries, India, Pakistan, Malaysia, the Philippines, and Fiji. English was implanted into these regions through colonial expansion and largely came to be adopted as a second language, partially also as a first language. The resulting varieties of English are known by such labels as Fiji English, Ghanaian English, Indian English, Malaysian English, Nigerian English, Pakistani English, Philippine English, South African English, and the like.

These varieties of English have been extensively researched, more recently by means of large corpora reflecting the use of English in the relevant countries (see the references in Kortmann et al. 2004 as well as Siemund 2013).[1] However, current research provides overarching generalizations that are likely to play out quite differently at the local and individual level. This is due to three reasons.

[1] Widely used corpora include the International Corpus of English (ice-corpora.net/ice/) and the Corpus of Global Web-Based English (www.english-corpora.org/glowbe/).

First, the communities speaking these varieties of English have always been extensively multilingual. Colonialism penetrated into linguistically diverse areas in which knowledge and use of several languages used to be the norm.[2] Moreover, at least some colonies rapidly developed into major targets of migration shortly after being established. They were in need of cheap labour attracting people from far away speaking different languages. To complicate the picture further, indentured labour, especially from Southern India, added to the already existing multilingual texture in other colonies (e.g. in Fiji, Malaysia, Singapore, and South Africa).[3]

Second, political borders were created rather artificially following colonial rule, not infrequently cutting across ethnic and linguistic groups. The idea of finding one variety of English to the left of a political border and another to its right cannot be but an oversimplification. What matters is the speech community, and this should be the unit of investigation (Schneider 2003: 273). On a similar note, urban centres tend to be different from the other parts of a country. English in Lagos is likely to be quite different from what is generally referred to as Nigerian English (Schreiber 2012).

Third, global migration is widely perceived of as flowing from developing to developed countries, silently passing over the fact that there is also extensive migration in the developing world. Expanding urban areas such as Accra, Lagos, Mumbai, Bangalore, Manila, and Cebu are as much targets of migration as are Toronto, London, and Dubai. They are densely populated linguistic melting pots with English being part of the mix.

The following observations can help to substantiate the above points. As for societal multilingualism, Table 6.1 offers a snapshot of the number of languages in a range of countries in 2021, based on the information provided by Ethnologue (Eberhard, Simons & Fennig 2022).[4] They bear witness to impressive degrees of multilingualism, especially in regard to India, Malaysia, Nigeria, the Philippines, and Tanzania.

Evidently, such figures need to be interpreted with care, as the distinction between languages and dialects is diffuse and Ethnologue does not systematically distinguish between indigenous and immigrant languages – although there is the category "non-indigenous." Moreover, the figures in Table 6.1 do not

[2] Regarding India and Pakistan, Mahboob and Jain (2017: 234) highlight their intensely multilingual and plurilingual traditions.

[3] South Africa witnessed the development of Indian South African English (or South African Indian English) as a concomitant of such migration streams (see Mesthrie 2002).

[4] Ethnologue counts languages in different categories, such as "developing," "dormant," "dying," "endangered," "established," "extinct," "indigenous," "institutional," "in trouble," "living," "non-indigenous," "unestablished," and "vigorous" languages. I here report the figures in the category of "established languages," accessed on 26 February 2021. Ethnologue keeps updating the figures.

Table 6.1. *Countries and their languages according to Ethnologue (Eberhard, Simons & Fennig 2022).*

Country	Languages	Country	Languages
Fiji	15	Nigeria	531
Ghana	83	Pakistan	76
Hong Kong	7	Philippines	186
India	463	Singapore	24
Kenya	69	South Africa	36
Malaysia	133	Tanzania	128

necessarily reflect the most recent information. Accordingly, they sometimes under-report languages, while over-reporting in other places. The figures for India, Nigeria, and the Philippines look impressive, but many languages are rather small and restricted to specific areas or islands. Crucially, the figures do not reflect the time of colonization. Singapore perhaps had fewer than twenty-four distinct languages in 1819, while Hong Kong likely counted more than seven in 1841.[5] We will come back to these issues in the subsequent sections. In sum, the New Englishes typically emerged and continue to emerge in territories and contexts that are characterized by strong degrees of multilingualism.

Concerning varieties of English in relation to current political divisions, one could alternatively postulate macro-units like West Africa, East Africa, a super region comprising India, Pakistan, and Sri Lanka, as well as one consisting of Singapore, Malaysia, and parts of Indonesia, where the Englishes in use show important commonalities and could be conceptualized in terms of dialect continua. The dendrograms provided in Nagy et al. (2006), Schmidtke and Kuperman (2017) as well as Szmrecsanyi and Kortmann (2008) offer some support for such a view, although further work is needed here. In a similar vein, classificatory labels like 'Indian English', 'Nigerian English', 'Philippine English', 'Singapore English', and the like are quite misleading in that they pass over variability in the representations of these Englishes in different locales of the same country or within unrelated speaker groups, but also in that they convey a degree of stasis that these Englishes simply do not possess. Ironically, the linguistic field of World Englishes has unconsciously contributed to the codification of these varieties, but given current globalization and migration processes, any such assumptions regarding stability are questionable. We need to factor in extensive fluidity (Blommaert 2010; see also Johnstone, Andrus & Danielson 2006 on enregisterment).

[5] These years reflect the respective time of colonization (see Sections 6.3 and 6.4).

Finally, with respect to migration within the territories where the New Englishes are spoken, recent figures suggest extensive internal population movements. For example, the Policy Brief on Internal Migration in the Philippines (UNESCO 2016b) states that "[a]pproximately 2.9 million Filipinos changed residence between 2005 and 2010," but that the share of international migrants contributed only 4.2 per cent. Not surprisingly, the lion's share of internal migration went to Metro Manila and the adjacent regions of Calabarzon and Central Luzon. One may suspect that people migrating to more prosperous international destinations induce flows of migration at home from rural to urban areas. As for Malaysia, internal migration accounted for 88.7 per cent of all migration (UNESCO 2016a). Amongst the most prominent destinations is the southern state of Johor which borders on Singapore. There is substantial daily commuting between its capital Johor Bahru and Singapore. I take it that similar data could be compiled for New Delhi, Mumbai, Bangalore, Hyderabad, Chennai, Accra, Banjul, Lagos, Nairobi, Dodoma, and others. Again, English can always be assumed to be part of the linguistic repertoire of these internal migrants.

6.2 Multilingual Strands, Migration Strands, and Transnational Migration

The New Englishes introduced above are characterized by differing degrees of nativization or endonormative stabilization in the sense of Schneider (2003, 2007), but they nevertheless remain embedded in their respective local multilingual ecologies with which they continue to interact and in which they develop further. The New Englishes have in fact been appropriated by the local populations and have become part of the local ecologies. It may seem odd to consider English an African or Asian language, but current realities suggest such an analysis. And although New Englishes as such have received extensive scholarly attention, much less is known about their interaction with and their embedding in the local multilingual textures (Leimgruber, Siemund & Terassa 2018; Siemund, Al-Issa & Leimgruber 2021; Siemund, Schulz & Schweinberger 2014). Schreiber (2012) describes impressive internal differentiation and social stratification for the English in Lagos.

In systematically distinguishing between "settler strands" and "indigenous strands," augmented by various "adstrate strands," the Dynamic Model proposed in Schneider (2003, 2007) takes the discussion of World Englishes significantly beyond Kachru's (1985) division into inner, outer, and expanding circle Englishes or that between English as a native, second, or foreign language. The development of the New Englishes in colonial and postcolonial settings can be conceptualized as complex language contact situations in which indigenous and settler strands converge over time and together forge a new variety of English. According to Schneider (2003, 2007), postcolonial Englishes traverse through five distinct stages, namely (i) foundation, (ii) exonormative stabilization, (iii) nativization, (iv) endonormative stabilization, and (v) differentiation. Due to important differences in the demographics, the languages involved, the acquisition processes, the communication patterns, migration patterns, attitudes and social evaluations, this general unidirectional process has led to unique outcomes depending on the postcolonial setting considered. For example, Schneider (2003) sees Fiji English in stage two, Hong Kong English in stage three,[6] and Singapore English in stage four. Irish English can be considered one of the earliest postcolonial Englishes and has been nativized to an extent that as of today it is hardly recognized as such and typically classified as an inner circle English. Nevertheless, it is full of Irish traces and since Irish is the first official language of Ireland – though it is not widely spoken – it remains in contact with it.[7] It should be clear that the rather abstract classification proposed by the Dynamic Model passes over important local differences and variation. Some age groups and social groups in Singapore can be expected to be in stage three, others in stage four, and yet others perhaps even in stage five. It could also be possible that individuals traverse through these stages in the course of their lifetime.

Furthermore, in the typical colonial and postcolonial setting, there is not only one indigenous strand but several (see Schneider 2003: 243). What is more, the individual indigenous strands are composed of multilingual individuals. To complicate matters further, there may be local lingua francas, such as Bazaar Malay in Singapore and Malaysia, enriching the repertoires of the multilingual speakers. Accordingly, the indigenous strands are highly heterogeneous. Apart from the largely monolingual stage five Englishes in the United States, Canada, Australia, and New Zealand, where the indigenous strands have strongly diminished, the New Englishes considered here have become part of the language repertoires of the multilingual speakers in the relevant areas. The aim of the following sections lies precisely in making these multilingual strands and the local language ecologies explicit.

It is usually possible to associate the postcolonial Englishes with a particular developmental stage in Schneider's (2003) Dynamic Model. However, recent targets of international migration where English comes to be widely adopted as a lingua franca, such as the Gulf Region, largely eschew a classification in this model. The United Arab Emirates, for example, is an independent country that attracts foreign labour to drive local infrastructure projects. There is no immediate colonial power taking English to the area, although the Arabian Peninsula

[6] After the reinstatement of Hong Kong to the People's Republic of China in 1997, Hong Kong English may in fact have moved in the opposite direction (see Section 6.4.3).

[7] Retrieved from www.britannica.com/place/Ireland, accessed on 11 May 2021.

Hyper-Central Variety
"Hub" of the World System of Englishes: American English

Super-Central Varieties
British English, Australian English, South African English, Nigerian English, Indian English, ...

Central Varieties
Irish English, Scottish (Standard) English, Jamaican English, Ghanaian English, Kenyan English, Sri Lankan English, Pakistani English, New Zealand English, ...

Peripheral Varieties
Maltese English, St. Kitts English, Cameroonian English, Papua New Guinea English, ...

Figure 6.1 The World System of Standard Englishes according to Mair (2013: 261).

has a long history of English. In fact, the power relations are here reversed. Moreover, foreigners outnumber local Emiratis by factor ten (see Chapter 1 and Section 6.5). English is used because it is the global lingua franca and incoming workers and professionals speak it as a second language – partially also as a first language. The driving force behind English is globalization, not colonialism. In spite of important parallels in the genesis of other New Englishes, such situations necessitate different models. Migration strands – often themselves multilingual – complement and even outweigh the earlier indigenous and settler strands. As a matter of fact, the development of English in at least Singapore and Malaysia equally cannot be understood without factoring in the relevant migration strands (see also Chapter 7). They deserve attention in the historical reconstruction of these varieties.

Mair (2013), building on de Swaan's (2001) World Language System (see Chapter 1), proposes the World System of Standard Englishes shown in Figure 6.1 that captures the hierarchical relationship behind World Englishes and likely paths of mutual influence (typically top-down). American English is considered the current hub variety providing a normative orientation for the other varieties. The super-central varieties could also be described as epicentres in their respective regions of influence (Mair 2013: 259; see also Peters 2009).

Mair (2013: 264) then goes on to include non-standard varieties into this model with the interesting consequence that non-standard varieties like African American Vernacular English and Jamaican Creole, amongst others, form a layer of non-standard super-central varieties. Jamaican Creole even ranks above the corresponding standard variety of Jamaican English. The motivation behind this ordering is that these varieties carry high covert prestige and exert strong global influences on specific cultural domains, such as music, entertainment, and media. Crucially, English as a lingua franca appears amongst the non-standard super-central varieties, which explains why it becomes the preferred medium of communication in migration contexts such as the United Arab Emirates.

However, although Mair's (2013) model captures important dependencies between different varieties of English, it does not incorporate their embedding in the local multilingual ecologies and the concomitant linguistic influences. For the context of Singapore, for example, we need a model that captures the interaction between Standard English, Standard Singapore English, Colloquial Singapore English (CSE), as well as the mother tongues and the other languages active in the area. In historical terms, all languages in the territory, except for Malay, count as immigrant languages.[8] Further differentiation appears necessary, as Colloquial Singapore English is not homogenous across ethnic groups (see Section 6.3.3).

6.3 Singapore and Singapore English

Both laypeople and specialists widely consider Singapore as the archetype of a multilingual society. There can be no doubt that this description is adequate for the foundational decades of the then British colony. However, due to fervent governmental intervention and language planning, Singaporean society has been moving towards individual bilingualism. More recently, we see a trend to espouse English as the most dominant language in peoples' language repertoires.

6.3.1 Historical Multilingualism

Separated by the Strait of Johor from the Malaysian peninsula, Singapore is a small island close to the equator in the Northern Hemisphere. There still are noticeable stretches of rain forest and wetland that can be taken to have been the primordial state before Sir Stamford Raffles arrived in 1819 and envisioned a special position for the location as a trading post in the British Empire. It is safe to assume that nobody then foresaw the ensuing population movements

[8] I consider this important for the understanding of the present status of English in Singapore. There is no country amongst the outer circle countries where English has advanced to a similar extent and is used in a comparable number of social sectors, including the home. I believe that it is easier for immigrant groups to shift to a new language than for indigenous groups, as the latter construct their identity from their home territory and their language (see Chapter 7). Needless to say, there are other important factors behind the promotion of English in Singapore.

and especially the linguistic developments. It took about 200 years for Singapore to mature into the current super-diverse high-tech conurbation. Needless to say, its current linguistic texture cannot be understood without an appraisal of its early decades.

In the centuries before the British arrival, population density in Singapore can be assumed to have been relatively low with people engaging in fishing, agriculture, and trading. Malay will have been spoken, most certainly in various dialectal forms. It is reasonable to believe that there was trade and migration between and across the adjacent archipelago. One can further assume that contact with people from Southern China enjoys a long history in the area, with there being extensive trade networks spanning the South China Sea (Lim 2010; Siemund & Li 2020).[9] The fact that Malaysia holds a strong Muslim population bears testimony to the extensive cultural and commercial networks operating in and beyond the area centuries before the British (and other Europeans) arrived.[10] Moreover, it is important to view Singapore in the context of previously established European trading posts such as Penang and Malacca. These European posts had been operated by other colonial powers – notably the Netherlands, Portugal, and Spain – before the British Empire incorporated them. These earlier colonial centres will have attracted migration in much the same way as Singapore later would. Many of these migrants and their descendants later moved on to Singapore seeking new opportunities. In any event, the foundation of Singapore as a major settlement and its development into an urban centre proved a far-sighted decision.

Current Singaporean officialdom stratifies the local population ethnically into Malays, Chinese, Indians, and others. Chapter 1 introduced the 2019 figures regarding their proportions relative to the entire population, namely 15.0, 76.0, 7.5, and 1.5 per cent, respectively (Singapore Department of Statistics 2021). It is obvious that the Chinese represent the biggest group numerically although they are historically immigrants to the area. These proportions used to be quite different in the early years of the colony. Table 6.2 reports the population figures from a selection of time points starting in 1824 (Lim 2010: 22). Not surprisingly, Malay people then constituted the most sizeable group, but the figures reveal a rapid increase of the Chinese population so that by 1901 the current proportions had almost been reached. One can also see a strong population growth

[9] Li (2021: 26–28), in fact, argues that the common interpretation of precolonial Singapore as an insignificant fishing location is a misconception. Apparently, the excellent strategic position of Singapore had been discovered and made use of in the centuries before Raffles' arrival in 1819. An earlier name for Singapore was *Temasek* (Javanese *tumasik* 'sea town'; see Li 2021: 26).

[10] Islam was disseminated in what is today Malaysia by Arab and Indian traders between the thirteenth and the seventeenth century and was quickly adopted by the local populations (retrieved from www.britannica.com/place/Malaysia, accessed on 12 May 2021).

Table 6.2. *Population development in Singapore (adapted from Lim 2010: 22; see also Li 2021 for further details).*

Year	Population	Chinese %	Malay %	Indian %	Others %
1824	10,683	31.0	60.2	7.1	1.7
1849	52,891	52.9	32.2	11.9	3.0
1901	226,842	72.1	15.8	7.8	4.3
1931	557,745	75.1	11.7	9.1	4.2
1980	2,413,945	76.9	14.6	6.4	2.1

apparently primarily propelled by Chinese immigration. The proportional size of the Indian population has remained relatively constant and so has the group of others (primarily Europeans and Eurasians).

What is also interesting is that even the earliest figures are already based on the ethnic divisions still employed today. This is by no means obvious as all groups were – and still are – strongly stratified internally. The group of Indians especially was very heterogeneous in terms of origin, language, and religion (Lim 2010: 25–26). Accordingly, the modern Singapore nomenclature finds its roots in the very early history of the then colony. Lim (2010: 22), following Bloom (1986: 352), argues that this system of ethnic compartmentalization is in fact much older and had already been used in Malacca. It went hand in hand with territorial allocations so that the ethnic groups came to reside in distinct areas of Singapore. The contemporary, largely touristic destinations of China Town, Kampong Glam (Kampung Gelam), and Little India can be traced back to these earlier territorial confinements. Modern Singapore pursues a policy of ethnic integration by which certain quotas in the distribution of the ethnic groups across neighbourhoods need to be observed (Sin 2002).

The language ecology created by the early streams of migration must have been quite diverse and also multilingual – in spite of the ethnic compartmentalization. The broad ethnic labels in Table 6.2 represent cover terms for extensive ethnic and linguistic diversity. Lim (2010: 23) states that the bulk of Chinese immigrants originates in the southern coastal provinces of China, in particular "Xiamen in southern Fujian (the Hokkiens), Chaozhou in the east of Guangdong (the Teochews), and Guangdong itself (the Cantonese)." In addition, there was a "sizeable representation of Hakkas and Hainanese" as well as "small numbers from the coastal counties of northern Fujian and 'Three Rivers People' from northern and central China" (Lim 2010: 23). Indians primarily came from Southern India representing "Tamil, Telugu, and Malayalam language communities," but also from Northern India speaking Punjabi and Bengali (Lim 2010: 25–26). The Malays were perhaps the most homogenous internally, although this group "included immigrants from various parts of the Malay archipelago" speaking Austronesian languages including Javanese, Buginese, and Boyanese (Lim 2010: 23).

One cannot but start wondering how communication proceeded in this colonial Babel. Since the British ruled Singapore and likely did not learn the various local languages, English must have been imposed from above on this newly created community from early on.[11] This can only have worked through intermediaries versatile in English and the other languages. Lim (2010: 24–25) informs us that it was especially the Straits-born Chinese or Peranakans who served as such intermediaries (see also Bao 2021). An early education system installed by British rule provided tuition in English and used English as a medium of instruction (see below). At the same time, there were local pidginized forms of Malay available that had already established themselves as interethnic communication systems (lingua francas) across the Malay peninsula and the surrounding archipelago. Amongst the most prominent are Bazaar Malay and Baba Malay (Lim 2010: 26–27). As contact languages, they represent restructured forms of Malay with various lexical and grammatical influences from the immigrant languages, especially Hokkien. Baba Malay used to be widely spoken in the community of the Straits Chinese (Peranakans) who originate in families formed by local Malay women and assimilated Chinese settlers. Singaporean Babas (Peranakans) stem from Penang and Malacca from where they traversed southwards to Singapore (Lim 2010: 24–25). Interestingly enough, English only began to replace Bazaar Malay as the local lingua franca after Singapore reached independence in 1965, primarily due to the ensuing language policy decisions. By then, English had already established itself in its distinct localized form of Colloquial Singapore English (Singlish). Again, this is a contact language that can be analyzed as a restructured and relexified form of a Sinitic variety enriched by influences from Malay and Tamil (Ho & Platt 1993; Platt 1975). We will look at Colloquial Singapore English in more detail in Section 6.3.3.

Modern Singapore has established an "ethnic-specific, English-centric bilingualism" (Bao 2021: 19). Malay, Mandarin, and Tamil are officially assigned to the three most important ethnic groups as mother tongues with English supposed to be known by everyone. This bilingual language policy was vigorously promoted by the Singaporean government after independence, but its roots can be reconstructed in early decisions by the colonial government. Bao (2021: 21–22) writes that it was Raffles himself who envisioned an education system for the colony that aimed to educate the local elites in English and to provide education in the local languages to others. These local languages would be Malay, Chinese, and Tamil (besides perhaps other Indian

[11] Platt and Weber (1980: 7) characterize the linguistic situation as "polyglossic" with several H-varieties and L-varieties interacting.

languages). The sciences in particular were decreed to be taught in English, which still is a widely encountered educational philosophy in other postcolonial countries (see Chapter 5). Raffles' ideas were institutionally enshrined in the Singapore Institution in 1823, known as Raffles Institution from 1868 on.[12] It has survived to this very day and is counted amongst the most prestigious schools in Singapore. Crucially, these early decisions foreshadow the contemporary functional division of languages that views English as connecting Singapore to the world, whereas the local ethnic languages provide cultural anchors. Moreover, it introduced important social stratification with English coming to be the preferred language in the upper social strata (Bao 2021: 22). Modern Singapore continues these divisions, albeit on a broader social basis.

The extension of the moniker 'Chinese' has changed substantially over time, especially after the Chinese Revolution in 1911. In the early decades, it referred to the Chinese immigrant languages taken to Singapore, notably Cantonese, Hokkien, and Teochew. One can assume that early Chinese education reflected these languages. The foundation of the Republic of China in 1912 triggered strong efforts to create a national language, leading to the promotion of Mandarin in the education system (see Chapter 5). The repercussions of these processes on the mainland of China could be perceived even in faraway Singapore, with efforts starting to promote the use of Mandarin in Chinese-based education (Bao 2021: 23). After independence in 1965, education in Chinese and the other local languages slowly gave way to English as the preferred medium of instruction until in 1987 English came to be selected as the only option. Again, this conversion was foreshadowed much earlier, as parts of the Chinese community – especially the Straits-born Peranakans – showed a strong preference for English, while other parts leaned towards the use of Chinese (Bao 2021: 23; Lim 2010: 24–25).[13]

Despite the relatively detailed information available on the different ethnic groups and languages historically interacting in the area, the situation at the individual levels remains speculation. In keeping with the spirit of the preceding chapters, one would like to know more about the individual language dominance and acquisition patterns as well as the resulting types of bilingualism and multilingualism. Moreover, it would be revealing to learn about the individual migration trajectories and interactional patterns in the different languages. Li, Lorenz and Siemund (2022) as well as Li (2021) probe into the Oral History Interviews held by the National Archives of Singapore (OHI-NAS 2020) and

[12] See Li (2021: 57–58) for a more detailed account of the development of the Singaporean educational landscape.

[13] To quote Bao (2021: 23) on this point: "Within the Chinese community, the labels Chinese-educated and English-educated became thoroughly politicized, and the two languages acquired new indexical meanings – English as progressive and modern, and Chinese as backward and uncool."

discover fascinating personal narratives bearing testimony to the above points. For example, they report the case of Elsie Quah (OHI-000213-EQ) born in 1899 into a Hokkien-speaking family of immigrants from China. They spoke Hokkien at home, but Elsie also learnt Malay in a mission school. She received training as a midwife in Kuala Lumpur before returning to Singapore where she worked the rest of her life. The interview proceeds in Colloquial Singapore English, but Elsie was most certainly also fluent in Bazaar Malay. Language repertoires like that of Elsie Quah are still partially mirrored in the current population of Singapore. The next section looks at these from a contemporary perspective.

6.3.2 Societal Multilingualism

Despite the official bilingual policy pursued by the Singaporean government that assigns a so-called mother tongue to each of three main ethnic groups in conjunction with English, the observable individual language repertoires still are considerably more heterogeneous and diverse. Nevertheless, the declaration of Mandarin, Malay, and Tamil as the respective ethnic mother tongues after independence effected a dwindling of the linguistic diversity present during colonial times. In particular, the Chinese community went through a process of language shift from the Sinitic immigrant vernaculars to Mandarin, but similar shifting processes can also be observed in the other ethnic groups (Cavallaro & Ng 2021: 134). In 2015, English, Mandarin, and Malay were the most widely used home languages with English in top position (see Chapter 1). For many speakers in Singapore, the mother tongues are in fact second languages, primarily acquired in the education system (Cavallaro & Ng 2021: 134–135). There can be no doubt that the Speak Mandarin Campaign initiated in 1979 and the conversion of the entire education system to English as the medium of instruction in 1987 are in a fundamental way responsible for these changes (Bao 2021; Cavallaro & Ng 2021; Leimgruber, Siemund & Terassa 2018; Siemund, Schulz & Schweinberger 2014). Cavallaro and Ng (2021: 135) point out that "[f]or a great majority of Singaporeans, English is their most competent language, regardless of the language(s) they speak at home."

The idea of an "ethnic-specific, English-centric bilingualism" (Bao 2021: 19), as introduced above, represents the reigning ideology in Singapore. However, underneath this ideological layer substantial linguistic diversity can still be observed, partially stratified by social parameters. In addition, when people report that they speak English, this can mean Standard Singapore English, Colloquial Singapore English, or both. For example, Leimgruber, Siemund and Terassa (2018) as well as Siemund, Schulz and Schweinberger (2014) studied the language repertoires, self-reported proficiencies, attitudes, and usage

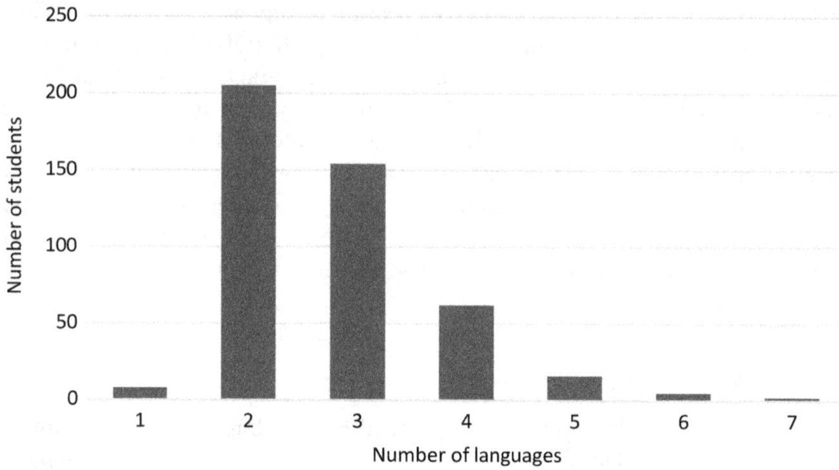

Figure 6.2 Number of languages spoken by students.
Adapted from Leimgruber, Siemund and Terassa (2018: 290).

patterns in three cohorts of 450 students altogether. They represent university students, polytechnic students, as well as students from the Institute of Technical Education (ITE). The latter is a type of vocational school and was included in order for the three institutions to serve as proxies for differences in social background. Each institution contributed 150 students. Figure 6.2 shows that most students in the sample are bilingual and trilingual. A sizeable number of students reported four languages. Monolingualism is the exception with only eight cases in the sample. In other words, many students know other languages apart from English and their mother tongue.

The languages reported by the students are documented in Figure 6.3. One can see here that English is spoken by everyone and that a sizeable majority knows Mandarin. Interestingly, the Chinese vernaculars Hokkien, Cantonese, and Teochew also feature in the students' language repertoires. Hokkien even ranges before Malay, while Tamil accrues the lowest number of speakers in the sample.[14] The presently attested languages still mirror the historical immigration patterns discussed in Section 6.3.1.

The language repertoires owned by the students can be gleaned from Figure 6.4. Not surprisingly, English in combination with Mandarin is the most widely reported profile, but it is somewhat unexpected that trilingualism of

[14] The languages in the category "Others" include Japanese, Korean, and Bahasa Indonesia, amongst others.

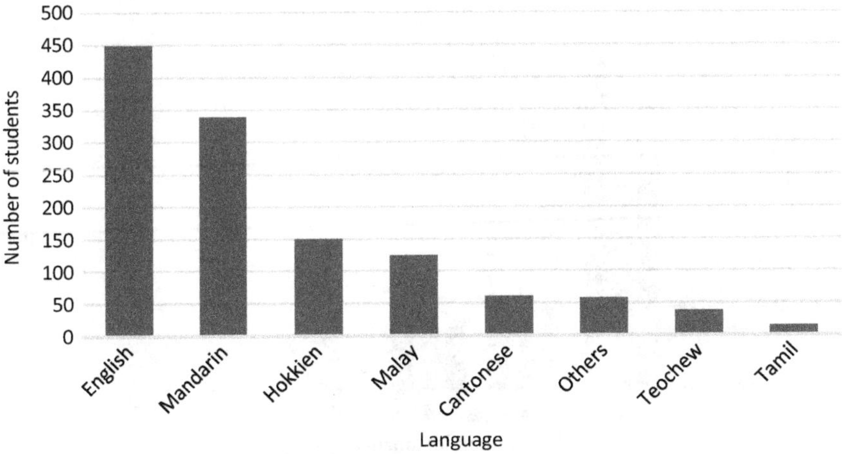

Figure 6.3 Languages spoken by students.
Adapted from Leimgruber, Siemund and Terassa (2018: 291).

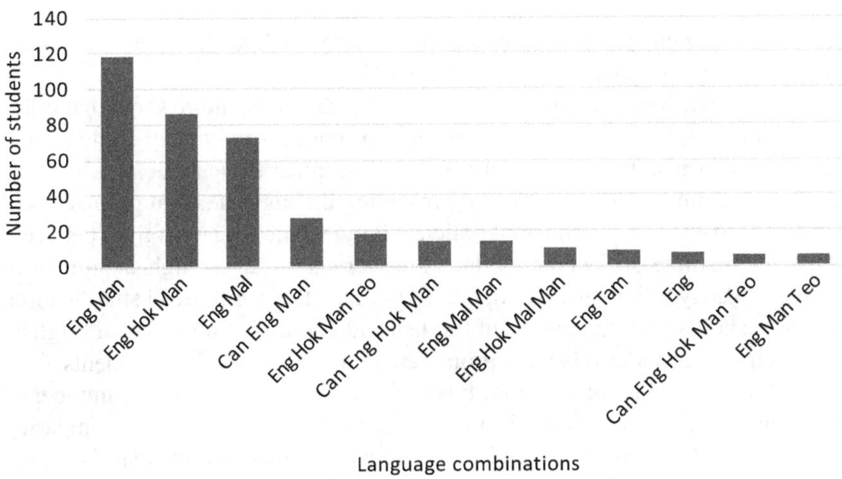

Figure 6.4 Language combinations amongst students that occur at least five times.
Adapted from Leimgruber, Siemund and Terassa (2018: 292–293).
Note: Can = Cantonese, Eng = English, Hok = Hokkien, Mal = Malay, Man = Mandarin, Tam = Tamil, Teo = Teochew.

English, Hokkien, and Mandarin is attested more frequently than bilingualism of English and Malay or English and Tamil. In addition, we can see that Hokkien is typically part of the repertoires and that Malay occurs together with Chinese

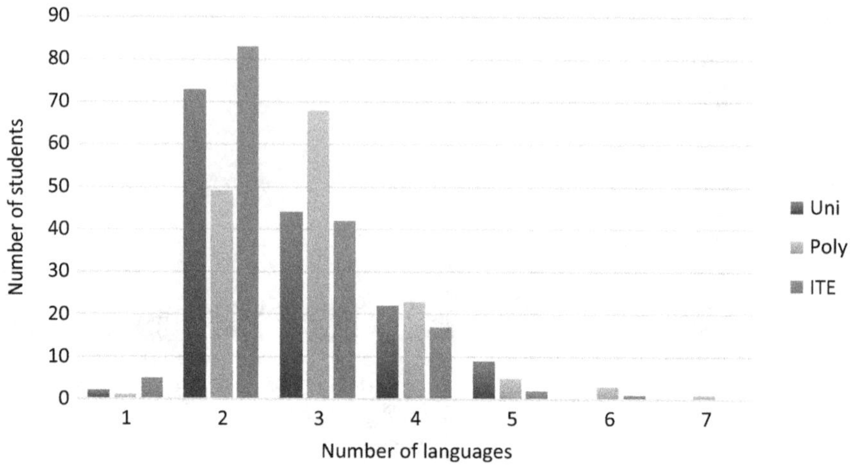

Figure 6.5 Number of languages spoken by university (Uni), polytechnic (Poly), and ITE students (ITE).
Adapted from Leimgruber, Siemund and Terassa (2018: 294).

languages. Again, English here is a cover term for both Standard Singapore English and Colloquial Singapore English.[15]

Leimgruber, Siemund and Terassa (2018: 293) furthermore show that bilingualism of English and Mandarin is highest amongst university students and lowest with students from the Institute of Technical Education. This is to be expected, as university students – representing the highest social groups – will conform closest to governmental policies. Polytechnic students fall in between. Also, the Institute of Technical Education accrues by far the highest number of English–Malay bilinguals, pointing to important ethnic and social stratification. The same holds for bilingualism of English and Tamil. Trilingualism of English, Hokkien, and Mandarin is most prominent amongst polytechnic students.

Students from the three school types differ systematically in the number of languages they report. This is illustrated in Figure 6.5. When comparing university with polytechnic students, one can see that bilingualism is higher in the first group. Trilingualism is more widespread in the second group. Again, the linguistic behaviour of university students corresponds more closely to official policies. These differences are mainly driven by Chinese students. There are also many bilingual students at the Institute of Technical Education, but this bilingualism is largely ethnic-specific and induced by the high number of Malay students in this educational track.

[15] The eight most frequently attested language profiles account for 80 per cent of all attested profiles (Leimgruber, Siemund & Terassa 2018: 292).

Table 6.3. *Mean rankings of languages across schools. The highest rank is "1." Languages are ordered alphabetically.*

School	Can	Eng	Hok	Mal	Man	Tam	Teo
Uni	2.74	1.13	3.14	3.00	1.96	2.00	3.43
Poly	3.03	1.17	2.90	2.42	2.02	2.00	3.45
ITE	3.44	1.37	3.05	1.73	1.90	2.00	3.29
Total	3.00	1.22	3.02	2.03	1.97	2.00	3.41

Note: Can = Cantonese, Eng = English, Hok = Hokkien, Mal = Malay, Man = Mandarin, Tam = Tamil, Teo = Teochew.

The questionnaire used in the studies by Siemund, Schulz and Schweinberger (2014) and Leimgruber, Siemund and Terassa (2018) also asked students to rank the languages in their repertoires according to proficiency. The ranking is based on self-assessments and serves as a proxy for the corresponding objective proficiencies. With the exception of two students, the ranking involved at most four languages per students. Table 6.3 details the mean rankings for seven languages according to school type.

Evidently, English is the language all students feel most proficient in, there being a slight downslope from university to ITE students. English is followed by the three official mother tongues in terms of proficiency. Noticeably, Malay is reported as the weakest mother tongue with regard to the total means. The Chinese vernaculars of Cantonese, Hokkien, and Teochew received the lowest proficiencies. This ranking nicely reflects the social prestige associated with these languages (recall the hierarchy of languages introduced in Chapter 1). It furthermore underlines the difficulty of achieving balanced bilingualism even in a society that officially promotes bilingualism. With some caution one may interpret the ranking as the incipient development towards monolingualism in English. This may be an overinterpretation. However, since monolingualism is never pure but a matter of degree, it is already built into the imbalanced system.[16]

[16] The questionnaire utilized in Leimgruber, Siemund and Terassa (2018) further contained an item relating to the students' first language. The question was "What is the first language you spoke as long as you can remember?" Interestingly, 200 out of the 450 students reported English as their first language, followed by Mandarin (n=170), Malay (n=56), Hokkien (n=7), Teochew (n=6), and Tamil (n=4). Moreover, the students with English as their first language are more or less equally distributed across the three institutions (university: n=64; polytechnic: n=68; ITE: n=68). The Singapore Department of Statistics (2021) reports a home language use of English of 36.9 per cent for 2015 and 48.2 per cent for 2020 (see Chapter 1). With 44.4 per cent, the ratio of English as a first language reported by the students lies in between the official home language figures. Given their young age, this is not unexpected. There is another item in the questionnaire enquiring about the languages learnt at home ("What language or languages did you learn at home?"). Here, 269 students or 59.8 per cent responded with English (university: n=103; polytechnic: n=100; ITE: n=66).

Table 6.4. *Absolute language rankings. The highest rank is "1." Languages are ordered alphabetically.*

Rank	Can	Eng	Hok	Mal	Man	Tam	Teo
1	5	355	3	27	51	1	1
2	4	85	12	70	250	14	3
3	36	5	110	11	33	1	11
4	14	1	21	10	2	0	16
5	0	0	0	0	0	0	1
6	0	0	0	0	1	0	0
n/a	391	4	304	332	113	434	418
Total	450	450	450	450	450	450	450

Note: Can = Cantonese, Eng = English, Hok = Hokkien, Mal = Malay, Man = Mandarin, Tam = Tamil, Teo = Teochew.

Table 6.4 catalogues the absolute number of students in the relevant language rankings. English rank one accumulated the highest number of students. For Malay, Mandarin, and Tamil, this is rank two. Chinese vernaculars are strong in ranks three and four, especially Hokkien. Leimgruber, Siemund and Terassa (2018: 295) further calculated the self-assessed proficiencies averaged across listening and reading comprehension as well as spoken and written production. On a five-point Likert scale, students reported an average of 1.68 for their rank one language (mostly English) and 2.28 for their rank two language (mostly one of the mother tongues). The languages at rank three were assessed at 3.0, again on average. One can see a clear monotonic decrease, but also that students do not consider themselves as fully proficient even in their rank one language. Not surprisingly, there are differences across schools and the domains considered (spoken vs. written). The assessment of the rank one language as imperfect may be due to students' supposedly high levels of metalinguistic awareness, but could also be viewed as a consequence of the strong competition exerted by the Singaporean education system.

The proficiency rankings provided by the students are further supported by language use data that reveal important differences across speaker groups. Consider Figure 6.6: students' preferred language for communication with their siblings is English, while we find usage of English and Mandarin with their parents. They hardly use English to talk to their grandparents. Between parents, English is used alongside the other languages, including Chinese vernaculars. English hardly matters in the communication between grandparents. Malay is used more consistently across all types of interlocutors.[17]

[17] Cavallaro and Ng (2021: 150) contend that "the Malay community is more resilient to language shift from Malay to English in the home domain compared to the Chinese and Indian communities."

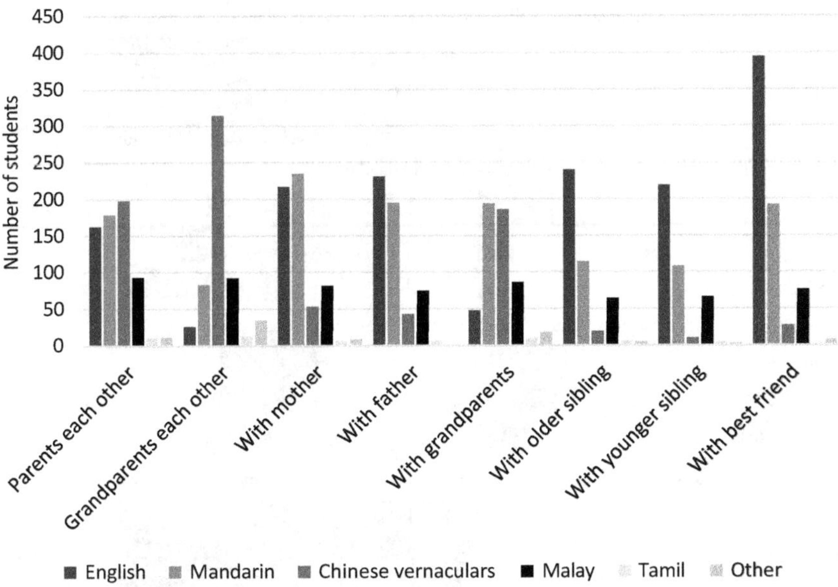

Figure 6.6 Differences in language use.
Adapted from Siemund et al. (2021: 115).

Notably, students' use of English is highest in communication with their best friends. Such data underline the ongoing language shift to English.

The studies by Siemund, Schulz and Schweinberger (2014) as well as Leimgruber, Siemund and Terassa (2018) also tried to uncover the attitudes that students from different social backgrounds associate with English and the mother tongues. To that end, they confronted students with the following seven statements asking them to rate these statements on a seven-point Likert scale.

1. Proficiency in English is more important than mother tongue proficiency.
2. The mother tongues should only be maintained if it is not done at the expense of English.
3. It is normal for Singapore speakers to speak only in English.
4. You are still a Singaporean even if you don't speak your mother tongue very often.
5. You are still a Singaporean even if you can't speak your mother tongue.
6. I don't think speaking my mother tongue is a critical part of my self-definition.
7. I think speaking Singlish is a critical part of my self-definition.

The responses to these statements can be gleaned from Figure 6.7. Regarding statement number one, all students assign more weight to English than the

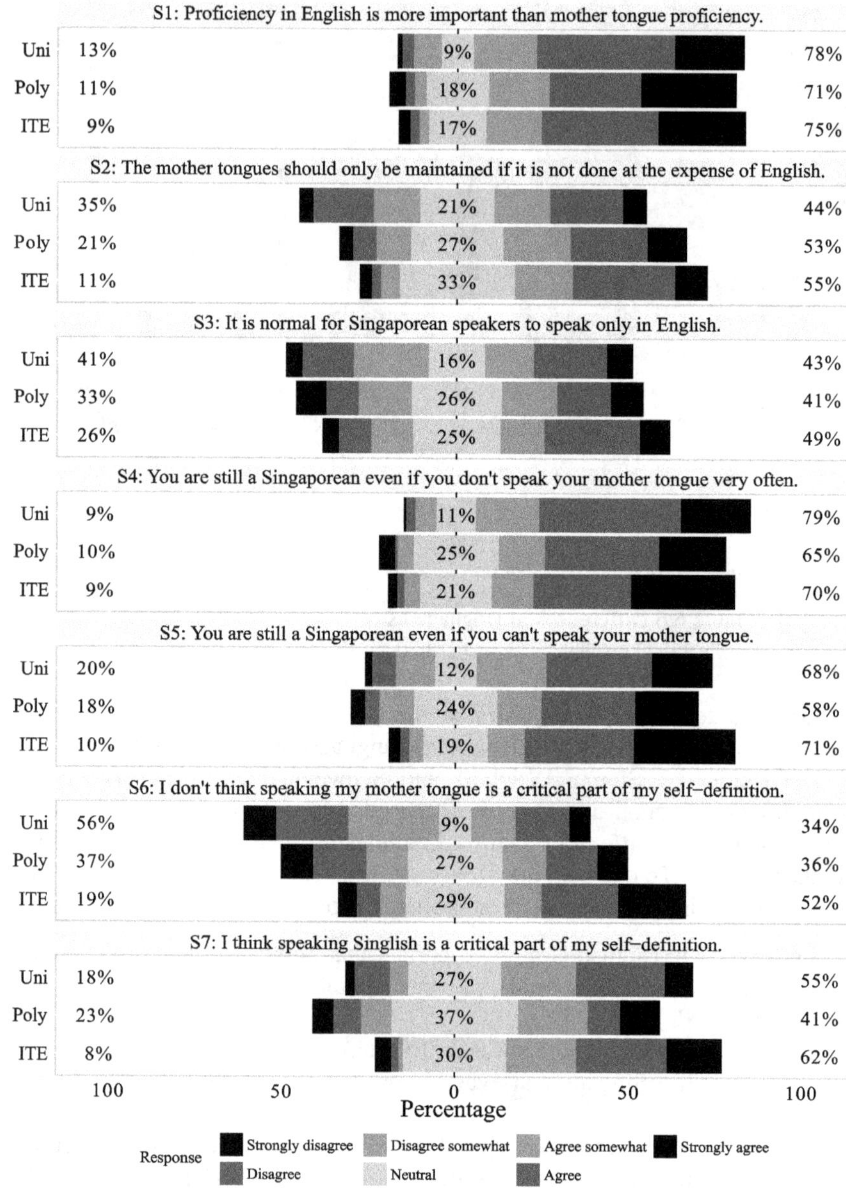

Figure 6.7 Attitudes towards English, Singlish, and mother tongue.
Adapted from Leimgruber, Siemund and Terassa (2018: 297).

mother tongues, corroborating various observations made above. However, the responses to statements two and three suggest that university students more strongly embrace the mother tongues in comparison to the two other cohorts. This can be interpreted as greater compliance with official policies, but it perhaps also suggests that the social elite values the mother tongues as cultural anchors. The responses to statements four and five can be taken to mean that a Singaporean identity is not strictly tied to mother tongue knowledge, and all groups are in agreement here. One may conclude that English represents the more important carrier of national identity. However, university students in particular consider the mother tongues important for their personal identity conceptions. They rather strongly disagree with statement six. Finally, it is interesting to note that all student groups view Colloquial Singapore English (Singlish) as a critical part of their self-definition. This underlines the importance of Singlish as a national identity marker that is also embraced by the socially most prestigious group of university students – in fact, more so than by polytechnic students. This is surprising, as in 2000 the Singaporean government launched a dedicated campaign – the Speak Good English Movement – to encourage its citizens to speak standard English rather than Colloquial Singapore English (Siemund, Schulz & Schweinberger 2014: 341). Evidently, this campaign has not been able to destroy the covert prestige of Singlish.

The historical and current situations of Singapore underline observations made earlier in the present book that multilingualism represents a complex and highly dynamic mix at both the individual and societal level. There are overarching trends, but also massive individual differences. Overall, official language policy has produced a greater degree of homogeneity since independence, elevating English to the most dominant language at the expense of the mother tongues, the original vernaculars, and also the traditional lingua francas. Levels of multilingualism have been lowered, rather than increased. Ironically, the language most strongly stratified internally now seems to be English.

6.3.3 Singapore English

In the context of Singapore, the label 'English' serves as a cover term for a spectrum of codes ranging from a basilectal form of Colloquial Singapore English to a standard variety – Standard Singapore English – that is not fundamentally different from Standard British or American English, especially in its written form. Singapore English has been extensively studied and there is no need to duplicate these research findings here (Ho & Platt 1993; Leimgruber 2013; Platt 1975; Platt & Weber 1980). However, there are two topical issues that deserve attention, namely (i) the historical reconstruction of Colloquial Singapore English and (ii) its internal stratification by social factors. These will be explored in what follows, based on two salient grammatical phenomena of Colloquial Singapore English: *already* as a marker of completive aspect and pragmatic particles.

The use of the adverb *already* to signal the completion of a situation counts amongst the most salient markers of Colloquial Singapore English. Its occurrence can be readily motivated by substrate influence from Chinese where the particle *le* 了 serves as the functional equivalent. Illustration of this use of *already* is provided in example (1). Besides completion, CSE *already* also possesses inchoative or inceptive uses (*It rain already*. 'It has started to rain.' Bao 2005: 241; Li 2021) that, however, are not relevant here.

(1) Colloquial Singapore English (Bao 2005: 239)
  a. I see the movie already.
     'I saw the movie.'
  b. I wash my hand already.
     'I have washed/washed my hand.'

Example (2) provides illustration of the coding in Chinese, making the correspondence visible.[18]

(2) Chinese (Lijun Li)

我	吃	过	了。
Wǒ	chī	guò	le.
1SG	eat	PAST	ASP

'I have eaten.' CSE: *I eat already.*

Siemund and Li (2017) compared the raw frequencies of the adverb *already* in corpora of British and Singapore English (International Corpus of English: British Component, ICE-GB; Singapore Component, ICE-SG).[19] They detected more than twice as many occurrences of *already* in the spoken component of the Singapore Corpus, in comparison to the one sampling British English (see Table 6.5). The two corpora are nearly identical in size. The most likely cause underlying this difference is the use of *already* as an aspectual marker in CSE.

In a more recent study, Li and Siemund (2021) probe into historical data of CSE using the Oral History Interviews stored at the National Archives of Singapore (OHI-NAS 2020). The oldest speaker in their sample was born in 1899 and recorded in 1979. They make two observations. First, the use of aspectual *already* is more prominent with speakers who have a Chinese background. This is perhaps not surprising but underlines that CSE is internally differentiated and not homogenous. Figure 6.8 illustrates these

[18] The following glosses are used in example (2): 1 = first person; ASP = aspect; PAST = past tense; SG = singular.

[19] The International Corpus of English can be accessed through the following website: ice-corpora.net/ice/, accessed on 11 May 2021.

Table 6.5. *Frequencies of* already *in ICE-GB and ICE-SG (Siemund & Li 2017: 22).*

	Words	*already*	*already* (ptw)
ICE-GB	630,903	208	0.33
ICE-SG	601,980	491	0.82

Note: ptw = per thousand words.

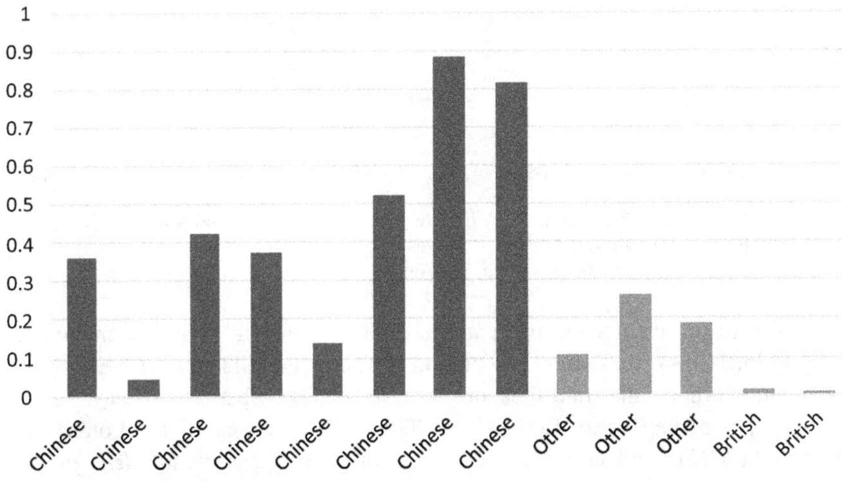

Figure 6.8 Frequency of *already* per page amongst speakers of different ethnic backgrounds.
Adapted from Li and Siemund (2021: 528).

differences. The group named "other" includes speakers with a Malay, Indian, or Peranakan background. Notably, the Chinese group is not at all homogenous internally, perhaps due to various social background variables.

Second, Li and Siemund (2021) show that aspectual *already* occurs with all speakers of Chinese background independent of their year of birth (see Figure 6.9, based on a sample of eight speakers; see Li 2021 for a more extensive data set). Although there are important differences across the individual speakers, there does not seem to be an increase or decrease over time. Speakers of CSE seem to use aspectual *already* today much in the same way as they did 100 years ago. These findings point to substantial diachronic stability of CSE.[20]

[20] Li (2021: 276) in fact argues that the data from the Oral History Interviews suggest a slight increase in the use of aspectual *already* over time.

Figure 6.9 Frequencies of *already* per page of individual speakers born between 1899 and 1948.
Adapted from Li and Siemund (2021: 528).

Similar results emanate from an analysis of CSE pragmatic particles in the Oral History Interviews (Li, Lorenz & Siemund 2022). As is well known, CSE is rich in pragmatic particles that find their origin in the Sinitic substrates, Malay, Bazaar Malay, and perhaps also Tamil (Lim 2007). The analysis of Li, Lorenz and Siemund (2022) involves 1,910 occurrences of the particles *ah, lah, leh, lor,* and *meh* from 101 speakers born between 1899 and 1983 with interviews conducted between 1979 and 2009. The particles are used to modulate the illocutionary force of utterances in various ways, as illustrated in the examples below.[21]

(3) a. That was just after the 1968 *ah*? [OHI-003206-MA]
b. I got a certificate for 25 years of service *ah*. [OHI-E000284-CNS]

(4) a. Only two big food stalls *lah* I remember. [OHI-002951-JY]
b. So, I apply for Health Visitor *lah*. [OHI-000213-EQ]

(5) a. Probably after he left *leh*? [OHI-E000462-LWK]
b. [. . .], we have almost a hundred people *leh*. [OHI-000416-TCH]

(6) I forgot *lor*. [OHI-001631-OCN]

(7) They are the shopkeepers who extended their goods on the five-foot-way and on the road *meh*. [OHI-002107-CPK]

[21] The particles possess a range functions. The three particles *ah*, *meh*, and *leh* indicate uncertainty and may be classified as question markers. The particles *lah* and *lor* express persuasiveness and obviousness (see Lim 2007 for more details). There are more particles in Colloquial Singapore English than the five expressions discussed here (Leimgruber et al. 2020).

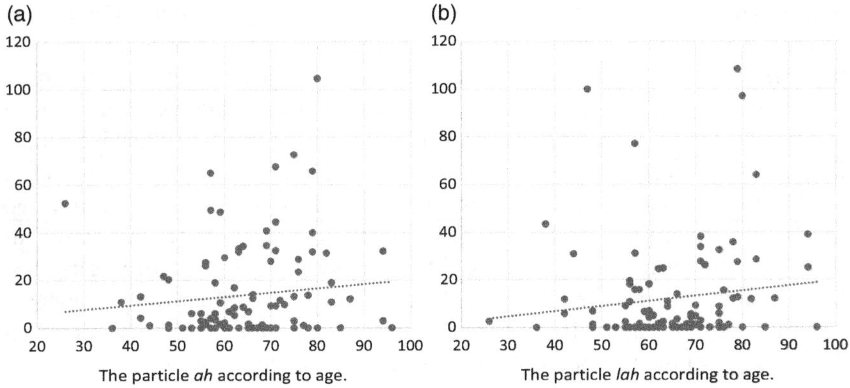

Figure 6.10 Normalized (per 10,000 words) frequency of occurrence of the particles *ah* (left) and *lah* (right) according to speaker age.
Adapted from Li, Lorenz and Siemund (2022).

The scatterplots in Figure 6.10 depict the normalized frequencies of the particles *ah* and *lah*, which represent the most commonly used particles, against the age of the speakers. The trend lines suggest a slight increase with speaker age, but since the group of 50–70 year olds is over-represented in the sample (*n*=60), these trends need to be viewed with caution. Be that as it may, the findings indicate that the pragmatic particles were widely used in the early twentieth century. The most likely source languages are Hokkien and/or Bazaar Malay (Lim 2007). We may further note that some speakers in the sample did not produce any particles.

Regarding social predictors like gender and level of education, Li, Lorenz and Siemund (2022) demonstrate that the particle *ah* is associated with male and *lah* with female gender. In addition, *ah* is over-represented amongst speakers of high (university) education, while *lah* is preferred in the speaker group with medium (secondary) levels of education. Speakers with an Indian or Malay background favour *ah* and disfavour *lah.* Using random forests to predict the occurrence of *ah* versus *lah*, Li, Lorenz and Siemund (2022) can show that speaker identity is the strongest predictor, followed by interview year, level of education, gender, ethnicity, age, and year of birth. As in the case of *already*, the data point to a fundamental stability of Colloquial Singapore English as well as an early differentiation along social background variables (see also Buschfeld 2021; Leimgruber et al. 2020).

6.3.4 *Summary*

The preceding survey of Singaporean multilingualism has essentially produced three results. First, a substantial portion of the currently observable multilingual texture can be traced back to the founding years of the then British colony. It is quite remarkable how persistent the early decisions are, in spite of the many dedicated governmental policy initiatives and activities – not only related to language. Second, post-independent policy initiatives did produce effects, especially regarding the streamlining of the formerly extensive multilingualism into the official bilingual model of English in combination with a mother tongue. The main losers are the vernaculars and early lingua francas, much as in other parts of the world. English is developing into the dominant and most widely used language. And third, Colloquial Singapore English has been maintained despite its officially bad reputation. Moreover, it appears socially stratified internally to a greater extent and with a longer history than previously assumed. Evidently, there is scope for much more work here.

6.4 Hong Kong and Hong Kong English

A former British colony like Singapore, Hong Kong never developed into an independent state. Instead, it remained a British colony until it was reinstated as part of the People's Republic of China in 1997, after the 99-year British lease of the territory ceased. Following the handover, Hong Kong was declared a Special Administrative Region (SAR) of China for another fifty years. As we will see in the following sections, these differences in relation to Singapore entail important consequences for the development of its multilingual ecology and for the position of English in it.

6.4.1 Historical Multilingualism

When Hong Kong Island became a British colony in 1842, it quickly developed into an extensively multilingual place. Bolton and Lee (2021: 38) inform us that the island was sparsely populated before the arrival of the British, there being a few fishing villages and boat dwelling communities. Much as in Singapore, the newly established colony soon became a magnet for immigration, but in the case of Hong Kong this primarily involved people from nearby Southern China, especially the Guangdong and Fujian provinces (Bolton & Lee 2021: 40). These immigrants transplanted mainly three languages to Hong Kong, namely Cantonese (also known as 'Punti'), Hakka (Hok-ha), and Hokkien (Hoklo). The Hakka represent former immigrants from Northern China who migrated South due to social unrest, upheaval, and invasion preceding the fourth century C.E. (Constable 1996: 9). This early immigration established an ethnic and language ecology that in one way or another has been continued to the present day. The first Hong Kong census from 1911 reports almost half a million inhabitants – a sharp increase from the approximately 5,000 precolonial inhabitants (Bolton & Lee 2021: 38, 42).

Table 6.6. *The 1911 Hong Kong census results on languages (Bolton & Lee 2021: 42).*[22]

District	Hong Kong Island and Kowloon	New Territories, Northern District	New Territories, Southern District	Total	Percentage
Punti	311,992	31,595	16,395	359,982	81.0
Hakka	22,822	37,053	7,321	67,196	15.1
Hoklo	6,949	75	1,369	8,393	1.9
Others	2,864	124	–	2,988	0.7
Not stated	5,791	275	39	6,105	1.3
Total	350,418	59,122	25,124	444,664	100.0

Table 6.6 shows that the Punti or Cantonese represented the major part of the population.

Until 1997, Hong Kong remained largely unaffected by the linguistic developments in Mainland China, which saw a strong promotion of the national language Putonghua and, with the proclamation of the People's Republic in 1949, the development of a simplified character script (Bolton, Bacon-Shone & Lee 2021: 161; see also Chapter 5). The British colony practically served as a shelter where the use of Cantonese and the traditional script could be continued.[23] Not surprisingly, the influence of Putonghua increased after 1997.

Much as with Singapore English, the origin of Hong Kong English can be traced back to the early colonial years and, again as in Singapore, the education system played an important role in its promotion. Bolton and Lee (2021: 47) relate early Hong Kong English to "Canton jargon" or Chinese Pidgin English, widely used in Southern China (especially Guangzhou and Macau) before Hong Kong became a colony and itself heavily influenced by Cantonese (see also Schneider 2007: 133). Like the Raffles Institution in Singapore, the Government Central School of Hong Kong, opened in 1862 and renamed as Queen's College in 1894, introduced formal education in Chinese and English and laid the foundation for all subsequent English-medium and Chinese-medium education in the area. It still counts as one of Hong Kong's most prestigious schools. For a long time until the handover to China in 1997, the language ecology of Hong Kong was characterized by a small proportion of monolingual English speakers, a bilingual Chinese–English speaking local elite, and a great majority of Chinese speakers (mostly Cantonese) with strongly varying command of

[22] Bolton and Lee (2021: 42) further note that the "total population in 1911 was 456,739."
[23] The use of traditional characters was also continued in Taiwan as a consequence of language policy measures exported to the island before 1949 (see Klöter 2020: 144).

English (Schneider 2007: 135–137). Chinese–English bilingualism became more widely distributed through the population during the last decades of British colonial rule.

What I find remarkable is that in neither the context of Singapore nor Hong Kong does one find a narrative of negative effects associated with bilingual education or multilingualism in general. The establishment of Chinese-medium education, besides English-medium education, does not suggest a general devaluation of Chinese. In contrast, the conflictual relationships of the British Empire with the Celtic populations in Wales, Ireland, and Scotland, as well as the indigenous populations in North America and Australia rather produced a devaluation of the relevant languages, if they were recognized as languages at all. One may recall from Chapter 1 that the study of Welsh–English bilingualism produced some of the earliest publications arguing for negative cognitive effects associated with bilingualism. Multilingualism in Singapore only came to be questioned after independence when it began to be streamlined into today's ethnic-based bilingual model. Nevertheless, this did not produce a discourse on monolingual advantages or bilingual disadvantages (and mainly affected the vernaculars).

6.4.2 *Societal Multilingualism*

During most of its colonial history, Hong Kong's only official language was English. Chinese was attributed co-official status in 1974 (Bolton, Bacon-Shone & Lee 2021: 173; Wang & Kirkpatrick 2021: 229). In practical terms, this mostly meant Cantonese. When Hong Kong was repatriated to China in 1997, the status of Putonghua suddenly increased elevating it to another official language in the area. This new situation was formally sanctioned in the Biliterate and Trilingual (兩文三語政策) language policy (BT policy) that recognizes Cantonese, English, and Putonghua as official languages and promotes literacy in both the Chinese and Latin scripts (Wang & Kirkpatrick 2021: 231). One consequence of this arrangement appears to be a decline in English proficiencies, due to compulsory Chinese-medium instruction (Poon 2021: 104–105). Arguably, Hong Kong is currently witnessing a recalibration of the status of English from a second to a foreign language, subject to ongoing change (see below). There is a concomitant increase in the ability to speak Putonghua, namely from 25.3 per cent in 1996 to 48.6 per cent in 2016, promoted by radio broadcasting in Putonghua, public announcements, and community activities (Poon 2021: 107). One is reminded of the Speak Mandarin Campaign in Singapore.

Contemporary societal ethnic and linguistic diversity, however, goes considerably beyond Chinese and English. Bolton, Bacon-Shone and Lee (2021: 173) provide the summary shown in Table 6.7, inter alia illustrating

Table 6.7. *Numbers and percentages of Hong Kong residents claiming selected ethnicities (Bolton, Bacon-Shone & Lee 2021: 173).*

Ethnicity	Number	Percentage
Chinese	6,752,202	92.0
Filipino	184,081	2.5
Indonesian	153,299	2.1
White	58,209	0.8
Indian	36,462	0.5
Nepalese	25,472	0.3
Pakistani	18,094	0.2
Thai	10,215	0.1
Japanese	9,976	0.1
Other Asian	19,589	0.3
Others	584,383	8.0
Total	7,336,585	100.0

Table 6.8. *Percentage of the population five years old and above able to speak selected languages (Bolton, Bacon-Shone & Lee 2021: 162).*

Language/dialect	As usual language		As another language		Total percentages	
	2011	2016	2011	2016	2011	2016
Cantonese	89.5	88.9	6.3	5.7	95.8	94.6
Putonghua	1.4	1.9	46.5	46.7	46.1	48.6
English	3.5	4.3	42.6	48.9	47.8	53.2
Hakka	0.9	0.6	3.8	3.5	4.7	4.2
Chiu Chau	0.7	0.5	3.1	2.9	3.8	3.4
Fukien	1.1	1.0	2.3	2.6	3.5	3.6
Bahasa Indonesia	0.3	0.3	2.2	2.4	2.4	2.7
Filipino	0.2	0.4	1.4	2.3	1.7	2.7
Japanese	0.2	0.1	1.4	1.7	1.5	1.8
Shanghainese	0.3	0.2	0.9	0.9	1.1	1.1

the high numbers of Filipinos and Indonesians in the area. According to Poon (2021: 108), most of them work as domestic helpers.

Table 6.8 translates these ethnic figures into language use, detailing increases and decreases from 2011 to 2016. The situation is relatively stable, with slight increases regarding English and Putonghua. Use of English appears to be growing, despite the above complaints about its falling standards.

The graphs in Figure 6.11 portray language use in terms of the "usual spoken language" excluding Cantonese as the most widely used language.

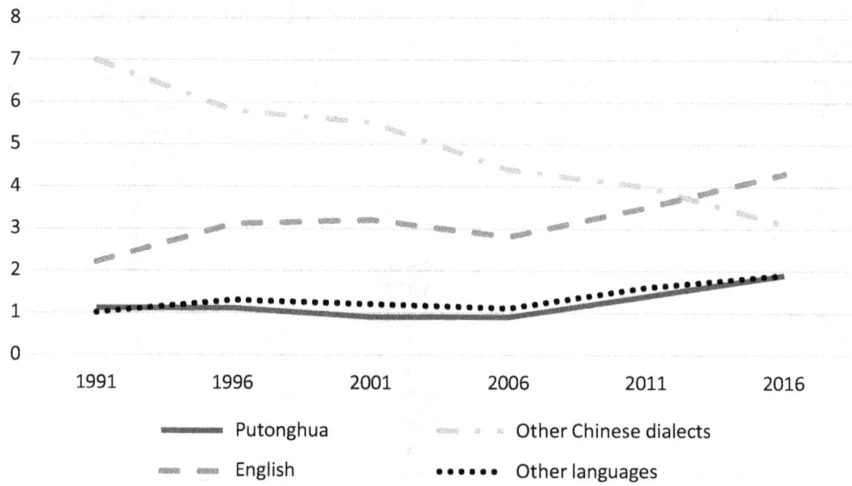

Figure 6.11 Usual spoken language, in per cent (population aged five or older), without Cantonese (Census and Statistics Department: Items A107, censuses and by-censuses 1991–2016.
Adapted from Fuchs (2021: 293). Reproduced by permission of Taylor and Francis Group, LLC, a division of Informa plc.

They attest a slight increase in English from 1991 to 2016, though only a very small increase in the use of Putonghua. Much as in Singapore and throughout China, the use of Chinese vernaculars is falling.

A different picture emerges from the development of the knowledge of second languages in the same time frame, as detailed in Figure 6.12. The data come from speakers for whom Cantonese is their first language. By 2016, knowledge of Putonghua had almost reached parity with English. As stipulated by the Biliterate and Trilingual language policy, Hong Kong Cantonese speakers have developed trilingualism of Cantonese, English, and Putonghua. To be sure, these figures reveal little about their objective (rather than their perceived) oral and written proficiencies.

Languages and ethnic groups are not evenly distributed across the territory of Hong Kong, as Bolton, Bacon-Shone and Lee (2021) demonstrate. Not surprisingly, English along with other Western languages is strongly concentrated on Hong Kong Island, that is, the original British dominion. The main Sinitic varieties of Cantonese, Chiu Chau (Teochew), Fukien, and Hakka predominate in the New Territories south of the Chinese border. Indian languages are strongly represented on Kowloon Peninsula. Figure 6.13 offers a succinct overview, with more detailed information provided in Bolton, Bacon-Shone and Lee (2021).

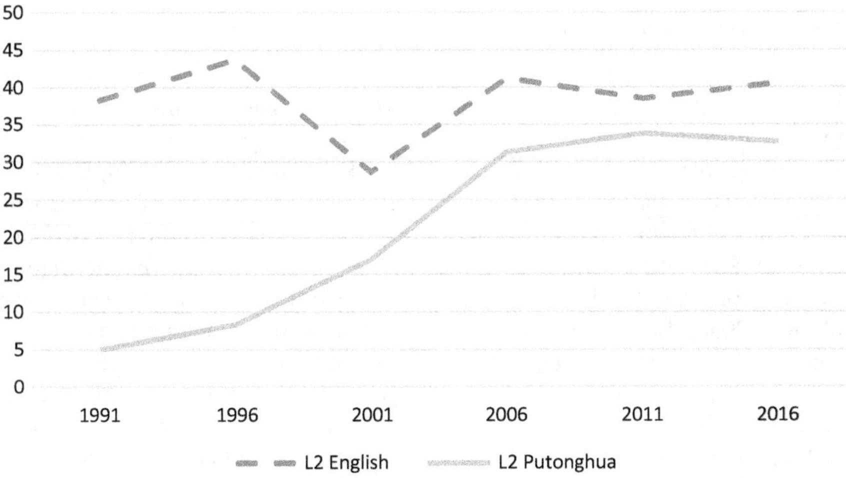

Figure 6.12 Knowledge of second languages, in per cent (population aged five or older), by L1 Cantonese-speakers born in Hong Kong (Census and Statistics Department, 2018: Items A123, censuses and by-censuses 1991–2016). Adapted from Fuchs (2021: 293). Reproduced by permission of Taylor and Francis Group, LLC, a division of Informa plc.

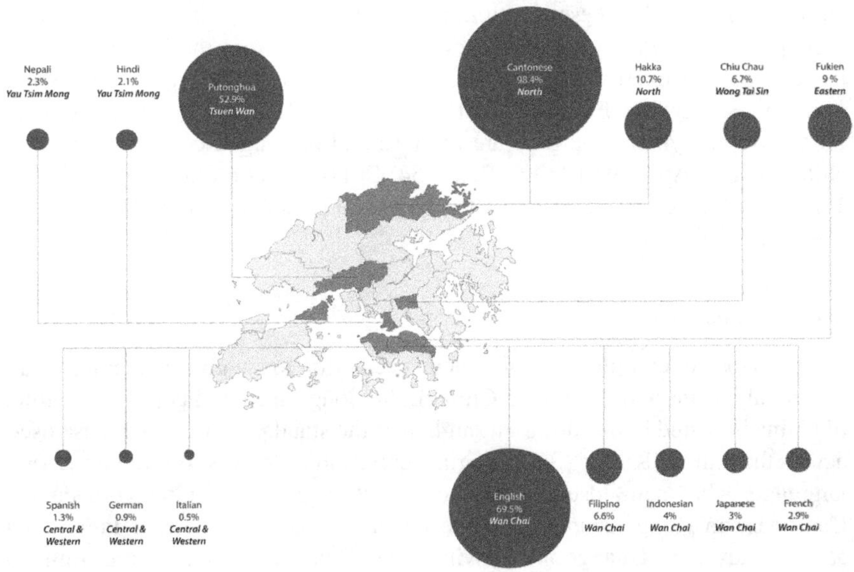

Figure 6.13 Chinese languages and other languages spoken in Hong Kong (Bolton, Bacon-Shone & Lee 2021: 172). Reproduced by permission of Taylor and Francis Group, LLC, a division of Informa plc.

6.4.3 *Hong Kong English*

Few scholars would perhaps doubt the existence of a distinct variety of Hong Kong English, but in comparison to Colloquial Singapore English it appears much harder to describe by reference to specific grammatical properties. According to Schneider (2007: 133), Hong Kong (and Hong Kong English) "can be regarded as having reached phase 3, with some traces of phase 2 still observable," but this assessment was made several years ago. Phases two and three in Schneider's (2003, 2007) Dynamic Model refer to "exonormative stabilization" and "nativization." The assessment rests on the distinct accent of Hong Kong English, many lexical borrowings from Cantonese, as well as some incipient morphosyntactic features identifying this variety (Schneider 2007: 138), especially regarding relative clause formation and finiteness (Gisborne 2000, 2009). Further grammatical variables are addressed in Fuchs (2021), but the majority of these attest frequency differentials in comparison to other varieties.

Hong Kong English, as other postcolonial varieties of English, received and keeps receiving its special characteristics from the various contact languages present in the local language ecology. There can be no doubt that Cantonese has been most influential, but according to Fuchs (2021: 287) several additional channels of influence need to be recognized, including South Asian varieties of English. These are summarized in Table 6.9.

Apparently, the high number of domestic helpers from the Philippines can be assumed to exert a disproportionately strong influence on Hong Kong English, as speaking English – that is, Philippine English – is a prerequisite for their employment and they are in close and prolonged contact with small children (see also Bolton & Lee 2021: 54; Bolton, Bacon-Shone & Lee 2021: 172; Poon 2021: 100). Similar patterns emerge in Dubai and the Gulf Region (see Section 6.5).[24]

6.4.4 *Summary*

It is perhaps not completely unfounded speculation to suggest that Hong Kong will amalgamate with Mainland China in the long run. The People's Republic of China is vested in installing Putonghua as the standard form of Chinese used across the nation (Klöter 2020). English comes in as the first foreign or second language. The main losers in this competition are the Sinitic vernaculars. Cantonese in Hong Kong may come under the same pressure of Putonghua as it already is in Guangdong Province (see Chapter 5). Hong Kong English

[24] Franceschini (2013: 2) points out that slaves in Ancient Rome were often of Greek origin and "also worked as teachers in upper-class families," thus disseminating Greek.

Table 6.9. *Historical and contemporary sources of influence on Hong Kong English along the ethnic/L1 dimension (Fuchs 2021: 287).*

L1/Ethnic group	Influence on Hong Kong English (HKE)
Cantonese	Substrate influence/L1 transfer, as Cantonese is widely spoken.
Caucasian/L1 varieties of English	British English is the superstrate language. In addition, speakers of various L1 varieties of English have influenced HKE through their work as teachers and their presence in the city.
South Asian (English)	Although small in size, this population might have played a disproportionately large role in shaping HKE.
Philippine (English)	Guest workers employed domestically in child care transmit their variety of English to the children they care for.
Putonghua	Increasing numbers of Putonghua-speaking immigrants, increasing role of Putonghua in official and commercial contexts within HK.
Returnees	Cantonese-speaking people from HK who have spent time in other countries, having been exposed to the English spoken there, and who have returned to HK.

(*Konglish*) would then come to align with Chinese English (*Chinglish*), however that is to be defined.

6.5 Dubai and Gulf English

The territory of what is today the United Arab Emirates (UAE) never was a British colony – only a protectorate. After the discovery of oil in the middle of the twentieth century, the UAE along with other so-called Gulf States experienced an unforeseen economic boom. An extensive expatriate labour force hailed from practically all parts of the world producing a strong imbalance between the local Arab population and the international residents. The foreign population amounts to as much as 90 per cent, as observed in Chapter 1. This created the need for a common language. Even though Arabic is the official language of the UAE, English has developed into the de facto lingua franca of the country and the entire Gulf area.[25] It is common for native Emiratis to speak English with the expatriate labour force. There are signs that English is developing a localized form of Gulf English or UAE English (Boyle 2012, 2014; Fussell 2011).

[25] Ricento (2015a) contains several highly readable contributions on the role of English as a global means for communication. Ricento (2015b) explores three alternative conceptions of English, namely as "(1) a form of linguistic imperialism, (2) a vehicle for social and economic mobility, or (3) a global lingua franca necessary for a global *demos* necessary to achieve global justice" (Ricento 2015b: 28). A critical discussion of English as a global lingua franca can be found in Ricento (2015c).

6.5.1 *Historical Multilingualism*

Before the oil-based economic developments started, the Gulf Coast along the Arabian Peninsula used to be sparsely populated territory. Society was organized in clans – their economy being based on agriculture, fishing, and pearling. The original forts, around which the villages were organized and which offered protection in times of crisis, can still be visited in the presently seven emirates of Abu Dhabi, Ajman, Dubai, Fujairah, Ras Al Khaimah, Sharjah, and Umm al Quwain. They bear testimony to the pre-modern social structure that appears not so far away from the Scottish Highland clans or the central German compartmentalized castle system. The East Coast at the Gulf of Oman is considerably more fertile due to water captured by and under the Hajar Mountain ridge. The local Arab population can be assumed to have spoken a variety of local dialects, there perhaps being individual multi-dialectism. The early nineteenth century beginnings are in fact not too different from what we observed for Singapore and Hong Kong above.

British interest in the region arose around the turn of the nineteenth century when the local Arab clans apparently began to engage too extensively in piracy and warfare, interfering with the British sea routes to India (Pacione 2005; Siemund, Al-Issa & Leimgruber 2021). This provoked British naval intervention in 1819, followed by a series of peace treaties between the various sheikdoms and continued British presence in the area. The peace treaties inspired the coinage of the so-called Trucial States (also Trucial Coast), signifying an assemblage of sheikdoms under British supervision and partial governance. The Trucial States lasted until 1971 when the seven emirates introduced above formed a federation known as the United Arab Emirates today.[26] Oman and Bahrain formed independent states. The Trucial States thus were a British protectorate and this signals an important difference relative to Singapore and Hong Kong. Little is known about the exact extent to which British rule penetrated into the local structures, but it seems clear that the roots of the present dominance of English – including English culture – in the area can be traced back to these early social interactions. The oldest English-speaking school in Dubai and the entire UAE is the Dubai English Speaking School (DESS), founded in 1963.[27] By comparison, the Singapore Institution was formed in 1823 and the Government Central School of Hong Kong in 1862. We can see a time lapse of around 100 years (see Sections 6.3.1 and 6.4.1).

After 1900, the Gulf Region experienced increasing population growth that began to gain momentum after the discovery of oil and the establishment of the United Arab Emirates. Some milestone figures can be taken from Table 6.10.

[26] Retrieved from www.britannica.com/place/United-Arab-Emirates, accessed on 28 May 2021.
[27] Retrieved from www.dessc.sch.ae/, accessed on 26 May 2021.

Table 6.10. *Population development in Dubai (Pacione 2005: 257).*

Year	Population
1833	1,500
1900	10,000
1968	59,000
1985	370,788
1995	689,420
2000	862,387

By 2010, the figures had already risen to 1,905,476 to reach a staggering 3,411,200 people in 2020 (Dubai Statistics Center 2020). To recall, more than 90 per cent of these represent foreigners, mirroring the broader immigration patterns in Singapore and Hong Kong surprisingly closely.[28] The share of indigenous Malays in Singapore has been hovering at around 15 per cent for a long time. There are probably no descendants of precolonial indigenous Hong Kongers, as the present majority group of Cantonese are in fact immigrants themselves. Regarding the United Arab Emirates, an important difference is that the ownership of the territory has always remained in the hands of the indigenous Arab people and that immigrants have the legal status of foreigners (expatriates).[29]

6.5.2 Societal Multilingualism

The varieties of English in Singapore and Hong Kong developed during times when sea and land traffic was still relatively slow and dangerous, and the number of people shippable within a temporal reference unit was rather limited. Today's air traffic is fast, cheap, and extremely reliable. Cheap labour (construction workers, taxi drivers, domestic helpers, nannies, shop assistants, cleaners, etc.) travels from poor to prosperous regions at an enormous pace and in very high numbers. The digital flow of money and the easy use of social media allow their families to remain in the source areas of migration, but still continue to be functional units. Personal remittances to the Philippines, to cite just one salient case, amounted to nearly 10 per cent

[28] Foreign residents in the UAE are highly transient and they are typically male. Of the 3,411,200 Dubai residents reported in 2020, 2,362,255 are male and 1,048,945 are female (Dubai Statistics Center 2020; see also the population pyramids discussed in Pacione 2005: 261). Interestingly, Li (2021: 38) reports a similar pattern for the early colonial decades of Singapore.

[29] Residency and work permits require an Emirati sponsor and guarantor under the kafala system (Theodoropoulou 2021: 78; Hopkyns 2021: 253).

of the national GDP in 2019.[30] As argued in Section 6.4.3, there is evidence that Hong Kong English is being influenced by the English spoken by the numerous Philippine nannies working there (Fuchs 2021: 286). Similar claims have also been made in the context of the UAE. According to Hopkyns (2021: 254), 94 per cent of the Dubai Emirati families employ domestic helpers who typically speak English with the Emirati children.

Foreign residents to the UAE to a large extent come from former colonial countries where English has been maintained as an official or co-official language. Reliable figures are practically impossible to find, but Siemund, Al-Issa and Leimgruber (2021: 194) estimate that 51 per cent of the foreign population in Dubai comes from India, 17 per cent from Pakistan, 9 per cent from Bangladesh, 3 per cent from the Philippines, and 20 per cent from various other countries (see also Theodoropoulou 2021: 66). They speak specific varieties of English, such as Indian English, Pakistani English, or Philippine English. This gives rise to an interesting new dialect laboratory in which language contact and change in the context of the encounter of different varieties of English can be studied in real time, as it were.[31] Piller (2018: 78) describes Dubai as a "multilingual and multicultural utopia."

The official language of the UAE is Arabic, but the language most widely used is English (Al-Issa 2021; Theodoropoulou 2021).[32] This establishes a situation of diglossia – in fact triglossia, as Arabic bifurcates into Modern Standard Arabic and Gulf Arabic (Khaleeji). There is widespread concern that the younger generation is beginning to lose Arabic (especially in the written language), as English dominates public discourse and bears extremely high prestige (Romaine 2015; Theodoropoulou 2021: 68–69). Al-Issa (2021: 119) points out that "English becomes connected to all things modern, including business, education, and internationalism, while Arabic is relegated to a lower status as the language of religion, tradition, family, and home." Speakers of different forms of Arabic frequently fall back on English in their communicative encounters, rather than using Modern Standard Arabic (Al-Issa & Dahan 2011: 11).

Higher education in the UAE is almost universally based on English as the medium of instruction (Hopkyns 2021: 254–255). The government public schools officially use Arabic and teach English as a foreign language, but in

[30] Retrieved from data.worldbank.org/indicator/BX.TRF.PWKR.DT.GD.ZS, accessed on 26 May 2021.

[31] Dubai could be considered as replicating the dialect levelling processes in Milton Keynes, only on a global scale involving international varieties of English. Milton Keynes, one of the so-called new towns in the United Kingdom, is a product of urban planning, officially designated in 1967. Residents were attracted from different parts of the United Kingdom. The concomitant processes of dialect levelling were studied by Kerswill and Williams (2000).

[32] Arabic was formally established as the official language of the UAE in 2008 (Al-Issa 2021: 119).

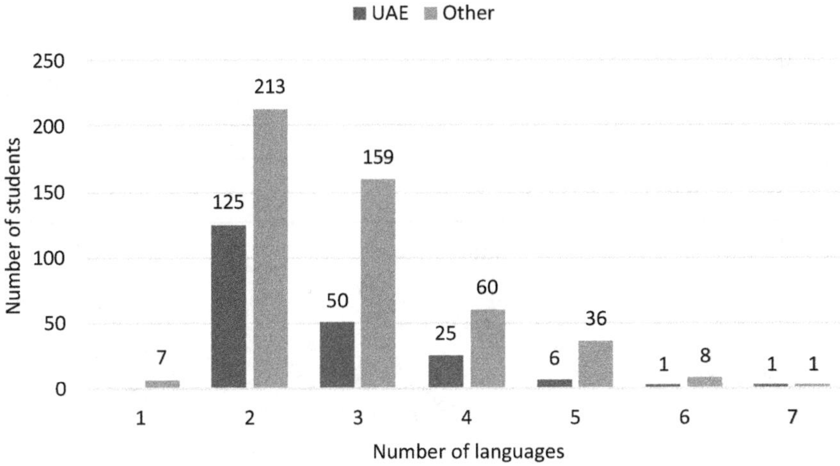

Figure 6.14 Number of languages declared, by citizenship.
Adapted from Siemund, Al-Issa and Leimgruber (2021: 199).

actual practice a substantial portion of the instruction proceeds in English (Al-Issa 2021: 122). The foreign population sends their children to private schools most of which are based on curricula developed in the United Kingdom or the United States. Since English is allotted such a high status, Emirati parents have developed a preference for sending their children to private schools, too, on the assumption that the standards of English are higher there (Al-Issa 2021: 122). In view of this situation, one can surmise that many, if not most Emirati children acquire English as a late first or early second language.

Siemund, Al-Issa and Leimgruber (2021), building on earlier research carried out in Singapore (Leimgruber, Siemund & Terassa 2018; Siemund, Schulz & Schweinberger 2014), studied the languages repertoires of 692 students at the American University of Sharjah in spring 2019. They encountered extensive multilingualism and linguistic diversity. Sharjah – one of the seven emirates – borders on Dubai with many students commuting between the two emirates. Differentiating between UAE citizens and other nationalities, Figure 6.14 charts the number of students by the number of languages they speak. As in Singapore, there is extensive bilingualism and trilingualism with the former being most prominent (see Section 6.3.2). Figure 6.14 looks surprisingly similar to Figure 6.2.

Figure 6.15 reveals the languages spoken by the students, again differentiating between UAE nationals and other nationalities. Not surprisingly, English was declared by the highest number of students in both groups – in fact all students – followed by Arabic, other languages, French, Urdu, and Hindi.

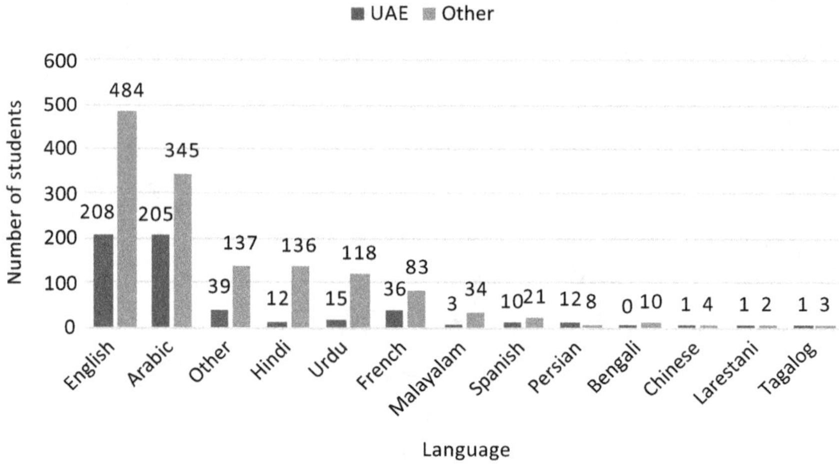

Figure 6.15 Languages used ordered by frequency of attestation, by citizenship.
Adapted from Siemund, Al-Issa and Leimgruber (2021: 199).

English is a prerequisite for enrolling in the American University. Evidently, there are many students from other Arabic-speaking countries (such as Egypt, Syria, Saudi Arabia, and Jordan). Urdu and Hindi are also strongly represented amongst non-UAE students.

The most frequently reported language combinations are shown in Figure 6.16. Besides the expectable combination of Arabic and English, this language profile also features French, apparently acquired as a foreign language. English alone or in combination with Arabic further profiles with the Asian languages Hindi, Malayalam, and Urdu, bearing witness to the considerable number of students with South Asian roots. Amongst the most common other languages count Turkish, Tamil, German, Korean, Swahili, Russian, and Japanese. The language combinations in Figure 6.16 together make up 75.87 per cent of all reported combinations. The combination of Arabic plus English alone accounts for 43.64 per cent of all cases.[33]

As in the context of Singapore, students were further asked to rank their languages according to their self-assessed proficiencies. The outcome of this ranking can be gathered from Table 6.11. English was ranked highest by all students, closely followed by Arabic in the group of UAE citizens. It is noteworthy that even UAE students rank English highest, again mirroring the results

[33] These percentages refer to the totals and do not discriminate between UAE nationals and students of other nationalities.

Table 6.11. *Mean rankings of languages. The highest rank is "1." Languages are ordered alphabetically.*

	Ara	Ben	Eng	Hin	Mal	Per	Tag	Urd
UAE	1.58	n.a.	1.55	3.08	1.67	3.00	3.00	2.67
Other	1.97	3.09	1.38	2.89	2.41	2.75	2.33	2.45
Total	1.83	3.09	1.43	2.91	2.35	2.90	2.50	2.47

Note: Ara = Arabic, Ben = Bengali, Eng = English, Hin = Hindi, Mal = Malayalam, Per = Persian, Tag = Tagalog, Urd = Urdu.

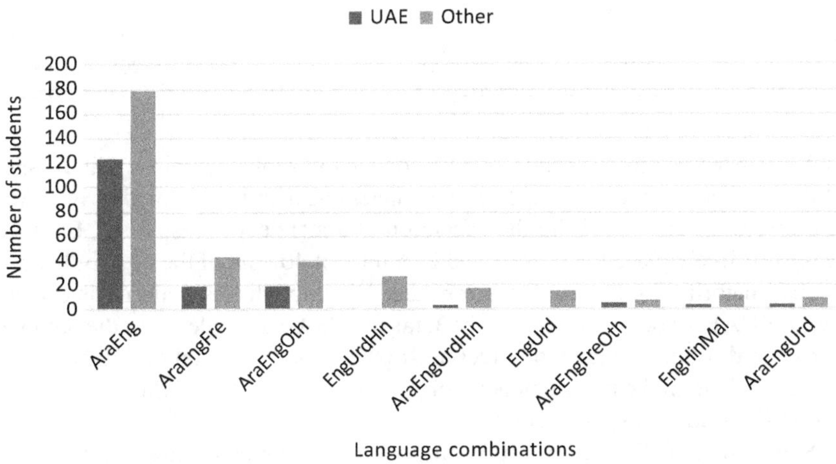

Figure 6.16 Most frequent language combinations, by citizenship.
Adapted from Siemund, Al-Issa and Leimgruber (2021: 200).
Note: Ara = Arabic, Eng = English, Fre = French, Hin = Hindi, Mal = Malayalam, Oth = Other, Urd = Urdu.

found in Singapore. These findings lend some credence to the discourse on losing Arabic, as introduced above. Interestingly, the Asian languages are equally found in the lower ranks, with the exception of Malayalam (based on five students). One may suspect that these students come from internationally mobile families who primarily use English.[34]

[34] The questionnaire used further presented the students with items regarding their first language and their home language. The item "What was the first language you spoke as long as you can remember?" returned 416 positive responses for Arabic (60.1%), 106 for English (15.3%), and 170 for other languages (24.6%). A total of 178 UAE students reported Arabic as their first language, while 238 such students came from other countries. Eighteen UAE students indicated that English is their first language. Eighty-eight students from other countries reported English as their first language. The item "What language or languages does your family primarily speak at home?" returned 449 positive responses for Arabic and 202 for English. Out of the 449

Table 6.12. *Absolute language rankings. The highest rank is "1." Languages are ordered alphabetically.*

Rank	Arabic		English		Hindi		Urdu	
	UAE	Other	UAE	Other	UAE	Other	UAE	Other
1	112	138	94	308		2		13
2	79	139	114	169	1	40	7	59
3	6	26		7	9	72	6	29
4	4	29			2	17	2	14
5	4	11				6		3
6		3						
n/a	3	138			196	347	193	363
Total	208	484	208	484	208	484	208	484

Table 6.12 details the individual responses for Arabic, English, Hindi, and Urdu (the most frequently reported languages) against the distinction of UAE and non-UAE citizens. With the exception of a mere seven responses, English was exclusively placed at ranks 1 and 2. A total of 402 out of the 692 students – a clear majority – positioned it at top rank.[35] Although this majority is driven by non-UAE students, 94 out of the total of 208 UAE students in the sample considered it the language they feel most proficient in. A total of 250 students reported their highest proficiency for Arabic, not English. Hindi and Urdu primarily occur at ranks 2 and 3.

Siemund et al. (2021: 101–103) further report the mean self-assessed proficiencies in the four CEFR domains (Council of Europe 2020) of spoken and written production as well as listening and reading comprehension. Measured across all students, they find slightly better assessments for English in comparison to Arabic. Moreover, the range of self-assessed proficiencies in Arabic is wider. Given the high share of international students at the American University of Sharjah, this is certainly expected. In addition, the authors examine the mean proficiencies for English and Arabic in the cohorts of Emirati students, South Asian students, and students from other areas. Here, the mean proficiency in Arabic is practically identical for Emirati students and students from other countries (advanced level). This makes sense since these other countries are often Arabic-speaking. Knowledge of Arabic reaches only

Arabic-speaking homes, 183 involved UAE nationals (40.8%) and 266 students of other nationalities (59.2%). The 202 English-speaking homes were reported by 31 UAE students (15.3%) and 171 students from other countries (84.7%).

35 This response contrasts with the observation that students did not assess English as their most frequent first language or home language (see Note 34).

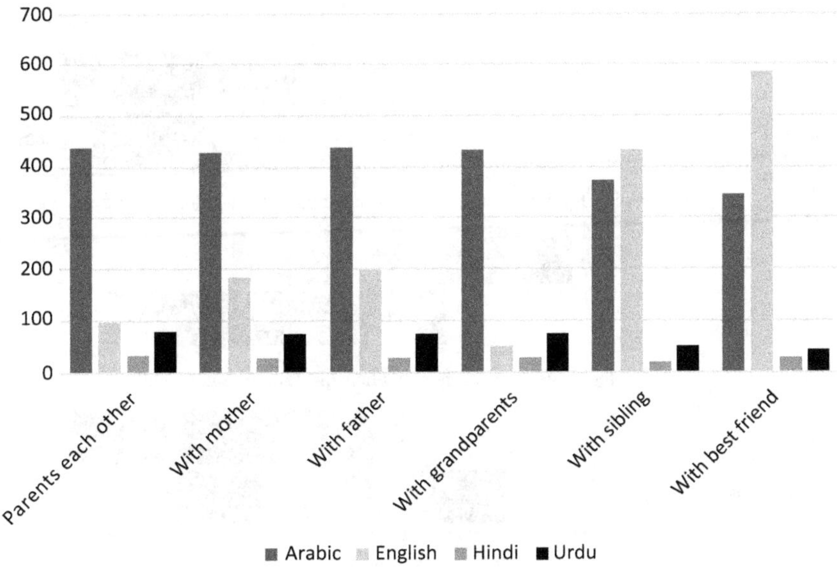

Figure 6.17 Differences in language use (based on own project data).

intermediate values amongst South Asian students. As far as English is concerned, South Asian students score highest (near mastery) followed by students from other countries. These findings reveal something about the high status of English in South Asian countries. Emirati students consider themselves advanced speakers of English.

Just as in the case of Singapore in Section 6.3.2, it is also instructive to consider language use data. Figure 6.17 manifests a strong use of Arabic with and amongst parents and grandparents, but English overtakes as the primary medium of communication with siblings and best friends. Regarding the use of English, one can identify similar trends as in Singapore (recall Figure 6.6). Hindi and Urdu also play a role in the family domain, but are used less frequently with siblings and friends. The pattern is suggestive of an ongoing language shift to English.

The student data reported from here also permit a reconstruction of the attitudes towards English and Arabic along the dimensions of status and solidarity. The responses to the following three statements reveal interesting attitudinal differences.

1. Knowing English/Arabic will increase my opportunities to find employment.
2. Knowing English/Arabic is a significant part of my cultural identity.
3. I feel confident and secure when speaking English/Arabic.

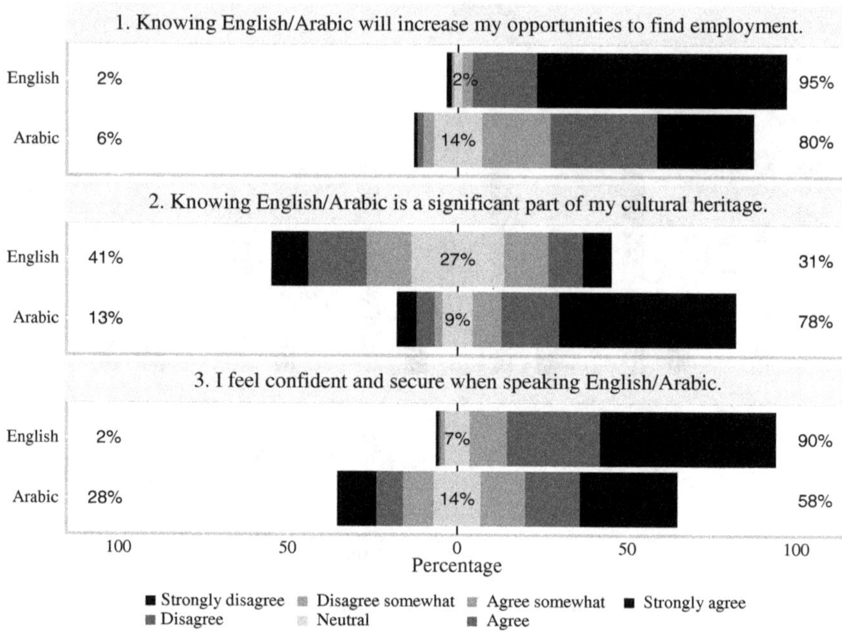

Figure 6.18 Attitudes to English and Arabic.
Adapted from Siemund et al. (2021: 104–107).

As can be gleaned from Figure 6.18, English in the UAE is strong along the status dimension, but figures less prominently in terms of solidarity. Students associate a high economic value with it, but are divided about its significance in regard to their cultural identity. The inclusion of the background of the students would most certainly reveal further differences. Students also express great confidence in their English abilities (see also Leimgruber et al. 2022).

Knowledge of Arabic, in contrast, is associated with less economic opportunity, but greater cultural significance. Consider Figure 6.18 again. It stands to reason that a distinction between students from Arabic and non-Arabic-speaking countries would reveal additional differences. Students generally do not feel particularly confident when using Arabic, mirroring the results from the rankings and proficiencies discussed above.

In contrast to Singapore, English in the Gulf Region and the UAE in particular does not yet seem to be associated with a specific local identity. Arabic remains a very strong cultural and also religious anchor (Siemund et al. 2021). This is consonant with the relatively short history of English in the area, the status of Arabic as the official language of the UAE, and the high mobility and diversity of the foreign population. For example, the sample of

692 students introduced above comprises citizenships of no fewer than 50 separate countries, notably the United Arab Emirates (208), India (105), Egypt (60), Pakistan (45), Syria (33), Saudi Arabia (31), Jordan (29), the United States (22), Palestine (20), Lebanon (20), Canada (15), and Iraq (10). This listing points to a complicated mix of native and non-native speakers. They use English as a lingua franca with comparably high proficiency levels, the specific properties of which will be followed up in Section 6.5.3. To be sure, this use of English cannot be representative of the situation in the UAE at large, but there are practically no studies that could be consulted here (see Siemund, Al-Issa & Leimgruber 2021).

6.5.3 English as a Lingua Franca and Gulf English

In the multilingual university campus context introduced above, the boundaries between English as a native language, as a second language, as a foreign language, as an additional language, and as a lingua franca begin to blur and become indistinct. It challenges the conceptual and definitional distinctions underlying these constructs (Filppula et al. 2017; Kecskes 2019; Mauranen 2018; McKay 2002; Ricento 2015c; Seidlhofer 2004). The few (in fact only seven) monolingual native speakers of English are in a clear minority. Students from the UAE, as outlined in Section 6.5.2, can mostly be assumed to have acquired English as a late first or early second language. Students from other Arab countries are likely to have learnt English as a second or foreign language. For the South Asian students, English will be either a first, second, or additional language. One may recall that 402 out of the 692 students consider English as the language they feel most proficient in. Depending on who talks to whom, different interactional contexts arise. If this particular student population were to continue their lives on a remote and secluded island, a novel and distinct variety of English would probably quickly develop. However, since the student cohorts keep changing from term to term, the interactional context as a whole is leaning towards the use of English as lingua franca (ELF). Nevertheless, this ELF context is rather different from that found at European universities where ELF interactions are much less frequent. We are here witnessing the emergence of a new variety of English (Gulf English, UAE English) in its incipient stages that, due to the external circumstances, keeps being interrupted in its further development (Leimgruber & Siemund 2021: 12).

English lingua franca communication and interaction in one of the New Englishes overlap, as, at least for subgroups in territories where New Englishes are spoken (India, Nigeria, the Philippines, etc.), interaction in English is qualitatively similar to lingua franca communication. For example, speakers of Indian English may have learnt English relatively late in life and speak different first languages (say, Hindi and Malayalam). In regard to the emergence of Singapore English and Hong Kong English, the current situation in the UAE is reminiscent of these former colonial contexts during their early decades. English-medium universities like the University of Sharjah display parallels to the Raffles Institution (Singapore) and the Government Central School (Hong Kong) in the nineteenth century (see Sections 6.3.1 and 6.4.1). Levels of English can be assumed to have been high in these institutions, but these were certainly not representative of the wider population. The same can be said about the UAE today where interactional sequences like those in (8) can be frequently encountered.

(8) Gulf English (Parra-Guinaldo & Lanteigne 2021: 307–308)
  a. Want taxi Dubai you?
     'Do you want a taxi to Dubai?'
  b. Not good karak.
     'The karak is not good.'
  c. You can go the other room. There is one patient.
     'We'll use a different room because there's a patient in this one.'
  d. Next Friday I clean? Put water? Outside?
     'Do you want me to clean the driveway next Friday using water?'
  e. One madam telling. After pharmacy asking 'this one'.
     'One day a madam told me about this medicine. After that I asked the pharmacy if they had this one.'

According to Mauranen (2012: 8), English as a lingua franca is "a vehicular language used by speakers who do not share a first language." Crucially, it is not their first or native language (see also Kecskes 2019: 2). Lingua francas are primarily defined by reference to the specific communicative situations in which they are used, and not in terms of their linguistic properties. We will see below, however, that the communicative strategies employed by lingua franca speakers produce recurrent and identifiable linguistic phenomena. Mauranen (2012: 3–4) further points out that the same language may be a learner language and also be employed as a lingua franca. Situational and functional differences can be used to discriminate between the two (see also Seidlhofer 2011).

Lingua franca communication produces a special type of language contact between what Mauranen (2012: 29) refers to as "similects," understood as mutually intelligible idiolects influenced by the speakers' L1 (or other) substrate. The background languages of the speakers thus always participate in lingua franca communications. This produces cases of second-order language contact, or contact between hybrids (Mauranen 2012: 29). Adopting this perspective, numerous languages in fact interact in the campus situation described in Section 6.5.2, and by no means only English. The same holds, mutatis mutandis, for similar language contact scenarios in other parts of the world and other eras. The degree of complexity of such situations increases

Table 6.13. *Morpho-syntactic processes (Parra-Guinaldo & Lanteigne 2021: 308–309).*

Process	Example	Gloss
Omission	Put boxes where?	Where should I put the boxes?
	Before cake yellow colour.	The cake you made before was yellow.
	Problem not mine.	This is not my problem.
Insertion	Trust you make.	Trust me.
	What's the hell is going on?	What the hell is going on?
Substitution	Me want return.	I want a refund.
	Wrap you make.	Can you wrap the item?

with the number of languages involved, with multilingually raised lingua franca speakers contributing more complexity than their monolingually raised peers. In a similar way, linguistically highly diverse ecologies in which English is used as a lingua franca are more complex than those in which just two or three languages partake besides English.

As the primary aim of lingua franca speakers is to bring their message across – rather than standard English formal correctness, the communication process is characterized by a number of recurrent morpho-syntactic strategies that by and large result in a highly pragmatically organized code. Parra-Guinaldo and Lanteigne (2021), based on a self-compiled corpus of 179 naturalistic utterances containing 417 non-standard specimens, identify the processes shown and illustrated in Table 6.13. Omissions are very frequent and represent nearly half of all non-standard forms, whereas insertions and substitutions are relatively rare.

These morpho-syntactic processes target a number of salient grammatical categories, particularly those identified in Table 6.14. Here, we see differences in the use of the progressive and the past tense, dislocations, invariant negative particles, and non-standard expressions of number and agreement. The question in topicalized declarative form (*Yogurt you don't want?*) is reminiscent of Indian English (see Siemund 2013: 242).

By and large, the processes and categories described in Tables 6.13 and 6.14 have also been observed in other ELF contexts (Mauranen 2012; Seidlhofer 2004). Parra-Guinaldo and Lanteigne (2021: 318) make the laudable attempt to contrast their data with findings from other ELF encounters and are able to identify various non-standard specimens that appear unique to the UAE context.[36] It remains to be seen, however, whether these are sufficiently concrete to define a distinct form of Gulf or UAE English.

[36] The authors there discuss specific types of omissions, insertions, and substitutions. The interested reader is referred to Parra-Guinaldo and Lanteigne (2021: 318).

Table 6.14. *Morpho-syntactic categories (Parra-Guinaldo & Lanteigne 2021: 310–312).*

Category	Example	Gloss
Tense	I no know what you say.	I don't understand what you're saying.
	The rest you fill all?	You filled out all the rest?
Word order	Professor I will tell him.	I will tell the professor.
	Yogurt you don't want?	You don't want yogurt?
Negation	Plastic no have.	We don't have it in plastic.
Number	Ma'am, if I give you small bill, is it ok?	Ma'am, is it ok if I give you small bills?
	Two shrimps box.	Two boxes of shrimp.
3rd person *-s*	This also white have.	This [new multicoloured sheet] also comes in white.

Before closing this chapter, let us briefly take up again the question of putative linguistic advantages of multilingual over monolingual speakers, as described inter alia in Agustín-Llach (2019), Bialystok (2001, 2018), Cenoz (2013b), Maluch et al. (2015), and Maluch, Neumann and Kempert (2016). The extensively multilingual ELF context encountered in the UAE could give rise to the hypothesis that those speakers with strongly multilingual backgrounds are in fact the more versatile ELF users. This hypothesis connects to the discussion of self-assessments of language proficiencies in Chapter 4. Based on Mueller (2018) as well as Siemund and Mueller (2021), it was shown that multilingually raised ELF users provide stronger self-assessments regarding their English proficiencies in comparison to their monolingually raised peers (measured across all CEFR domains). A preliminary analysis of the data collected at the University of Sharjah indeed confirms this hypothesis. Students with a multilingual background rate their English proficiencies higher relative to students with a monolingual background, but this initial comparison warrants a separate study.

6.5.4 Summary

It may not be entirely adequate to consider Gulf English (UAE English) as another postcolonial New English, but I cannot resist the temptation to position it within Schneider's (2003, 2007) Dynamic Model. Of the five stages distinguished there, that is, (i) foundation, (ii) exonormative stabilization, (iii) nativization, (iv) endonormative stabilization, and (v) differentiation, we can readily rule out stages four and five. The information provided in the preceding sections as well as my personal experience gathered in the UAE supports the idea of incipient nativization, as English represents a very natural part of the local multilingual ecology. In fact, one cannot successfully navigate the UAE without English. Nevertheless, all official language use in the administration or the education system is under strong exonormative pressure, with American English being the most important point of reference. There are as yet no signs of endonormative stabilization.

6.6 Chapter Summary

Chapter 6 aimed to illustrate the major themes of the present book – globalization, migration, urban areas, multilingual advantages, cross-linguistic influence, language acquisition and learning, language policies, identities, and attitudes – in the context of the New Englishes where interaction between multilingual speakers is abundant. The concepts and categories introduced and developed through Chapters 1–5 were applied to specific multilingual ecologies that demonstrate their relevance and mutual dependence. Singapore, Hong Kong, and the United Arab Emirates served as three case studies.

The comparison of the multilingual ecologies of Singapore, Hong Kong, and Dubai revealed important commonalities, but also crucial differences. There is extensive linguistic diversity in all three cities, but Dubai stands out in terms of density and transience. It is also the youngest multilingual global city of the three. Singapore became an independent country in 1965 and has made significant investments into organizing its multilingual ecology since. The linguistic texture of Singapore has become less diverse and more homogeneous within the bounds of its bilingual model. Hong Kong never achieved independence, but was returned to China in 1997 as a former colonial possession. It remains to be seen what happens to its long-lasting Cantonese–English bilingualism under the new Biliterate and Trilingual language policy (BT policy). With Singapore English – including its colloquial variety, the city state of Singapore has developed its own marker of national identity.

Multilingual contexts shaped by international migration, such as Dubai, pose new challenges for established models describing the global spread of English. Essential to Schneider's (2003, 2007) Dynamic Model is the distinction between a settler strand (the colonizers), on the one hand, and an indigenous strand (the colonized), on the other (Schneider 2003: 242). Apart from international investment as perhaps the modern equivalent of former physical settling, there is no distinguishable settler strand in Dubai or the UAE. Instead, we find an indigenous strand in the form of the local Arab population and a highly internally stratified international migration strand. There are in fact several migration strands. Further reflection reveals that the assumption of three separate strands is also necessary for adequately describing the early multilingual ecology of Singapore. The Malay represent the indigenous strand *sensu stricto*, while the Chinese and the Indian population groups form the most important migration strands. Most Cantonese people in Hong Kong are descendants of former immigrants, although their area of origin was the nearby Guangdong Province. The assumption of just two strands, indigenous and settler, works best for the United States, Australia, and New Zealand. In these locales, the early settler and indigenous strands were only much later complemented by newly arriving international migration strands. In sum, I here see the need for a model that incorporates immigrants as a separate strand, especially as they bring in their own varieties of English.

7 Patterns and Limits of Multilingualism

Monolingualism, bilingualism, and multilingualism represent concepts of individual upbringing and social organization of extreme impact and scope. Any policy decisions in this domain need to be grounded on a sound scientific basis. The present book provided a critical reassessment of the field, introducing and evaluating novel research findings. In addition, it offers crucial orientation for new research initiatives, research administrators, and policymakers.

All in all, I attempted to guide the reader from a multilingualism-as-problem to a multilingualism-as-resource perspective. However, I also argued that multilingualism cannot work wonders and should not be considered a goal in itself. Any ideological thinking invites suspicion. Running a multilingual society can produce many beneficial effects, but maintaining several languages at the same time also incurs costs that a society must be prepared to burden and share. Language learning and development – especially when it comes to literacy and academic language – will always remain hard work and necessitate substantial investments, both in terms of time and material resources (Berthele 2019). It is crucial to know which boundary conditions tip the balance from burden to benefit, or vice versa.

The final chapter tries to condense the content of the book into a coherent message. Section 7.1 summarizes the factors influencing multilingual development. There are many, as we have seen, both linguistic and extra-linguistic, and they interact in multifarious ways. Successful multilingual development requires specific factor arrangements, and not necessarily just one, contingent on the socio-historical context and the relevant multilingual ecology. Crucially, if the domineering cultural mindset is one of monolingualism and homogeneity, it becomes difficult to appreciate multilingualism and linguistic diversity. Ironically, modern education systems in their competitive model of flawless, highly normative literacy tend to work against multilingual development, in spite of widespread rhetoric to the contrary.

The preceding chapters revealed that most observable differences between monolinguals, bilinguals, and multilinguals – be they cognitive, linguistic, or educational – are typically statistical, not categorical. Generally speaking, one finds particular effects in particular cohorts. These offer snapshots of reality, but they should not be equated with reality itself. All observable differences require interpretations and Section 7.2 enquires into the bases of the presently entertained interpretations. Evidently, statistical significance is different from practical relevance and its concrete importance tends to be overrated. There are critical additional parameters. The conception of advantages is often driven by particular interests. What one group views as an advantage may be viewed as a disadvantage by another. An advantage in one context may turn out to be a problem in another context. Here, I argue for a more considerate stance regarding all political and practical implications.

Section 7.3 argues for a continuum from monolingualism to multilingualism. Multilingualism represents a spectrum of experiences (DeLuca et al. 2019; Leivada et al. 2020). Similarly, there are multiple forms of monolingualism as well as an extensive grey area between monolingualism and multilingualism. There is in fact no pure monolingualism much as there is no pure, or rather perfect, multilingualism. Social and individual forms of language organization are too multifarious and evade simple categorizations. Any speech community and essentially every individual speaker is linguistically stratified. I believe that conceptualizations of the field in terms of black and white are likely to hinder progress. Needless to say, the very term 'language' is riddled with problems and not without ideological biases. Monolingualism, bilingualism, and multilingualism only arise as categories once languages are labelled and can be identified. The most common individual and social model in the world appears to be domain-specific multilingualism.

Section 7.4 introduces a novel typology of English in multilingual contexts, distinguishing between English in heritage contexts, English in bilingual heritage contexts, English in contexts of balanced bilingualism, English in indigenous multilingual contexts, English in postcolonial multilingual immigrant contexts, and English as a lingua franca in modern multilingual immigrant contexts. This model considers the position of English from the local language ecology and offers a perspective that is significantly different from Kachru's (1985) differentiation between inner, outer, and expanding circle Englishes or Schneider's (2003, 2007) historical-dynamic approach to postcolonial Englishes.

Section 7.5 develops ideas for future research. I argue that we need more extensive and also more fine-grained comparisons of multilingual and linguistically diverse areas. Building on the comparison of the multilingual ecologies of Singapore, Hong Kong, and Dubai in Chapter 6, I develop ideas of how to advance this research to a globally representative scale.

7.1 Factors Influencing Multilingual Development

Multilingual development is not just language acquisition; it is much more. While there is plenty of information about child language acquisition, second

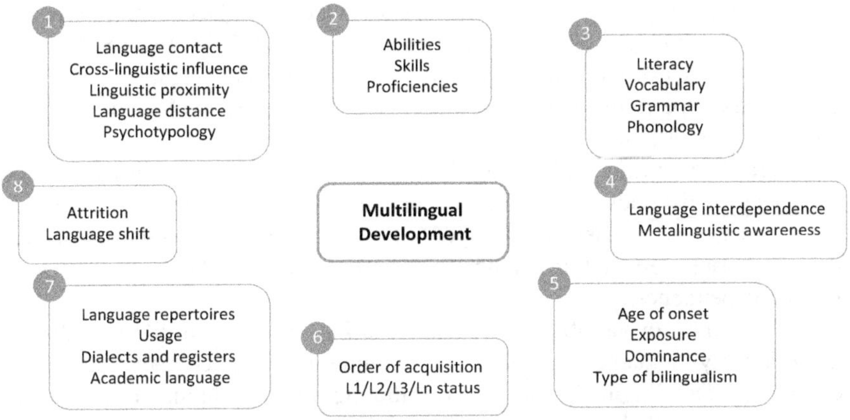

Figure 7.1 Multilingual development: linguistic factors.

language acquisition, and more recently also third or additional language acquisition, traditional research in these fields tends not to be embedded in social and educational development. However, we acquire languages in a multitude of different social settings and spend a substantial time of our lives in the education system. Therefore, it is crucial to relativize multilingual acquisition and learning to the relevant contexts where it occurs and to consider the various variables influencing them.

Multilingual development is conditioned by the underlying multilingual ecologies and the social as well as linguistic interactions within them. There are both linguistic and extra-linguistic variables. The former pertain to language proper, while the latter concern cognitive, social, educational, and political influences. The present book tries to consider multilingual development in the context of all these conditioning variables. Sections 7.1.1 and 7.1.2 recapitulate linguistic and extra-linguistic factors consecutively. Some factors involve both linguistic and extra-linguistic dimensions, but are only listed where I consider their contribution more important.[1]

7.1.1 Linguistic Factors

The most important linguistic factors contributing to multilingual development are summarized in Figure 7.1, arranged around the explanandum in the centre.

[1] Hufeisen (2018) considers a large battery of factors influencing the acquisition of a first, second, third, fourth, and further language. There is partial overlap with the factors discussed in what follows, but the focus here is on multilingual development.

They concern properties of the languages involved as well as different types of language knowledge, as noted in boxes 1, 2, and 3 in Figure 7.1 (see Chapters 3 and 4). Other factors define patterns of multilingualism in terms of language repertoires and usage, which are also subject to change over time (boxes 7 and 8). Several factors jointly define the cognitive status of the languages in a multilingual's mind (boxes 5 and 6). Language interdependence and metalinguistic awareness (box 4), besides influencing multilingual development, can also be viewed as important outcomes of it. As a matter of fact, the categories depicted in Figure 7.1 represent a complicated network of mutual dependencies.

The factors – or variables – assembled in Figure 7.1 span different disciplines, notably language acquisition and learning, language contact studies, and education. The linguistic factors contributing to multilingual development need to be modelled at the intersection of these disciplines.

7.1.2 Extra-Linguistic Factors

Multilingual development cannot be understood without the inclusion of extra-linguistic factors. Moreover, I consider it important to underline the interplay of linguistic and extra-linguistic factors. Not surprisingly, studies with a linguistic orientation tend to focus on linguistic factors, while educational and psychological research takes a keen interest in extra-linguistic factors. However, it is important to consider them in tandem.

The extra-linguistic factors shown in Figure 7.2 essentially capture individual differences, parameters relating to populations and the institutions they live and work in, functional differentiations, ideological and political dimensions, attitudes and perceptions, identity, status and prestige, as well as standards and norms. They all contribute to multilingual development in complicated ways.

Some of these factors impact multilingual development more strongly than others. For example, cognition, social status (socio-economic status), and age revealed themselves as strong factors, whereas gender turned out to be less important (box 1 in Figure 7.2; see Chapter 4). The influence of the attitudinal and motivational variables is generally quite strong (box 4). I consider that issues of language policy and planning, as well as ideological factors, are highly important (box 2), even though I am not aware of studies that would measure their influence. After all, these are highly consequential for the languages of instruction as well as the pedagogical approaches used in the educational institutions (box 8). Standards and norms define languages (box 5). Without them, many linguistic codes considered languages would be dialects (see Section 7.3). In multilingual ecologies, languages typically come to be associated with different functional domains manifesting as diglossia and polyglossia (box 3). In heritage situations, differentiations between home and

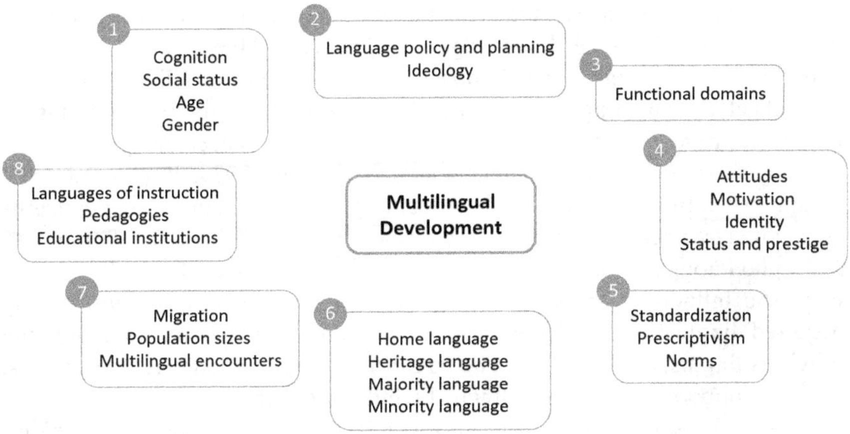

Figure 7.2 Multilingual development: extra-linguistic factors.

other contexts, as in box 6, arise yielding competing contexts of language learning and use (family, environment, classroom, etc.). Multilingual development further comes to be determined by migration and the populations in contact (box 7).

7.1.3 *The Interplay of Linguistic and Extra-Linguistic Factors*

The following points try to summarize the interrelations of linguistic and extra-linguistic factors with multilingual development. They result from the discussions in Chapters 1–6, without repeating all the research and sources on which they are based. They need to be viewed as partially programmatic, and not absolute.

Languages support one another. There is no such thing as deficient or harmful linguistic knowledge. Any such negative interpretations result from social inequalities, violations of prescriptive norms, and concomitant negative perceptions. The concept of language interdependence, as formulated by Cummins (1979, 2009), emphasizes the enhancing effects of languages on one another. Language interdependence primarily concerns the transfer of encyclopaedic concepts and academic conventions from one language to another. Given their similarity across languages, at least in the Western World, the net effect is typically positive.

Additive bi- and multilingualism impact language interdependence more strongly, and more positively than subtractive bi- and multilingualism. In a similar way, balanced bi- and multilingualism increase language interdependence and its positive aspects. However, balanced bi- and multilingualism appear to be the exception rather than the norm. We usually find functional differentiation due to social, cultural, and economic considerations.

Language proficiencies, the lexicon, grammar, and phonology represent different types of language knowledge (see Chapter 4). They respond differently to multilingual development and impact it in distinctive ways. Bilingual heritage students at a younger age can, apparently, draw on their previous multilingual experience more successfully than students in more advanced age groups.

Language interdependence in the sense of Cummins (1979, 2009) needs to be distinguished from cross-linguistic influence proper. While the former concerns conceptual transfer in a wider sense, the latter relates to the transfer of grammatical, phonological, and lexical properties *sensu stricto*. Crucially, cross-linguistic influence can be enhancing or inhibitory. This is because newly acquired linguistic knowledge may violate the language norms regulating previous linguistic knowledge. The larger the individual language repertoires, the more opportunity for cross-linguistic influence there is.

Cross-linguistic influence can, in principle, take any direction, but forward influence is more likely than backward influence. All previously acquired languages can influence subsequent language acquisition. Bilingual heritage speakers tend to experience more influence from the (dominant) majority language than their heritage language. Cross-linguistic influence is further modulated by linguistic proximity, language distance, and psychotypology.

Cognition impacts multilingual development positively, although it should itself not be regarded as a prerequisite for becoming multilingual. Highly developed multilingualism, especially in the written academic register, is widely considered an emblem of high education. This is not surprising, as it is a consequence of educational development.

Metalinguistic awareness is a function of the languages that one speaks. It increases with each new language learnt. Explicit language education further enhances metalinguistic awareness. It is currently unclear how much explicit language education contributes to the development of metalinguistic awareness. I submit that its influence is larger than we may be aware of.

Attitudes, identity issues, and prestige interact with multilingual development, both positively and negatively. Language learners are likely to invest in languages that they value, whose speech communities they wish to identify with, and which offer an increase in cultural and economic status. Having said that, languages also represent important cultural anchors that people cling to for reasons of identity. Otherwise, they would forfeit important social capital that they need for their well-being or in times of crisis.

Ideology as well as language policy and planning influence multilingual development. They can either enhance or inhibit it. Socially devalued languages are unlikely to attract speaker investment in contrast to those that receive political support. Furthermore, languages need continuous planning along the status and corpus dimension to remain attractive for their speakers (see Chapter 5). Otherwise, speakers may shift to different languages, such as English.

Languages of instruction, pedagogies, language syllabi, and language didactics are direct and indirect outcomes of language policy and planning. They determine the language repertoires of future generations and thus the languages that are allowed to survive. English has developed into a widely used language of instruction in non-native English-speaking countries, both as the sole medium of instruction as well as in content and language integrated courses.

Globalization and migration, both at a national and international level, promote the distribution and use of English. Postcolonial anglophone countries bear ample testimony to this claim, but the spread of English, including changes in its status, is also visible in other countries – notably in smaller polities like the Scandinavian countries and the Netherlands.

7.1.4 Summary

This section recapitulated the linguistic and extra-linguistic factors contributing to multilingual development. Moreover, it tried to capture their most important interactions in a listing of quasi-programmatic statements. These are based on the research results reported in Chapters 1–6, awaiting further testing and refinement.

7.2 Statistical Significance, Effect Sizes, and Practical Relevance

One way to read the contemporary discourse on multilingual advantages is as a rebuttal against earlier claims that associated bilingualism with certain cognitive deficits (see Chapter 1). Although entirely plausible and laudable, this, strictly speaking, represents an unwarranted justification of multilingualism. As argued in Section 7.1.3, the whole idea of deficient linguistic knowledge is fundamentally flawed. As if knowledge of languages – or knowledge of anything – could as such be defective and harmful. I must admit that before developing an interest in multilingualism, I had not been aware that knowledge of language could be conceived as a problem. The deficit discourse only makes sense in a competitive world of strong social asymmetries where some languages are valued while others are not. It is a political and normative problem.

In searching for multilingual advantages, unfortunately, we are unintentionally perpetuating competition and social asymmetries. Much of the research discussed in the present book, including my own work, represents benchmark studies that compare the performance of multilinguals against monolingual controls. Current research typically tries to refute the null hypothesis that monolinguals and multilinguals are not different, but the implicit understanding now is that the multilingual groups show superior performance. One hundred years ago, this used to be exactly the other way around. Again, this is unfortunate, as languages represent cultural goods that should be outside such considerations. Languages are valuable just by themselves and speakers have a right to use them. Having said that, they also have the right not to use certain languages. In any event, languages are beautiful human artefacts that reveal fundamental aspects of ourselves.[2]

Benchmarking in the sense introduced above tends to be based on tests of statistical significance and effect sizes. One needs to bear in mind that in big populations, small absolute differences quickly produce statistical significance. For example, when throwing a dice, the expectation (null hypothesis) is that each face appears with exactly the same probability (1/6). Throwing the dice, say, 60,000 times, we expect each face to be on top 10,000 times. Evidently, the reality will be different, but one may note that a deviation of merely ±150 already produces a significant *p*-value of 0.01912.[3] In other words, this imaginary dice produces biased results. I think we need to be careful to extrapolate such patterns to comparisons of multilingual and monolingual human populations. After all, the practical relevance in regard to human populations is low, especially as they tend to differ along many other dimensions.

Statistical significance looks for deviations from some expected pattern measured as probability of error, but it does not reveal what produces this deviation. In the above dice example, the observed deviations could be due to the table surface, the throwing angle, properties of the dice, or manipulation, for instance. Effect sizes – typically operationalized in terms of "small," "medium," and "large" – compute the impact of one variable on another in a standardized manner, and provided the data is free from multicollinearities, they are suggestive of causal relationships. Coming back to the above fictitious dice example, we can use Cramer's V to detect a very weak effect only.[4] In other words, despite the statistically significant skewing regarding the occurrence of its faces, the dice can be expected to perform well regarding all practical purposes.

Considering the studies to which I contributed, the effect sizes relating to the impact of a previous multilingual experience on the acquisition of subsequent

[2] I wish to add that I possess enough common sense to understand that this is a romantic illusion. Nevertheless, it serves as a reminder that we ourselves are responsible for social asymmetries and language prestige differentials. There is a more fundamental conflict between disciplines here. Linguists tend to understand languages as independent cognitive objects. There is the famous saying that language is "un système oú tout se tient," attributed to Ferdinand de Saussure (Koerner 1997). The species metaphor likens linguistic diversity to biodiversity and within that metaphorical space language diversity is considered in need to be preserved much as biodiversity. Education studies largely view language as cultural capital, following Bourdieu (1991). A concomitant of this economic perspective is competition between languages.

[3] I am assuming the following distribution of the 6 faces: 10,150; 10,150; 10,150; 9,850; 9,850; 9,850. The *p*-value was calculated in R using the chi-square function to perform a goodness-of-fit test. Martin Schweinberger needs to be credited for the necessary calculations.

[4] Using a confidence interval of 95 per cent, Cramer's *V* is between 0.00 and 0.01 (0.00671). According to Cohen (1988), the observed effect is practically negligible.

languages were generally rather low – especially when compared to the impact of extra-linguistic variables (see Chapter 4). For example, the impact of heritage language proficiency and proficiency in German on proficiency in English when learnt as a further language is relatively weak, albeit measurable. The impact of German is generally higher than that of the heritage languages. However, it would not be valid to conclude from such findings that the relevance of these background languages is generally low or that the heritage languages are irrelevant, as they may strongly determine the identity of the speakers and be essential in the relevant communities. Moreover, I am certain that increasing the time spent on heritage languages in terms of teaching and use would increase their relevance and impact on English – quite likely in a positive way. Whether that is desirable is a political and perhaps also a personal decision. Someone may wish to refuse to speak certain languages and rather remain monolingual. Such considerations make clear that study results and practical relevance are different pairs of shoes. Benchmark studies in their focus on particular aspects of language are deceptive. They fail to capture the complexities of our linguistic experiences.

Leivada et al. (2020: 4) critically remark that what counts as an advantage is subject to the perspective taken. For example, observable delayed onsets of mental illnesses in multilingual populations (see Chapter 2) may be tantamount to a delayed diagnosis and thus a disadvantage. In a similar vein, the measured reaction time differences between monolingual and multilingual cohorts are small and it stands to reason where these differences could become practically relevant. Studies need to state effect sizes in addition to significance values. Furthermore, all the language proficiency gains discussed in Chapter 4 presuppose some normative evaluative grid in the background. I believe that one could easily design language tests that favour monolinguals in much the same way as others favour multilinguals. Nevertheless, whenever monolingual and multilingual cohorts respond differently to the same test, that is an interesting observation in itself in need of explanation. However, as Leivada et al. (2020: 4) argue, we should first and foremost view this as an effect independently of any concomitant evaluations.

7.3 Monolingualism and Multilingualism within a Space of Linguistic Diversity

This section argues that the definition of monolingualism, bilingualism, and multilingualism crucially depends on our understanding of the term ‘language’. All these expressions represent fuzzy constructs harnessed by the linguistic and extra-linguistic factors summarized in Section 7.1. Here, I discuss different approaches to categorize the underlying space of linguistic diversity and explore ways of being monolingual, bilingual, and multilingual.

It is proposed to reconceptualize monolingualism and multilingualism with reference to the two dimensions of homogeneity and heterogeneity.

7.3.1 *Defining Languages*

The discourse on monolingualism, bilingualism, and multilingualism – especially in relation to putative advantages associated with the two latter forms of language experience – is complicated by the fact that the term 'language' is not without problems and subject to various political and ideological concerns. We typically explain to beginner students of linguistics that the boundary between dialects and languages is indistinct, or at least blurry, opposing issues of mutual intelligibility with political considerations and decisions. Dialect continua like those established by Germanic, Romance, or Slavic languages are used for illustration and contrasted with contemporary polities. According to a famous slogan, a "language is a dialect with an army and navy" – although its exact provenance is somewhat unclear.[5] Monolingualism, bilingualism, and multilingualism are ideological constructs that hover over linguistic reality, which is much more diverse. The number of recognized languages could easily be increased or reduced, depending on where one wishes to draw the line (see also Berthele 2021: 97–98).[6] Still, everybody agrees that Japanese is different from German and Twi is different from Malay. Nobody would dispute their status as separate languages. Apparently, typological differences are as important as political divisions. Moreover, writing systems increase the recognizability of languages as separate categorical entities. If two principally mutually intelligible dialects are written in different scripts (say Cyrillic and Latin), they become ipso facto two different languages.

The above, of course, is a more general problem of categorization. The reality around us is relatively amorphous so that categorical divisions can be imposed on it in different places and along different lines. Categories – as well as the mental models built on them – are indispensable and help us to navigate this complicated world, but they are to a certain extent arbitrary and sometimes deceptive. We know this from lexical semantics and phonology where different languages reconstruct the underlying semantic and phonetic spaces in often surprisingly heterogeneous, though also homogenous ways.[7] The resulting

[5] Maxwell (2018: 264) attributes it to linguist Max Weinreich (1894–1969), but the latter apparently only noted the "witticism" down and circulated it.

[6] Ricento (2006b: 13) argues that the number of languages as well as the dividing lines between them are at least partially a function of extensive field work and the production of grammatical descriptions.

[7] For example, allophonic distinctions in one language may be used as phonemic contrasts in another. Russian possesses distinct colour terms for dark blue (*синий siniy*) and light blue (*голубой goluboy*) where English uses only one to cover both light and dark blue.

patterns and limits of variation are the very food of linguists. Although the exact theoretical reconstruction, analysis, and interpretation of these differences are subject to (sometimes passionate and ardent) scholarly debate, the controversies are of little political impact, as they remain confined to the linguistic community. In contrast, the definition of languages affects our societies at large. Phonemes and morphemes are (mostly) innocent, languages are highly political. Language labels are associated with political influence and economic resources. They can literally decide the fate of entire populations. And once something has been politicized, it becomes difficult to talk about in objective terms.

Language labels serve as symbols of group identity. Linguistic differences can be exploited for political reasons. They can be maximized to exclude unwanted individuals or subgroups or be minimized to include desirable people. Humans possess enormous flexibility in their categorization, in my view. Communities who can communicate in principle may refuse to talk to one another for political reasons, thus maximizing differences over time. New dialects and languages develop. At the same time, there are mixed communities who initially cannot communicate verbally, but wish or simply need to interact in socially meaningful ways. Mixed languages like Michif, Medneyj Aleut, or Media Lengua must have arisen out of such social constellations (Evans 2018a: 918; Thomason 2001: 198–203; Thomason 2015: 50–52). To a good extent, language labels simply identify social groups passing over extensive linguistic heterogeneity within these groups. They are descriptors of identity, as stated above.

If it is the case that the underlying linguistic reality is amorphous with language labels relatively arbitrarily superimposed on it, this has consequences for the definition of monolingualism, bilingualism, and multilingualism. People may be conceptually bilingual or trilingual, even though they are officially monolingual. Others may be notionally bilingual, although they are in reality multilingual. Here, I wish to argue that few people are monolingual other than in a political sense. Monolingualism is an ideological construct that passes over substantial linguistic heterogeneity. Everyone's mind is linguistically heterogenous and in this sense, everyone is multilingual. Franceschini (2016: 97) points out that "[w]hen the focus is on the multilingual individual, the concept of separable individual languages can no longer be strictly applied." She here refers to the minds of the speakers, which underlines the tension between linguistic and political categorization.

Berthele (2021) convincingly argues that current research strands working on multilingualism adopt radically different perspectives on the identifiability of languages in the human mind. While the translanguaging paradigm (García & Wei 2014) conceptualizes the various codes in the multilingual mind as one coherent system, that is, as practically one language, researchers working on language contact and cross-linguistic influence happily identify different languages, defining precise input and output conditions across subsystems and modules in their mutual interactions. Parameters and universals are assumed to constrain the general architecture of language. By and large, these assumptions can be reconstructed as the legacy of structuralism. Evidently, the discussions in Chapters 3 and 4 of the present book adopted this latter perspective. Dynamic systemic approaches, as advocated by Herdina and Jessner (2002), combine assumptions from both perspectives. As far as I can see, all of these approaches are valid and correct in their own way. They do not contradict one another, but are reflective of the immensely flexible and plastic categorization possibilities of the human mind. Languages and the divisions between them are cognitive constructs. Crucially, they determine the ways in which bilingualism and multilingualism can be used as predictor variables for certain cognitive advantages or other effects (Berthele 2021: 107).

7.3.2 *Ways of Being Monolingual, Bilingual, and Multilingual*

Even if someone is officially monolingual, that is, a notional speaker of Chinese, English, German, Malay, etc., they are in fact able to control multiple codes or registers and in that sense they are multilingual (see also Fishman 1967: 32–33). As already stated, nobody is monolingual in the strict sense of the word. Officially monolingual modern societies expect their members to control the spoken and the written code of the relevant national language. The written code tends to be substantially different from the spoken one and is systematically developed in the education system. For example, German written academic language contains a host of 'upmarket' lexical items that would sound inadequate in the spoken registers, uses extensive complex clause structures, and the word order patterns in main and subordinate clauses are different. The education system instils in students different text types and genres. I know from experience that children spend considerable time on mastering these issues.[8] Once we include dialectal and other variation, many otherwise monolingual countries become highly multilingual spaces (see also Franceschini 2016: 101). The majority of British people are dialect speakers in one way or another and can typically speak a local dialect besides the standard variety. The written academic standard is quite different from the oral language, especially when it comes to mastering the exuberant English lexicon. Academic English is a register that requires substantial training and constitutes a major international business. Most speakers of English are not monolingual provided spoken dialects and academic language are counted, even though

[8] Modern Standard Arabic furnishes another convincing case to illustrate the difference between spoken and written language. This code nearly exclusively occurs in written form, while local Arabic dialects serve as spoken media of communication.

they technically speak one language only. Also, if Austrian or Swiss German were known by different names (say just Austrian and Swiss), the relevant territories would become officially bilingual instead of bi-dialectal (i.e. Standard German in combination with Austrian or Swiss; see Berthele 2021: 103). German as a label hides extensive linguistic diversity. The moniker 'Chinese' conceals even more complexity (see Chapter 5).

Mathematics as a school subject introduces a new language with its own lexicon, syntactic rules, and operators – perhaps even its own mode of thinking. It accompanies students throughout their careers and effectively expands their linguistic repertoire. By the time they graduate from school, students from officially monolingual countries control the respective spoken and written codes as well as the language of mathematics.[9] Many speak a local dialect. Students from non-English-speaking monolingual countries will also have acquired English as another language. Regarding Germany, for example, English, German, and mathematics are designated "core subjects" in the curriculum. Evidently, these codes are regarded as essential to manoeuvre modern society successfully.[10]

I consider it a fallacy to compare members of modern, script-based, officially monolingual societies with members of older multilingual clan-based societies who exclusively communicated through the oral medium (see Berthele 2019: 2 for a similar point of view in relation to "multilingual societies with low literacy rates"). Although our forefathers can be expected to have been able to master several oral codes representing different clan languages, they did not have to worry about orthography, writing, and educational attainment. Even when writing systems began to be used more widely, literacy in the general population remained very low. For example, levels of literacy in China were still only just above 65 per cent in 1982, to reach 96.8 per cent in 2018.[11] Literacy used to be reserved for a small elite in earlier times. The bilingual or multilingual elite capable of writing in several languages must have been even smaller. Few people will have been able to read the inscriptions on the Rosetta Stone, not to mention being able to produce them.

Provided the above observations are correct, we can discern a shift in the use of our linguistic capacity over the centuries and millennia. I believe that this capacity as such has not changed substantially, but the way we use it has changed tremendously. Today's multilingualism is different from historical

9 I ignore the learning of foreign and other languages here. These, of course, further expand the students' linguistic repertoires.

10 One may wish to include other subjects (chemistry, biology, geography, physics), but I believe that these mainly expand one's lexicon and, of course, one's conceptual knowledge.

11 Retrieved from data.worldbank.org/indicator/SE.ADT.LITR.ZS?end=2018&locations=CN&start=1982&view=chart, accessed on 2 February 2021.

multilingualism. There has been a universal drift from oral to written cultures. Bilingualism, trilingualism, or multilingualism, in general, are not a problem for the human mind. We have seen that these experiences are culturally precious and can be beneficial in different ways. However, developing and maintaining multiple written (academic) registers concurrently – in often rather artificially standardized forms – represents a significant investment that presupposes the allocation of resources. Few people outside academia can afford this, and we as academics need to be careful when we generalize from our lofty positions into the wider population.

7.3.3 Homogeneity versus Heterogeneity

In what follows, I propose to reconceptualize monolingualism and multilingualism in terms of homogeneity and heterogeneity, insisting from the outset that these categories need to be interpreted devoid of any evaluative associations. From that perspective, monolingualism is a fiction as there is no absolutely homogenous speech community in the sense of Chomsky (1965: 3). Neither is there a homogenous speaker. We always find individual variation as well as social, regional, and functional stratification – even in the smallest and most isolated communities.[12] The closest one can perhaps get are (artificial) computer languages, but even here one finds dialects and programmers' preferences for particular structures. Homogeneity – including the idea of purity – represent romantic ideals far removed from reality. These ideas impacted European languages strongly during the period of standardization (Baugh & Cable 2002: 253–295). Language academies like the Italian *Accademia della Crusca* (founded in 1582) and the French *Académie Française* (founded in 1635) emerged with the aim to regularize and purify language (Baugh & Cable 2002: 263–264), typically with reference to the classical languages Latin and Greek. Languages became the target of prescriptivism. Although attempts at establishing a corresponding *English Academy* failed (Baugh & Cable 2002: 269), issues of standardization were widely and ardently discussed in England, nevertheless. This period saw the emergence of numerous dictionaries and grammars of the hitherto vernacular languages, leading to the explicit codification of lexicon and grammar (notably Samuel Johnson's *A Dictionary of the English Language* published in 1755). Arguably, it was the outcome of these standardization processes that made the proper identification of languages possible. Languages became defined by their respective handbooks. Standardization can thus be viewed as an important

[12] Nevertheless, I consider it absolutely legitimate to abstract away from these differences for the sake of theory building.

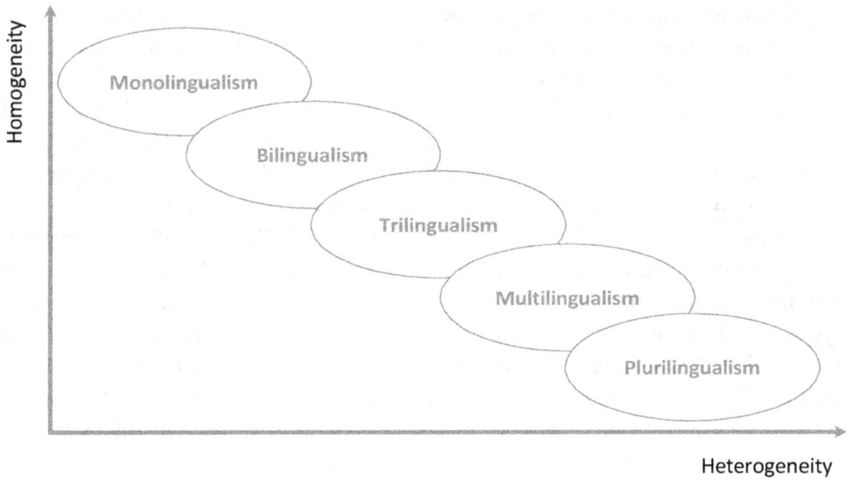

Figure 7.3 Homogeneity versus heterogeneity.

instrument to achieve monolingualism, but it mainly targets written language. Spoken language is too elusive.[13]

Figure 7.3 employs the two dimensions of homogeneity and heterogeneity to map out a space of linguistic diversity ranging from monolingualism to multilingualism and plurilingualism.[14] This space can be read in relation to both individuals and societies. More diversity in terms of phonological categories, lexical means of expression, and grammatical structures is tantamount to higher levels of heterogeneity. An increase in heterogeneity along the horizontal axis leads to a concomitant decrease in homogeneity mapped along the vertical axis, and vice versa.[15] At the individual level, the space is

[13] If, as a consequence of standardization, language variation is curtailed and specific variants are proscribed over others, this effectively leads to an increase in homogeneity. There are many examples, including the avoidance of split infinitives and preposition stranding, the use of certain pronominal forms in coordinations and comparatives, negative concord, variation in the use of the third person *s*-suffix, relative pronouns, etc. It is interesting why some instances of variation – for example, *s*-genitive versus *of*-genitive – have been spared. Moreover, the German dative possessive *dem Paul sein Bruder* the.DAT Paul his brother 'Paul's brother' (DAT = dative) is heavily stigmatized and restricted to colloquial language. Apparently, our cognitive apparatus associates extensive socio-cultural usage information with each lexical item and each grammatical construction. Linguistic homogeneity and heterogeneity, thus, serve as emblems and gatekeepers of social group membership.

[14] The term 'plurilingualism' is here understood as defined in Chapter 1, that is, as a perspective on multilingualism that defocusses the boundaries between languages and emphasizes their interrelations.

[15] In addition, homogeneity typically indexes accuracy, consistency, and normativity, while heterogeneity is tantamount to flexibility, fluidity, and expressivity. These are difficult concepts that are culturally laden. One needs to be careful in their application and interpretation.

populated by different language repertoires. Multilingualism generally represents a more heterogeneous state of mind than monolingualism. Considering the evidence gathered in the present book, it would appear that bilingualism and trilingualism – of different types – are amongst the most widely attested models of linguistic organization, both at the individual and societal level. Note that there is overlap between the categories in Figure 7.3. The space as such is amorphous with certain focal areas superimposed on it.[16]

The model in Figure 7.3 needs to be extended by additional dimensions that cannot be depicted in this simple graphic representation. The first is language dominance. Bilingualism and trilingualism must not be restricted to balanced types based on early child language acquisition, which I, by and large, consider idealized states – much like cardinal vowels. Most natural occurrences of bilingualism and trilingualism appear to be of an unbalanced and/or functional type, involving varying ages of onset as well as lengths and intensities of exposure. I consider balanced bilingualism or trilingualism to comprise more structural heterogeneity than the corresponding unbalanced states. Bilinguals and trilinguals who are strongly dominant in one language lean towards more homogeneity, that is, they show more overlap with monolinguals. We may recall that cross-linguistic influence in unbalanced bilingual heritage speakers, in their acquisition of English as an additional language, primarily originated in the stronger majority language (see Chapter 4). They effectively showed a behaviour resembling monolingual learners of second languages.

Another dimension is typological proximity. I consider the language repertoires of multilinguals that contain closely related languages as more homogeneous than those comprising typologically and genetically diverse languages. To illustrate, multilingualism of Danish, Dutch, Low German, Norwegian, and Swedish is more homogenous than that involving Arabic, Chinese, Cree, Yoruba, and Wardaman. A person speaking the latter five languages would control a highly heterogeneous language repertoire. Such a person probably does not exist (other than perhaps in the academic field of linguistics), while someone exhibiting multilingualism of the former more homogenous type might indeed be encountered outside academia. One could also say that the latter language repertoire is more complex than the former, since it contains a greater diversity of structures.

The third dimension not depicted in Figure 7.3 relates to the separability of languages (see Aronin & Singleton 2012: 106–108 for discussion). The labels bilingualism, trilingualism, multilingualism, plurilingualism, and also

[16] Evans' (2018a: 906) conception of language as a social technology implies a continuous elaboration of this technology. This can be interpreted as an increase in heterogeneity. As far as I can see, Construction Grammar in the sense of Goldberg (2006) matches this perspective most adequately.

translanguaging describe different forms of heterogeneity, ranging from internally structured heterogeneity to nearly chaotic states of affairs. Bilingualism and trilingualism may be used as labels for double or triple monolingualism, with all languages being neatly compartmentalized and no cross-linguistic influence. Alternatively, they may describe situations in which the languages overlap, heavily interact, and merge. The former situation represents structured heterogeneity, while the latter leans more towards loosely structured chaos. This distinction applies to both individuals and societies where double and triple monolingualism finds its equivalent in diglossic or triglossic societies (in the sense of Ferguson 1959 and Fishman 1967). Here, the different languages are used for specific functional domains. Pidginization and creolization processes manifest less structure and more chaos. They occur in linguistically unstable societies. Translanguaging as a theoretical construct describes less structured communicative situations, judged from the normative perspective of distinct and identifiable languages. Much as monolingualism represents an idealized fiction, so does multilingualism when it is understood as complete heterogeneity or chaos. The reality is somewhere in between.

Register differences represent another important dimension, as people may develop a multilingual spoken repertoire, but control the written register of just one language. This is not uncommon, in my view, and more frequent than the opposite scenario. This latter scenario, where someone commands more written than spoken languages, is best represented by the monolingually socialized scholar of classical languages who can read and write Latin, Greek, and Sanskrit – although they cannot speak these languages. When English was relegated to a spoken language after the Norman Conquest in Medieval England, the spoken and written registers came to be based on two different languages, as written communication was conducted in French. Nowadays, English is the main language used in academia. I speak German with my family and friends but mostly write and teach in English. The spoken registers can be more homogeneous or heterogeneous depending on the population group considered. Adolescents have a different understanding of normativity than academic adults.

The fifth dimension concerns attitudinal issues, as language prestige, identity, and motivation heavily interact with the concepts depicted in Figure 7.3. When there is a strong delta in social prestige between the languages of a bilingual speaker, the person may come to behave like an unbalanced bilingual – quasi monolingual – even though they in fact possess extensive knowledge of the allegedly weaker language. I need to flag this as anecdotal evidence, but I have encountered parents of heritage communities who practically denied knowledge of their heritage language for the presumed benefit of their children. I have also met adolescents who curtailed their linguistic repertoire to conform to their majority language-speaking peer group. Knowledge of language can be construed as a liability. These are unfortunate situations, but they become understandable when issues of identity and prestige are factored in. Pressure from norm-conformity can make our linguistic repertoires more homogenous, but perhaps also more heterogeneous.

Finally, there is the political or ideological dimension. Polities – whatever their size and political orientation – impose or recognize official language labels on the basis of different criteria. Officially monolingual, bilingual, or trilingual countries may hide extensive linguistic diversity with languages counting in the hundreds (see Chapters 1 and 5). In recognizing eleven official languages, for example, South Africa tries to establish a relatively close match between linguistic reality (thirty-six languages according to Ethnologue, Eberhard, Simons & Fennig 2022) and political categorization.

7.3.4 Summary

It must remain a matter of speculation why the space of linguistic diversity established by homogeneity and heterogeneity is harnessed in so many different ways across the world. The modern nation state stands out in its monolingual orientation. Apparently, technological advances provided the means to create linguistically and ideologically coherent population clusters of unforeseen dimensions. However, I believe that the underlying group formation processes are much older.[17] There are additional factors. For example, linguistic diversity within Germany was apparently also reduced as a consequence of extensive population relocations after World War II and concomitant dialect mixing and levelling (see Erdmann 1992: 88 on Low German).

Despite all monolingual ideologies, the world has remained a multilingual space and my present conjecture is that this will not change – although the number of recognized languages is bound to fall further. Social gravitational forces are strong and are likely to create new group structures in need of displaying their identity. Languages here tend to be the means of choice. Most of the world currently appears to be converging on some bilingual or trilingual model in which English plays a crucial role.[18] Speech communities need to develop some form of multilingualism to remain functional. Arguably, such models strike a workable compromise between communicative function, identity formation, and economic considerations. Which languages are included in these models, however, will remain a matter of great debate.

[17] Again, I wish to draw attention to the "one-clan one-language ideal" (Evans 2018b: 30), as discussed in Chapter 1.

[18] These may be analyzed as Dominant Language Constellations, as extensively discussed in Aronin and Singleton (2012: 59) as well as Lo Bianco and Aronin (2020).

7.4 English in Multilingual Contexts

This section adopts a perspective on English from within the multilingual ecologies in which it occurs. Kachru's (1985) concentric circle model, which distinguishes between inner, outer, and expanding circle Englishes, rests on the mode of acquisition as the primary discriminator. Inner circle Englishes are characterized by the use of English as a first language (norm-providing), outer circle varieties by that of English as a second language (norm-developing), while expanding circles varieties correspond to the use of English as a foreign language (norm-dependent). Schneider's (2003, 2007) Dynamic Model distinguishes between "settler," "indigenous," and "adstrate" strands, offering another dimension along which the different Englishes can be classified. However, the various immigrant groups and their languages have not been sufficiently identified as a separate strand or strands, but they are important to understand the linguistic forces in the local multilingual ecologies.[19] The following sections develop a taxonomy of the multilingual ecologies in which English can be currently encountered.

7.4.1 English in Heritage Contexts

Although the traditional settler countries of the United States, Canada, Australia, and New Zealand were mainly populated by English speakers during the foundational periods of colonization, supplanting the respective indigenous groups, these were subsequently followed by immigrants from other countries. Migration was driven by many factors, including the escape from religious and political oppression, famines and diseases, family reunifications, and the quest for economic opportunities. Before the World Wars, immigration to the above settler destinations primarily originated in European countries (Germany, Greece, Ireland, Italy, the Scandinavian Countries, Scotland, etc.). After World War II, we see a noticeable shift to Asian countries as the main source of immigration. For example, Germans established a sizeable diaspora in Southern Australia around the city of Adelaide in the middle of the nineteenth century (Hahndorf, Barossa Valley).[20] These German settlers must have been dialect speakers. Similar examples could be procured from the other settler countries and immigrant communities (see Clyne 1991 for the context of Australia). Chapter 1 provided extensive illustration of the contemporary heritage

[19] Cenoz and Jessner (2001b: viii–ix) advance a typology of contexts where English is acquired as a third language that shows some overlap to the systematics offered here. My perspective is that of the multilingual ecology in which English is used and acquired.

[20] The State Library of Southern Australia offers valuable information, including passenger lists and immigration schemes: guides.slsa.sa.gov.au/c.php?g=410226&p=2796017, accessed on 10 February 2021.

communities and their languages in London, Toronto, Vancouver, New York City, San Francisco, Sydney, Melbourne, and Auckland. To be sure, English as the surrounding majority language is part of people's language repertoires.

Given the long history of immigration, the above settler countries must also have experienced a long history of multilingualism. The immigrants likely did not speak English when they arrived. I am not aware of detailed comparative studies of the multilingual ecologies that arose out of these immigration streams, that is, across the different settler countries. However, Clyne (1991) provides a very readable and informative overview of the Australian situation.[21] Moreover, there are no studies comparing these earlier multilingual immigrant ecologies with those established more recently. It is well known that the two World Wars in combination with the extreme political orientations of certain European countries considerably and persistently damaged the social prestige of the associated languages, leading to faster assimilation and shift to English in the immigrant countries. We learnt in Chapter 1 that urban areas like New York City, San Francisco, Sydney, Melbourne, and Auckland nowadays witness levels of bilingualism and multilingualism exceeding 50 per cent of their populations. Perhaps the multilingual ecologies of the nineteenth century were not that different, just on a smaller scale.

7.4.2 English in Bilingual Heritage Contexts

The phenomenon of learning English in bilingual heritage contexts is by and large restricted to Western Europe. It could only arise after English developed into the hub language of the world (de Swaan 2001), or the global lingua franca, and Western Europe experienced rising levels of immigration. With increasingly lowered levels of onset, English complements a bilingual experience consisting of a heritage language and the relevant national or majority language. In view of the fact that around 50 per cent of the school children in major European urban areas have a migration background (Gogolin 2020: 2; see also Romaine 2017: 554), bilingual heritage contexts have developed into a prominent part of the local multilingual ecologies. In addition, and especially for the younger age groups, English serves as an important emblem of global identity (Fuller 2020). Since the heritage languages usually receive little institutional support outside their respective communities, they now find themselves in competition not only with the national languages, but also English.

[21] For example, Clyne (1991: 24–25) identifies four "phases of policies towards multilingualism" in Australia: (i) "*Accepting but* laisses-faire (up to the mid-1870s)," (ii) "*Tolerant but restrictive* (1870s–early 1900s)," (iii) "*Rejecting* (c. 1914–c. 1970)," and (iv) "*Accepting* (c. 1970)" (emphasis in the original). These may find parallels in the other settler countries.

As we saw in Chapters 3 and 4, the use of English in bilingual heritage contexts sparked two by now highly visible research areas. On the one hand, there is the question of which of the background languages determines the acquisition process of English in matters of cross-linguistic influence. On the other hand, researchers ask whether the bilingual experience of the heritage students can be exploited in such a way as to produce advantages for subsequent language learning. The discussion in Chapters 3 and 4 revealed that cross-linguistic influence in such contexts primarily emanates in the relevant majority languages (i.e., the national languages), although the heritage languages also become visible to a certain extent – especially during the early stages in the acquisition process. The majority languages typically represent the more dominant language of the students. Although learning advantages have been observed, they appear tied to specific contexts and apparently also learner groups. Moreover, students' previous multilingual experience can be accessed more successfully during the early stages in the acquisition of English, with all students converging on the relevant educational norms over time. As pointed out before, the notion of advantages needs to be defined adequately.

7.4.3 English in Contexts of Balanced Bilingualism

Some territories have a history of bilingualism involving languages other than English – for different reasons – and in these contexts, English currently comes to be learnt as an additional language. One may subsume these contexts under third language acquisition, as English typically is the third language in the acquisition chronology. Chapter 3 elaborated on the associated taxonomic problems. However, I here see a specific multilingual ecology and acquisition context. Bilingualism tends to be of a balanced or quasi-balanced type. Moreover, the context is one of childhood bilingualism, not adult bilingualism. As in bilingual heritage contexts, English is typically transmitted through the education system.

Presently, the most prominent and best researched contexts matching this type are Catalunya and the Spanish part of the Basque Country. Bilingualism of Catalan and Spanish, as well as Basque and Spanish, is widespread in these regions. Moreover, Basque, Catalan, and Spanish possess the status of official languages in these regions and enjoy high social prestige (see Chapter 5). In principle, many other European regional minority contexts conform to this type, but levels of bilingualism – especially balanced bilingualism – tend to be less pronounced there and the relevant minority languages may be associated with less social prestige and receive less official and educational support.

The countries formerly assembled within the Soviet Union provide further bilingual contexts where English is now widely taught and learnt as an additional language. Armenia, the Baltic States, Georgia, Kazakhstan, and Ukraine may serve as illustration, but it should be clear that there are important differences both across and within these countries. The Soviet Union, and formerly the Russian Empire, implanted Russian in these countries so that extensive bilingualism developed of Russian in combination with the indigenous languages. We also find dense multilingual ecologies, as there may be more than one indigenous language. Georgia may serve as a prominent example. Russian used to be the official language across the Soviet Union much as English was across the British Empire. After the fall of the Iron Curtain, English developed into a prominent competitor in these language ecologies. One might have expected that English replaces Russian, but this does not seem to happen. Rather, English comes to be learnt in addition to Russian and the many local languages. With increasing levels of English in China, ethnic minorities speaking non-Sinitic languages besides Putonghua yield further bilingual contexts where the acquisition of English could be studied. The Bai languages spoken in the Yunnan province of Southern China provide illustration (Wang 2005), but little is known about the acquisition of English in the relevant communities. Bilingualism of Spanish or Portuguese in combination with one of the many indigenous languages of South America provides yet another context where the acquisition of English could be explored.

The acquisition of English in the bilingual contexts of Catalunya and the Basque Country is a relatively prominent research area (see Chapter 4). Much of what we know about the acquisition of English by bilingual speakers relates to research carried out in these territories. In contrast, other European bilingual minority contexts as well as the many bilingual contexts produced by the former Soviet Union appear rather under-researched. I am not aware of any studies on such bilingual communities from China or South America.

Moreover, Catalunya and the Spanish part of the Basque Country offer an interesting contrast, as Catalan and Spanish are closely related languages, whereas Basque and Spanish are not. This likely affects the acquisition process of English in different ways. Evidently, the other bilingual contexts introduced above offer a great number of highly interesting language constellations in which the acquisition of English could be studied.

7.4.4 English in Indigenous Multilingual Contexts

Colonialism and globalization have transplanted English into many territories characterized by extensive language density, linguistic diversity, and multilingualism. This description applies to many parts of Africa, India, Indonesia, Papua New Guinea, and the Philippines – perhaps others. In principle, North America and Australia need to be mentioned in this context, too, but as

European settlements, they developed into largely English-speaking areas with substantial portions of the autochthonous linguistic diversity lost or relegated to the fringes of society.

Language density and linguistic diversity have been defining characteristics of the aforementioned areas for a very long time. They are not the result of recent immigration. These areas bear testimony to the primordial character of multilingualism. It appears nearly impossible to compute a precise number of languages for Africa, but the combined figures for Ghana, Kenya, Nigeria, South Africa, and Tanzania already amount to 847 (Ethnologue, Eberhard, Simons & Fennig 2022; see Chapter 6). The total figure for the continent could easily reach 2,000. India counts 463 languages, Indonesia 722, Papua New Guinea 852, and the Philippines 186 (Ethnologue, Eberhard, Simons & Fennig 2022).[22] To be sure, the majority of these languages will be used by rather small communities of speakers and be confined to particular locations and contexts. However, precisely these speakers of smaller languages can be assumed to be multilingual. This follows from de Swaan's (2001) World Language System, as discussed in Chapter 1. A typical multilingual repertoire will consist of a local language, a regional language, a national language, and English.

In the indigenous multilingual contexts, English is added to the multilingual repertoires either in the form of standard or near-standard English, or a nativized variety of English (e.g. Nigerian English). Furthermore, it occurs in the form of Creoles or Pidgin Englishes, such as Naija in Nigeria or Tok Pisin in Papua New Guinea. There will also be several learner varieties. For all practical purposes, English can now be considered as another language of the relevant territories, complementing the indigenous languages.

7.4.5 English in Postcolonial Multilingual Immigrant Contexts

Although Singapore has been widely treated as a postcolonial context similar to that of India and several African countries, it is in fact very different. The reason is that the majority of its population is – in historical terms – not indigenous to the area, but represents the descendants of various immigrant communities. As I pointed out in Chapter 1, the indigenous Malay population amounted to merely 15.0 per cent in 2019. A total of 76.0 per cent were ethnic Chinese, 7.5 per cent were Indians, and 1.5 per cent belonged to other ethnic groups (Singapore Department of Statistics 2021). In other words, 85.0 per cent of the Singaporean population possess non-indigenous roots. Chapter 6 showed that the current population balance has a long history and can be traced

[22] According to Ethnologue (Eberhard, Simons and Fennig 2022), Papua New Guinea is the country with the highest number of languages (852), followed by Indonesia (722), Nigeria (531), and India (463). The figures relate to the category of "established languages."

back at least to around 1900. Singapore is an immigrant country, although a substantial part of the immigration occurred during colonial times and before the country was officially established in 1965. Regarding its broad pattern of immigration, Singapore aligns with modern Dubai and less with, say, Lagos, Manila, or Mumbai.[23]

I believe that immigration is an important reason why Singapore has embraced English more strongly than any other postcolonial country outside the traditional settler countries and why it has developed into such an important factor in the identity formation of Singaporeans. Language shift to the surrounding majority language is widespread in immigrant communities. What makes Singapore different from other immigrant communities is that the majority language – English – was itself transplanted to the area. Moreover, in terms of the attitudes to and the emotions associated with, English represents a relatively neutral language for the different immigrant groups. It is certainly no coincidence that the Singaporean Malay community lags behind in their adoption of English and may resist language shift longest (Cavallaro & Ng 2021).

Although Hong Kong is a colonial immigrant community in historical terms, the situation here is again different. During colonial rule, immigrants hailed primarily from the nearby Cantonese-speaking province of Guangdong. Moreover, the greater part of Hong Kong was only leased to the British Empire. Technically, it remained part of China until the lease ended in 1997 and Hong Kong was reconstituted as part of the People's Republic of China. These broad facts help to motivate the different status of English in Hong Kong in comparison to Singapore.[24]

7.4.6 *English as a Lingua Franca in Modern Multilingual Immigrant Contexts*

Dubai is the pivotal global city in the Gulf Region outshining other conurbations along the Gulf Coast. As pointed out in Chapters 1 and 6, it is primarily inhabited by immigrants who practically run the city, although they do not rule it. Dubai replicates the history of Singapore, but what attracted immigration and established English in the area is not primarily colonialism but globalization. However, immigration to Dubai is different from that flowing into Singapore inasmuch as the number of source countries is considerably higher and the immigrants are more transient. Also, many immigrants come from countries

[23] Nevertheless, these cities experience substantial immigration from within Africa, the Philippines, and India (see Chapter 5).
[24] Although created more recently and on a much bigger scale than Hong Kong, nearby Shenzhen can be viewed as a pan-Chinese immigrant city.

where English is an official language and used widely (India, Pakistan, the Philippines). English has developed into the de facto official language, as the many immigrant groups and the indigenous Arab population were in need of a common language. Apparently, Arabic could not assume this function.

As far as I can tell, the multilingual immigrant context established by Dubai and the United Arab Emirates, in general, is unique and unparalleled in the contemporary world. Although English serves as a lingua franca in the city and the country, it has been accommodated to such an extent that it appears more adequately analyzed as a second language. Its overwhelming prominence in the education system underlines this analysis.

7.4.7 Summary

According to Ethnologue (Eberhard, Simons & Fennig 2022), English "is spoken in 171 countries, as an established language or by a substantial immigrant group."[25] It is the language that accrues the highest number of speakers, although Chinese outnumbers English in terms of native speakers.[26] The preceding sections proposed a typology of the most prominent multilingual contexts in which English is currently used. This perspective complements models of English based on the mode of acquisition (as a native, second, or foreign language; Kachru 1985), national borders (a substantial portion of the World Englishes paradigm), and degree of nativization (Schneider 2003, 2007). Moreover, this perspective highlights the importance of immigrant groups in the local multilingual ecologies.

Adopting a perspective from the multilingual ecologies in which English is used brings to the fore the parameters that proved important throughout the present book. If one wishes to understand multilingual development in the context of English around the world, one needs to factor in the surrounding languages, their status, indigenous and immigrant groups, individual language repertoires, types of bilingualism and multilingualism, language dominance, types of acquisition and use, and so on and so forth. There is definitely potential for more research here.

7.5 Towards a Global Comparison of Multilingual Ecologies

Depending on where one is born in this world and into which social circumstances, one's life trajectory and one's linguistic biography – especially in

[25] Retrieved from www.ethnologue.com/enterprise-faq/which-language-spoken-most-countries-how-many-countries, accessed on 27 February 2021.

[26] Retrieved from www.ethnologue.com/guides/most-spoken-languages, accessed on 27 February 2021.

one's early years – will be very different. Although there are many multilingual cities in this world, it matters whether one is born and raised in Singapore, Hong Kong, Dubai, London, Hamburg, Toronto, Vancouver, New York City, San Francisco, Sydney, Melbourne, Auckland, Cape Town, Lagos, Manila, Mumbai, or Shanghai. Even moving from one neighbourhood to another may make a crucial difference. Multilingual development means something different in these places, though English is of great importance in all of them.

The final section of the book is a plea for more extensive and more systematic research on multilingual development in different, especially urban areas of the world. Based on our current understanding, the book has compiled and discussed the most important parameters that contribute to and determine multilingual development as well as their mutual interactions. Nevertheless, they locally play out differently contingent on the specific multilingual ecologies, the local language practices and interactions, ideologies and policies, as well as the attitudes held towards the languages present. The long-term objective, then, would be to work towards a unified, global typology of multilingual ecologies.

As early as 1972, Einar Haugen envisioned the systematic study of language ecologies as defined by the following nine parameters, formulated as research questions. Considering a particular language, these questions are (i) "What is its classification in relation to other languages?"; (ii) "Who are its users?"; (iii) "What are its domains of use?"; (iv) "What concurrent languages are employed by its users?"; (v) "What internal varieties does the language show?"; (vi) "What is the nature of its written tradition?"; (vii) "To what extent has its written form been standardized, i.e. unified and codified?"; (viii) "What kind of institutional support has it won, either in government, education, or private organizations, either to regulate its form or to propagate it?"; (ix) "What are the attitudes of its users towards the language, in terms of intimacy and status, leading to personal identification?" (Haugen 1972: 336–337). Evidently, the parameters underlying these questions have been intensely discussed in the present book, but as the summary in Section 7.1 has shown, several additional parameters have an effect on language development in multilingual ecologies.

Siemund and Leimgruber (2021) represent a first attempt at comparing and systematizing multilingual global cities focusing on Singapore, Hong Kong, and Dubai, paying heed to the special status of English in them. They propose to analyze these polities from the following five perspectives: (i) socio-historical multilingualism, in which diachronic accounts of the cities' multilingual realities are established; (ii) the management of languages and social diversity, focusing on governmental and bottom-up policies (both regarding linguistic and other social diversity); (iii) institutional and societal multilingualism, in which a more synchronic approach is taken; (iv) multilingual language acquisition, dealing with the linguistic outcomes in the next generation of speakers; and (v) structural features in the Englishes of multilingual global cities, offering comparative analyses of the respective varieties of English (Leimgruber & Siemund 2021).

In the long run, such a comparison of multilingual global cities and language ecologies, in general, would also need to consider multilingual literacy development (see Berthele & Lambelet 2018 as well as Usanova 2019 for recent approaches and overviews). While the present book did not really venture into this issue, many of the problems raised in the preceding chapters are also relevant here. Most importantly and much as with languages in general, people are often confronted with and have to learn new scripts as a concomitant of global migration. Additional areas of interest include the social prestige associated with different script systems (e.g. Hangul and Chinese characters in Korea), the interdependence and processing of different script systems (e.g. Cyrillic and Latin scripts in bilingual heritage speakers), metalinguistic awareness in speakers who are able to handle multiple scripts, learning advantages from one script system to another, the mutual influence of different script systems in the multilingual speaker, various language policy and planning issues related to scripts, identity issues as scripts are easily perceptible symbolic systems, the hybridization of scripts, and the loss of writing proficiencies in multilingual situations (Al-Issa 2017).

Multilingual advantages or effects will remain a prominent research topic in linguistics, psychology, and especially education studies for some time to come, as the political stakes are high. My expectation, however, is that this research will continue to produce somewhat unstable results that remain difficult to replicate. Some of the central concepts represent fuzzy constructs in need of definition. The number of confounds is extremely high and multilingual advantages proper are likely to resist their disentangling from more general cognitive effects. This does not mean that this research should not be pursued further. After all, it produces highly insightful case studies with impressive degrees of methodological sophistication. Still, the most important advantage of multilingualism lies in the fact that it helps to preserve linguistic diversity. Only if we use them can languages remain alive.

References

Agustín-Llach, María del Pilar. 2019. The impact of bilingualism on the acquisition of an additional language: Evidence from lexical knowledge, lexical fluency, and (lexical) cross-linguistic influence. *International Journal of Bilingualism* 23(5), 888–900.

Al-Issa, Ahmad. 2017. English as a medium of instruction and the endangerment of Arabic literacy: The case of the United Arab Emirates. *Arab World English Journal* 8(3), 3–17.

Al-Issa, Ahmad. 2021. Multilingualism, language management, and social diversity in the United Arab Emirates. In Peter Siemund & Jakob Leimgruber (eds.) *Multilingual Global Cities: Singapore, Hong Kong, Dubai.* Multilingual Asia Series. Singapore: Routledge, pp. 116–130.

Al-Issa, Ahmad & Laila Dahan. 2011. Global English and endangered Arabic in the United Arab Emirates. In Ahmad Al-Issa & Laila Dahan (eds.) *Global English and Arabic.* Bern: Peter Lang, pp. 1–22.

Antoniou, Mark, Eric Liang, Marc Ettlinger & Patrick Wong. 2015. The bilingual advantage in phonetic learning. *Bilingualism: Language and Cognition* 18(4), 683–695.

Århammar, Nils. 2008. Das Nordfriesische, eine bedrohte Minderheitensprache in zehn Dialekten: Eine Bestandsaufnahme. In Horst Haider Munske (ed.) *Sterben die Dialekte aus? Vorträge am Interdisziplinären Zentrum für Dialektforschung an der Friedrich-Alexander-Universität Erlangen-Nürnberg, 22.10.–10.12.2007.* Erlangen/Nürnberg, Friedrich-Alexander-Universität Erlangen-Nürnberg. urn:nbn:de:bvb:29-opus-9529 (accessed 11 July 2021).

Aronin, Larissa. 2005. Theoretical perspectives of trilingual education. *The International Journal of the Sociology of Language* 2005(171), 7–22.

Aronin, Larissa & David Singleton. 2012. *Multilingualism.* Amsterdam: John Benjamins.

Australian Bureau of Statistics. 2016a. Census of population and housing. General community profile. Sydney significant urban area. G13 Language spoken at home by proficiency in spoken English/language by sex. www.abs.gov.au/ (accessed 20 April 2021).

Australian Bureau of Statistics. 2016b. Census of population and housing. General community profile. Melbourne significant urban area. G13 Language spoken at home by proficiency in spoken English/language by sex. www.abs.gov.au/ (accessed 20 April 2021).

Australian Bureau of Statistics. 2016c. Census of population and housing. Australia. G13 Language spoken at home by proficiency in spoken English/language by sex. www.abs.gov.au/ (accessed 20 April 2021).

Aveledo, Fraibet, Yolanda Higueras, Theodoros Marinis, Arpita Bose, Christos Pliatsikas, Ariana Meldaña-Rivera, María Luisa Martínez-Ginés, José Manuel García-Domínguez, Alberto Lozano-Ros, Juan Pablo Cuello & Haydee Goicochea-Briceño. 2021. Multiple sclerosis and bilingualism. Some initial findings. *Linguistic Approaches to Bilingualism* 11(4), 551–577.

Baker, Colin. 2011. *Foundations of Bilingual Education and Bilingualism*. Clevedon: Multilingual Matters.

Bao, Zhiming. 2005. The aspectual system of Singapore English and the systemic substratist explanation. *Journal of Linguistics* 41(2), 237–267.

Bao, Zhiming. 2015. *The Making of Vernacular Singapore English: System, Transfer and Filter*. Cambridge: Cambridge University Press.

Bao, Zhiming. 2021. The origins of Singapore English: A sociohistorical sketch. In Peter Siemund & Jakob Leimgruber (eds.) *Multilingual Global Cities: Singapore, Hong Kong, Dubai*. Multilingual Asia Series. Singapore: Routledge, pp. 19–37.

Bardel, Camilla. 2015. Lexical cross-linguistic influence in third language development. In Hagen Peukert (ed.) *Transfer Effects in Multilingual Language Development*. Amsterdam: John Benjamins, pp. 111–128.

Bardel, Camilla & Ylva Falk. 2007. The role of the second language in third language acquisition: The case of Germanic syntax. *Second Language Research* 23(4), 459–484.

Bardel, Camilla & Ylva Falk. 2012. The L2 status factor and the declarative/procedural distinction. In Jennifer Cabrelli Amaro, Suzanne Flynn & Jason Rothman (eds.) *Third Language Acquisition in Adulthood*. Amsterdam: John Benjamins, pp. 61–78.

Baugh, Albert Croll & Thomas Cable. 2002. *A History of the English Language*. London: Routledge.

Behörde für Schule und Berufsbildung, Hamburg. 2020. Schuljahreserhebung, Schuljahr 2019/20. Version: 1.0.0. Das Institut für Bildungsmonitoring und Qualitätsentwicklung. Dataset. www.hamburg.de/bsb/ifbq/ (accessed 24 August 2021).

Behörde für Schule und Berufsbildung, Hamburg. 2021. Herkunftssprachenunterricht. Regelungen und Umsetzungshinweise für den Herkunftssprachenunterricht (HSU) in Hamburg. www.hamburg.de/contentblob/14666512/ce646698551635b452707 3e7ab6d7583/data/rahmenvorgaben.pdf (accessed 3 September 2021).

Berkes, Éva & Suzanne Flynn. 2012. Further evidence in support of the cumulative-enhancement model. In Jennifer Cabrelli, Suzanne Flynn & Jason Rothman (eds.) *Third Language Acquisition in Adulthood*. Amsterdam: John Benjamins, pp. 143–164.

Bernstein, Basil. 1971. *Class, Codes and Control: Volume 1. Theoretical Studies toward a Sociology of Education*. London: Routledge & Kegan Paul.

Berry, John. 1997. Immigration, acculturation, and adaptation. *Applied Psychology: An International Review* 46(1), 5–68.

Berthele, Raphael. 2019. Policy recommendations for language learning: Linguists' contributions between scholarly debates and pseudoscience. *Journal of the European Second Language Association* 3(1), 1–11.

Berthele, Raphael. 2021. The extraordinary ordinary: Re-engineering multilingualism as a natural category. *Language Learning* 71(S1), 80–120.

Berthele, Raphael & Amelia Lambelet (eds.). 2018. *Heritage and School Language Literacy Development in Migrant Children: Interdependence or Independence?* Bristol: Multilingual Matters.

Berthele, Raphael & Isabelle Udry. 2022. Multilingual boost vs. cognitive abilities: Testing two theories of multilingual language learning in a primary school context. *International Journal of Multilingualism* 19(1), 142–161.

Berthele, Raphael & Jan Vanhove. 2020. What would disprove interdependence? Lessons learned from a study on biliteracy in Portuguese heritage language speakers in Switzerland. *International Journal of Bilingual Education and Bilingualism* 23(5), 550–566.

Berthelheimer, Lennart, Britta Hufeisen & Simona Montanari. 2019. Multilingualism in Europe. In Simona Montanari & Suzanne Quay (eds.) *Multidisciplinary Perspectives on Multilingualism: The Fundamentals*. Boston, MA: De Gruyter Mouton, pp. 51–75.

Bialystok, Ellen. 2001. *Bilingualism in Development: Language, Literacy, and Cognition*. New York: Cambridge University Press.

Bialystok, Ellen. 2018. Bilingualism and executive function: What's the connection? In David Miller, Fatih Bayram, Jason Rothman & Ludovica Serratrice (eds.) *Bilingual Cognition and Language: The State of the Science across Its Subfields*. Amsterdam: John Benjamins, pp. 283–305.

Bialystok, Ellen. 2020. Null results in bilingualism research: What they tell us and what they don't. *Journal of Multilingual Theories and Practices* 1(1), 8–22.

Bialystok, Ellen, Fergus Craik & Morris Freedman. 2007. Bilingualism as a protection against the onset of symptoms of dementia. *Neuropsychologia* 45(2), 459–464.

Bialystok, Ellen, Fergus Craik & Gigi Luk. 2012. Bilingualism: Consequences for mind and brain. *Trends in Cognitive Sciences* 16(4), 240–250.

Bialystok, Ellen, Fergus Craik, Raymond Klein & Mythili Viswanathan. 2004. Bilingualism, aging, and cognitive control: Evidence from the Simon Task. *Psychology and Aging* 19(2), 290–303.

Bialystok, Ellen, Gigi Luk, Kathleen Peets & Sujin Yang. 2010. Receptive vocabulary differences in monolingual and bilingual children. *Bilingualism: Language and Cognition* 13(4), 525–531.

Biber, Douglas. 2006. *University Language: A Corpus-Based Study of Spoken and Written Registers*. Amsterdam: John Benjamins.

Bissoonauth, Anu. 2018. Language practices and attitudes of Australian children of Indian descent in a primary education setting. *International Journal of Multilingualism* 15(1), 54–71.

Biville, Frédérique. 2018. Multilingualism in the Roman World. *Oxford Handbooks Online*. www.oxfordhandbooks.com/view/10.1093/oxfordhb/9780199935390.001.0001/oxfordhb-9780199935390-e-101 (accessed 5 June 2020).

Blommaert, Jan. 2010. *The Sociolinguistics of Globalization*. Cambridge: Cambridge University Press.

Bloom, David. 1986. The English language and Singapore: A critical survey. In Basant Kapur (ed.) *Singapore Studies: Critical Surveys of the Humanities and Social Sciences*. Singapore: Singapore University Press, pp. 337–452.

Boas, Franz. 1911. Introduction to Handbook of American Indian Languages. In Franz Boas (ed.) *Bulletin Bureau of American Ethnology*, no. 4, part 1. Washington, DC: Government Printing Office, pp. 1–83.

Bolton, Kingsley & Siu-Lun Lee. 2021. A socio-historical approach to multilingualism in Hong Kong. In Peter Siemund & Jakob Leimgruber (eds.) *Multilingual Global Cities: Singapore, Hong Kong, Dubai*. Multilingual Asia Series. Singapore: Routledge, pp. 38–62.

Bolton, Kingsley, John Bacon-Shone & Siu-Lun Lee. 2021. Societal multilingualism in Hong Kong. In Peter Siemund & Jakob Leimgruber (eds.) *Multilingual Global Cities: Singapore, Hong Kong, Dubai*. Multilingual Asia Series. Singapore: Routledge, pp. 160–184.

Bonnet, Andreas & Peter Siemund. 2018a. Multilingualism and foreign language education: A synthesis of linguistic and educational findings. In Andreas Bonnet & Peter Siemund (eds.) *Foreign Language Education in Multilingual Classrooms*. Amsterdam: John Benjamins, pp. 1–29.

Bonnet, Andreas & Peter Siemund (eds.). 2018b. *Foreign Language Education in Multilingual Classrooms*. Amsterdam: John Benjamins.

Bosma, Evelyn, Elma Blom & Arjen Versloot. 2017. Language balance and cognitive advantages in Frisian–Dutch bilingual children. In Fraser Lauchlan & Maria del Carmen Parafita Couto (eds.) *Bilingualism and Minority Languages in Europe: Current Trends and Developments*. Newcastle upon Tyne: Cambridge Scholars Publishing, pp. 141–158.

Bourdieu, Pierre. 1991. *Language and Symbolic Power*. Cambridge: Cambridge Polity Press.

Boyle, Ronald. 2012. Language contact in the United Arab Emirates. *World Englishes* 31(3), 312–330.

Boyle, Ronald. 2014. Economic migrants, social networks, and the prospect of koinéization in the United Arab Emirates. *English World-Wide* 35(1), 32–51.

Braunmüller Kurt. 1996. Forms of language contact in the area of the Hanseatic League: Dialect contact phenomena and semicommunication. *Nordic Journal of Linguistics* 19(2), 141–154.

Braunmüller Kurt. 2019. Historical multilingualism. In David Singleton & Larissa Aronin (eds.) *Twelve Lectures on Multilingualism*. Bristol: Multilingual Matters, pp. 299–328.

Braunmüller, Kurt & Gisella Ferraresi. 2003. *Aspects of Multilingualism in European Language History*. Amsterdam: John Benjamins.

Braunmüller Kurt & Juliane House (eds.). 2009. *Convergence and Divergence in Language Contact Situations*. Amsterdam: John Benjamins.

Brehmer, Bernhard, Dominika Steinbach & Vladimir Arifulin. 2021. Heritage languages and the 'multilingual boost': Intercomprehension skills of Russian and Polish heritage speakers in Germany. *Multilingua: Journal of Cross-Cultural and Interlanguage Communication* 40, 839–858.

Bromham, Lindell, Russell Dinnage, Hedvig Skirgard, Andrew Ritchie, Marcel Cardillo, Felicity Meakins, Simon Greenhill & Xia Hua. 2021. Global predictors of language endangerment and the future of linguistic diversity. *Nature Ecology & Evolution* 6, 163–173.

Brown, R. & A. Gilman. 1960. The pronouns of power and solidarity. In T. A. Sebeok (ed.) *Style in Language*. Cambridge, MA: MIT Press, pp. 253–276.

Bunyi, Grace & Leila Schroeder. 2017. Bilingual education in Sub-Saharan Africa: Policies and practice. In Ofelia García, Angel Lin & Stephen May (eds.) *Bilingual and Multilingual Education: Encyclopedia of Language and Education* (3rd ed.). Cham: Springer Nature, pp. 311–328.

Bührig, Kristin & Bernd Meyer. 2013. *Transferring Linguistic Know-How into Institutional Practice*. Amsterdam: John Benjamins.

Buschfeld, Sarah. 2021. Multilingual language acquisition in Singapore: Heterogeneity and homogenization tendencies in the emergence of a new first language variety of English. In Peter Siemund & Jakob Leimgruber (eds.) *Multilingual Global Cities: Singapore, Hong Kong, Dubai*. Multilingual Asia Series. Singapore: Routledge, pp. 205–228.

Byram, Michael. 2018. Language education in and for a multilingual Europe. In Andreas Bonnet & Peter Siemund (eds.) *Foreign Language Education in Multilingual Classrooms*. Amsterdam: John Benjamins, pp. 33–56.

Cabrelli Amaro, Jennifer, Suzanne Flynn & Jason Rothman (eds.). 2012a. *Third Language Acquisition in Adulthood*. Amsterdam: John Benjamins.

Cabrelli Amaro, Jennifer, Suzanne Flynn & Jason Rothman. 2012b. Introduction. Third language (L3) acquisition in adulthood. In Jennifer Cabrelli Amaro, Suzanne Flynn & Jason Rothman (eds.) *Third Language Acquisition in Adulthood*. Amsterdam: John Benjamins, pp. 1–7.

Cabrelli Amaro, Jennifer & Magdalena Wrembel. 2016. Investigating the acquisition of phonology in a third language – A state of the science and an outlook for the future. *International Journal of Multilingualism* 13(4), 395–409.

Cavallaro, Francesco & Bee Chin Ng. 2021. Multilingualism and multiculturalism in Singapore. In Peter Siemund & Jakob Leimgruber (eds.) *Multilingual Global Cities: Singapore, Hong Kong, Dubai*. Multilingual Asia Series. Singapore: Routledge, pp. 133–159.

Cenoz, Jasone. 2001. The effect of linguistic distance, L2 status and age on cross-linguistic influence in third language acquisition. In Jasone Cenoz, Britta Hufeisen & Ulrike Jessner (eds.) *Cross-Linguistic Influence in Third Language Acquisition: Psycholinguistic Perspectives*. Clevedon: Multilingual Matters, pp. 8–20.

Cenoz, Jasone. 2003. The additive effect of bilingualism on third language acquisition: A review. *The International Journal of Bilingualism* 7(1), 71–87.

Cenoz, Jasone. 2013a. The influence of bilingualism on third language acquisition: Focus on multilingualism. *Language Teaching* 46(1), 71–86.

Cenoz, Jasone. 2013b. Defining multilingualism. *Annual Review of Applied Linguistics* 33, 3–18.

Cenoz, Jasone & Durk Gorter. 2013. Towards a plurilingual approach in English language teaching: Softening the boundaries between languages. *TESOL Quarterly* 47(3), 591–599.

Cenoz, Jasone & Durk Gorter. 2017. Minority languages and sustainable translanguaging: Threat or opportunity? *Journal of Multilingual and Multicultural Development* 38(10), 901–912.

Cenoz, Jasone & Durk Gorter. 2020. Teaching English through pedagogical translanguaging. *World Englishes* 39(2), 300–311.

Cenoz, Jasone & Ulrike Jessner (eds.). 2001a. *English in Europe: The Acquisition of a Third Language*. Clevedon: Multilingual Matters.

Cenoz, Jasone & Ulrike Jessner. 2001b. Introduction. In Jasone Cenoz & Ulrike Jessner (eds.) *English in Europe: The Acquisition of a Third Language*. Clevedon: Multilingual Matters, pp. 1–12.

Cenoz, Jasone & Alaitz Santos. 2020. Implementing pedagogical translanguaging in trilingual schools. *System* 92, 1–9.

Cenoz, Jasone & José Valencia. 1994. Additive trilingualism: Evidence from the Basque Country. *Applied Psycholinguistics* 15, 197–209.

Cenoz, Jasone, Britta Hufeisen & Ulrike Jessner (eds.). 2001a. *Cross-Linguistic Influence in Third Language Acquisition: Psycholinguistic Perspectives*. Clevedon: Multilingual Matters.

Cenoz, Jasone, Britta Hufeisen & Ulrike Jessner. 2001b. Introduction. In Jasone Cenoz, Britta Hufeisen & Ulrike Jessner (eds.) *Cross-Linguistic Influence in Third Language Acquisition: Psycholinguistic Perspectives*. Clevedon: Multilingual Matters, pp. 1–7.

Census and Statistics Department Hong Kong. 2017. 2016 Population by-census. Hong Kong: Census and Statistics Department. www.bycensus2016.gov.hk/en/bc-index.html (accessed 24 August 2021)

Census and Statistics Department Hong Kong. 2019. Thematic Household Survey Report No. 66. Hong Kong: Census and Statistics Department. www.statistics.gov.hk/pub/B11302662019XXXXB0100.pdf (accessed 24 August 2021).

Cheshire, Jenny, Paul Kerswill, Sue Fox & Eivind Torgersen. 2011. Contact, the feature pool and the speech community: The emergence of Multicultural London English. *Journal of Sociolinguistics* 15(2), 151–96.

Chimbutane, Feliciano. 2018. Multilingualism and education in sub-Saharan Africa: Policies, practices and implications. In Andreas Bonnet & Peter Siemund (eds.) *Foreign Language Education in Multilingual Classrooms*. Amsterdam: John Benjamins, pp. 57–75.

Chomsky, Noam. 1965. *Aspects of the Theory of Syntax*. Cambridge, MA: MIT Press.

Chomsky, Noam. 1981. *Lectures on Government and Binding*. Dordrecht: Foris.

Chomsky, Noam. 1986. *Knowledge of Language: Its Nature, Origin and Use*. Westport, CT: Praeger.

Clyne, Michael. 1991. *Community Languages: The Australian Experience*. Cambridge: Cambridge University Press.

Clyne, Michael. 1992. Pluricentric languages – Introduction. In Michael Clyne (ed.) *Pluricentric Languages: Differing Norms in Different Nations*. Berlin: De Gruyter Mouton, pp. 1–9.

Cohen, Jacob. 1988. *Statistical Power Analysis for the Behavioral Sciences*. New York: Routledge.

Constable, Nicole. 1996. Introduction. What does it mean to be Hakka? In Nicole Constable (ed.) *Guest People: Hakka Identity in China and Abroad*. Seattle: University of Washington Press, pp. 3–35.

Cook, Vivian & Li Wei (eds.). 2016. *The Cambridge Handbook of Linguistic Multi-Competence*. Cambridge: Cambridge University Press.

Corum, Micah. 2015. *Substrate and Adstrate: The Origins of Spatial Semantics in West African Pidgincreoles*. Berlin: De Gruyter Mouton.

Council of Europe. 2020. *Common European Framework of Reference for Languages. Council of Europe*. www.coe.int/en/web/common-european-framework-reference-languages/home (accessed 24 April 2021).

Council of the European Union. 2014. *Conclusions on Multilingualism and the Development of Language Competences.* www.consilium.europa.eu/uedocs/cms_data/docs/pressdata/en/educ/142692.pdf (accessed 24 April 2021).

Craik, Fergus, Ellen Bialystok & Morris Freedman. 2010. Delaying the onset of Alzheimer disease. Bilingualism as a form of cognitive reserve. *Neurology* 75(19), 1726–1729.

Critten, Rory & Elisabeth Dutton. 2020. Medieval English Multilingualisms. *Language Learning* 71(S1), 12–38.

Cummins, James. 1976. The influence of bilingualism on cognitive growth: A synthesis of research findings and explanatory hypothesis. *Working Papers on Bilingualism* 9, 1–43.

Cummins, James. 1978. Bilingualism and the development of metalinguistic awareness. *Journal of Cross-Cultural Psychology* 9(2), 131–149.

Cummins, James. 1979. Linguistic interdependence and the educational development of bilingual children. *Review of Educational Research,* 49(2), 222–251.

Cummins, James. 1991. Conversational and academic language proficiency in bilingual contexts. In Jan Hulstijn & Johan Matter (eds.) *Reading in Two Languages.* Amsterdam: Free University Press. AILA-Review 8, pp. 75–89.

Cummins, James. 1996. *Negotiating Identities: Education for Empowerment in a Diverse Society.* Ontario, CA: California Association for Bilingual Education.

Cummins, James. 2000. *Language, Power and Pedagogy: Bilingual Children in the Crossfire.* Clevedon: Multilingual Matters.

Cummins, James. 2001. Putting language proficiency in its place. Responding to critiques of the conversational/academic language distinction. In Jasone Cenoz & Ulrike Jessner (eds.) *English in Europe: The Acquisition of a Third Language.* Clevedon: Multilingual Matters, pp. 54–83.

Cummins, James. 2007. Rethinking monolingual instructional strategies in multilingual classrooms. *Canadian Journal of Applied Linguistics* 10(2), 221–240.

Cummins, James. 2009. Pedagogies of choice: Challenging coercive relations of power in classrooms and communities. *International Journal of Bilingual Education and Bilingualism* 12(3), 261–271.

Curdt-Christiansen, Xiao Lan. 2018. Family language planning. In James Tollefson & Miguel Pérez-Milans (eds.) *The Oxford Handbook of Language Policy and Planning.* New York: Oxford University Press, pp. 420–441.

Curzan, Anne. 2014. *Fixing English: Prescriptivism and Language History.* Cambridge: Cambridge University Press.

Darvin, Ron & Bonny Norton. 2015. Identity and a model of investment in applied linguistics. *Annual Review of Applied Linguistics* 35, 36–56.

De Angelis, Gessica. 2007. *Third or Additional Language Acquisition.* Clevedon: Multilingual Matters.

De Angelis, Gessica & Larry Selinker. 2001. Interlanguage transfer and competing linguistic systems in the multilingual mind. In Jason Cenoz, Britta Hufeisen & Ulrike Jessner (eds.) *Cross-Linguistic Influence in Third Language Acquisition: Psycholinguistic Perspectives.* Clevedon: Multilingual Matters, pp. 42–58.

de Bruin, Angela, Barbara Treccani & Sergio Della Sala. 2015. Cognitive advantage in bilingualism: An example of publication bias? *Psychological Science* 26(1), 99–107.

DeLuca, Vincent, Jason Rothman, Ellen Bialystok & Christos Pliatsikas. 2019. Redefining bilingualism as a spectrum of experiences that differentially affects

brain structure and function. *Proceedings of the National Academy of Sciences of the United States of America (PNAS)* 116(15), 7565–7574.
de Swaan, Abram. 2001. *The World Language System: A Political Sociology and Political Economy of Language*. Cambridge: Polity.
Dicks, Joseph & Fred Genesee. 2017. Bilingual education in Canada. In Ofelia García, Angel Lin & Stephen May (eds.) *Bilingual and Multilingual Education: Encyclopedia of Language and Education* (3rd ed.). Cham: Springer Nature, pp. 453–467.
Dittmar, Norbert & Christine Paul. 2019. *Sprechen im Umbruch: Zeitzeugen erzählen und argumentieren rund um den Fall der Mauer im Wendekorpus*. Mannheim: Institut für Deutsche Sprache.
Donnelly, Seamus, Patricia Brooks & Bruce Homer. 2015. Examining the bilingual advantage on conflict resolution tasks: A meta-analysis. In D. C. Noelle, R. Dale, A. Warlaumont, J. Yoshimi, T. Matlock, C. D. Jennings & P. P. Maglio (eds.) *Proceedings of the 37th Annual Meeting of the Cognitive Science Society*. Austin, TX: Cognitive Science Society.
Dubai Statistics Center. 2020. Government of Dubai. www.dsc.gov.ae/en-us/ (accessed 27 July 2021).
Duchêne, Alexandre & Monica Heller (eds.). 2012. *Language in Late Capitalism: Pride and Profit*. London: Routledge.
Duguine, Maia. 2008. Silent arguments without pro. In Theresa Biberauer (ed.) *The Limits of Syntactic Variation*. Amsterdam: John Benjamins, pp. 311–329.
Duñabeitia, Andoni & Manuel Carreiras. 2015. The bilingual advantage: Acta est fabula? *Cortex* 73, 371–372.
Eberhard, David, Gary Simons & Charles Fennig (eds.). 2022. *Ethnologue: Languages of the World*. Twenty-fifth edition. Dallas, TX: SIL International. Online version: www.ethnologue.com.
Eckert, Penelope. 2012. Three waves of variation study: The emergence of meaning in the study of sociolinguistic variation. *Annual Review of Anthropology* 41, 87–100.
Edele, Aileen, Sebastian Kempert, & Kristin Schotte. 2018. Does competent bilingualism entail advantages for the third language learning of immigrant students? *Learning and Instruction* 58, 232–244.
Edwards, Alison. 2016. *English in the Netherlands: Functions, Forms and Attitudes*. Amsterdam: John Benjamins.
Edwards, John. 2009. *Language and Identity*. Cambridge: Cambridge University Press.
Edwards, John. 2012. *Multilingualism: Understanding Linguistic Diversity*. London: Continuum.
El Euch, Sonia. 2010. Attitudes, motivations et conscience métalinguistique chez des bilingues et des trilingues adultes: Effets, similarités et différences. *Language Awareness* 19(1), 17–33.
Erdmann, Ursula. 1992. *Language Maintenance versus Assimilation: A Study of the Fate of Low German in Northeast Lower Saxony since World War II*. Stuttgart: Franz Steiner Verlag.
Esser, Hartmut. 2009. Der Streit um die Zweisprachigkeit: Was bringt die Bilingualität? In Ingrid Gogolin & Ulla Neumann (eds.) *Streitfall Zweisprachigkeit – The Bilingualism Controversy*. Wiesbaden: VS Verlag für Sozialwissenschaften, pp. 69–88.
Evans, Nicholas. 2011. A tale of many tongues: Documenting polyglot narrative in north Australian oral traditions. In Brett Baker, Ilana Mushin, Mark Harvey & Rod

Gardner (eds) *Indigenous Language and Social Identity: Papers in Honour of Michael Walsh*. Canberra: Pacific Linguistics, pp. 275–295.

Evans, Nicholas. 2018a. Did language evolve in multilingual settings? *Biology & Philosophy* 32(6), 905–933.

Evans, Nicholas. 2018b. The dynamics of language diversity. In Rajend Mesthrie & David Bradley (eds.) *The Dynamics of Language: Plenary and Focus Lectures from the 20th International Congress of Linguists*. Cape Town: UCT-Press, pp. 12–35.

Extra, Guus. 2013. Mapping increasing linguistic diversity in European and non-European countries. In David Singleton, Joshua A. Fishman, Larissa Aronin & Muiris Ó Laoire (eds.) *Current Multilingualism: A New Linguistic Dispensation*. Berlin: De Gruyter Mouton, pp. 139–162.

Extra, Guus & Kutlay Yağmur. 2004. *Urban Multilingualism in Europe: Immigrant Minority Languages at Home and School*. Clevedon: Multilingual Matters.

Falk, Ylva & Camilla Bardel. 2011. Object pronouns in German L3 syntax: Evidence for the L2 status factor. *Second Language Research* 27(1), 59–82.

Falk, Ylva, Christina Lindqvist & Camilla Bardel. 2015. The role of L1 explicit metalinguistic knowledge in L3 oral production at the initial state. *Bilingualism: Language and Cognition* 18(2), 227–235.

Fallah, Nader & Ali Akbar Jabbari. 2018. L3 acquisition of English attributive adjectives. Dominant language of communication matters for syntactic cross-linguistic influence. *Linguistic Approaches to Bilingualism* 8(2), 193–216.

Ferguson, Charles. 1959. Diglossia. *WORD* 15(2), 325–340.

Fettes, Mark. 2019. Language, land, and stewardship: Indigenous imperatives and Canadian policy. In Thomas Ricento (ed.) *Language Politics and Policies: Perspectives from Canada and the United States*. Cambridge: Cambridge University Press, pp. 263–280.

Filppula, Markku, Juhani Klemola, Anna Mauranen & Svetlana Vetchinnikova (eds.). 2017. *Global English: Global and Local Perspectives*. Berlin: De Gruyter Mouton.

Fishman, Joshua. 1967. Bilingualism with and without diglossia; Diglossia with and without bilingualism. *Journal of Social Issues* 23(2), 29–38.

Fleckenstein, Johanna, Jens Möller & Jürgen Baumert. 2018. Mehrsprachigkeit als Ressource. *Zeitschrift für Erziehungswissenschaft* 21(1), 97–120.

Flynn, Suzanne, Claire Foley & Inna Vinnitskaya. 2004. The Cumulative Enhancement Model for language acquisition: Comparing adults' and children's patterns of development in first, second and third language acquisition of relative clauses. *International Journal of Multilingualism* 1(1), 3–16.

Fortna, Benjamin. 2002. *Imperial Classroom: Islam, Education and the State in the Late Ottoman Empire*. Oxford: Oxford University Press.

Foulds, G. A. & J. C. Raven. 1950. An experimental survey with progressive matrices (1947). *British Journal of Educational Psychology* 20, 104–110.

Franceschini, Rita. 2013. History of multilingualism. In Carol Chapelle (ed.) *The Encyclopedia of Applied Linguistics*. West Sussex: Blackwell Publishing Ltd. doi.org/10.1002/9781405198431.wbeal0511.

Franceschini, Rita. 2016. Multilingualism research. In Vivian Cook & Li Wei (eds.) *The Cambridge Handbook of Linguistic Multi-Competence*. Cambridge: Cambridge University Press, pp. 97–124.

Friedmann, Naama & Dana Rusou. 2015. Critical period for first language: The crucial role of language input during the first year of life. *Current Opinion in Neurobiology* 35, 27–34.

Fuchs, Robert. 2021. Hong Kong English: Structural features and future prospects. In Peter Siemund & Jakob Leimgruber (eds.) *Multilingual Global Cities: Singapore, Hong Kong, Dubai*. Multilingual Asia Series. Singapore: Routledge, pp. 285–302.

Fuller, Janet. 2020. English in the German-speaking world: Immigration and integration. In Raymond Hickey (ed.) *English in the German-Speaking World*. Cambridge: Cambridge University Press, pp. 165–184.

Fussell, Blair. 2011. The local flavour of English in the Gulf. *English Today* 27(4), 26–32.

Gal, Susan. 2007. Multilingualism. In Carmen Llamas, Louise Mullany & Peter Stockwell (eds.) *The Routledge Companion to Sociolinguistics*. London: Routledge, pp. 149–156.

Gándara, Patricia & Kathy Escamilla. 2017. Bilingual education in the United States. In Ofelia García, Angel Lin & Stephen May (eds.) *Bilingual and Multilingual Education: Encyclopedia of Language and Education* (3rd ed.). Cham: Springer Nature, pp. 219–231.

Gao, Xuesong Andy & Weihong Wang. 2017. Bilingual education in the People's Republic of China. In Ofelia García, Angel Lin & Stephen May (eds.) *Bilingual and Multilingual Education: Encyclopedia of Language and Education* (3rd ed.). Cham: Springer Nature, pp. 439–452.

García, Ofelia. 2008. Multilingual language awareness and teacher education. In Jasone Cenoz & Nancy Hornberger (eds.) *Encyclopedia of Language and Education* (2nd ed.), Vol. 6: Knowledge about Language. Berlin: Springer, pp. 385–400.

García, Ofelia & Li Wei. 2014. *Translanguaging: Language, Bilingualism and Education*. London: Palgrave Pivot.

García Mayo, María del Pilar & Roumyana Slabakova. 2015. Object drop in L3 acquisition. *International Journal of Bilingualism* 19(5), 483–498.

Gast, Volker. 2007. *I gave it him* – On the motivation of the 'alternative double object construction' in varieties of British English. *Functions of Language* 14(1), 31–56.

Gill, Saran Kaur. 2014. *Language Policy Changes in Multi-Ethnic Malaysia*. Heidelberg: Springer.

Gisborne, Nikolas. 2000. Relative clauses in Hong Kong English. *World Englishes* 19 (3), 357–371.

Gisborne, Nikolas. 2009. Aspects of the morphosyntactic typology of Hong Kong English. *English World-Wide* 30(2), 149–169.

Göbel, Kerstin, Dominique Rauch & Svenja Vieluf. 2011. Leistungsbedingungen und Leistungsergebnisse von Schülerinnen und Schülern türkischer, russischer und polnischer Herkunftssprachen. *Zeitschrift für Interkulturellen Fremdsprachenunterricht* 16(2), 50–65.

Gogolin, Ingrid. 2008. *Der monolinguale Habitus der multilingualen Schule*. Münster: Waxmann.

Gogolin, Ingrid. 2020. Multilingualism: A threat to public education or a resource in public education? European histories and realities. *European Educational Research Journal* 20(3), 297–310.

Gogolin, Ingrid, Peter Siemund, Monika Schulz & Julia Davydova. 2013. Multilingualism, language contact, and urban areas: An introduction. In Peter Siemund, Ingrid Gogolin, Monika Schulz & Julia Davydova (eds.) *Multilingualism and Language Contact in Urban Areas: Acquisition – Identities – Space – Education*. Amsterdam: John Benjamins, pp. 1–15.

Goldberg, Adele. 2006. *Constructions at Work: The Nature of Generalization in Language*. Oxford: Oxford University Press.

Gombert, Jean Emile. 1992. *Metalinguistic Development*. New York: Harvester Wheatsheaf.

Gorter, Durk & Eli Arocena. 2020. Teachers' beliefs about multilingualism in a course on translanguaging. *System* 92, 1–10.

Gorter, Durk & Jasone Cenoz. 2011. Multilingual education for European minority languages: The Basque Country and Friesland. *International Review of Education / Internationale Zeitschrift Für Erziehungswissenschaft / Revue Internationale de l'Education* 57(5/6), 651–666.

Grosjean, François. 1997. The bilingual individual. *Interpreting* 2(1/2), 163–187.

Grosjean, François & Krista Byers-Heinlein. 2018. Bilingual adults and children: a short introduction. In François Grosjean & Krista Byers-Heinlein (eds.) *The Listening Bilingual: Speech Perception, Comprehension, and Bilingualism*. Hoboken, NJ: Wiley Blackwell, pp. 4–24.

Hakuta, Kenji. 1989. *Bilingualism and Intelligence Testing: An Annotated Bibliography. Bilingual Research Group Working Papers*. University of California, Santa Cruz.

Hakuta, Kenji & Rafael Diaz. 1985. The relationship between degree of bilingualism and cognitive ability: A critical discussion and some new longitudinal data. In Keith Nelson (ed.) *Children's Language*, Vol. 5. Hillsdale, NJ: Lawrence Erlbaum Associates, Inc., pp. 319–344.

Hamann, Cornelia, Esther Rinke & Dobrinka Genevska-Hanke. 2019. Bilingual language development: The role of dominance. *Frontiers in Psychology* 10, Article 1064. www.frontiersin.org/articles/10.3389/fpsyg.2019.01064/full

Hammarberg, Björn. 2001. Roles of L1 and L2 in L3 production and acquisition. In Jason Cenoz, Britta Hufeisen & Ulrike Jessner (eds.) *Cross-Linguistic Influence in Third Language Acquisition: Psycholinguistic Perspectives*. Clevedon: Multilingual Matters, pp. 21–41.

Hammarberg, Björn. 2010. The languages of the multilingual: Some conceptual and terminological issues. *IRAL, International Review of Applied Linguistics in Language Teaching* 48(2), 91–104.

Hammarberg, Björn. 2018. L3, the tertiary language. In Andreas Bonnet & Peter Siemund (eds.) *Foreign Language Education in Multilingual Classrooms*. Amsterdam: Benjamins, pp. 127–150.

Hansegard, Nils-Erik. 1968. *Tvasprakighet eller Halvsprakighet? (Bilingualism or Semilingualism?)* Stockholm: Aldus/Bonniers.

Harris, Chester. 1948. An exploration of language skill patterns. *Journal of Educational Psychology* 39(6), 321–336.

Harris, D. P. & L. A. Palmer. 1970. *CELT Technical Manual*. New York: McGraw-Hill.

Haspelmath, Martin. 2001. The European linguistic area: Standard Average European. In Martin Haspelmath, Ekkehard König, Wuld Oesterreicher & Wolfgang Raible (eds.) *Language Typology and Language Universals (Handbücher zur*

Sprach- und Kommunikationswissenschaft vol. 20.2). Berlin: Walter de Gruyter, pp. 1492–1510.

Haugen, Einar. 1950. The analysis of linguistic borrowing. *Language* 26(2), 210–231.

Haugen, Einar. 1966. Dialect, language, nation. *American Anthropologist* 68(4), 922–935.

Haugen, Einar. 1972. The ecology of language. In Anwar Dil (ed.) *The Ecology of Language*. Stanford: Standford University Press, pp. 325–339.

Haugen, Einar. 2001. The ecology of language. In Alvin Fill & Peter Mühlhäusler (eds.) *The Ecolinguistics Reader. Language, Ecology, and Environment*. London: Continuum, pp. 57–66.

Haukås, Åsta. 2016. Teachers' beliefs about multilingualism and a multilingual pedagogical approach. *International Journal of Multilingualism* 13(1), 1–18.

Heine, Bernd & Tania Kuteva. 2005. *Language Contact and Grammatical Change*. Cambridge: Cambridge University Press.

Heinrich, Patrick. 2012. *The Making of Monolingual Japan: Language Ideology and Japanese Modernity: Multilingual Matters 146*. Bristol: Multilingual Matters.

Heller, Monica. 2003. Globalization, the new economy, and the commodification of language and identity. *Journal of Sociolinguistics* 7(4), 473–492.

Herdina, Philip & Ulrike Jessner. 2002. *A Dynamic Model of Multilingualism*. Clevedon: Multilingual Matters.

Hermas, Abdelkader. 2010. Language acquisition as computational resetting: Verb movement in L3 initial state. *International Journal of Multilingualism* 7(4), 343–362.

Hermas, Abdelkader. 2014. Multilingual transfer: L1 morphosyntax in L3 English. *International Journal of Language Studies* 8(2), 1–24.

Hilchey, Matthew & Raymond Klein. 2011. Are there bilingual advantages on nonlinguistic interference tasks? Implications for the plasticity of executive control processes. *Psychonomic Bulletin & Review* 18(4), 625–658.

Hill, Richard. 2017. Bilingual education in Aotearoa/New Zealand. In Ofelia García, Angel Lin & Stephen May (eds.) *Bilingual and Multilingual Education: Encyclopedia of Language and Education* (3rd ed.). Cham: Springer Nature, pp. 329–345.

Hirosh, Zoya & Tamar Degani. 2018. Direct and indirect effects of multilingualism on novel language learning: An integrative review. *Psychonomic Bulletin & Review* 25(3), 892–916.

Ho, Mian Lian & John Platt. 1993. *Dynamics of a Contact Continuum: Singaporean English*. Oxford: Clarendon Press.

Hobsbawm, Eric. 1990. *Nations and Nationalism since 1780: Programme, Myth, Reality*. Cambridge: Cambridge University Press.

Hofer, Barbara & Ulrike Jessner. 2019. Multilingualism at the primary level in South Tyrol: How does multilingual education affect young learners' metalinguistic awareness and proficiency in L1, L2 and L3? *The Language Learning Journal* 47 (1), 76–87.

Hoffmann, Charlotte. 2001. Towards a description of trilingual competence. *International Journal of Bilingualism* 5(1), 1–17.

Hopkyns, Sarah. 2021. Multilingualism and linguistic hybridity in Dubai. In Peter Siemund & Jakob Leimgruber (eds.) *Multilingual Global Cities: Singapore, Hong Kong, Dubai*. Multilingual Asia Series. Singapore: Routledge, pp. 248–264.

Hopp, Holger. 2019. Cross-linguistic influence in the child third language acquisition of grammar: Sentence comprehension and production among Turkish–German and

German learners of English. *International Journal of Bilingualism* 23(2), 567–583.

Hopp, Holger, Teresa Kieseier, Markus Vogelbacher & Dieter Thoma. 2018. L1 effects in the early L3 acquisition of vocabulary and grammar. In Andreas Bonnet & Peter Siemund (eds.) *Foreign Language Education in Multilingual Classrooms*. Amsterdam: John Benjamins, pp. 305–330.

Hopp, Holger, Markus Vogelbacher, Teresa Kieseier & Dieter Thoma. 2019. Bilingual advantages in early foreign language learning: Effects of the minority and the majority language. *Learning and Instruction* 61, 99–110.

Hopp, Holger, Jenny Jakisch, Sarah Sturm, Carmen Becker & Dieter Thoma. 2020. Integrating multilingualism into the early foreign language classroom: Empirical and teaching perspectives. *International Multilingual Research Journal* 14(2), 146–162.

Hopper, Paul & Elizabeth Closs Traugott. 2003. *Grammaticalization*. Cambridge: Cambridge University Press.

Howatt, Anthony. 1984. *A History of English Language Teaching*. Oxford: Oxford University Press.

Hu, Adelheid. 2018. Plurilingual identities. On the way to an integrative view on language education? In Andreas Bonnet & Peter Siemund (eds.) *Foreign Language Education in Multilingual Classrooms*. Amsterdam: John Benjamins, pp. 151–172.

Huddleston, Rodney & Geoffrey Pullum. 2002. *The Cambridge Grammar of the English Language*. Cambridge: Cambridge University Press.

Hufeisen, Britta. 2018. Models of multilingual competence. In Andreas Bonnet & Peter Siemund (eds.) *Foreign Language Education in Multilingual Classrooms*. Amsterdam: John Benjamins, pp. 173–189.

Hulstijn, Jan. 2015. *Language Proficiency in Native and Non-Native Speakers: Theory and Research*. Amsterdam: John Benjamins.

Igboanusi, Herbert. 2014. The English-only language education policy in The Gambia and low literacy rates. *International Journal of Bilingual Education and Bilingualism* 17(5), 558–569.

Imaz Agirre, Ainara & María del Pilar García Mayo. 2017. Transfer effects in the acquisition of double object constructions in English as an L3. In Tanja Angelovka & Angela Han (eds.) *L3 Syntactic Transfer: Models, New Developments and Implications*. Amsterdam: John Benjamins, pp. 143–171.

Imaz Agirre, Ainara & María del Pilar García Mayo. 2018. Proficiency and transfer effects in the acquisition of gender agreement by L2 and L3 English learners. In Jacee Cho, Michael Iverson, Tiffany Juddy, Tania Leal & Elena Shimanskaya (eds.) *Meaning and Structure in Second Language Acquisition: In Honor of Roumyana Slabakova*. Amsterdam: John Benjamins, pp. 203–227.

Ionin, Tania, Heejeong Ko & Kenneth Wexler. 2004. Article semantics in L2 acquisition: The role of specificity. *Language Acquisition* 12(1), 3–69.

Ivanova, Iva & Albert Costa. 2008. Does bilingualism hamper lexical access in speech production? *Acta Psychologica* 127, 277–288.

Jarvis, Scott. 2000. Methodological rigor in the study of transfer: Identifying L1 influence in the interlanguage lexicon. *Language Learning* 50(2): 245–309.

Jarvis, Scott & Aneta Pavlenko. 2008. *Crosslinguistic Influence in Language and Cognition*. London: Routledge.

Jeffery, Jill & Catherine van Beuningen. 2020. Language education in the EU and the US: Paradoxes and parallels. *Prospects* 48, 175–191.

Jessner, Ulrike. 1999. Metalinguistic awareness in multilinguals: Cognitive aspects of third language learning. *Language Awareness* 8(3–4), 201–209.

Jessner, Ulrike. 2006. *Linguistic Awareness in Multilinguals: English as a Third Language*. Edinburgh: Edinburgh University Press.

Jessner, Ulrike. 2008. A DST model of multilingualism and the role of metalinguistic awareness. *The Modern Language Journal* 92(2), 270–283.

Johanson, Lars. 2002. *Structural Factors in Turkic Language Contacts*. Richmond: Curzon.

Johnstone, Barbara. 2010. Indexing the local. In Nikolas Coupland (ed.) *Handbook of Language and Globalization*. Malden, MA: Wiley Blackwell, pp. 386–405.

Johnstone, Barbara, Jennifer Andrus & Andrew Danielson. 2006. Mobility, indexicality, and the Enregisterment of 'Pittsburghese'. *Journal of English Linguistics* 34(2), 77–104.

Jones, W. R. 1960. A critical study of bilingualism and nonverbal intelligence. *British Journal of Educational Psychology* 30(1), 71–76.

Jones, W. R. & W. A. Stewart. 1951. Bilingualism and verbal intelligence. *British Journal of Psychology* 4(1), 3–8.

Joseph, John. 2004. *Language and Identity: National, Ethnic, Religious*. Basingstoke: Palgrave Macmillan.

Kachru, Braj. 1985. Standards, codification and sociolinguistic realism: The English language in the outer circle. In Randolph Quirk & Henry Widdowson (eds.) *English in the World: Teaching and Learning the Language and Literatures*. Cambridge: Cambridge University Press and the British Council, pp. 11–30.

Kahnemann, Daniel. 2012. *Thinking, Fast and Slow*. London: Penguin.

Kaltenböck, Gunther, Bernd Heine & Tania Kuteva. 2011. On thetical grammar. *Studies in Language* 35(4), 848–893.

Kaplan, Robert & Richard Baldauf Jr. 1997. *Language Planning: From Practice to Theory*. Clevedon: Multilingual Matters.

Kecskes, Istvan. 2010. Dual and multilanguage systems. *International Journal of Multilingualism* 7(2), 91–109.

Kecskes, Istvan. 2019. *English as a Lingua Franca: The Pragmatic Perspective*. Cambridge: Cambridge University Press.

Kecskes, Istvan & Tünde Papp. 2000. *Foreign Language and Mother Tongue*. Mahwah, NJ: Lawrence Erlbaum Associates.

Kellerman, Eric. 1983. Now you see it, now you don't. In Susan Gass & Larry Selinker (eds.) *Language Transfer in Language Learning*. Rowley, MA: Newbury House, pp. 112–134.

Kerswill, Paul & Ann Williams. 2000. Creating a New Town koine: Children and language change in Milton Keynes. *Language in Society* 29(1), 65–115.

King, Kendall, Mengying Liu & María Cecilia Schwedhelm. 2018. Language policy, language study, and heritage language education in the U.S. In Andreas Bonnet & Peter Siemund (eds.) *Foreign Language Education in Multilingual Classrooms*. Amsterdam: John Benjamins, pp. 77–98.

Klieme, Eckhard, Wolfgang Eichler, Andreas Helmke, Rainer Lehmann, Günter Nold, Hans-Günter Rolff, Konrad Schröder, Günther Thomé & Heiner Willenberg.

2006. *Unterricht und Kompetenzerwerb in Deutsch und Englisch: Zentrale Befunde der Studie Deutsch-Englisch-Schülerleistungen-International (DESI).* Frankfurt am Main: DIPF.

Kloss, Heinz. 1978. *Die Entwicklung neuer germanischer Kultursprachen seit 1800.* Düsseldorf: Schwann.

Klöter, Henning. 2020. One legacy, two legislations. Language policies on the two sides of the Taiwan Strait. In Henning Klöter & Mårten Söderblom Saarela (eds.) *Language Diversity in the Sinophone World.* London: Routledge, pp. 101–121.

Klöter, Henning & Mårten Söderblom Saarela (eds.). 2020. *Language Diversity in the Sinophone World.* London: Routledge.

Koerner, E. 1997. Notes on the history of the concept of language as a system 'Où tout se tient'. Linguistica *Atlantica* 19, 1–20. journals.lib.unb.ca/index.php/la/article/view/22501 (accessed 30 April 2021).

Kopečková, Romana. 2016. The bilingual advantage in L3 learning: A developmental study of rhotic sounds. *International Journal of Multilingualism* 13(4), 410–425.

Kopečková, Romana. 2018. Exploring metalinguistic awareness in L3 phonological acquisition: The case of young instructed learners of Spanish in Germany. *Language Awareness* 27(1–2), 153–166.

Kopečková, Romana, Marta Marecka, Magdalena Wrembel & Ulrike Gut. 2016. Interactions between three phonological subsystems of young multilinguals: The influence of language status. *International Journal of Multilingualism* 13(4), 426–443.

Kortmann, Bernd, Kate Burridge, Rajend Mesthrie, Edgar Werner Schneider & Clive Upton (eds.). 2004. *A Handbook of Varieties of English. Volume 1: Phonology; Volume 2: Morphology and Syntax.* Berlin: Mouton de Gruyter.

Krashen, Stephen. 1985. *The Input Hypothesis: Issues and Implications.* London: Longman.

Krulatz, Anna, Anne Dahl & Mona Flognfeldt. 2018. *Enacting Multilingualism: From Research to Teaching Practice in the English Language Classroom.* Oslo: Cappelen Damm Akademisk.

Kupisch, Tanja, Neal Snape & Ilse Stangen. 2013. Foreign language acquisition in heritage speakers: The acquisition of articles in L3-English by German–Turkish bilinguals. In Joana Duarte & Ingrid Gogolin (eds.) *Linguistic Superdiversity in Urban Areas.* Amsterdam: John Benjamins, pp. 99–122.

Landesinstitut für Lehrerbildung und Schulentwicklung, Hamburg. 2021a. *Bildungsplan Grundschule Herkunftssprachen.* li.hamburg.de/contentblob/3850336/af094d8482d393867909a3ad4f6bd537/data/download-pdf-rp-herkunftsspr-unterricht-gs.pdf (accessed 24 April 2021).

Landesinstitut für Lehrerbildung und Schulentwicklung, Hamburg. 2021b. *Regelungen im Herkunftssprachlichen Unterricht.* li.hamburg.de/contentblob/3850334/4948f404a3dafa711dcf2d7485dddadd/data/download-pdf-regelungen-im-herkunftssprachlichen-unterricht.pdf (accessed 24 April 2021).

Lasagabaster, David. 1998. The threshold hypothesis applied to three languages in contact at school. *International Journal of Bilingual Education and Bilingualism* 1 (2), 119–133.

Lasagabaster, David. 2001. The effect of knowledge about the L1 on foreign language skills and grammar. *International Journal of Bilingual Education and Bilingualism* 4(5), 310–331.

Lechner, Simone & Peter Siemund. 2014. Double threshold in bi- and multilingual contexts: Preconditions for higher academic attainment in English as an additional language. *Frontiers in Psychology* 5, 546.

Lehtonen, Minna, Anna Soveri, Aini Laine, Janica Järvenpää, Angela de Bruin & Jan Antfolk. 2018. Is bilingualism associated with enhanced executive functioning in adults? A meta-analytic review. *Psychological Bulletin* 144(4), 394–425.

Leimgruber, Jakob. 2013. *Singapore English: Structure, Variation and Usage*. Cambridge: Cambridge University Press.

Leimgruber, Jakob, Ahmad Al-Issa, Eliane Lorenz & Peter Siemund. 2022. Managing and investing in hybrid identities in the globalized United Arab Emirates. *Journal of Language, Identity & Education*. DOI: 10.1080/15348458.2022.2070849

Leimgruber, Jakob & Peter Siemund. 2021. The multilingual ecologies of Singapore, Hong Kong, and Dubai. In Peter Siemund & Jakob Leimgruber (eds.) *Multilingual Global Cities: Singapore, Hong Kong, Dubai*. Multilingual Asia Series. Singapore: Routledge, pp. 1–15.

Leimgruber, Jakob, Peter Siemund & Laura Terassa. 2018. Singaporean students' language repertoires and attitudes revisited. *World Englishes* 37(2), 282–306.

Leimgruber, Jakob, Jun Jie Lim, Wilkinson Daniel Wong Gonzales & Mie Hieramoto. 2020. Ethnic and gender variation in the use of Colloquial Singapore English discourse particles. *English Language and Linguistics* 25(3), 601–620.

Leivada, Evelina, Marit Westergaard, Jon Andoni Duñabeitia & Jason Rothman. 2020. On the phantom-like appearance of bilingualism effects on neurocognition: (How) should we proceed? *Bilingualism: Language and Cognition* 24(1), 197–210.

Leung, Yan-Kit. 2005. L2 vs. L3 initial state: A comparative study of the acquisition of French DPs by Vietnamese monolinguals and Cantonese–English bilinguals. *Bilingualism: Language and Cognition* 8(1), 39–61.

Li, Lijun. 2021. *Language Contact: A Historical Sociolinguistic Reconstruction of Colloquial Singapore English in Relation to its Chinese Substrates*. PhD Dissertation, University of Hamburg.

Li, Lijun & Peter Siemund. 2021. From phasal polarity expression to aspectual marker: grammaticalization of already in Asian and African varieties of English. In Raija Kramer (ed.) *The Expression of Phasal Polarity in African Languages*. Berlin: De Gruyter Mouton, pp. 509–537.

Li, Lijun, Eliane Lorenz & Peter Siemund. 2022. The ages of pragmatic particles in Colloquial Singapore English: A corpus study based on oral history interviews. *English World-Wide*. DOI: 10.1075/eww.21016.li

Liang, Sihua. 2020. Speakers of "Mother Tongues" in multilingual China. Complex linguistic repertoires and identity construction. In Henning Klöter & Mårten Söderblom Saarela (eds.) *Language Diversity in the Sinophone World*. London: Routledge, pp. 185–204.

Lim, Lisa. 2007. Mergers and acquisitions: On the ages and origins of Singapore English particles. *World Englishes* 26(4), 446–473.

Lim, Lisa. 2010. Migrants and 'Mother Tongues': Extralinguistic forces in the ecology of English in Singapore. In Lisa Lim, Anne Pakir & Lionel Wee (eds.) *English in Singapore: Modernity and Management*. Hong Kong: Hong Kong University Press, pp. 19–54.

Lo Bianco, Joseph & Larissa Aronin (eds.). 2020. *Dominant Language Constellations*. Cham: Springer Nature.

Lo Bianco, Joseph & Yvette Slaughter. 2017a. Language policy and education in Australia. In Teresa McCarty & Stephen May (eds.) *Language Policy and Political Issues in Education: Encyclopedia of Language and Education* (3rd ed.). Cham: Springer Nature, pp. 449–461.

Lo Bianco, Joseph & Yvette Slaughter. 2017b. Bilingual education in Australia. In Ofelia García, Angel Lin & Stephen May (eds.) *Bilingual and Multilingual Education: Encyclopedia of Language and Education* (3rd ed.). Cham: Springer Nature, pp. 347–360.

London Census. 2011a. Census first results: London boroughs' populations by age by sex. CIS2012–01. *Census Information Scheme.* data.london.gov.uk/census/2011-census/ (accessed 8 May 2020).

London Census. 2011b. Census Snapshot: Main Language. CIS2013–01. *Census Information Scheme.* data.london.gov.uk/census/2011-census/ (accessed 8 May 2020).

London Census. 2011c. Census Snapshot: Household Language. CIS2012–10. *Census Information Scheme.* data.london.gov.uk/census/2011-census/ (accessed 8 May 2020).

Longva, Anh Nga. 2005. Neither autocracy nor democracy but ethnocracy: Citizens, expatriates and the socio-political system in Kuwait. In Paul Dresch & James Piscatori (eds.) *Monarchies and Nations: Globalisation and Identity in the Arab States of the Gulf.* London: I.B. Tauris, pp. 114–135.

Lorenz, Eliane. 2018. "One day a father and his son going fishing on the Lake." A study on the use of the progressive aspect of monolingual and bilingual learners of English. In Andreas Bonnet & Peter Siemund (eds.) *Foreign Language Education in Multilingual Classrooms*. Amsterdam: John Benjamins, pp. 331–357.

Lorenz, Eliane. 2019. *The Use of Tense and Aspect in the Additional Language English by Monolingual Speakers and Bilingual Heritage Speakers*. PhD Dissertation. University of Hamburg. ediss.sub.uni-hamburg.de/handle/ediss/6317 (accessed 24 August 2021).

Lorenz, Eliane & Peter Siemund. 2019. Differences in the acquisition and production of English as a foreign language. A study of bilingual and monolingual students in Germany. In Eva Vetter & Ulrike Jessner (eds.) *International Research on Multilingualism: Breaking with the Monolingual Perspective*. Berlin: Springer, pp. 81–102.

Lorenz, Eliane & Peter Siemund. 2020. The acquisition of English as an additional language by multilingual heritage speakers. In Matthias Meyer & Ulrich Hoinkes (eds.) *Der Einfluss der Migration auf Sprach- und Kulturräume – The Impact of Migration on Linguistic and Cultural Areas*. Bern: Peter Lang, pp. 111–134.

Lorenz, Eliane, Yevheniia Hasai & Peter Siemund. 2021. Multilingual lexical transfer challenges monolingual educational norms: Not quite! *Multilingua: Journal of Cross-Cultural and Interlanguage Communication* 40, 791–813.

Lorenz, Eliane, Tugba Elif Toprak & Peter Siemund. 2021. English L3 acquisition in heritage contexts: Modelling a path through the bilingualism controversy. *Poznań Studies in Contemporary Linguistics* 57(2), 273–298.

Lorenz, Eliane, Tugba Elif Toprak & Peter Siemund (2022) Why are they so similar? The interplay of linguistic and extra-linguistic variables in monolingual and bilingual learners of English. *Pedagogical Linguistics*. DOI: 10.1075/pl.21016.lor

Lorenz, Eliane, Ulrike Schackow, Sharareh Rahbari & Peter Siemund. 2020. Does bilingualism correlate with or predict higher proficiency in L3 English? A contrastive study of monolingual and bilingual learners. *Journal of Multilingual Theories and Practices* 1(2), 185–217.

Lorenz, Eliane, Richard Bonnie, Kathrin Feindt, Sharareh Rahbari & Peter Siemund. 2019. Cross-linguistic influence in unbalanced bilingual heritage speakers on subsequent language acquisition: Evidence from pronominal object placement in ditransitive clauses. *International Journal of Bilingualism* 23(6), 1410–1430.

Lynch, Andrew. 2018. Spatial reconfigurations of Spanish in postmodernity. In Jeremy King & Sandro Sassarego (eds.) *Language Variation and Contact-Induced Change: Spanish across Space and Time*. Amsterdam: John Benjamins, pp. 11–34.

MacQuarrie, Sarah & Fiona Lyon. 2017. Practitioner engagement with research in minority language contexts: Evidence from research regarding Gaelic medium education. In Fraser Lauchlan & Maria del Carmen Parafita Couto (eds.) *Bilingualism and Minority Languages in Europe: Current Trends and Developments*. Newcastle upon Tyne: Cambridge Scholars Publishing, pp. 34–47.

MacSwan, Jeff. 2000. The Threshold Hypothesis, semilingualism, and other contributions to a deficit view of linguistic minorities. *Hispanic Journal of Behavioral Sciences* 22(1), 3–45.

Mahboob, Ahmar & Rashi Jain. 2017. Bilingual education in India and Pakistan. In Ofelia García, Angel Lin & Stephen May (eds.) *Bilingual and Multilingual Education. Encyclopedia of Language and Education* (3rd ed.). Cham: Springer Nature, pp. 233–246.

Mair, Christian. 2013. The World System of Englishes. Accounting for the transnational importance of mobile and mediated vernaculars. *English World-Wide* 34(3), 253–278.

Mair, Victor. 2013. The classification of Sinitic languages: What is 'Chinese'? In Guangshun Cao, Hilary Chappell, Redouane Djamouri & Thekla Wiebusch (eds.) *Breaking down the Barriers: Interdisciplinary Studies in Chinese Linguistics and Beyond*. Taipei: Academia Sinica, pp. 735–754.

Mairs, Rachel. 2016. *The Hellenistic Far East: Archaeology, Language, and Identity in Greek Central Asia*. Oakland, CA: The University of California Press.

Malabarba, Taiane. 2019. 'In English, sorry': Participants' orientation to the English-only policy in beginning-level EFL classroom interaction. In Hanh thi Nguyen & Taiane Malabarba (eds.) *Conversation Analytic Perspectives on English Language Learning, Teaching, and Testing in Global Contexts*. Bristol: Multilingual Matters, pp. 244–267.

Maluch, Jessica Tsimprea & Sebastian Kempert. 2019. Bilingual profiles and third language learning: The effects of the manner of learning, sequence of bilingual acquisition, and language use practices. *International Journal of Bilingual Education and Bilingualism*, 22(7), 870–822.

Maluch, Jessica Tsimprea, Marko Neumann & Sebastian Kempert. 2016. Bilingualism as a resource for foreign language learning of language minority students?

Empirical evidence from a longitudinal study during primary and secondary school in Germany. *Learning and Individual Differences* 51, 111–118.

Maluch, Jessica Tsimprea, Sebastian Kempert, Marko Neumann & Petra Stanat. 2015. The effect of speaking a minority language at home on foreign language learning. *Learning and Instruction* 36, 76–85.

Matras, Yaron. 2009. *Language Contact*. Cambridge: Cambridge University Press.

Mauranen, Anna. 2012. *Exploring ELF: Academic English shaped by non-native Speakers*. Cambridge: Cambridge University Press.

Mauranen, Anna. 2018. Second language acquisition, World Englishes, and English as a Lingua Franca (ELF). *World Englishes* 37(1), 106–119.

Maxwell, Alexander. 2018. When theory is a joke. The Weinreich witticism in linguistics. *Beiträge zur Geschichte der Sprachwissenschaft* 28(2), 263–292.

McCarty, Teresa. 2019. Indigenous language movements in a settler state. In Thomas Ricento (ed.) *Language Politics and Policies: Perspectives from Canada and the United States*. Cambridge: Cambridge University Press, pp. 173–191.

McKay, Sandra Lee. 2002. *Teaching English as an International Language*. Oxford: Oxford University Press.

Meisel, Jürgen. 2004. The bilingual child. In Tej Bhatia & William Ritchie (eds.) *The Handbook of Bilingualism*. Malden, MA: Blackwell Publishing, pp. 90–113.

Meisel, Jürgen. 2011. *First and Second Language Acquisition: Parallels and Differences*. Cambridge: Cambridge University Press.

Meisel, Jürgen. 2013. Sensitive phases in successive language acquisition: The critical period hypothesis revisited. In Cedric Boeckx & Kleanthes Grohmann (eds.) *The Cambridge Handbook of Biolinguistics*. Cambridge: Cambridge University Press, pp. 69–85.

Melo-Pfeifer, Silvia. 2018. The multilingual turn in foreign language education. Facts and fallacies. In Andreas Bonnet & Peter Siemund (eds.) *Foreign Languages in Multilingual Classrooms*. Amsterdam: John Benjamins, pp. 191–212.

Menocal, María Rosa. 2002. *The Ornament of the World: How Muslims, Jews, and Christians Created a Culture of Tolerance in Medieval Spain*. Boston: Little Brown.

Mesthrie, Raj (eds.). 2002. *Language in South Africa*. Cambridge: Cambridge University Press.

Mithun, Marianne. 1999. *The Languages of Native North America*. Cambridge: Cambridge University Press.

Mohanty, Ajit. 2013. Multilingual education in India. In Peter Siemund, Ingrid Gogolin, Monika Schulz & Julia Davydova (eds.) *Multilingualism and Language Contact in Urban Areas: Acquisition – Identities – Space – Education*. Amsterdam: John Benjamins, pp. 305–326.

Mollin, Sandra. 2020. English in Germany and the European context. In Raymond Hickey (ed.) *English in the German-Speaking World*. Cambridge: Cambridge University Press, pp. 31–52.

Montrul, Silvina. 2008. *Incomplete Acquisition in Bilingualism: Re-examining the Age Factor*. Amsterdam: John Benjamins.

Montrul, Silvina. 2016. *The Acquisition of Heritage Languages*. Cambridge: Cambridge University Press.

Mueller, Jessica Terese. 2018. English as a lingua franca at the multilingual university: A comparison of monolingually and multilingually raised students and instructors. In Andreas Bonnet & Peter Siemund (eds.) *Foreign Language Education in Multilingual Classrooms*. Amsterdam: John Benjamins, pp. 359–380.

Mufwene, Salikoko. 2001. *The Ecology of Language Evolution*. Cambridge: Cambridge University Press.

Muysken, Pieter. 2013. Language contact outcomes as the result of bilingual optimization strategies. *Bilingualism: Language and Cognition* 16(4), 709–730.

Nagy, Naomi, Xiaoli Zhang, George Nagy & Edgar Schneider. 2006. Clustering dialects automatically: A mutual information approach. *University of Pennsylvania Working Papers in Linguistics* 12(2), Papers from NWAV 34. repository.upenn.edu/pwpl/vol12/iss2/ (accessed 24 August 2021).

Naqvi Rahat, Anne McKeough, Keoma Thorne & Christina Pfitscher. 2013. Fostering early literacy learning using dual language books: Language as a cultural amplifier. In Peter Siemund, Ingrid Gogolin, Monika Schulz & Julia Davydova (eds.) *Multilingualism and Language Contact in Urban Areas: Acquisition – Identities – Space – Education*. Amsterdam: Benjamins, pp. 327–348.

Na Ranong, Sirirat & Yan-kit Ingrid Leung. 2009. Null objects in L1 Thai–L2 English–L3 Chinese: An empiricist take on a theoretical problem. In Yan-kit Ingrid Leung (ed.) *Third Language Acquisition and Universal Grammar*. Clevedon: Multilingual Matters, pp. 162–191.

Nevalainen, Terttu. 2006. Negative concord as an English "Vernacular Universal": Social history and linguistic typology. *Journal of English Linguistics* 34(3), 257–278.

Norton, Bonny. 2013. *Identity and Language Learning: Extending the Conversation*. Bristol: Multilingual Matters.

Norton, Bonny. 2018. Identity and investment in multilingual classrooms. In Andreas Bonnet & Peter Siemund (eds.) *Foreign Language Education in Multilingual Classrooms*. Amsterdam: Benjamins, pp. 237–252.

Odlin, Terence. 1989. *Language Transfer: Cross-Linguistic Influence in Language Learning*. Cambridge: Cambridge University Press.

Odlin, Terence. 2003. Cross-linguistic influence. In Catherine Doughty & Michael Long (eds.) *The Handbook of Second Language Acquisition*. Malden, MA: Blackwell, pp. 436–486.

Odlin, Terence. 2010. *Language Transfer: Cross-Linguistic Influence in Language Learning*. Cambridge: Cambridge University Press.

OECD. 2019. *International Migration Outlook 2019*. Paris: OECD Publishing. doi.org/10.1787/c3e35eec-en (accessed 19 March 2020).

OHI-NAS. 2020. Oral History Interviews. *National Archives of Singapore*. www.nas.gov.sg/archivesonline/oral_history_interviews (accessed 15 May 2021).

Olusola, Adesope, Tracy Lavin, Terri Thompson & Charles Ungerleider. 2010. A systematic review and meta-analysis of the cognitive correlates of bilingualism. *Review of Educational Research* 80(2), 207–245.

Onysko, Alexander. 2007. *Anglicisms in German: Borrowing, Lexical Productivity, and Written Codeswitching*. Berlin: Walter de Gruyter.

Opoku-Amankwa, Kwasi. 2009. English-only language-in-education policy in multilingual classrooms in Ghana. *Language, Culture and Curriculum* 22(2), 121–135.

Paap, Kenneth & Zachary Greenberg. 2013. There is no coherent evidence for a bilingual advantage in executive processing. *Cognitive Psychology* 66(2), 232–258.

Paap, Kenneth, Hunter Johnson & Oliver Sawi. 2015. Bilingual advantages in executive functioning either do not exist or are restricted to very specific and undetermined circumstances. *Cortex* 69, 265–278.

Paap, Kenneth, Hunter Johnson & Oliver Sawi. 2016. Should the search for bilingual advantages in executive functioning continue? *Cortex* 74, 305–314.

Pacione, Michael. 2005. City profile Dubai. *Cities* 22(3), 255–265.

Pahta, Päivi, Janne Skaffari & Laura Wright (eds.). 2018. *Multilingual Practices in Language History: English and Beyond.* Berlin: De Gruyter Mouton.

Pan, Jinger, Shuang Song, Mengmeng Su, Catherine McBride, Hongyun Liu, Yuping Zhang, Hong Li & Hua Shu. 2015. On the relationship between phonological awareness, morphological awareness and Chinese literacy skills: Evidence from an 8-year longitudinal study. *Developmental Science* 19(6), 982–991.

Parra-Guinaldo, Victor & Betty Lanteigne. 2021. Morpho-syntactic features of English as a lingua franca in Dubai and Sharjah. In Peter Siemund & Jakob Leimgruber (eds.) *Multilingual Global Cities: Singapore, Hong Kong, Dubai.* Multilingual Asia Series. Singapore: Routledge, pp. 303–320.

Patrick, Donna. 2019. Promises, acts, and action: Indigenous language politics in Canada. In Thomas Ricento (ed.) *Language Politics and Policies: Perspectives from Canada and the United States.* Cambridge: Cambridge University Press, pp. 244–262.

Pavlenko, Aneta & Adrian Blackledge (eds.). 2004a. *Negotiation of Identities in Multilingual Contexts.* Clevedon: Multilingual Matters.

Pavlenko, Aneta & Adrian Blackledge. 2004b. Introduction: New theoretical approaches to the study of negotiation of identities in multilingual contexts. In Aneta Pavlenko & Adrian Blackledge (eds.) *Negotiation of Identities in Multilingual Contexts.* Clevedon: Multilingual Matters, pp. 1–33.

Pavlenko, Aneta & Scott Jarvis. 2002. Bidirectional transfer. *Applied Linguistics* 23(2), 190–214.

Peal, Elizabeth & Wallace Lambert. 1962. The relation of bilingualism to intelligence. *Psychological Monographs: General and Applied* 76(27), 1–23.

Perez, Danae, Marianne Hundt, Johannes Kabatek & Daniel Schreier (eds.). 2021. *English and Spanish: World Languages in Interaction.* Cambridge: Cambridge University Press.

Peters, Pam. 2009. Australian English as a regional epicenter. In Thomas Hoffmann & Lucia Siebers (eds.) *World Englishes – Problems, Properties and Prospects.* Amsterdam: John Benjamins, pp. 107–124.

Petrovic, John. 2019. Alienation, language work, and the so-called commodification of language. In Thomas Ricento (ed.) *Language Politics and Policies: Perspectives from Canada and the United States.* Cambridge: Cambridge University Press, pp. 66–77.

Philips, Susan. 2015. Language ideologies. In Deborah Tannen, Heidi Hamilton & Deborah Schiffrin (eds.) *The Handbook of Discourse Analysis.* Vol. 7. Blackwell Handbooks in Linguistics. New York: John Wiley & Sons, pp. 557–574.

Phillips, Beth, Jeanine Clancy-Menchetti & Christopher Lonigan. 2008. Successful phonological awareness instruction with preschool children: Lessons from the classroom. *Topics in Early Childhood Special Education* 28(1), 3–17.

Piller, Ingrid. 2016. *Linguistic Diversity and Social Justice*. Oxford: Oxford University Press.

Piller, Ingrid. 2017. *Intercultural Communication: A Critical Introduction*. Cambridge: Cambridge University Press.

Piller, Ingrid. 2018. Dubai: Language in the ethnocratic, corporate and mobile city. In Dick Smakman & Patrick Heinrich (eds.) *Urban Sociolinguistics: The City as a Linguistic Process and Experience*. Abingdon: Routledge, pp. 77–94.

Pinto, Maria Antonietta, Renzo Titone & Francesca Trusso. 1999. *Metalinguistic Awareness: Theory, Development and Measurement Instruments*. Pisa and Rome: Istituti Editoriali e Poligrafici Internazionali.

Platt, John. 1975. The Singapore English Speech Continuum and Its Basilect 'Singlish' as a 'Creoloid.' *Anthropological Linguistics* 17(7), 363–374.

Platt, John & Heidi Weber. 1980. *English in Singapore and Malaysia: Status, Features, Functions*. New York: Oxford University Press.

Polinsky, Maria. 2018. *Heritage Languages and their Speakers*. Cambridge: Cambridge University Press.

Poon, Anita. 2021. Multilingualism, language policy, and social diversity in Hong Kong. In Peter Siemund & Jakob Leimgruber (eds.) *Multilingual Global Cities: Singapore, Hong Kong, Dubai*. Multilingual Asia Series. Singapore: Routledge, pp. 99–115.

Puig-Mayenco, Eloi, Jorge Gonzáles Alonso & Jason Rothman. 2020. A systematic review of transfer studies in third language acquisition. *Second Language Research* 36(1), 31–64.

Rampton, Ben. 1995. *Crossing: Language and Ethnicity among Adolescents*. London: Longman.

Reder, Fanny, Nathalie Marec-Breton, Jean-Emile Gombert & Elisabeth Demont. 2013. Second-language learners' advantage in metalinguistic awareness: A question of languages' characteristics. *British Journal of Educational Psychology* 83(4), 686–702.

Ricento, Thomas (ed.). 2006a. *An Introduction to Language Policy: Theory and Method*. Oxford: Blackwell.

Ricento, Thomas. 2006b. Language policy: Theory and practice – An introduction. In Thomas Ricento (ed.) *An Introduction to Language Policy: Theory and Method*. Oxford: Blackwell, pp. 10–23.

Ricento, Thomas (ed.). 2015a. *Language Policy and Political Economy: English in a Global Context*. Oxford: Oxford University Press.

Ricento, Thomas. 2015b. Political economy and English as a "global" language. In Thomas Ricento (ed.) *Language Policy and Political Economy: English in a Global Context*. Oxford: Oxford University Press, pp. 27–47.

Ricento, Thomas. 2015c. "English," the Global Lingua Franca? In Thomas Ricento (ed.) *Language Policy and Political Economy: English in a Global Context*. Oxford: Oxford University Press, pp. 276–304.

Ricento, Thomas (ed.). 2019a. *Language Politics and Policies: Perspectives from Canada and the United States*. Cambridge: Cambridge University Press.

Ricento, Thomas. 2019b. Introduction. In Thomas Ricento (ed.) *Language Politics and Policies: Perspectives from Canada and the United States*. Cambridge: Cambridge University Press, pp. 1–24.

Ricento, Thomas, Yael Peled & Peter Ives (eds.). 2015. *Language Policy and Political Theory: Building Bridges, Assessing Breaches*. Berlin: Springer.

Ringbom, Håkan. 1987. *The Role of the First Language in Foreign Language Learning*. Clevedon: Multilingual Matters.

Ringbom, Håkan. 2001. Lexical transfer in L3 production. In Jasone Cenoz, Britta Hufeisen & Ulrike Jessner (eds.) *Cross-Linguistic Influence in Third Language Acquisition: Psycholinguistic Perspectives*. Clevedon: Multilingual Matters, pp. 59–68.

Ringbom, Håkan. 2007. *Cross-Linguistic Similarity in Foreign Language Learning*. Clevedon: Multilingual Matters.

Rochette, Bruno. 2012. Language policies in the Roman Republic and Empire. In James Clackson (ed.) *A Companion to the Latin Language*. Oxford: Blackwell, pp. 549–563.

Romaine, Suzanne. 2015. Linguistic diversity and global English: The PushmiPullyu of language and political economy. In Thomas Ricento (ed.) *Language Policy and Political Economy: English in a Global Context*. Oxford: Oxford University Press, pp. 252–275.

Romaine, Suzanne. 2017. Multilingualism. In Mark Aronoff & Janie Rees-Miller (eds.) *The Handbook of Linguistics*. Oxford: Wiley-Blackwell, pp. 541–556.

Ross, Malcolm. 1991. Refining Guy's sociolinguistic types of language change. *Diachronica* 8(1), 119–129.

Rothman, Jason. 2011. L3 syntactic transfer selectivity and typological determinacy. The typological primacy model. *Second Language Research* 27(1), 107–127.

Rothman, Jason & Jennifer Cabrelli Amaro. 2010. What variables condition syntactic transfer? A look at the L3 initial state. *Second Language Research* 26(2), 189–218.

Rothman, Jason, Jorge Gonzáles Alonso & Eloi Puig-Mayenco. 2019. *Third Language Acquisition and Linguistic Transfer*. Cambridge: Cambridge University Press.

RSNZ. 2013. *Languages in Aotearoa New Zealand*. Royal Society of New Zealand. Royalsociety.org.nz/assets/Uploads/Languages-in-Aotearoa-New-Zealand.pdf (accessed 24 August 2021).

Ruíz, Richard. 1984. Orientations in language planning. *NABE Journal/National Association for Bilingual Education* 8(2), 15–34.

Rutgers, Dieuwerke & Michael Evans. 2017. Bilingual education and L3 learning: Metalinguistic advantage or not? *International Journal of Bilingual Education and Bilingualism* 20(7), 788–806.

Ryan, Ellen Bouchard, Howards Giles & Richard Sebastian. 1982. An integrative perspective for the study of attitudes towards language variation. In Ellen Bouchard Ryan & Howard Giles (eds.) *Attitudes Towards Language Variation: Social and Applied Contexts*. London: Edward Arnold, pp. 1–19.

Saer, D. J. 1923. The effect of bilingualism on intelligence. *British Journal of Psychology. General Section* 14(1), 25–38.

Safont Jordà, Maria Pilar. 2003. Metapragmatic awareness and pragmatic production of third language learners of English: A focus on request acts realizations. *The International Journal of Bilingualism* 7(1), 43–69.

Safont Jordà, Maria Pilar. 2005. *Third Language Learners: Pragmatic Production and Awareness*. Clevedon: Multilingual Matters.

Sagasta Errasti, María Pilar. 2003. Acquiring writing skills in a third language: The positive effects of bilingualism. *International Journal of Bilingualism* 7(1), 27–42.

Sağın-Şimşek, Sultan Çiğdem. 2005. *Turkish–German bilingual students' acquisition of English word order in a German educational setting*. Münster: Waxmann.

Şahingöz, Yasemin. 2014. Schulische Mehrsprachigkeit bei Türkisch–Deutsch Bilingualen Schülern: Erwerb und Auswirkungen. PhD Dissertation. Universität Hamburg. Ediss.sub.uni-hamburg.de/handle/ediss/5998 (accessed 24 August 2021).

Sanders, Marianne & Guust Meijers. 1995. English as L3 in the elementary school. *ITL: Review of Applied Linguistics* 107/108, 59–78.

Sanz, Cristina. 2000. Bilingual education enhances third language acquisition: Evidence from Catalonia. *Applied Psycholinguistics* 21, 23–44.

Sanz, Cristina. 2012. Multilingualism and metalinguistic awareness. In Carol Chapelle (ed.) *The Encyclopedia of Applied Linguistics*. Oxford: John Wiley and Sons, Inc., pp. 3933–3942.

Schendl, Herbert & Laura Wright (eds.). 2011. *Code-Switching in Early English*. Berlin: De Gruyter Mouton.

Schmid, Monika. 2002. *First Language Attrition, Use and Maintenance*. Amsterdam: John Benjamins.

Schmidtke, Daniel & Victor Kuperman. 2017. Mass counts in World Englishes: A corpus linguistic study of noun countability in non-native varieties of English. *Corpus Linguistics and Linguistic Theory* 13(1), 135–164.

Schneider, Edgar. 2003. The dynamics of New Englishes: From identity construction to dialect birth. *Language* 79(2), 233–281.

Schneider, Edgar. 2007. *Postcolonial English: Varieties around the World*. Cambridge: Cambridge University Press.

Schreiber, Henning (with Clement Odoje & Djeneba Obot). 2012. Linguistic solidarity against ultra-hyper-diversity: Nigerian Pidgin in Lagos. In Klaus Beyer & Raija Kramer (eds.) *Language Change under Multilingual Conditions: Frankfurter Afrikanistische Blätter* 24, pp. 51–72.

Schwartz, Bonnie & Rex Sprouse. 1996. L2 cognitive states and the full transfer/full access model. *Second Language Research* 12(1), 40–72.

Schwartz, Mila, Esther Geva, David Share & Mark Leikin. 2007. Learning to read in English as a third language: The cross-linguistic transfer of phonological processing skills. *Written Language and Literacy* 10(1), 25–52.

Scotland's Census. 2011. www.scotlandscensus.gov.uk/ethnicity-identity-language-and-religion (accessed 24 April 2021).

Seidlhofer, Barbara. 2004. Research perspectives on teaching English as a lingua franca. *Annual Review of Applied Linguistics* 24(1), 209–239.

Seidlhofer, Barbara. 2011. *Understanding English as a Lingua Franca*. Oxford: Oxford University Press.

Sharwood Smith, Michael & Eric Kellerman. 1986. Crosslinguistic influence in second language acquisition: An introduction. In Eric Kellerman & Michael Sharwood Smith (eds.) *Crosslinguistic Influence in Second Language Acquisition*. Oxford: Pergamon Press, pp. 1–9.

Shohamy, Elana. 2006. *Language Policy: Hidden Agendas and New Approaches*. New York: Routledge.

Shohamy, Elana & Durk Gorter. 2008. *Linguistic Landscape: Expanding the Scenery*. London: Routledge.

Siemund, Peter. 2008. Language contact: Constraints and common paths of contact induced change. In Peter Siemund & Noemi Kintana (eds.) *Language Contact and Contact Languages*. Amsterdam: John Benjamins, pp. 3–11.

Siemund, Peter. 2013. *Varieties of English: A Typological Approach*. Cambridge: Cambridge University Press.

Siemund, Peter. 2018a. Modeling World Englishes from a cross-linguistic perspective. In Sandra Dehors (ed.) *Modeling World Englishes: Assessing the Interplay of Emancipation and Globalization of ESL Varieties*. Amsterdam: John Benjamins, pp. 133–162.

Siemund, Peter. 2018b. *Speech Acts and Clause Types: English in a Cross-Linguistic Context*. Oxford: Oxford University Press.

Siemund, Peter. 2022. Englisch als weitere Sprache im Kontext herkunftsbedingter Mehrsprachigkeit. In Thorsten Klinger, Ingrid Gogolin & Birger Schnoor (eds.) *Sprachentwicklung im Kontext von Mehrsprachigkeit – Hypothesen, Methoden, Forschungsperspektiven*. Wiesbaden: Springer VS, 193–210.

Siemund, Peter & Simone Lechner. 2015. Transfer effects in the acquisition of English as an additional language by bilingual children in Germany. In Hagen Peukert (ed.) *Transfer Effects in Multilingual Language Development*. Amsterdam: John Benjamins, pp. 147–160.

Siemund, Peter & Jakob Leimgruber (eds.). 2021. *Multilingual Global Cities: Singapore, Hong Kong, Dubai*. Multilingual Asia Series. Singapore: Routledge.

Siemund, Peter & Lijun Li. 2017. Towards a diachronic reconstruction of Colloquial Singapore English. In Debra Ziegeler & Bao Zhiming (eds.) *Negation and Contact: With Special Focus on Singapore English*. Amsterdam: John Benjamins, pp. 11–32.

Siemund, Peter & Lijun Li. 2020. Multilingualism and language policy in Singapore. In Henning Klöter & Mårten Söderblom Saarela (eds.) *Language Diversity in the Sinophone World*. London: Routledge, pp. 205–228.

Siemund, Peter & Eliane Lorenz. 2023. Multilingual advantages: On the relationship between type of bilingualism and language proficiency. In Kleanthes Grohmann (ed.) *Multifaceted Multilingualism*. Amsterdam: John Benjamins.

Siemund, Peter & Jessica Terese Mueller. 2021. Are multilinguals the better academic ELF users? Evidence from a questionnaire study measuring self-assessed proficiencies. In Anna Mauranen & Svetlana Vetchinnikova (eds.) *Language Change: The Impact of English as a Lingua Franca*. Cambridge: Cambridge University Press, pp. 234–266.

Siemund, Peter, Ahmad Al-Issa & Jakob Leimgruber. 2021. Multilingualism and the role of English in the United Arab Emirates. *World Englishes* 40(2), 191–204.

Siemund, Peter, Julia Davydova & Georg Maier. 2012. *The Amazing World of Englishes: A Practical Introduction*. Berlin: De Gruyter Mouton.

Siemund, Peter, Stefanie Schröter & Sharareh Rahbari. 2018. Learning English demonstrative pronouns on bilingual substrate: Evidence from German heritage speakers of Russian, Turkish, and Vietnamese. In Andreas Bonnet & Peter

Siemund (eds.) *Foreign Language Education in Multilingual Classrooms*. Amsterdam: John Benjamins, pp. 381–405.

Siemund, Peter, Monika Schulz & Martin Schweinberger. 2014. Studying the linguistic ecology of Singapore: A comparison of college and university students. *World Englishes* 33(3), 340–362.

Siemund, Peter, Ahmad Al-Issa, Sharareh Rahbari & Jakob Leimgruber. 2021. Multilingualism and the role of English in the United Arab Emirates, with views from Singapore and Hong Kong. In Alexander Onysko (ed.) *Research Developments in World Englishes*. London: Bloomsbury, 95–119.

Siemund, Peter, Ingrid Gogolin, Monika Schulz & Julia Davydova (eds.) 2013. *Multilingualism and Language Contact in Urban Areas: Acquisition – Identities – Space – Education*. Amsterdam: John Benjamins.

Silva-Corvalán, Carmen & Jeanine Treffers-Daller (eds.). 2016. *Language Dominance in Bilinguals: Issues of Measurement and Operationalization*. Cambridge: Cambridge University Press.

Silverstein, Michael. 1979. Language structure and linguistic ideology. In Paul Clyne, William Hanks & Carol Hofbauer (eds.) *The Elements: A Parasession on Linguistic Units and Levels*. Chicago: Chicago Linguistic Society, pp. 193–247.

Sin, Chih Hoong. 2002. The quest for a balanced ethnic mix: Singapore's ethnic quota policy examined. *Urban Studies* 39(8), 1347–1374.

Singapore Department of Statistics. 2021. www.singstat.gov.sg (accessed 24 August 2021).

Singleton, David & Larissa Aronin (eds.). 2019. *Twelve Lectures on Multilingualism*. Bristol: Multilingual Matters.

Slabakova, Roumyana. 2017. The scalpel model of third language acquisition. *International Journal of Bilingualism* 21(6), 651–665.

Slabakova, Roumyana & María del Pilar García Mayo. 2015. The L3 syntax–discourse interface. *Bilingualism: Language and Cognition* 18(2), 208–226.

Snape, Neal, Maria Del Pilar García-Mayo & Ayşe Gürel. 2013. L1 transfer in article selection for generic reference by Spanish, Turkish and Japanese L2 learners. *International Journal of English Studies* 13(1), 1–28.

Snow, Don. 2013. Revisiting Ferguson's defining cases of diglossia. *Journal of Multilingual and Multicultural Development* 34(1), 61–76.

Spellerberg, Stine Marie. 2016. Metalinguistic awareness and academic achievement in a linguistically diverse school setting: A study of lower secondary pupils in Denmark. *International Journal of Multilingualism,* 13(1), 19–39.

Spolsky, Bernard. 2004. *Language Policy: Key Topics in Sociolinguistics*. Cambridge: Cambridge University Press.

Spolsky, Bernard. 2009. *Language Management*. Cambridge: Cambridge University Press.

Starr, Rebecca Lurie & Mie Hiramoto. 2019. Inclusion, exclusion, and racial identity in Singapore's language education system. *International Journal of Applied Linguistics* 29(3), 341–355.

Statistics Canada. 2017a. Toronto, C [Census subdivision], Ontario and Ontario [Province] (table). Census Profile. 2016 Census. Statistics Canada Catalogue no. 98-

316-X2016001. Ottawa. Released November 29, 2017. www12.statcan.gc.ca/census-recensement/2016/dp-pd/prof/index.cfm?Lang=E (accessed 9 February 2021).

Statistics Canada. 2017b. Vancouver, CY [Census subdivision], British Columbia and Canada [Country] (table). Census Profile. 2016 Census. Statistics Canada Catalogue no. 98-316-X2016001. Ottawa. Released November 29, 2017. www12.statcan.gc.ca/census-recensement/2016/dp-pd/prof/index.cfm?Lang=E (accessed 9 February 2021).

Statistics Canada. 2017c. Montréal, V [Census subdivision], Quebec and Canada [Country] (table). Census Profile. 2016 Census. Statistics Canada Catalogue no. 98-316-X2016001. Ottawa. Released November 29, 2017. www12.statcan.gc.ca/census-recensement/2016/dp-pd/prof/index.cfm?Lang=E (accessed 9 February 2021).

Statistics New Zealand. 2018. Auckland. nzdotstat.stats.govt.nz (accessed 24 August 2021).

Statistisches Amt für Hamburg und Schleswig-Holstein. 2020. www.statistik-nord.de (accessed 24 August 2021).

Stavans, Anat & Charlotte Hoffmann. 2015. *Multilingualism*. Cambridge: Cambridge University Press.

Stockwell, Robert, Donald Bowen & John Martin. 1965. *The Grammatical Structures of English and Spanish: An Analysis of Structural Differences between the two Languages*. Chicago, IL: The University of Chicago Press.

Sun, Wenyang & Xue Lan Rong. 2018. Globalization, national identity, and multiculturalism and multilingualism: Language policy and practice in education in Asian countries. In Andreas Bonnet & Peter Siemund (eds.) *Foreign Language Education in Multilingual Classrooms*. Amsterdam: John Benjamins, pp. 99–123.

Szmrecsanyi, Benedikt & Bernd Kortmann. 2008. The morphosyntax of varieties of English worldwide: A quantitative perspective. *Lingua* 119(11), 1643–1663.

Tabouret-Keller, Andrée. 2006. Bilingualism in Europe. In Taj Bhatia & William Ritchie (eds.) *The Handbook of Bilingualism*. Malden, MA: Blackwell, pp. 662–688.

Te Puni Kōkiri (Ministry of Māori Development). 2019. *The Crown's Strategy for Māori Language Revitalisation 2019–2023*. www.tpk.govt.nz/en/a-matou-mohiotanga/language/crowns-strategy-for-maori-language-revitalisation (accessed 2 June 2021).

Theodoropoulou, Irene. 2021. Socio-historical multilingualism and language policies in Dubai. In Peter Siemund & Jakob Leimgruber (eds.) *Multilingual Global Cities: Singapore, Hong Kong, Dubai*. Multilingual Asia Series. Singapore: Routledge, pp. 63–80.

Thomason, Sarah. 2001. *Language Contact: An Introduction*. Edinburgh: Edinburgh University Press.

Thomason, Sarah. 2015. *Endangered Languages*. Cambridge: Cambridge University Press.

Thomason, Sarah & Terrence Kaufman. 1991. Language Contact, Creolization, and Genetic Linguistics. *First Paperback Printing*. Berkeley, CA: University of California Press.

Tibategeza, Eustard & Theodorus du Plessis. 2012. Language-in-education policy development in Tanzania: An overview. *Language Matters* 43(2), 184–201.

Titone, Debra, Jason Gullifer, Sivaniya Subramaniapillai, Natasha Rajah & Shari Baum. 2017. History-inspired reflections on the bilingual advantages hypothesis.

In Margot Sullivan & Ellen Bialystok (eds.) *Growing Old with Two Languages: Effects of Bilingualism on Cognitive Aging*. Amsterdam: John Benjamins, pp. 265–295.

Tomasello, Michael. 2003. *Constructing a Language: A Usage-Based Theory of Language Acquisition*. Cambridge, MA: Harvard University Press.

Tucker, G.R. & Alison d'Anglejan. 1971. Some thoughts concerning bilingual education programs. *The Modern Language Journal* 55(8), 491–493.

Tupas, Ruanni & Isabel Pefianco Martin. 2017. Bilingual and mother tongue-based multilingual education in the Philippines. In Ofelia García, Angel Lin & Stephen May (eds.) *Bilingual and Multilingual Education: Encyclopedia of Language and Education* (3rd ed.). Cham, Switzerland: Springer Nature, pp. 247–258.

UNESCO. 2016a. *Policy Brief on Internal Migration in Malaysia*. UNESCO Bangkok. Asia and Pacific Regional Bureau for Education. bangkok.unesco.org/content/policy-briefs-internal-migration-southeast-asia (accessed 24 April 2021).

UNESCO. 2016b. *Policy Brief on Internal Migration in the Philippines*. UNESCO Bangkok. Asia and Pacific Regional Bureau for Education. bangkok.unesco.org/content/policy-briefs-internal- migration-southeast-asia (accessed 24 April 2021).

Usanova, Irina. 2019. *Biscriptuality: Writing Skills among German–Russian Adolescents*. Amsterdam: John Benjamins.

U.S. Census Bureau. 2018. American Community Survey. Language spoken at home by the ability to speak English for the population 5 years and over. data.census.gov/cedsci/table?q=B16001&g=310M400US35620,41860&hidePreview=true&tid=ACSDT1Y2018.B16001 (accessed 9 February 2021).

Valian, Virginia. 2015. Bilingualism and cognition. *Bilingualism: Language and Cognition* 18(1), 3–24.

van Coetsem, Frans. 1988. *Loan Phonology and the Two Transfer Types in Language Contact*. Dordrecht: Foris.

van der Maas, Han, Kees-Jan Kan & Denny Borsboom. 2014. Intelligence is what the intelligence test measures. Seriously. *Journal of Intelligence* 2(1), 12–15.

Van Gelderen, Amos, Rob Schoonen, Kees De Glopper, Jan Hulstijn, Patrick Snellings, Annegien Simis & Marie Stevenson. 2003. Roles of linguistic knowledge, metacognitive knowledge and processing speed in L3, L2 and L1 reading comprehension: A structural equation modelling approach. *International Journal of Bilingualism* 7(1), 7–25.

Vendler, Zeno. 1957. Verbs and times. *Philosophical Review* 66(2), 143–160.

Vennemann, Theo. 2003. *Europa Vasconica – Europa Semitica*. Trends in Linguistics. Studies and Monographs. Berlin: De Gruyter Mouton.

Vertovec, Steven. 2007. Super-diversity and its implications. *Ethnic and Racial Studies* 30(6), 1024–1054.

Wang, Feng. 2005. On the genetic position of the Bai language. *Cahiers de Linguistique – Asie Orientale* 34(1), 101–127.

Wang, Lixun & Andy Kirkpatrick. 2021. Medium of instruction issues in trilingual Hong Kong primary schools. In Peter Siemund & Jakob Leimgruber (eds.) Multilingual Global Cities: Singapore, Hong Kong, Dubai. Multilingual Asia Series. Singapore: Routledge, pp. 229–247.

Wasserfall, Julia. 2019. *Prestige and Pretentiousness: The English Language in Taiwan and Singapore*. PhD Dissertation, Humboldt-Universität zu Berlin.

Wee, Lionel. 2021. The state of/and language planning in Singapore. In Peter Siemund & Jakob Leimgruber (eds.) *Multilingual Global Cities: Singapore, Hong Kong, Dubai*. Multilingual Asia Series. Singapore: Routledge, pp. 83–98.

Wei, Li. 1994. *Three Generations, Two Languages, One Family: Language Choice and Language Shift in a Chinese Community in Britain*. Bristol: Multilingual Matters.

Weinreich, Uriel. 1953. *Languages in Contact: Findings and Problems*. New York: Publications of the Linguistic Circle of New York 1.

Westergaard, Marit, Natalia Mitrofanova, Roksolana Mykhaylyk & Yulia Rodina. 2017. Crosslinguistic influence in the acquisition of a third language: The linguistic proximity model. *International Journal of Bilingualism* 21(6), 666–682.

Wiese, Heike. 2012. *Kiezdeutsch: Ein neuer Dialekt entsteht*. München: Beck.

Wiley, Terence. 2019. The rise, fall, and rebirth of bilingual education in California and the ongoing American dilemma. In Thomas Ricento (ed.) *Language Politics and Policies: Perspectives from Canada and the United States*. Cambridge: Cambridge University Press, pp. 135–152.

Williams, Glyn. 1977. Social and cultural change in contemporary Wales. *Current Anthropology* 18(4), 737–743.

Williams, Sarah & Björn Hammarberg. 1998. Language switches in L3 production: Implications for a polyglot speaking model. *Applied Linguistics* 19(3), 295–333.

Wilson, Charles & Margaret Deuchar. 2017. Extralinguistic factors influencing the pronunciation of English by Welsh–English Bilinguals. In Fraser Lauchlan & Maria del Carmen Parafita Couto (eds.) *Bilingualism and Minority Languages in Europe: Current Trends and Developments*. Newcastle upon Tyne: Cambridge Scholars Publishing, pp. 48–69.

Winford, Donald. 2005. Contact-induced changes: Classification and processes. *Diachronica* 22(2), 373–427.

Woll, Nina. 2020. Towards crosslinguistic pedagogy: Demystifying pre-service teachers' beliefs regarding the target-language-only rule. *System* 92, 1–11.

Wrembel, Magdalena. 2013. Metalinguistic awareness in third language phonological acquisition. In Karen Roehr & Gabriela Adela Ganem-Gutierrez (eds.) *The Metalinguistic Dimension in Instructed Second Language Learning*. London: Bloomsbury, pp. 119–143.

Wright, Wane & Virak Chan. 2019. Multilingualism in North America. In Simona Montanari & Suzanne Quay (eds.) *Multidisciplinary Perspectives on Multilingualism: The Fundamentals*. Boston, FL: De Gruyter Mouton, pp. 77–100.

Worthington, Ian. 2005. *Alexander the Great: A Reader*. London: Routledge.

Young, Nia, Mirain Rhys, Ivan Kennedy & Enlli Thomas. 2017. The linguistic, cognitive and emotional advantages of minority language bilingualism. In Fraser Lauchlan & Maria del Carmen Parafita Couto (eds.) *Bilingualism and Minority Languages in Europe: Current Trends and Developments*. Newcastle upon Tyne: Cambridge Scholars Publishing, pp. 120–140.

Zakharia, Zeena. 2017. Bilingual education in the Middle East and North Africa. In Ofelia García, Angel Lin & Stephen May (eds.) *Bilingual and Multilingual Education: Encyclopedia of Language and Education* (3rd ed.). Cham: Springer Nature, pp. 281–293.

Ziegeler, Debra. 2014. Replica grammaticalisation as recapitulation: The other side of contact. *Diachronica* 31(1), 106–141.

Index

CPSIA information can be obtained
at www.ICGtesting.com
Printed in the USA
LVHW081908181222
735470LV00004B/282

9 781108 844024